Introduction to
Palaeolithic Cave Paintings in Northern Spain

César González Sainz
Roberto Cacho Toca
Takeo Fukazawa

Translation to English by Peter Smith

Texnai

Introduction to Palaeolithic Cave Paintings in Northern Spain
B/W Edition

Authors:
César González Sainz, Prof. of University of Cantabria
Roberto Cacho, Toca, University of Cantabria
Takeo Fukazawa, Photographer & Writer, President of Texnai

Translation to English: Peter Smith
Photos: Takeo Fukazawa, Pedro Saura(Altamira, La Garma)
Maps and ground plan: University of Cantabria, Texnai inc.

Printed by CreateSpace, USA

Published by Texnai Inc.
Based on Multimedia Database "Palaeolithic Cave Arts in Northern Spain", 2004
ISBN:978-4-907162-13-9

Texnai Inc.
#318, 2-1 Udagawa-cho, Shibuya-ku, Tokyo, Japan Zip:150-0042
Tel: +81-3-3464-6927 Fax: +81-3-3476-2372   info@texnai.co.jp
http://www.texnai.co.jp/   http://www.muse.or.jp

This edition is dedicated
to Mr. Max Ernst André Müller
who supported a young Japanese Artist during his stay
in Cortaillod, Switzerland, 1964~65

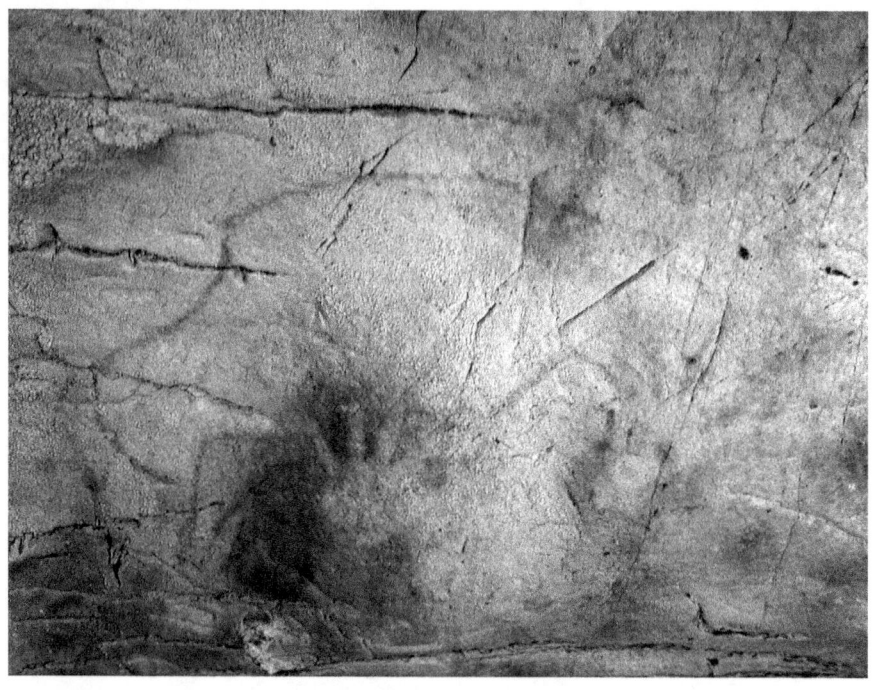

Prof. Alistair Pike of University of Bristol, UK reported in *Science* on June 15, 2012, that Uranium-series disequilibrium dating was executed for calcite deposits overlying art found in 11 caves in Northern Spain and the results demonstrated that some paintings of El Castillo extended back at least to the Early Aurignacian period, with minimum ages of 40.8 thousand years for a red disk, 37.3 thousand years for a negative hand.

Preface 2013

From 1997 to 2004, we executed Photographic VR shooting of Palaeolithic cave paintings in 23 major caves and about 150 Mobile Arts in 5 museums in Northern Spain as a co-project between the University of Cantabria, Spain and Texnai, Inc., Japan and the result was published in Spanish and English in 2003 by GOBIERNO de CANTABRIA as "ARTE PALEOLITICO EN LA REGION CANTABRICA, PALAEOLITHIC ARTS IN NORTHERN SPAIN" with a DVD ROM of the image database. This book is published based on these book and database in POD(Publishing On Demand) format. For this publishing, the images of cave paintings and mobile arts are scheduled to be published as the catalog editions in POD so that readers are able to see those images without PC. Books of paper are actually more convenient than those of electronic medium and even from the view point of preservation it must be better than magneto-optical media. I am thinking like this recently, but the reason why we decided to re-publish this book in POD now was not only for that.

On August 23, 1993 a joint Japan-Syria excavation team uncovered a set of almost complete fossilized Palaeolithic human skeleton at the Dederiyeh Cave that is located some 400 km north of Damascus. The skeleton was that of a Neanderthal child who lived in the Middle Palaeolithic era (ca. 200,000 to 40,000 years ago). One year later, thanks to an invitation by Prof. Takeru Akazawa of the University of Tokyo, the team leader of the joint excavation team, I got an opportunity to visit the Dederiyeh Cave as a photographer and learnt that Neanderthals and anatomically modern humans were living in the same area, the Dead Sea Rift Valley in those days. Since that time, the relationship of those two kinds of human and the replacement of Neanderthals by Modern Human that was progressively happened in the world later have been one of my major concerns.

For the replacement of Neanderthals by Modern Human, Prof.Akazawa and his colleagues launched a new research project in 2011 based on the theory of evolutionary models of learning. And on June 15, 2012, an extremely interesting report on the cave paintings of Northern Spain was published in *Science*. The report was written by Prof. Alistair Pike of University of Bristol, UK and his colleagues and it was reported that Uranium-series disequilibrium dating was executed that year for calcite deposits overlying art found in 11 caves in Northern Spain and the results demonstrated that some paintings of El Castillo extended back at least to the Early Aurignacian period, with minimum ages of 40.8 thousand years for a red disk, 37.3 thousand years for a negative hand.
It was surprising because if this dating is correct, the red disk becomes about

4.000 years earlier than the paintings of Grotte Chauvet that has been said to be the world's oldest, and not only that, it can not be ruled out that the earliest paintings were created by Neanderthals, which were estimated to present in the Cantabrian regions until at least 42,000 to 36,000 years B.P..

For the Palaeolithic cave paintings in Northern Spain, as I have already written, we had executed a series of photoVR shooting at 23 major caves and built the multimedia database, but the estimated chronology of the paintings was however not older than 35,000 years B.P. and all paintings were believed to be created by anatomically modern humans, Cro-magnons in that area. So we believed that the Palaeolithic Cave Arts including the Mobile Arts were totally indifferent from Neanderthals. However, from June 15, 2012, by the dating research of Prof. Pike's team, this common sense has become no longer 100% true. "We should make more attention to the cave paintings of Northern Spain". This was the main reason why we decided to re-publish this book in POD.

From November 18th to 24th, half a year after the Science's report, an International Symposium on the replacement of Neanderthals by Anatomically Modern Human was held in Tokyo inviting many specialists from overseas and a guest from the University of Barcelona, Prof. Joao Zilhao made a presentation on the Replacement in Europe. Coincidentally Prof. Joao Zilhao was a member of Prof.Pike's team and a very good friend of our partner and an author of this book, Prof. César González Sainz and was saying that they would continue the dating and he has just come from Santander after the meeting at El Castillo cave. I expect thier fruitful results.

August 15, 2013, Tokyo
Takeo Fukazawa, Texnai

Contents

Preface 2013 --- 5
Preface 2003-1 --- 9
Preface 2003-2 --- 15

1. The Art of Upper Paleolithic hunters
   Introduction to cave art in the Iberian Peninsula ------------------- 19

2. The Central Cantabrian Valleys
   Introduction to Paleolithic Cave Art in Cantabria ------------------- 49
   2.1 Cueva de Chufín -- 62
   2.2 Cueva de Altamira -- 68
   2.3 Cueva de Hornos de la Peña ----------------------------------- 84
   2.4 Cueva del Castillo --- 90
   2.5 Cueva de Las Chimeneas --------------------------------------- 100
   2.6 Cueva de La Pasiega -- 106
   2.7 Cueva de Las Monedas --- 120
   2.8 Cueva de Santian --- 126
   2.9 Cueva de El Pendo -- 132
   2.10 Cueva de La Haza --- 136
   2.11 Cueva de Covalanas --- 142
   2.12 Cueva de Pondra -- 148
   2.13 Cueva de La Garma -- 152

3. The western Cantabrian Region
   Introduction to Paleolithic Cave Art in Asturias -------------------- 159
   3.1 Cueva de la Peña de Candamo ----------------------------------- 172
   3.2 Cueva de La Lluera I -- 178
   3.3 Cueva de Tito Bustillo -- 184
   3.4 Cueva de El Buxu -- 192
   3.5 Cueva de El Pindal -- 198
   3.6 Cueva de La Loja -- 204

4. The End of the Cantabrian Corridor
   Introduction to Paleolithic Art in the Basque Country --------------- 209
   4.1 Cueva de Venta de la Perra ------------------------------------ 220
   4.2 Cueva de Arenaza -- 226
   4.3 Cueva de Santimamiñe -- 232
   4.4 Cueva de Ekain -- 238

5. General Bibliography -- 247

Preface 2003-1

Takeo Fukazawa
Texnai, Tokyo

Paleolithic cave art in Europe that was only known by the names of Altamira and Lascaux was, for myself, the world we could reach only in a couple of books for long time. However, in the middle of March in 1996, the world of Paleolithic cave art suddenly became real in my life by an unexpected e-mail from Seville of Spain.

"Could you let me know more about what you are doing for QuickTime VR?"

The sender of this mail was a multimedia photographer called Jose Maria Requena who was going to try the QuickTime VR for his multimedia productions.

I have been involved in computer imaging business for about 20 years, but at that time, our main business was going to be shifted from hardware business to software business and we had already started to be involved in a couple of digital archives of cultural heritage by using new image processing technologies such as QuickTime VR.

The QuickTime VR is one of the VR (Virtual Reality) technologies developed by Apple Computer, Inc. in the U.S. There are two different kinds of QuickTime VR. The one is QuickTime VR panorama movie that allows us to create an interactive panoramic movie by using 12 or 16 still pictures shot around one point. The other is QuickTime VR object movie that allows us to create an interactive omniview image of a 3-dimentional object by using 36 or 360 still pictures shot from all angles around the object.

My first encounter with the QuickTime VR was at the Sybold show that was held in San Francisco in 1994. I still remember the small Venus of Milo rotating slowly on the Macintosh display monitor at the exhibition site. The image size was not bigger than 160 x 160 pixels. It seemed to be a 3D computer graphics, but it looked too real as a computergenerated image.

When I learnt that the QuickTime VR object movie could be created using ordinary still pictures, I immediately recognized that it should be very useful for digital archives of cultural heritage. Because it is natural that interactive and omniview image is much more interesting for us than an ordinary single still picture and the photographic image quality can maintain its value as an academic material. We called this kind of VR image created by using photographs "PhotoVR"

"The image size is still too small, but it is due to the lack of computer power and it will be possible to create much bigger in near future". However, it was a new challenge for us to shoot such large number of pictures at a certain same interval from all angles around an object.

2 years later, to solve the problem, we had already developed a two-axis computer controlled rotator that allows us to shoot a 3-dimentional material and create QuickTime VR object movie almost automatically. We named this "AutoQTVR".

When I received a mail from Jose Maria, we had already finished an experimental shooting of Jomon potteries by AutoQTVR at an archeological museums located near Tokyo. Including Panoramic VR, some of the results had been open to the public at our website, then searching our QTVR site, Jose Maria tried to keep in touch with us by e-mail.

There was one more interesting photographic VR called IPIX that was getting popular at that time. IPIX is a software-integrated technology developed by Ipix, Inc. in the U.S. and it allows us to create an interactive spherical panorama by using a pair of front and back pictures shot by using a fish-eye lens. When opening an IPIX file, we can see a 360-degree-by 360-degree spherical view of a closed space including the ceiling and the ground by simple mouse operations.

Exchanging ideas on these latest PhotoVR technologies, our e-mail communication between Tokyo and Seville continued for a couple of weeks afterwards. And in this e-mail communication, I presented him my brief idea of shooting caves like Altamira and Lascaux that contains prehistoric wall paints such as bison and horses. "It must be pretty interesting if we could shoot such Paleolithic caves in Europe by using PhotoVR. Altamira is in Spain, so could you find some right person to talk about this idea?" It was only a few days later that I received a name of a young archeologist of the University of Cantabria. He was Roberto Cacho Toca who became later my indispensable partner to realize the digital archiving project in Spain.

Thanks to a lot of detail information from Roberto, I could learn that so many Paleolithic caves are widely distributed through out from the Cantabrian regions in the north of Spain up to the Dordogne regions in the south middle of France where the Lascaux is located. To tell the truth, I did not know anything about them but the names of Altamira and Lascaux until I started to make communications with Jose and Roberto. Even about the name of Santander, I have never heard of it until that time. "It might be very hard to shoot all of them, but if we could shoot some of the major caves, we will be able to create a beautiful PhotoVR Database. And it' s worth doing it. Because most of caves are not open to the public, so when creating such PhotoVR Database, everybody becomes able to see it and we can even feel the atmosphere of those caves in which Paleolithic peoples were living and working 12,000 years or more ago. How do you say?" Roberto' s answer was "Yes." He said that it would be useful even for students and specialists if it' s possible to create such PhotoVR database that covers the north of Spain and the middle south of France including Pyrenees. "Especially, if we can shoot Mobil arts by QTVR, it will be great because people can easily check all parts of those important materials."

Our views were in perfect harmony. However, like always, only the financial issue was left in front of us.

In the mean time, I had heard that the Ministry of International business and Industries of Japan was launching their supporting program for creating high quality digital contents and inviting proposals from multimedia companies in Japan. We had never applied this kind of supporting program by the government and our idea was of the matter of overseas countries, so it was supposed to be almost impossible to be adopted. However, I decided to join the competition with the idea of creating a PhotoVR database of Paleolithic cave art in Europe. "Let' s try, anyway. If it' s adopted, we can figure out the financial problem. Even if not, let us go and shoot some of the caves at our own cost since we have started talking like this, OK?"

It was three months later that I was invited to the 4th Congress of Japanese Studies in Spain held in Santander to present our ideas. The organizer was called Antonio Santos. He was a librarian of the University of Cantabria and an extremely earnest researcher of Japanese films. His position was indifferent from Paleolithic art, but he was always friendly with us and gave us his warm-hearted understandings and advice in behind until today.

"I am much younger than expected, am I?" Said Roberto in English to me first on my first arrival at the Santander airport. I had never asked his age, but he was really young and looked a student of 24 or 25 years old. However, he was truly sincere young man and he earnestly responded to my hundreds of e-mail during the project.

Fortunately on my leaving for the opening ceremony of the Congress of Japanese Studies, I was informed by a fax from Tokyo that our proposal for the digital contents supporting program was going to be adopted. Then, at the congress, together with a couple of specialists of Japanese cultures such as "Chadoh (Tea Ceremony)" and "Ikebana (Flower Arrangement)", I introduced our recent experience of archeological database and strongly presented at the end our joint project for creating PhotoVR database of Paleolithic cave art in Europe. During the period of the congress, Antonio Santos was showing a series of Kurosawa' s films at the auditorium of the city. I was so impressed to know that such many peoples in the north end of Spain were interested in Japanese culture.

After the congress, I was introduced to Dr. César González Sainz, a professor of the Department of Historical Sciences at the University of Cantabria. He was one of the most experienced experts in this region for the research of Paleolithic arts, but our proposal was willingly accepted and he showed me his deep understanding with our digital archiving project. It was thanks to his great efforts that we could have an opportunity to shoot such many important caves and that we could have completed our database with such detailed scientific comments. Like this way, we got such strong partners in Santander and the Japanese government officially adopted our proposal before long.

Our project started in March 1997 as a joint project between Texnai and the University of Cantabria. From the practical point of view, we excluded Pyrenees and Dordogne this time and 22 major caves located in Astrius, Cantabria, Vizcaya and Guipúzcoa in the north of Spain and about 150 Mobil arts in the possession of each archeological museum of those regions were selected to execute photoVR shooting.

Two different teams were organized to shoot Cave arts and Mobil arts at the same time, and in the mean time, our programmer was starting to write the database management program in Tokyo. I believed that the project would be a great job.

When looking back to the days we were walking around the valley of Cantabria, what I was impressed first was the rain and the tranquility. For most of ordinary Japanese, when talking about Spain, it is the country of the sunshine and the country of bullfight and flamenco or the country of passion. However, when arriving in Santander, it rains almost every day and peoples are relatively quite, and neither flamenco, nor bullfight could be seen there. "Is this Spain?" "No, this is Cantabria". It was due to my ignorance, but it took a couple of weeks until I realized this simple matter. Spain was bigger than I imagined and like any other countries, each region has their own features and characters.

However, the rain of Cantabria made me easily understand soon the reason why Paleolithic people chose this area to live for thousands of years. The Cantabrian region is a long narrow land that is located from the west to the east between the Cantabrian range and the Atlantic Ocean so even during the glacial period; this land should have had a rich rainfall. And thanks to this rich rainfall, the land was always covered by vegetation; it should be a very good location for Paleolithic peoples to make hunting. Adding to this climate, most of mountains of this region are covered by limestone, so the Paleolithic peoples could easily find their shelters to live. Actually, when standing in front of an entrance of those natural shelters in the mountain, the front view is always open to the spacious green valley, and it was easy to understand that the location of their shelters were strategically chosen for their hunting life. In addition, when getting such a splendid panoramic view from there, I happen to guess that the Paleolithic peoples might have almost the same sense as ours for the beauty of the landscape. I called those valleys "the Palolithic Route of Cantabria".

In those caves, it was a little hard at the beginning to discriminate the wall paints from the natural shape, but as getting to be used to the darkness, many kinds of paintings and engravings were going to be caught even by my eyes. So called "Points", "Macaroni", "Rectangular Shapes", "Vulva", etc., etc. Those abstract shapes were so mysterious. "What do they represent?" The answer by specialists was always like this. "We can not tell you exactly what they mean, but the similar kind of symbols can been seen all over from this area, from the west end of the Cantabrian regions up to the south middle of France". Of course, there were various kinds of animals as well in the caves. "Bison", "Horses", "Deers", "Wild cows", etc., etc. Most of them had already lost their original shapes and colors, so it was often difficult to identify the shapes of animals especially in case only a part of body could be seen. Even though, I was so impressed by the talents of Paleolithic peoples who described such wild animals so vividly and exactly. Most animals were not so spectacular like those of Altamira and Lascaux, but even a small engraving or a drawing by charcoal stick, their representations were surprisingly exact and strong, so it was almost like we ware looking at the sketches of Picasso. "What kinds of peoples created such drawings?"

In the archeological museums in each region, we could shoot a lot of important Mobil arts by using a mini-type AutoQTVR that we brought from Tokyo. Most of them were not open to the public, but thanks to warm-hearted understandings of the persons concerned, we were allowed to make omni-view shooting of the original pieces by using the computercontrolled rotators. In this database are contained approximately 150 QTVR object movies of those artifacts, but I believe that they are very useful for the peoples who want to study about the Paleolithic Mobil art.

As continuing our shooting in the Paleolithic Route, a couple of simple questions started sprouting in my mind.

"Who was the people who left such excellent paints and engravings in the caves?"

"From where did they come to the north of Iberian Peninsula? From the west or from the east?"

"What did such painting mean for them and where did they go afterwards leaving such paints and drawings?"

"Such as so called Venus, many Mobil arts that represent a human shape can be found in the north from of Pyrenees, but no Venus can be found in the Cantabrian regions. Why?"

There must be many theories that can respond to these questions. However, it seems, even for my eyes, that we still need more researches, especially more international co-researches from the worldwide viewpoints to illuminate these simple questions. A recent co-research made between Japan and Russia using a DNA analysis says that the root of most Jomon people in the Japanese islands was, against expectations, not the south Asia but Siberia. When looking over the remains that were found in Siberia, such as a bone-made human statue, many similar artifacts to those of Europe can be seen. Japanese might not be fully indifferent from the Paleolithic peoples of the Cantabrian regions.

Paleolithic art can be said to be the most original spiritual works of humanity. So it might be worth paying a little more attention to the world of 12,000 years ago today. If this database proves to be useful in knowing more about the peoples of Paleolithic period, it will be our great pleasure.

The database is going to be published soon. It is all thanks to the understandings and efforts of all the peoples concerned. It is impossible to list all the peoples here, but I would like to express my gratitude to all of them.

Preface of 2003-2

César González Sainz
Department of Historical Sciences, University of Cantabria

With these lines we would like to present the main result of a project that we developed in 1998 and part of 1999. It is equally the work of a group of postgraduate students in the Department of Historical Sciences at the University of Cantabria, led by Roberto Cacho Toca, who committed themselves to the project, and made it possible. Much of the first year was taken up seeking advice, defining objectives, organizing the fieldwork and writing the texts that accompany the photographs in the Database. These were taken by the magnificent team of photographers and multimedia experts belonging to Texnai Inc. of Tokyo, who deployed the latest techniques in virtual reproduction in prehistoric caves and museums throughout the Cantabrian Region.

Essentially, the Database offers people interested in Paleolithic art a full photographic record, making use of virtual reality techniques in order to overcome traditional limitations. In this way, it becomes possible to understand the rock art inside the chambers of a cave, or handle a decorated object and appreciate its tiniest details.

From the point of view of prehistoric cave art research, the Database provides a good opportunity to learn the latest information about Paleolithic works of art in the Cantabrian Region. This natural region had its own cultural characteristics in the Upper Paleolithic, and certain intra-regional differences. Furthermore the Database introduces an integrated approach, covering both rock art in caves and the surprising miniatures created in portable objects. It includes not only the large, internationally famous sites such as Altamira, Tito Bustillo or Ekain, but also less spectacular caves, like La Loja, Pondra and Arenaza, which we believe to be equally necessary in order to obtain a truer idea of the plural reality of the art.

The Database contains a large number of interrelated photographs, and information about decorated objects and cave paintings, about the depictions in certain caves, and about prehistoric art in the region. The twenty-two caves that it covers include several that are closed to the general public or with serious limitations in the number of visits (such as Peña Candamo, La Lluera, Chimeneas and Pasiega, Altamira, Pondra, Arenaza, Santimamiñe and Ekain). These measures are taken in order to conserve the paintings adequately, or because the art is located in narrow passages that are not suitable for tourist visits. However, the technology employed here allows the user to understand the interior layout of the caves, and assess the works of art in their spatial and physical context, in a more complete way than is obtained from the two-dimensional view of traditional photographs. This is of vital importance, as prehistoric art was produced on surfaces that varied greatly in quality, size and position, and the Paleolithic artists showed their mastery in the way they incorporated the irregularities in the walls and ceiling into their depictions of animals and signs. In the same way, the decorated areas are quite variable in their ease of access, their capacity and the possibilities for viewing the figures at a distance.

The photographs of mobiliary art illustrate unique objects that, at best, are normally only seen in a glass case in a museum, usually from only one side. Here it is possible to observe the techniques used in the preparation of these artifacts and their decoration, often better than with the original in our hand, as the light does not fluctuate, and our hands do not shake. We can rotate the object to examine the other side, or enlarge the photograph and see the smallest detail, such as the remains of red coloring on the ibex head from Cueva de Tito Bustillo, the tiny hairs on the ears of the hinds on the staff from El Pendo, or how the barbs were cut in the harpoons found in many Magdalenian sites.

Finally, the Database includes a large number of scenic views of the region, from the Pyrenees in the north of Navarra to the Nalón valley in the center of Asturias. These photographs are interesting to give an idea of the landscape in which the groups of Paleolithic hunters lived. In some cases (such as the circular panoramas from the tops of Peña de Candamo, Ardines hill, Monte Castillo and Ekain hill) they are quite spectacular views and rarely known even by specialists in Paleolithic archeology. They make it possible to visualize the territory around the site and the strategic value of the locations chosen by Paleolithic hunters.

The team at the Department of Historical Sciences at the University of Cantabria, in close and friendly collaboration with the photographers and software experts of Texnai, have worked together in order to offer a complete version of our Paleolithic artistic heritage, in an up-to-date product intended for the general public at a medium to high level. However, we believe that this Database will also be of interest to researchers in prehistoric art, given the possibilities it provides for the study of manufacturing and decoration techniques in bone and antler, of the composition of cave art panels, and the discovery of new figures, among other aspects. We aim, therefore, to contribute to a wider diffusion of information about this early, spectacular, artistic development, and at the same time, to its more efficient conservation. We also hope to arouse in the user the same emotion that we have felt while working in the caves in the Cantabrian region. An emotion that is linked to the vividness and expression of many of the figures of animals, and also, despite the great cultural and chronological distance separating us, to the recognition of the pulse of humanity beating in all these paintings created by our ancestors at the end of the Ice Age.

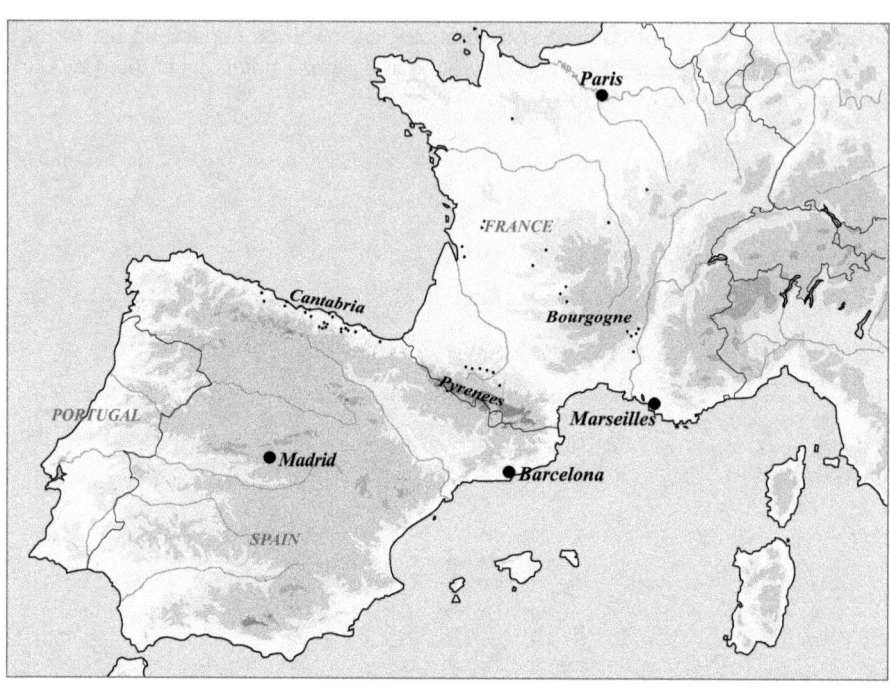
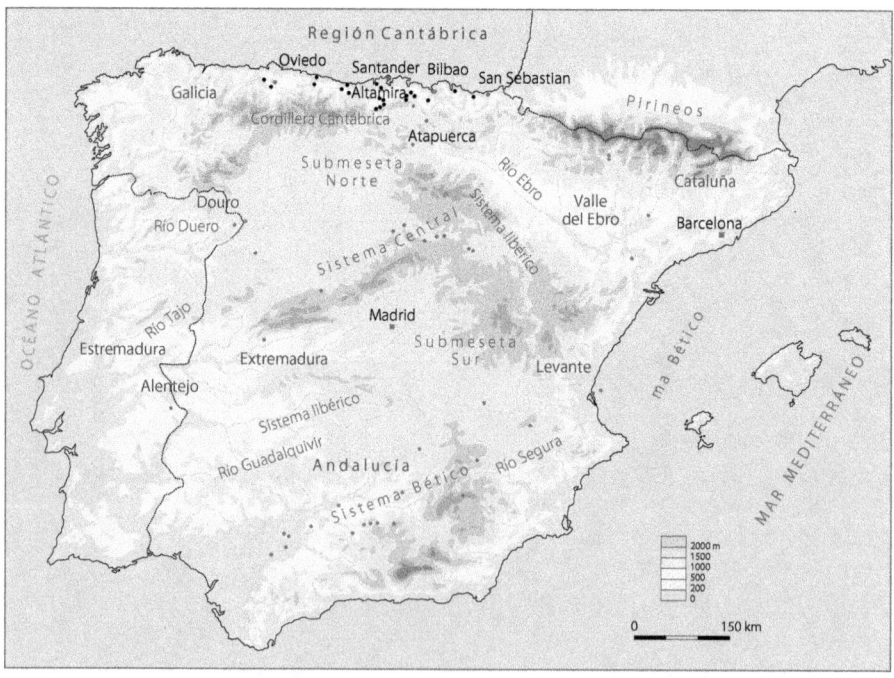

Chapter 1
The Art of Upper Paleolithic Hunters.
Introduction to Cave Art in the Iberian Peninsula

1. Introduction

During the last stages of the Würm glaciation, the groups of hunters living in Europe developed the first artistic cycle, which still surprises us today with the great esthetic value of many of the paintings, or their careful execution with techniques that are, nonetheless, very simple. We are equally struck by the unity of style over vast geographical areas, and its continuity during such a long period of time. Between approximately 35,000 and 11,000 years before the present, the continent saw the growth of this first example of figurative graphic expression, with its two variants: cave or rock art, on fixed surfaces (cave walls, floors and roofs, or open-air rock outcrops such as those recently located in the Iberian Peninsula), and a mobiliary art on portable objects (perforated staffs, harpoons, pendants ... and also on stone or bone plaques, statuettes etc).

Between these two variants, small differences can be detected in the distribution of the motifs represented, the techniques used, and in the composition of the figures and their thematic associations. These are due to the different conditions, such as size or hardness, of the surfaces to be decorated, and to the presumably different functions of the art. Their geographical distribution is partly different too. Whereas decorated objects are found in almost all of Europe, cave art is located essentially in the southwest of the continent. This means it is limited, apart from isolated exceptions, to the whole of the Iberian Peninsula, central and southern France, and to a lesser extent, Italy.

The Europe where this first art appeared and developed was very different to present day Europe; colder and inhospitable, wild and empty. Large glaciers had formed in mountainous areas, while a great ice sheet covered the north of Europe. Thus the northern limits of the inhabitable continent were in the center of what is now Great Britain and the north of Germany. At the same time, the water locked in this great mass of ice resulted in sea level dropping as much as 120m below the present level in the coldest period, which was from about 20,000 to 18,000 BP. This caused a regression in the coastline, of varying amount depending on the location, and the consequent enlargement in the territory avail-

Chapter1: The Art of Upper Paleolithic Hunters. Introduction to Cave Art in the Iberian Peninsula.

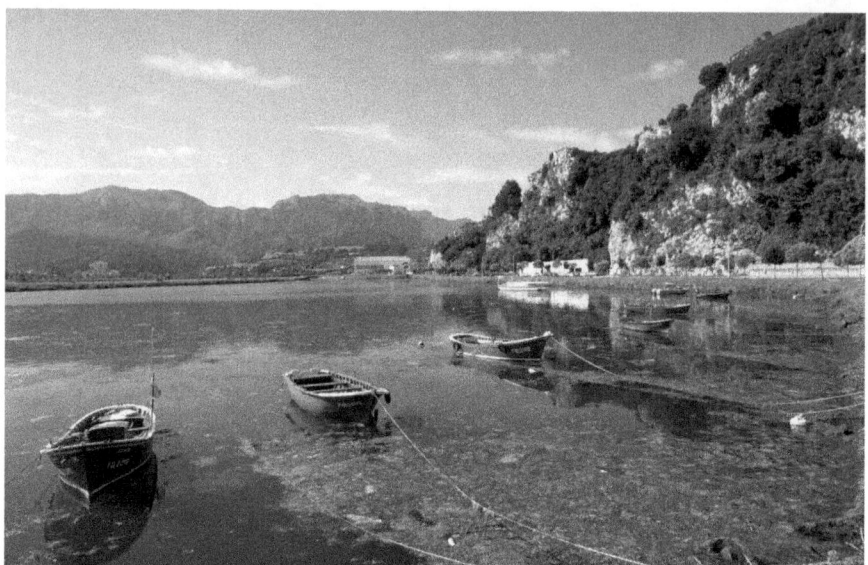

In the limestone hill of Ardines, Ribadesella is located La Cueva de Titto Bustillo, one of the most important Palaeolithic cave in Cantabrian region.

able to the human groups and the herds of wild animals. Where the present day underwater continental platform is wide and flat, there was a greater increase in the territory (so Great Britain was joined to the continent). On the other hand, the regression was much smaller where there is no platform, such as in the Straits of Gibraltar, between the European and African continents.

The ecosystems known in Upper Pleistocene Europe varied greatly, but they were always colder and more severe than nowadays. The differences among them depended, as today, on their continentality or proximity to the sea, the latitude, or altitude and soil types, and other factors. In southwestern Europe, where art developed, the differences among the most characteristic regions (Dordogne and the French Pyrenees, the Cantabrian Region, the Duero Valley, and in the extreme south, the coast and hills of Andalucia) were equally important. Despite this, everywhere the landscape was more open and barer of vegetation than we have known in historical times. There were fewer trees, and a much larger proportion of grasslands. The forests began to spread when the climate improved (first about 13,500 BP, and then irreversibly from 10,200 BP onwards). In those open spaces a great variety of wild animals roamed, again with significant differences between the colder periods and places, and warmer moments or more southern and temperate zones. In the former, the more characteristic faunal type, although not the only one, consisted of the great herds of gregarious ungulates (reindeer, horse, bison... and saiga antelope in drier periods), together with

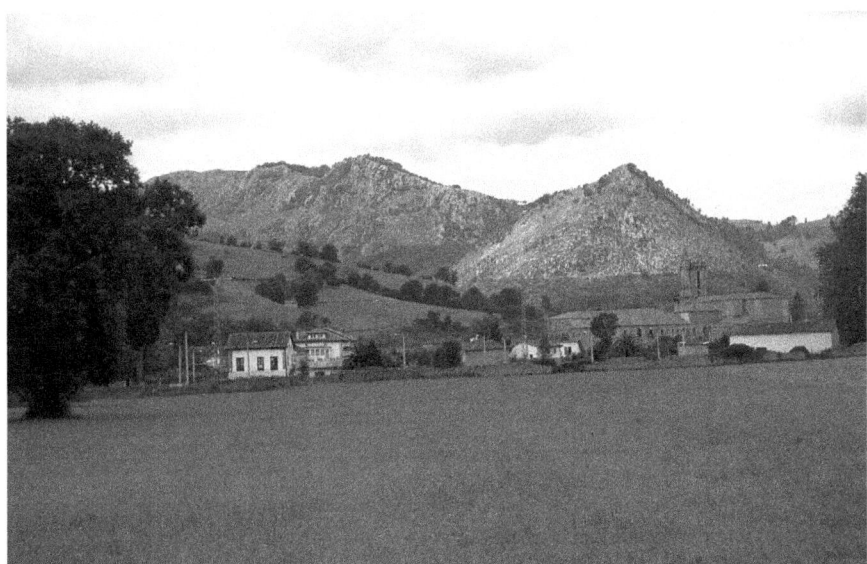
Mt. El Castillo located at the east end of La Sierra del Dobra, Cantabria. Four major Palaeolithic caves that contain cave paintings are situated in this mountain.

mammoths, and carnivores such as the polar fox or wolf. In the opposite conditions, smaller groups of ungulates better adapted to a more forested vegetation (red deer, chamois, and roe deer or wild boar in temperate moments), aurochs on flatland, and ibex on steep, rocky slopes. We can appreciate this environmental gradient from North to South in the animals represented in the Paleolithic cave art of the Iberian Peninsula, as significant differences exist between the faunal compositions in the Cantabrian Region, the central mesetas, and Andalucia.

Paleolithic art is therefore due to groups of hunters who lived in territories generally more open and colder than exist nowadays, where they exploited natural food resources by hunting, fishing, and gathering plants and fruit. As the variety, quantity and location of these resources changed with each season, and as they became slowly exhausted in any one place, it was necessary for the population to move relatively frequently, taking with them a few objects, as well as their ideas and knowledge. This enabled long-range interaction, which fixed tastes and a graphic style with many elements in common all across Europe, in a time when no stable paths or roads existed, only the migratory routes of the herds of ungulates. And the only way of transmitting images was on pendants and other light objects which were no burden for the journey, and, of course, in the artist's retina and mind.

The appearance of figurative art in Europe coincides with that of Homo

Chapter1: The Art of Upper Paleolithic Hunters. Introduction to Cave Art in the Iberian Peninsula.

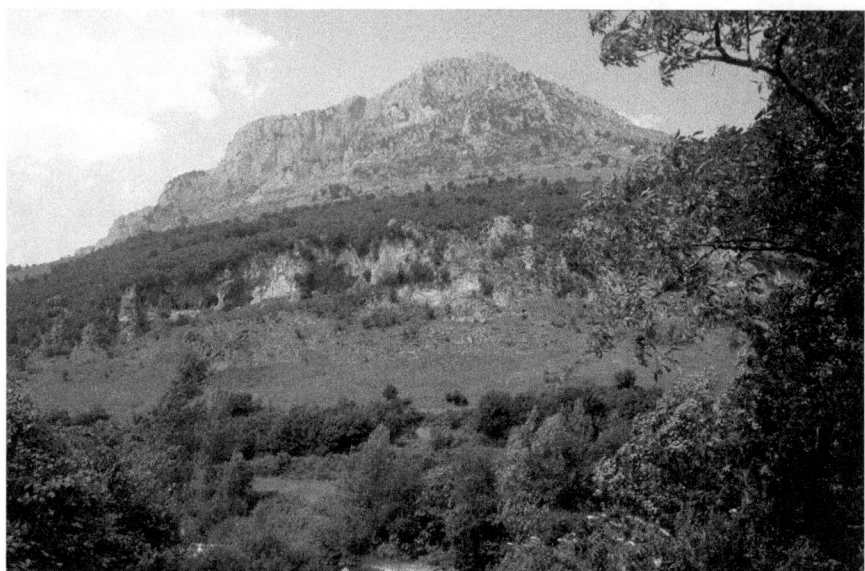

The Carranza valley that is located on the boundary between the proivinces of Cantabria and Vizcaya. Numerous Palaeolithic caves are opened in this steep limestone slopes of both side of vallay.

sapiens sapiens, that is, with our direct ancestors. These substituted Neanderthal man, who had occupied western Europe alone from at least 150,000 to 40/30,000 BP. The processes of anthropological replacement must have been quite complex and varied, and given the limitations of archaeological method, are still difficult to precise (which has caused a fecund literary sub-genre). But the development of figurative art is not only the consequence of the greater intellectual capacity of our species, but also of more complex and flexible forms of organization, which required systems of social cohesion, and of collection and exchange of information, which were rather more sophisticated than what had existed until then. Cave art, and the ceremonies to which its production may have been linked, probably formed part of that baggage of tools of intragroupal cohesion, or of the fixation and transmission of information. This does not exclude, among other things, its role as a formula of artistic expression and of personal or collective affirmation. Precisely because it was not reduced to a tool of cohesion or transmission of information, the geographical distribution of cave art, which spread like a film of oil across southwest Europe, affected areas with very different environmental conditions, and was not limited to those with cold, open conditions. The study of the cave art in the Iberian Peninsula shows this clearly, as will be seen.

It should also be taken into account that when we speak of Paleolithic art, we are referring to the part that can be documented archaeologically, and not

Chapter1: The Art of Upper Paleolithic Hunters. Introduction to Cave Art in the Iberian Peninsula.

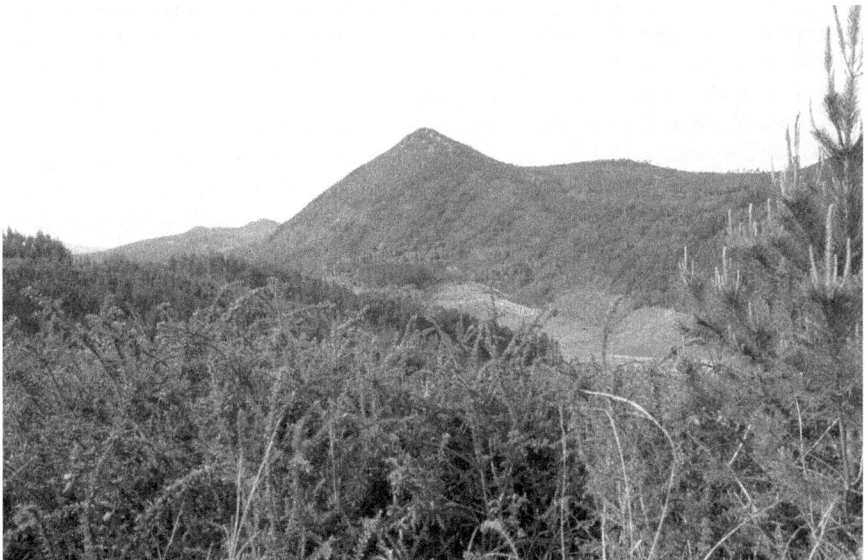

The Mt. of Ereñusarre, very near the village of Kortezubi, four kilometers from the town of Guernica. One of the most important Palaeolithic cave in Basque Country, La Cueva de Santimamiñe is located in this moutain.

to all that could have existed. We know nothing of other forms of expression such as tattoos or body paint, dancing, singing, or graphic art on short-lived organic surfaces, such as animal skins or wood. In any case, there must have been representations presumably linked to activities such as human burials, documented already among the Neanderthals. If we could know more about these other forms of artistic expression, and their similarities and differences with rock and mobiliary art, it would make it easier to understand the role played by art in Paleolithic societies.

Figurative art appears and develops, then, within a group of novelties protagonized by human groups in the Upper Paleolithic. These novelties are especially clear in the field of technology (new and more carefully selected raw materials and ways of working, new technical supports, more diverse tool assemblages, and development of tools on bone and antler), but they also affected the subsistence economy, and important processes of intensification are observed in many regions. The changes, without doubt, also implied more versatile and complex social structures, which would have shown regional differences, but which at the same time extended over larger areas of territory. In this context of novelties and accelerated cultural change (at least compared with the static situation of the long age of the Neanderthals), appears this new ability to create and use graphic symbols, specific to our species and, perhaps, one of its defining characteristics.

Chapter1: The Art of Upper Paleolithic Hunters. Introduction to Cave Art in the Iberian Peninsula.

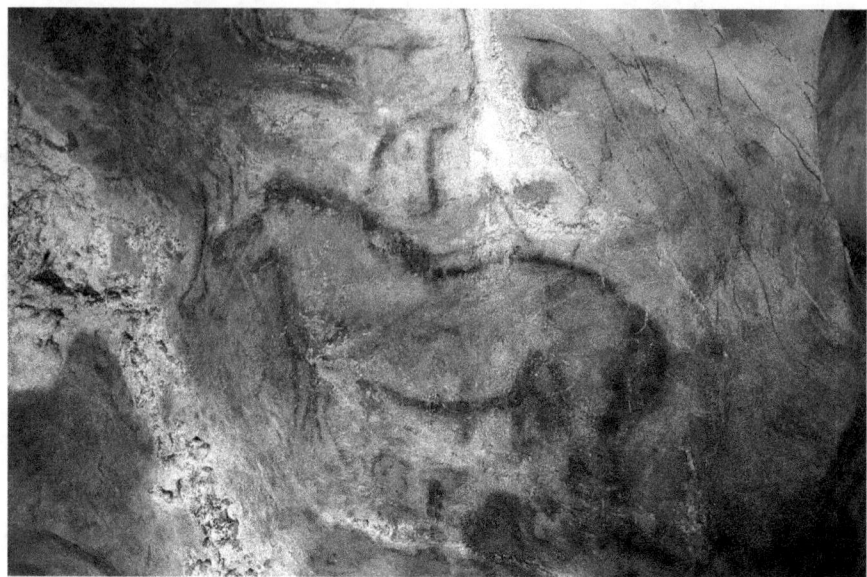

A horse facing left, Cueva de La Peña de Candamo, Asturias

This first great artistic cycle rapidly melted away in the last moments of the glaciation, as the milder environmental conditions allowed new territories to be colonized in the north of the continent, or in higher altitudes within the classic regions. At the same time as the flora and fauna was transformed in many areas, including the spread of the forests and the extinction of the typically Pleistocene mammals, like mammoth, reindeer, saiga or bison, the human groups tended to develop cultural systems that were more specific to each region, better adapted to highly variable local conditions. These systems were more intensive economically, directed more at the exploitation of less mobile and more predictable resources, increasing the gathering of vegetables, fruits and molluscs, and developing true fishing techniques in rivers and estuaries, and then in the open sea, as well as hunting birds and smaller mammals. This allowed the population to rise significantly in many regions, and each human group now tended to settle in a territory. Marriage systems and networks of interaction between groups were generally more closed geographically, and decorative styles were less unified than in the Upper Paleolithic, and frequently of a very different kind, with a greater proportion of abstract representations. In the Cantabrian region, occupying the northern rim of the Iberian Peninsula, only mobiliary art is found after 11,500 BP, and this is much less common than in the Magdalenian period, and reduced to abstract compositions usually of dots and lines. These non-figurative motifs from the Azilian period (c. 11,500 to 9,000 BP), engraved on spatulas and pendants or painted on stone cobbles, do however have extraregional connections, until

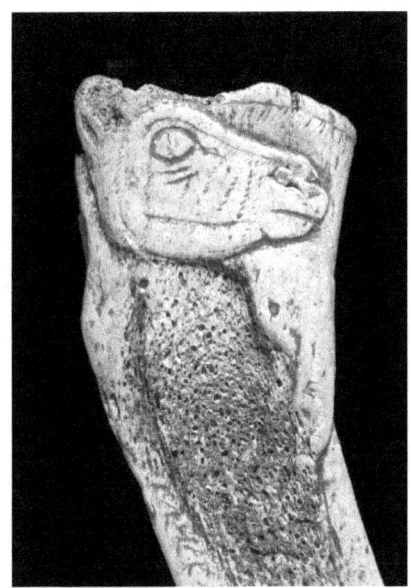 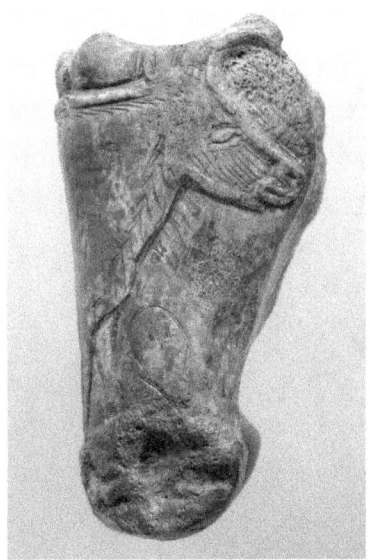

Decorated rib bone of La Garma   Decorated imb bone of La Garma

the expansion of the forests and regionalization were noticeably accelerated after about 10,000 BP.

2. Paleolithic cave art research

The Paleolithic art that we know today was always there. But it did not become the object of analysis until the scientific community, and soon afterwards society itself, were ready, as a result of the development and acceptance of the theory of evolution and the appearance of the very concept of Human Prehistory. Cave art research had its beginnings in Cueva de Altamira, in the center of the Cantabrian region. Here, M. Sanz de Sautuola proposed in 1880, for the first time (in a published article and after a logical and coherent discussion), that the astonishingly beautiful images of wild animals in the cave were of Paleolithic age. The bison on the incredible ceiling in Altamira remain the most spectacular example of cave art in the entire Cantabrian region, even today. After a long controversy, the artistic capacity of the Upper Paleolithic people slowly came to be accepted, and their graphic depictions, in caves and on artifacts, thus became the object of intense and exhilarating research throughout the century which has just come to an end.

This length of time can be divided into three main periods. The first

Chapter1: The Art of Upper Paleolithic Hunters. Introduction to Cave Art in the Iberian Peninsula.

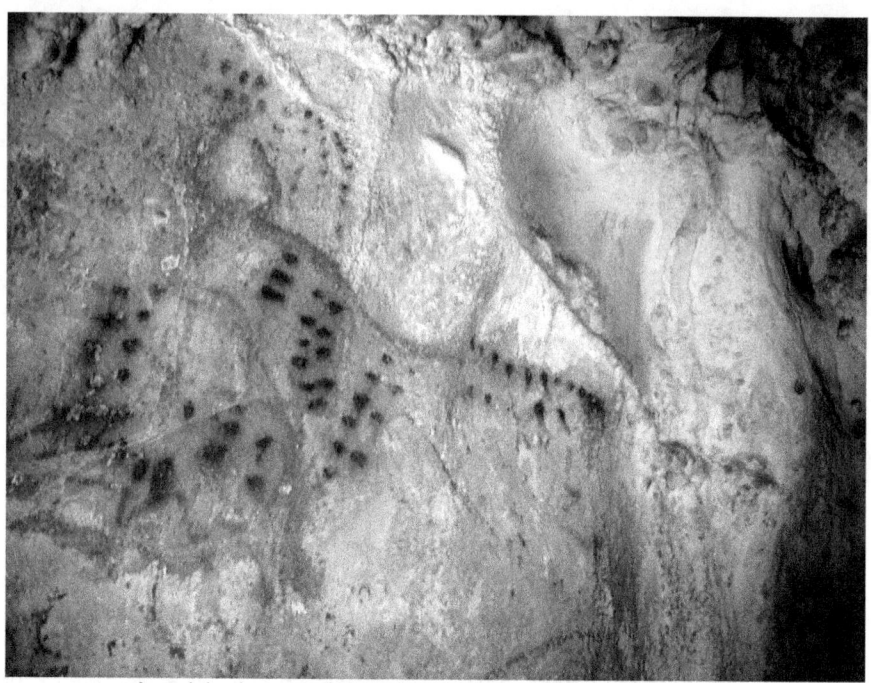

Auroch in sienna and black dots, La Peña de Candamo, Asturias

one, led by Henri Breuil until the mid-1950s, was focused on the exploration of hundreds of sites, and the publication of this amazing art. This occasioned the first chronological and interpretive synthesis (generally based on the comparison of Paleolithic societies with present day or historical primitive peoples and the principles of magic or totemism). Later, until 1980, research was dominated by A. Leroi-Gourhan and a structuralist perspective, explicit in his important book Prehistoire de l' art occidental, published in 1965. This study, a synthesis of his fieldwork during the previous decade, attempted to uncover the order existing in decorated caves, the graphic expression of ancestral myths, and to establish the chronology and rhythm of change during the Upper Paleolithic. In the last two decades, Paleolithic art research has come out of its European limits, and groups of cave art of the same age are now known in other parts of the world, like South Africa or Australia. At the same time, researchers of different intellectual traditions are taking greater part in the study of Paleolithic art in the southwest of Europe. Together with much more eclectic perspectives regarding interpretation, the main developments lie in the effects of the technological revolution. New systems of lighting, photography, surveying, computerized databases, digitalization and computer aided treatment of images, absolute dating and analysis of the pigments..., all these are changing each phase in the research process. Furthermore, the clear increase in the impact of human action on the land during the last

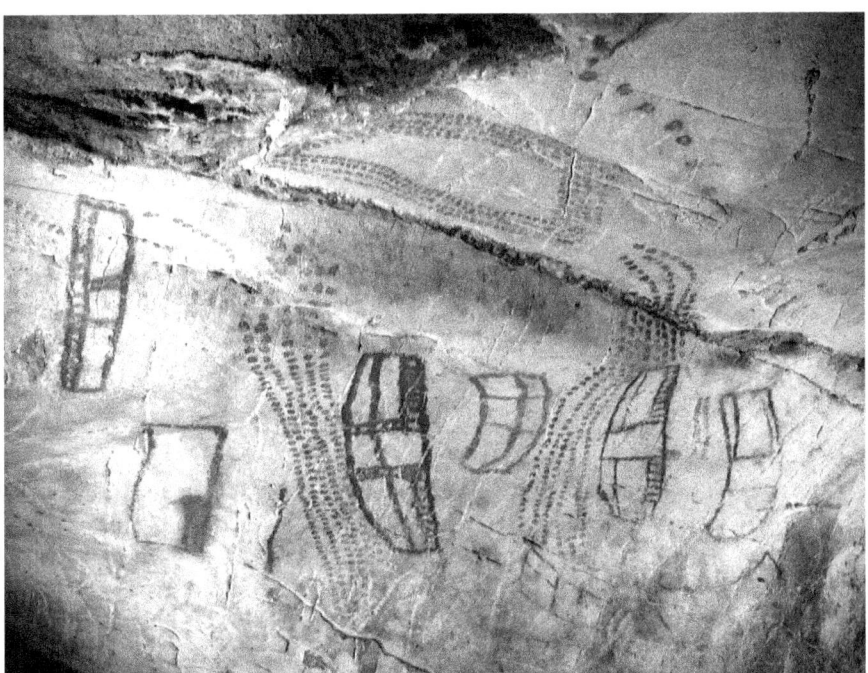
Quadrilateral signs and lines of dots, El Castillo, Cantabria

few decades, as in public works such as reservoirs, highways, and the plowing up of land, is making the extensive documentation of sites and the development of conservation policies even more necessary.

3. Main characteristics of Paleolithic cave art in SW Europe

Before entering in the Iberian Peninsula, with its own different regions and peculiarities, a brief account should be made of the basic characteristics of this first artistic cycle in all southwest Europe.

As mentioned above, this art displays great unity over wide geographical areas, above all in its mobiliary or portable version, but also in rock art. This unity is not seen again in the continent until the expansion of the Roman Empire, with very different economic, social and cultural bases. Furthermore, the same artistic tradition survives during a long lapse of time, covering all the Upper Paleolithic (c. 37,000-11,000 BP). Logically, regional peculiarities exist and styles change in time, yet these enrich, rather than detract from, this background unity. This is easily seen if figures of European Paleolithic art are compared with those of other prehistoric artistic cycles. It is, however, very difficult to define in a simple way. As will be shown, Paleolithic art does not have practically any aspects (referring to position, themes or contents, techniques or composition) which can be defined quickly and without needing to give exceptions.

1) Cave art is distributed in different parts of the caves, from right at the entrance - therefore coinciding with the living area - to the end of the cave. Together with panels in comfortably-sized passages, the figures can be found in small chambers only reached with difficulty. Hence, some figures are visible to only one person at a time, and from the same position in which they were produced. These dark, withdrawn places, far from noise and light, in the depths of a cave are possibly the most typical locations, but by no means the only ones. A good number of art assemblages in daylight have been known for many years. The fact that they show a limited range of techniques (deep engravings and bas-relief) is mainly due to the greater problems for the conservation of paint. But recently, many more sites with Paleolithic art on open-air rock outcrops have been discovered, both in Spain (the assemblages of Domingo García and Siega Verde) and in Portugal (Mazouco, and a number of sites in the Côa Valley), and occasionally in the south of France (Fornols Haut). It has even be noticed that some of the sites along the River Côa have large images of animals on the rock outcrops, which must have been visible at a considerable distance from the site itself.

In caves, artists produced their drawings and compositions on walls, floors and roofs. They used all types of accessible surfaces, and altered their techniques to suit the varying degrees of hardness, humidity or color of the rock surface. Sometimes they decorated smooth flat walls, or walls crossed by cracks and other irregularities which they used and frequently incorporated into their depictions. It is easy to see these same tendencies in the open-air panels of engravings, which are sometimes on horizontal beds of rock, as at Siega Verde, and other times on vertical or inclined walls. The use made of relief and discontinuities in the rock surface is the same as in caves.

2) In these areas they painted or engraved depictions of animals, usually mammals, but sometimes fish, birds or serpents; a few humans, generally caricatures; more or less conventionalized abstract "signs" (a good number of these "signs" are repeated in different caves); and other less striking manifestations, such as stains of color with random forms, and series of non-figurative engraved lines or paintings. That is to say, not all the known tangible realities were represented, but a selection of them. There are no evident depictions of plants, or habitational structures; nor are there any landscapes or weapons, although some animals have spears stuck in their bodies. And sometimes we can find figures of imaginary beings, mixtures of men and/or different animals.

Among the animals, the basis of Paleolithic art, bovines - bison and wild aurochs -, horses, deer and reindeer, goats and chamois are the principal figures. In other words, the animals which were most commonly hunted and consumed (although the proportions between the species depicted and consumed are not always the same, especially if these are evaluated at any particular site, rather than in the total number of sites in the region, or of any given period). But occasionally we find mammoths, rhinoceros, bears, carnivores, as well as fish, serpents and even insects.

The animals are usually depicted in a more natural style than are human figures, whose faces are conventionally omitted or deformed. Many of the abstract signs are specific to each region, as will be seen later.

3) The techniques used are very simple, but are applied in diverse and versatile ways, adapting them to the characteristics of each rock surface. Nearly all the figures were either engraved (with various objects, ranging from flint tools to finger-tips on soft clay surfaces) or painted (in black or in the palette of red colors - going from violet to yellow-, but neither white nor blue was used). In order to paint, they used charcoal or natural dyes (manganese, ocher or limonite), dissolved and applied with pieces of animal skins, brushes or sprayed, or as dry colors applied directly by hand. Besides these, many assemblages with bas-relief sculptures are known in the French Dordogne, or with clay models inside some caves in the Pyrenees. Furthermore many figures were made by chipping off small pieces of rock in order to produce the outline of the animal. This technique was used in some of the older French rockshelters, and was especially common in the open-air assemblages in the Duero Valley, in Portugal and Spain.

4) Regarding compositions of the figures on cave walls or at open-air sites, there are no fixed rules, but rather an extreme variety. Apart from very few exceptions, there are no narrative scenes, or at least, only a vivid imagination could interpret the compositions as such. But compositions of inter-related figures do exist, in which a sense of unity is perceived. These may go from pairs of animals facing each other to large compositions such as the central panel in La Lluera, the roof of Altamira, or the chamber in Santimamiñe, all in the Cantabrian region. And, of course, there are also panels with one, totally isolated figure, and even caves containing a single animal, such as the caves of San Antonio, Otero, Patatal and Sotarriza.

From another point of view we can find synchronic sites, generally with a small number of stylistically and technically homogeneous figures; and also great accumulations of figures, often superimposed on the same panel, which appear to have been produced during different periods and phases. These are found in the Cantabrian region in the caves of Candamo, Tito Bustillo, Llonín, Altamira, Castillo, Pasiega and La Garma.

Chapter1: The Art of Upper Paleolithic Hunters. Introduction to Cave Art in the Iberian Peninsula.

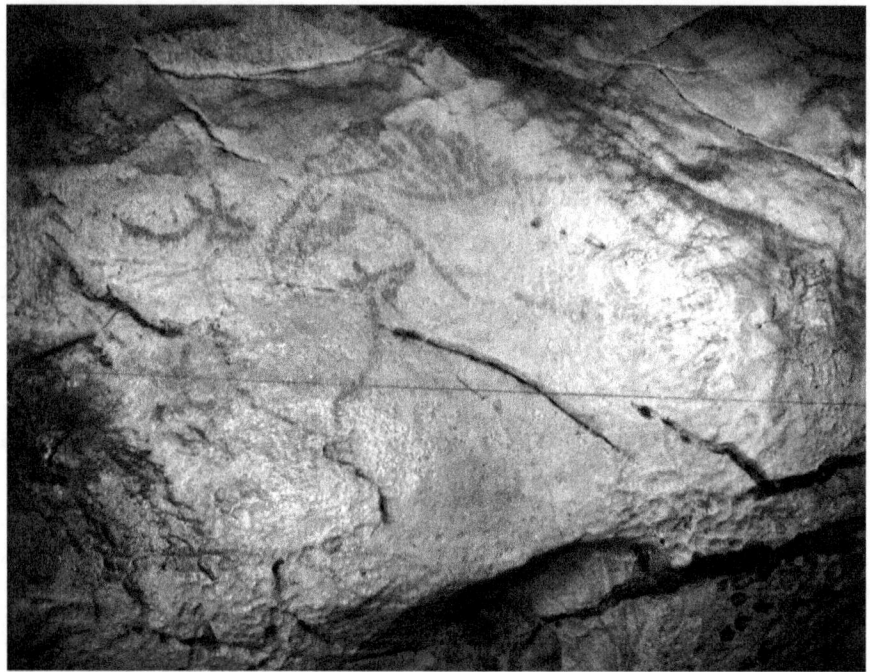

Panel with a large horse and hinds, Covalanas, Cantabria

The formulae of thematic association, as between animals and signs, or the association between certain themes and parts of the cave, are highly variable, but definitely do not occur at random, as was implicitly supposed until the 1960s. The main association of different animal species, as defined by structuralist researchers, is horse plus auroch or bison; with other animals, above all deer or goats, in marginal positions. This appears in a significant number of sites, especially in easily visible panels, painted with laborious techniques and represented by large-sized figures. But this is by no means the only formula of composition in synchronic assemblages, and is not found in the Cantabrian region in sites such as Chimeneas, Arenaza, Chufín entrance, La Loja or Cullalvera, and nor is it the most abundant. Indeed, other important formulae of association are found regionally: in the Cantabrian the hind-horse association is repeated at several sites particularly in the Solutrean period, or that of horse and reindeer at Late Magdalenian sites.

Equally, several tendencies of association between certain themes and parts of the cave are known. Again, here there is a great variety of possibilities, but one of the most significant is the concentration of abstract signs in hidden side-chambers, and not in panels of great visibility on the main route through the

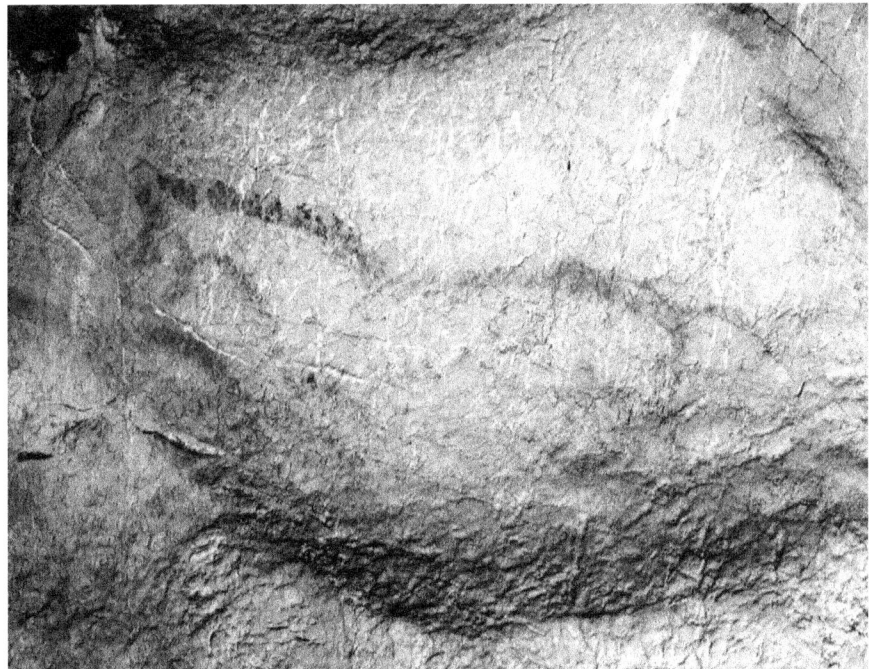
Horse in red. La Haza, Cantabria

cave. This is especially true of the quadrangular and other closed signs of Style III. The central, more visible panels tend to be filled by paintings of large animals, preferentially bison and horses.

5) Regarding the stylistic features of this art, just a few of what we consider to be the most important points, should be mentioned here. The depictions, as commented above, tend to reflect the most essential or characteristic aspects of the animals' bodies, while human figures appear deformed or highly simplified. On the other hand, the figures generally oscillate between a more or less realistic style and a schematic approach which reduces the form to its essential features without details. Both tendencies occur at the same times during the Upper Paleolithic, and occasionally in different figures of the same composition. This is more common in mobiliary art.

The animals are usually drawn as profiles, with their heads sometimes turned backwards or facing the spectator, but frontal views occur too. The former type of figure is usually represented with realism, whereas the latter are schematic, and normally consist of heads of animals with their horns or antlers, as the most common animals in this position are goats or occasionally deer.

Over time, it seems that there was a tendency to change in order to achieve a greater definition of the volume of the animals' bodies. This implied advances in the definition of depth (by different formulae of perspective in horns and limbs), and the reproduction of the different parts of the body (e.g. in the proportion of complete figures, or in the number of limbs depicted). Another development was in the construction of the interior of the animals' bodies, going from the mere indication of their outline, to the generalization of the lines of interior articulation, and the in-filling of parts with color or engraved bands. Similarly, there were changes in the co-ordination and animation of different parts of the body. These were, in any case very general tendencies of change throughout the Upper Paleolithic, and do not imply any strictly ordered or linear modifications during that period. The treatment given to any animal figure, the technique used or the degree of completeness, depended on many more factors than just the general level of artistic skill in each moment or the abilities of each artist.

Finally, it is necessary to add another feature which appears throughout the Paleolithic, although in varying proportions. It is usual to find animals with heavy, voluminous bodies, with insufficiently short limbs, and sometimes with long necks finishing in tiny heads. These conventional deformations affect the pictures of horses more than bovines, cervids or caprids, and are particularly common in the Gravettian and Solutrean periods (c. 27,000 to 17,000 BP), but not exclusively.

6) Dating Paleolithic art has been one of the central problems of research ever since its beginnings until the present time, when modern procedures such as the C14-AMS method have re-opened the subject with new controversy.

Various procedures have been used in different circumstances, either to confirm the chronology of cave art in the Upper Paleolithic, or to obtain a more precise date within that period. Some of the older arguments used were: the depiction of extinct animal species, like mammoth, reindeer or bison, whose bones were only found in Paleolithic sediments, or the use of natural dyes or lithic engraving tools like those found in the strata of Paleolithic occupation. Other arguments were the fact that stalagmitic layers covered some of the paintings, or that the entrances of decorated caves had been blocked by natural processes, and these were only uncovered by large scale public works, such as quarries or roads, or by using caving equipment or sophisticated diving techniques. Similarly, the start of some decorated cave passages may have been blocked by sediments of a later Paleolithic occupation, or walls with rock art were covered by occupation levels, or pieces of the wall containing art had broken off and become integrated in the stratigraphy.

Besides its link with the stratigraphy, the main criteria to date rock art was, and still is, its analysis compared with mobiliary art, which is found in stratigraphic sequences, and therefore has, at least, a relative date. In the early times of research, Breuil and other authors established a few "parallels" , or links between the two variants (figures which were characteristic in their themes, technique or stylistic features). They also used superimpositions of figures in panels to organize a technical and stylistic chronology, although this assumed that there always existed a great difference in time between the superimposed figures. Since the 1960s, dating has been based more on the paintings which are well recorded stratigraphically, and the stylistic and chronological analysis of the whole mobiliary corpus - which has become more abundant and of a more precise chronology - and its comparison with rock art. The "parallels" have gradually been revised, so that nowadays only a few are still accepted as sure. But these few are extraordinarily useful.

Since the 1980s it has been possible to date minimum amounts of charcoal from some of the black paintings, using the application of particle accelerators to the traditional method of radiocarbon dating. In this way absolute dates have been obtained for black figures in some twenty caves mainly in France and Spain (the caves of Altamira, Castillo, Covaciella, Monedas and Chimeneas in the Cantabrian region). The results have confirmed the Paleolithic date of the paintings, and roughly speaking, the stylistic chronology, especially in the late periods of the Upper Paleolithic. For older, Pre-Solutrean phases, however, some important contradictions have been produced, which have been the cause of fierce controversy. More recently it has become possible to date calcite layers associated with panels containing art, in caves like La Garma, Pondra and Venta de la Perra. This gives ante or post quem dates for all kinds of depictions, including engravings and paintings with inorganic pigments.

In our opinion, the comparison with mobiliary art, and the so-called stylistic method of dating are still valid in general, at least for broad chronological approximations. In certain regions like the Cantabrian or the southwest of France there does seem to have been a process of changes, in technique and above all expression, aimed at achieving a greater realism and a more faithful expression of the third dimension. But even if this happened it does not mean that it affected all the figures produced in that period in the same way, or that the process can be applied in a simple linear way, or that it is equally valid applied to isolated figures or to synchronic assemblages with many paintings. Not only have there been good and bad artists at any moment, but any painter may not have given all his works of art the same treatment, as he did not intend to achieve always the same degree of realism, or applied all his technical skills in every figure.

If we accept these tendencies to a general change, at least in regions like the Cantabrian, a succession of periods can be detected through the Upper

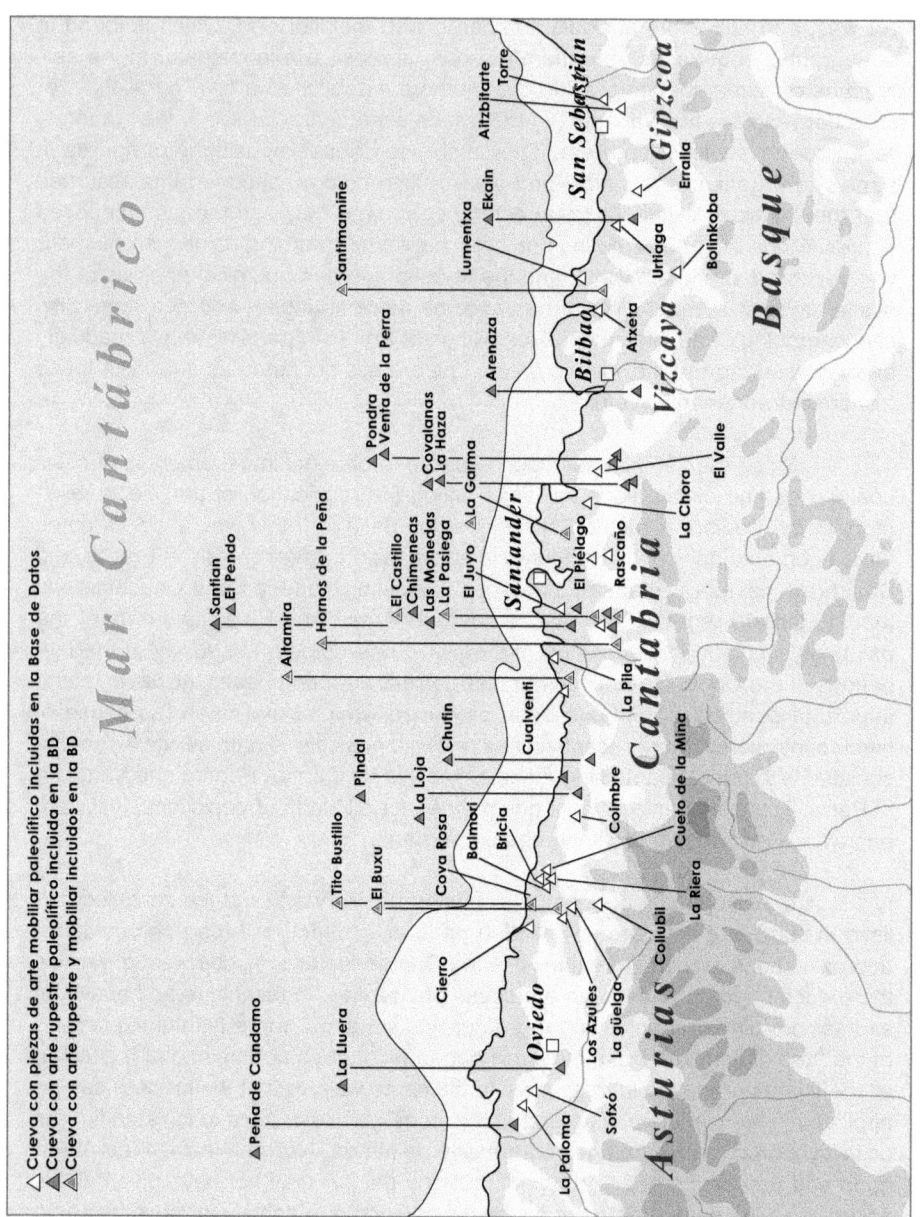

Paleolithic, shown above all by differences in the stylistic conventions applied to animals figures, but also by tendencies to change in the most usual techniques, in the abstract signs associated with them, and in the iconographic structure. Despite having some important problems, the best chronological synthesis is still the one devised by Leroi-Gourhan in the 1960s, and which we will follow, with a few adaptations, in the chronological order of the art of Asturias, Cantabria and the Basque Country.

7) It is very difficult to know the meaning of this art. It is a fact that there has been an absolute lack of continuity in cultural tradition between the Paleolithic and our society, unlike the situation in Baja California, among the Bushmen, and above all in Australia. This partly explains the little progress made in research on the meaning or reason of art during the Paleolithic, and that most studies prefer to concentrate on documenting the techniques, themes, composition and even on the chronological ordering of the art.

The studies aimed at interpreting the meaning have tended to reflect, unfailingly, the changes in mentality and the way of thinking and considering the past that have taken place, and continue to take place, in our society, as well as the ideology of each researcher. Nowadays, prehistorians usually trust little in sweeping single explanations, valid for the whole long period, whether these are ideas linking the art with good luck in hunting, with the expression of basic mythologies, or with rituals intended to maintain social cohesion, as these do not need to be mutually exclusive. Most studies are now based on the comparison between the different regions, and the different moments of the Upper Paleolithic, as a way of trying to understand the role played by the art, and hence, its meaning.

4. Paleolithic rock art in the Iberian Peninsula

The role of the Iberian Peninsula in the context of European Paleolithic art has changed decisively in the last few years. Until recently, peninsular rock art was limited to the Cantabrian region, which was a kind of maritime, western appendix to the French areas implicitly considered as central. A few isolated sites in Andalucia and the Mesetas were somewhat awkward to situate within the regions of European art. Nowadays we know cave art sites in almost the whole Peninsula, except in Galicia in the extreme northwest. Together with the great density of discoveries in the Cantabrian region, other prominent artistic groups are known in: the Mesetas and the Atlantic coast; the Andalucian area, with important prolongations to Murcia and the south of Levante, or to the west, and Extremadura and Alentejo. These regions now have important research projects being carried out by Spanish and Portuguese universities.

This decisive incorporation of the central and southern areas of the Peninsula is modifying our knowledge of Paleolithic rock art in more ways than just the quantitative aspects or the geographical distribution. Among these new discoveries, the open-air assemblages in the Duero Valley and a few other places have acquired a special scientific relevance. They alter and enrich the traditional identification of Paleolithic rock art as the art of the dark and mysterious underground world.

The number of Paleolithic caves and open-air sites in the Peninsula is now over 150. Of these, some 103 caves and rockshelters are in the Cantabrian region, 16 sites are in the Duero Valley (11 belonging to the River Côa network in Portugal), the Ebro Valley has 5 or 6 caves, there are 8 in the southern Meseta and Alentejo, 7 in the south of Levante, and about 17 in Andalucia.

These densities vary greatly due to several factors. One of these is the different exploration or tradition of this type of study in each region, and another is the different degree of conservation of the art. This too varies regionally, as in areas with many well-preserved caves, such as the Cantabrian, the importance of freeze-thaw weathering has made it difficult to conserve any possible open-air sites. But in areas which are not too high in Portugal or the northern Meseta, the greater dryness and the type of rock has enabled the survival of this kind of site. Furthermore, the density of human occupation during the Upper Paleolithic may have varied in different regions, together with the quantity, variety and continuity throughout the year of usable natural food resources.

The rock art of the Peninsula, and not only of the Cantabrian region, is clearly related with that of neighboring European areas. In the Peninsula, the art affected a series of regions of very different conditions of habitat and environment, and presumably of different organization of the subsistence economy during the Upper Paleolithic. Yet the art appears to extend through all the regions in a quite homogeneous way in general aspects. It does, nevertheless, show important differences in the structure of themes (animals and signs), and technique, among other aspects. The comparative analysis of these regional artistic groups, and of the environmental and ecological conditions of each area, is one of the fields for future research. It will equally be highly interesting, in coming years, to analyze the open-air sites spatially, as well as their relationship with the surrounding territory, and finally make comparisons between this kind of site and the caves in such classic aspects as themes, composition and distribution of depictions.

1) The Cantabrian Region. This forms a narrow West-East corridor across the north of the Iberian Peninsula, located between the Cantabrian Cordillera and the Basque Mountains to the south and the Bay of Biscay to the north. It

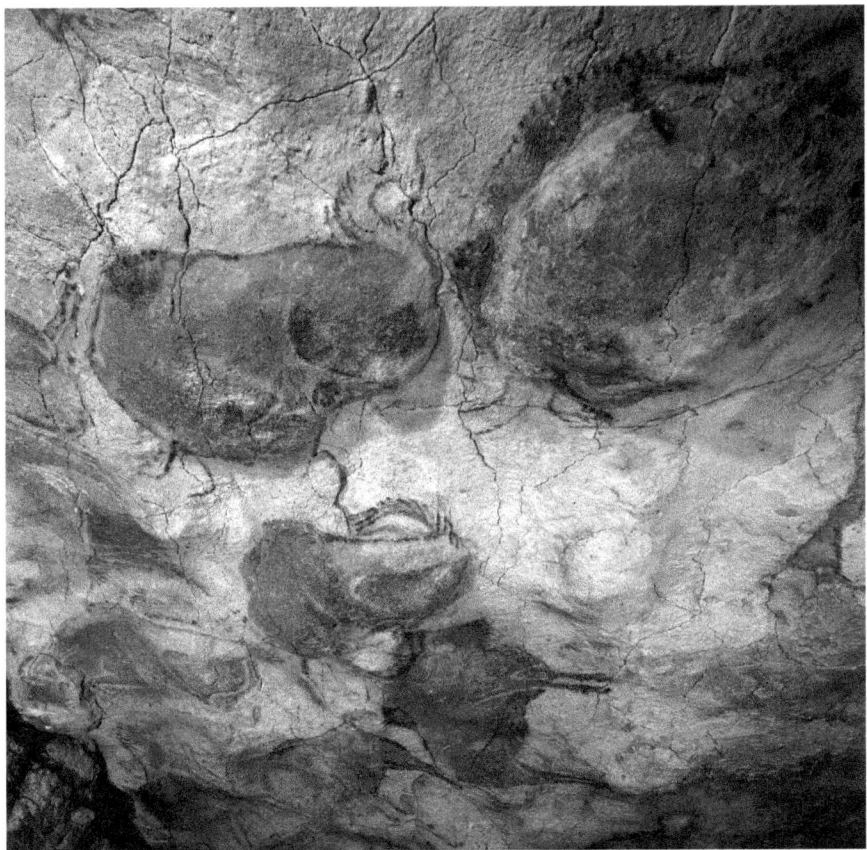
Chamber of the Polychromes, Altamira, Cantabria

is only a small region, about 400km long and 40km wide, connected at its eastern end with the regions of the south-west of France. It is known that there existed intense interaction with this part of France during the Upper Paleolithic, whereas the routes to the south were often blocked by the development of glaciers on the mountains of the cordillera, especially in the western and central sectors. At present, the Cantabrian region is divided into several administrative units, which are from west to east: Asturias, Cantabria, Basque Country, and northern Navarra.

This region had a quite large population during the Upper Paleolithic due to its relatively mild climate, and the abundance of hunting, fishing, seafood and plant resources. These were available to groups of hunter-gatherers in varied ecological environments, all located within close range. For those reasons, and the intense karstification of the area, it is easy to appreciate the abundance of well-preserved archaeological deposits, and the examples of mobiliary and rock

Chapter1: The Art of Upper Paleolithic Hunters. Introduction to Cave Art in the Iberian Peninsula.

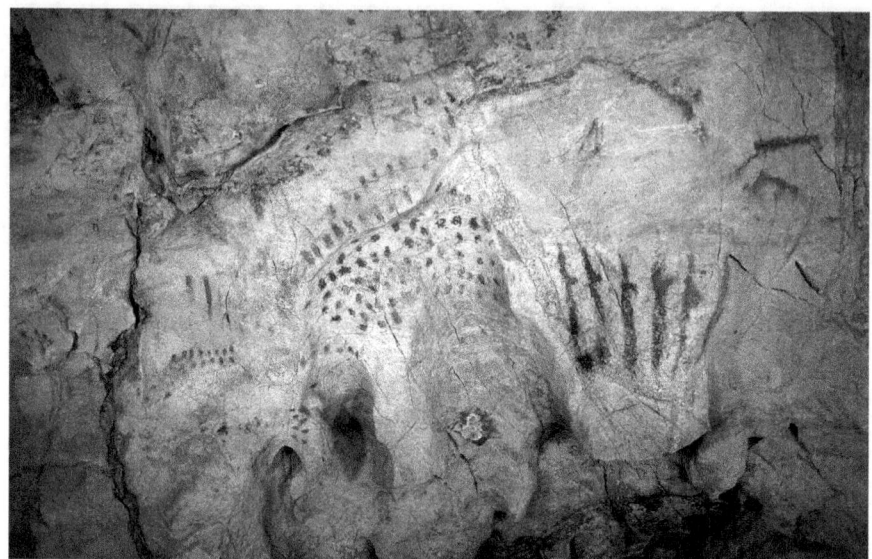

A panel of El Pindal that contains a group of six vertical red claviform signs

art, within the caves. On the other hand, it is difficult to locate Paleolithic archaeological sites in the open air.

After more than a century of research, about a hundred caves with art are known, distributed in an irregular pattern along the corridor. At the same time, decorated objects have been found in nearly all the excavations of Upper Paleolithic habitation sites, of which those with greatest stratigraphic interest are the Abrigo de La Viña, Cueto de la Mina and La Riera, El Castillo, Morín, Rascaño, Santimamiñe and the caves of Aitzbitarte. In these and many other deposits, it has been possible to study the development of the different phases of the Upper Paleolithic, between about 38,000 and 11,500 BP.

The distribution of caves with art is almost the same as the places of habitation. These are caves on the coastal strip, or more rarely, in the interior valleys, always at a low altitude. Nearly all the sites are below 200m above present sea level, and only exceptionally are they found as high as 600m. Human occupation of sites at higher altitudes are only known after 12,000 BP. Some of these caves were major centers, occupied repeatedly during the Upper Paleolithic, with many figures of different style and technique. At the other end of the spectrum, there are also caves with just one or two figures. All sites are, however, important to obtain a full view of the role played by art and the rituals linked to its production in the life of the hunters.

Chapter1: The Art of Upper Paleolithic Hunters. Introduction to Cave Art in the Iberian Peninsula.

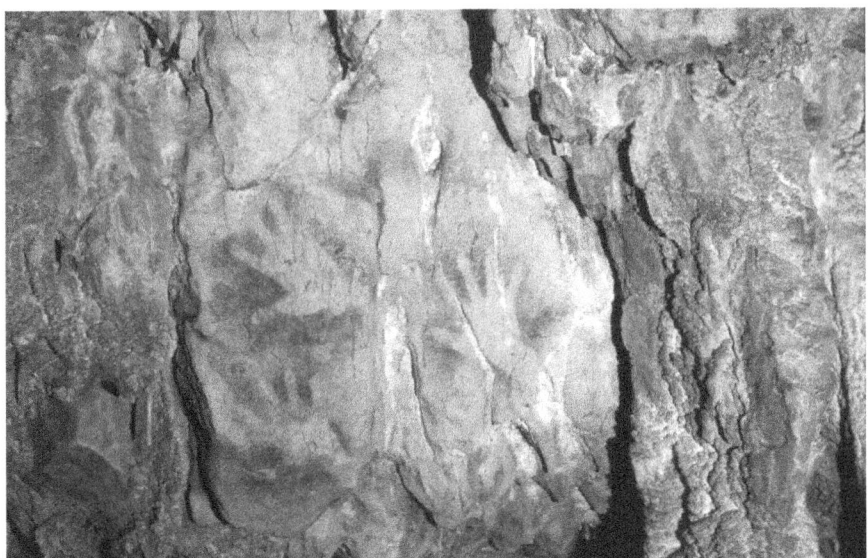

Negative hands that are found in Cueva de La Garma, Cantabria

Within the unity displayed by Paleolithic art across most of Europe, the Cantabrian region does have some distinctive features. One of these is the relatively peculiar distribution of animals, with many images of the most common ungulates here, such as red deer, and above all the females or hinds, as well as horses, goats, aurochs and bison, and fewer reindeer, mammoths and other cold climate species, although these are present in many sites. The representation of many more hinds than stags, while it may describe the reality perceived by the Paleolithic hunters because of the organization of these animals during much of the year, seems to be a purely stylistic feature. This is because it is different from the proportion of male and female red deer known in other regions nearest to the Cantabrian, like the Spanish Meseta, the Pyrenees, and the French Dordogne. Similarly, the Cantabrian region has a series of "signs" which are specific to the region, especially in the central and western zones. These abstract images appear with very similar forms in different caves, especially the quadrangular and oval signs, the quadrilaterals with a pointed protuberance midway along one side, and the "Cantabrian" claviforms.

Regarding the techniques used, we find similar types to those in other regions, with small peculiarities. There are no sculptures in low or medium relief either in stone as in Aquitaine, or in clay as in the Pyrenees. Neither was extensive use made of the chipping technique found in the open-air sites of the northern Meseta. In contrast, some techniques such as the red dotted lines, or bands of striated engraving, become very important in the region in certain periods. As

Chapter1: The Art of Upper Paleolithic Hunters. Introduction to Cave Art in the Iberian Peninsula.

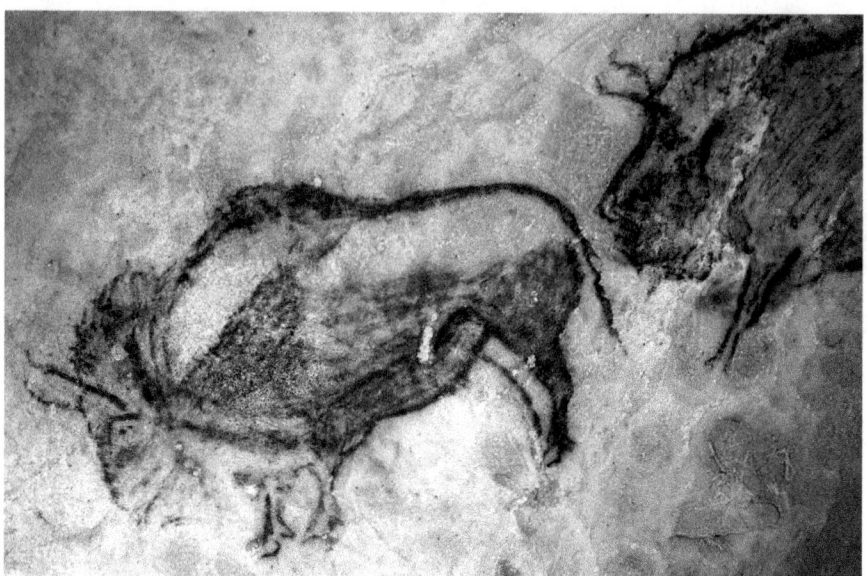

Black bison with two tails, antechamber of Cueva de Santimamiñe, Vizcaya

will be seen, in successive stages of the Upper Paleolithic, the characteristic art was: first the deep engravings in the daylight zone of caves (Abrigo de la Viña, La Lluera and Chufín); the groups of red outline or dotted line figures of Solutrean age (ie 21,000 to 16,500 BP) found in caves like Llonín, La Pasiega, Covalanas, Arco and Arenaza. These are often associated with quadrangular abstract signs, frequently subdivided internally, or with lines of dots, found therefore in the same sites and also in Chimeneas and El Castillo. Later came the great variety of technical and expressive devices used in the Magdalenian period (about 16,500 to 11,500 BP) generally aimed at reflecting reality more faithfully. These may be black paintings, as in Candamo, Cullalvera, Monedas or Santimamiñe, or in red, especially the abstract signs of the claviform type, and also engravings of different kinds, as in Tito Bustillo, Llonín, Hornos de la Peña and Altxerri. Some of the most characteristic engravings have striated areas inside the animals, which are most commonly hind' s heads. This period also sees the combination of different technical procedures in the bichromes and polychromes of Tito Bustillo, Altamira, Pasiega, Castillo and Ekain.

During the early times of cave art research, the excessive link made between the art and the greater intellectual capacity of Homo sapiens sapiens led to a chronological ordering which attributed a large number of the figures to the first period of the Upper Paleolithic, the Aurignacian (c. 33,000 to 27,000 BP). Nowadays, figurative art in its versions of mobiliary and cave art, is believed to have

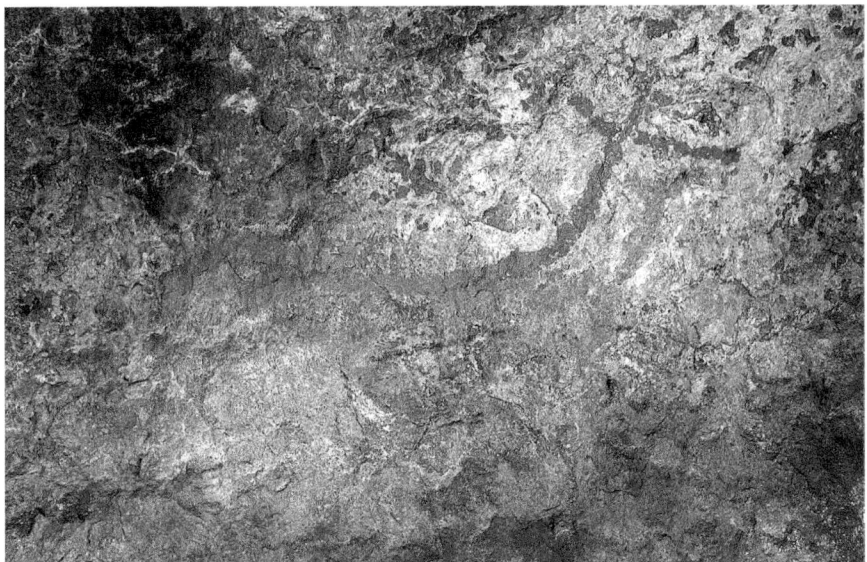
Hinds painted with red dotted lines, Cueva de Arenasa, Vizcaya

appeared much more slowly, growing a little more quickly after the Gravettian. As will be seen, an important increase in the quantity of cave art took place during the Solutrean (21,000-16,500 BP), and even more during the early Magdalenian (16,500-14,000 BP), moments when the region acquired a personality of its own. During the Magdalenian, Cantabrian art reached the highest levels of realism and formal virtuosity, while in its later phase, from 14,000 to 11,500, it is possible to see a greater interaction in style and themes with neighboring areas, especially with the French Pyrenees. As is to be seen, it was also during the Magdalenian, especially in its middle and late stages when the production of decorated bone and antler objects, and stone plaquettes, increased spectacularly.

2) Rock Art in the Mesetas and Portugal. The large drainage basins of the Duero and Tajo Rivers hold a number of Upper Paleolithic rock art sites, many of which have been found in recent years. But our knowledge of the Paleolithic population is, in most of this area, limited to these examples of art. Few Upper Paleolithic habitation sites remain in the caves of the Meseta, or if they exist, they still have not been found. Only in Portugal, especially in regions like Estremadura, to the north of the Tajo, have sites with quite important stratigraphic sequences been dug, as in the cave of Caldeirao. So in this area the industrial and economic development of the Upper Paleolithic is coming to be better known, from the Aurignacian to the Magdalenian.

Chapter1: The Art of Upper Paleolithic Hunters. Introduction to Cave Art in the Iberian Peninsula.

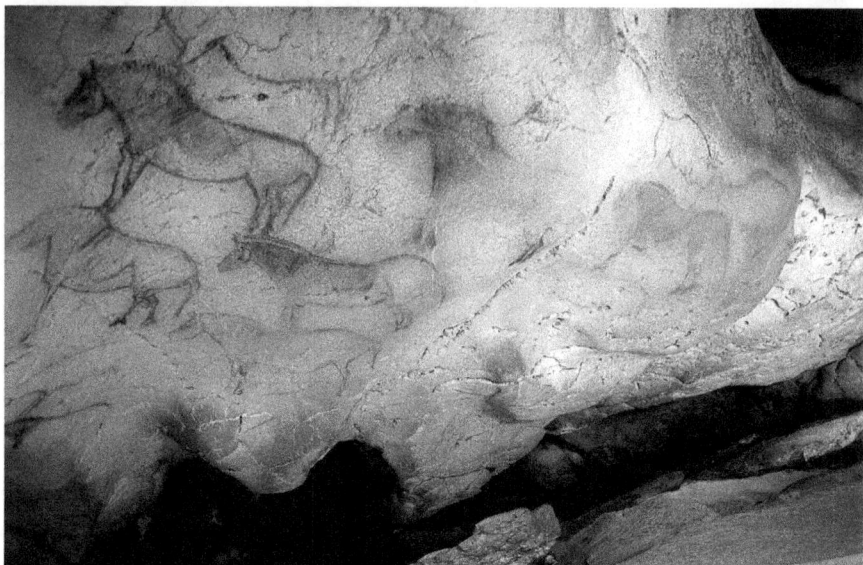

The panel of horses, Cueva de Ekain, Guipúzcoa, Basque Country

The caves with art are situated in the mountainous edges of both sub-mesetas, especially at the foot of the Central and Iberian Systems of mountains, or at lower altitude in the Portuguese hills, under the influence of the Atlantic. The open-air sites, so characteristic of this region, are located on outcrops of schist, and are located in more open or flatter areas, in many cases on the banks of the rivers themselves.

In the Duero Valley the most important sites are Cueva Mayor de Atapuerca in the North, near the passes to the Ebro Valley, and especially Cueva de la Griega in the northern slopes of the Central System, which has an exceptional group of engravings of horses, deer and signs, represented with conventions of pre-Magdalenian age. As well as these caves, an important number of open-air sites have been discovered in the last few decades. The style and chronology of these is doubtlessly Paleolithic. The figures in these assemblages were produced on rocky outcrops of schist with a characteristic technique of pecking and chipping, or with continuous fine engravings, such as are found on many cave walls, usually for the smaller drawings. These are the sites of Domingo García and Siega Verde in the northern Spanish Meseta, Mazouco and the impressive network of sites in the valley of the Côa River, a tributary of the Duero, in Portugal. This valley now has a dozen sites with rock art, especially Canada do Inferno, Penascosa, Ribeira de Piscos, Quinta de Barca; and an open-air habitation site has been dug at Cardina I, near Salto do Boi, with remains of camps, above all during the late Gravettian.

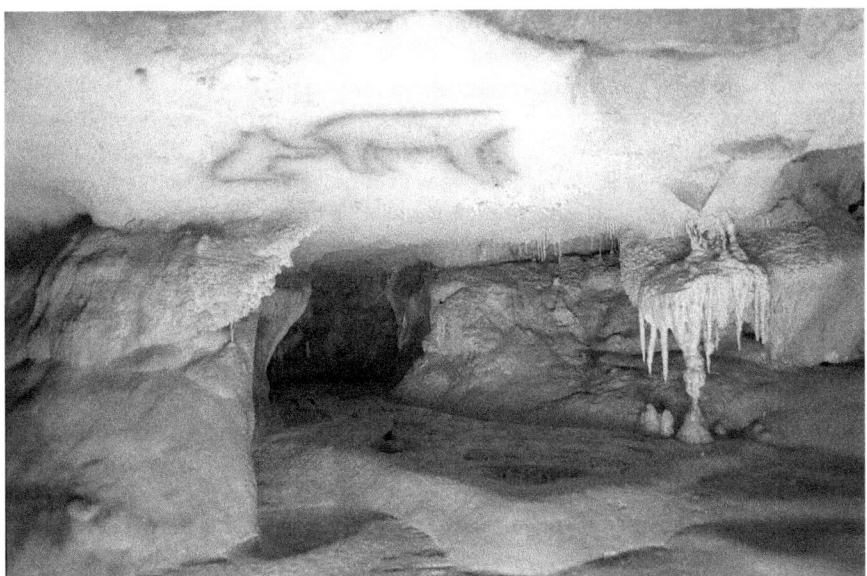

A pair of bears, Cueva de Ekain, Guipúzcoa, Basque Country

Most of these open-air sites are still being studied, but they are notable for the great numbers of aurochs, horses and stags, and occasionally caprids and other animals. A few characteristic abstract signs have been identified too, at least at Siega Verde. Regarding the forms of expression used, some interesting peculiarities include the association of several heads with one body, to give the idea of movement, and certain characteristic lines of interior articulation of the animals. Based on the stylistic assessment, a wide chronology has been proposed for these sites, from the Gravettian to the end of the Upper Paleolithic. However, the most abundant stylistic phase is that of the transition between Style III and early Style IV in the series devised by Leroi-Gourhan.

In the southern sub-meseta, Extremadura and Alentejo, two groups of caves can be differentiated. On one hand, those on the southern slopes of the Central System and in contact with the Iberian System. These form a ring of sites in the north of the provinces of Madrid and Guadalajara, including the caves of Reguerillo, Turismo, Reno and Cojo, and further to the West, Los Casares and La Hoz. They are caves in areas of karst altered by natural factors and sometimes human impact, especially in the case of El Reguerillo. The most important group is that of the engravings in Los Casares, which include an anthropomorph, a lion and a woolly rhinoceros, as well as deer, horses, goats and bovines.

On the other hand, in lower areas of the Tajo Valley, in the west of the region, we find caves in more open landscapes. These are the cave of Escoural in the Portuguese Alentejo, and the cave of Maltravieso near the city of Cáceres, in the Spanish Extremadura. These have a large number of paintings, which are unusual in the higher inland caves and even rarer in the open air, and with more archaic themes, different from the other areas. The most interesting figures are the positive and negative hands, and triangular signs and series of dots in Maltravieso. In Escoural they are black horses with large bellies and short legs, and red finger-marks and signs, as well as engravings of less precise chronology.

To summarize, the principal features of these sites in the Meseta and the Atlantic coast of the Peninsula are:

* The themes are quite different from those in the Cantabrian region. The typical abstract signs found in the North do not appear here, and signs in general are not too abundant, perhaps because of the smaller number of paintings than of engravings, as will be seen (although they do exist in several sites). The animals represented give little indication of the environmental conditions, as there is a clear predominance of horses and deer, with bovines and goats to a lesser degree. At least in the Mesetas, many of the more typically Pleistocene species can be seen, although their identification sometimes raises doubts. It has recently become clear that both bison and reindeer are depicted in Cueva de La Hoz. These figures thus accompany other Pleistocene species identified previously: a feline and possible glutton and rhinoceros in Los Casares, or a possible giant deer at Siega Verde.

The polarization in horses, deer, aurochs and goats is, in any case, greater than is found in the Cantabrian region. The faunal spectra also differ in the virtual lack of chamois among the caprids, or significantly, the greater frequency of stags, so that here they reach equal numbers with the hinds, unlike in the Cantabrian. Finally aurochs are much more abundant than bison, again in contrast with the situation in the north of the Peninsula. The images of fish and other rare species are even rarer here.

* The techniques are quite homogeneous in character, especially in the Meseta, with a strong polarization towards engraving, nearly always a simple, single line. Striated and scraped lines are found in Los Casares, while the technique of chipping off small pieces of rock, sometimes regularized with lines of abrasion, is typical of the open-air assemblages in the Duero Valley.

Paint is only predominant in the caves of Escoural and Maltravieso, with red finger-marks, and where the technique of spraying was used for the negative hands, and of printing for the positive hands. Figures in red, yellow and black paint are also known in Atapuerca, El Reno, La Hoz and Los Casares. They are nearly always simple lines, and color-wash was only used in Los Casares.

* Regarding the chronology, there is an immediate extra difficulty, which scarcely exists in the Cantabrian region, and that is distinguishing the Paleolithic figures from the art of other later periods belonging to the Holocene and sometimes existing in the same sites. The group of open-air sites on the River Côa, with dates based on the style of the figures going from the Gravettian to the late Magdalenian, summarizes the wide chronological range. Going into more detail, the oldest depictions are the paintings in the caves of Escoural and Maltravieso. The engravings in Cueva de la Griega are clearly of Style III, shown by the large-bellied animals, with characteristic long manes and heads, and few limbs. Finally, many other sites seem to be located between Leroi-Gourhan' s Styles III and IV. These are Los Casares, Domingo García, Siega Verde and part of the Côa sites. In other words, a true artistic explosion appears to have taken place between 18,000 and 14,000 BP.

3) The Ebro Valley and the Mediterranean Coast. The Mediterranean shore of the Iberian Peninsula has an important series of Paleolithic habitation sites, which are well-known due to having been studied since the early days of archaeological research. Some of them, especially Cueva del Parpalló in Valencia, provided a large collection of mobiliary art on stone plaquettes. These contain hundreds of figures, drawn with different kinds of engraving, and occasionally with paint, produced during the human occupation of the cave, and distributed throughout much of the Upper Paleolithic, from the Gravettian to the middle or late Magdalenian. The existence in this area of a mobiliary art of such a plainly Paleolithic style, was one of the main arguments which allowed the Levantine rock art, found in rock-shelters in this part of the Mediterranean, to be dated in the Holocene and to more advanced societies.

However, Paleolithic rock art was lacking, until in the last few decades when a number of sites have been discovered along the Mediterranean coast. Nevertheless, there are still very few decorated caves in relation with the number of known habitation sites, probably because of the important difficulties with conservation in this area, among other factors.

Beginning in the upper Ebro Valley, some caves have long been known, in areas in close contact with the northern Meseta. One is Cueva Palomera de Ojo Guareña, with a group of figures painted in black, in a unique style, but with animal species which are definitely Pleistocene. Another nearby cave is Penches, with animal engravings in a much more conventional Paleolithic style, and probably of Magdalenian age.

In the central Ebro Valley, only one site is known with definitely Paleolithic art: Cueva de la Fuente del Trucho. It has negative images of hands, in red and black, and always with bent or mutilated fingers, as well as horses and simple lines, meanders or finger-marks. Apart from the caves in the Cantabrian region, Fuente del Trucho, together with the caves of Maltravieso and Escoural, is one of the oldest assemblages in the Peninsula.

On the coast, to the south of Cataluña, only two figures have been located in a couple of caves. One is an engraved animal in Cova de la Taverna, attributed to the Paleolithic because of its naturalism and its location inside a cave. The other is an auroch in black, probably Paleolithic, in Cueva de la Moleta de Cartagena.

Just as in Cataluña, Levante has a full series of habitation sites, containing mobiliary art which is of great quality and abundance in Parpalló, or less so in Mallaetes or Cova Matutano. But rock art is limited to a handful of caves. The most interesting is Cueva de El Niño, near the headwaters of the River Mundo, in an area of transition with the southern sub-meseta, and very near the eastern Andalucian group of caves. It contains excellent red paintings of deer and goats. Nearer the coast, Cova Fosca has a good number of animal engravings, with deer, bovines and horses, of Style II or III. A short distance away, Cueva de Reinós is a small cave with just one goat painted in black.

The Segura Valley in Murcia has several caves which have recently been discovered, containing animal paintings of a clear and conventionalized Paleolithic style. Examples are the caves of Jorge, Las Cabras, and Arco I and II, with red paintings of horses, goats, hinds, and non-figurative marks. This group of caves leads on to another group in the east of Andalucia, which in cases like Cueva Ambrosio has art of a very similar style.

4) The First Andalucian Art. Situated in the extreme south-west of the European continent, Andalucia doubtlessly forms the last frontier of Paleolithic rock art, which does not exist in the north of Africa. A considerable number of decorated caves are known besides one open-air site at Piedras Blancas. And new discoveries are being made with a frequency that suggests more will be found in the future. The caves of La Pileta and Doña Trinidad, both in the province of Malaga, were discovered and studied at the beginning of the century. Since then, in the last twenty or thirty years, the paintings in the caves of Nerja and El Toro were discovered, and then the caves of Navarro, Malalmuerzo, Ambrosio and El Moro among other less clear ones. Furthermore, a number of interesting Upper Paleolithic habitation sites have been located; the caves of Nerja and Ambrosio mentioned above, and Cueva del Pirulejo, as well as the Gibraltar sites.

The rock art sites are distributed along the southern coast, at the western end of the Mediterranean Sea, from Gibraltar to Almeria, with a special concentration on the coast of Malaga. A second group is found in the inland hills of eastern Andalucia. So far, it seems that the art of the inland group (La Pileta and Doña Trinidad) tends to be of an archaic style, whereas a more recent Magdalenian style is more common on the coast, in the caves of Nerja, El Higuerón, El Toro and Cueva Navarro.

This first Andalucian art is clearly related to that of its neighboring areas. On its western edge it shows a continuity in its character with those sites in the Alentejo such as Escoural, and in the East with the caves of Murcia (Cueva del Arco) and Alicante. Its main characteristics, then, cannot be separated from those of its surrounding regions:

* The fauna is exclusively of temperate climates, and not specifically cold. Thus the fauna is much more similar to what is known historically in this region than to the animals represented in more northern zones, in which there was a simplification in the species of ungulates at the end of the Pleistocene, which did not happen in Andalucia. In this way, horses, aurochs, deer and goats are represented, as well as fish in Pileta and possible seals at Nerja. To put it another way, this southern third of the Peninsula does not have the cold Pleistocene fauna which is present, however scarcely, in the Mesetas.

* The assemblages discovered so far have quite a small number of figures, exceptions apart. Regarding the depictions themselves, there seems to be a relative abundance of abstract or simply non-figurative art. The simplest types are identical to depictions in northern regions, such as pairs of lines and series of dots. Other types are specific to the southern part of the Peninsula, and are stars, or lines forming grilles or reticules.

* The technical procedures seem to be less diverse than in the North. Simple, single line engravings are known in figures of an archaic style in Cueva del Moro, both in rock and in clay. Repeated and multiple line engravings exist in some cases too. Most of the paintings were produced with simple lines in black or red, or yellow in Doña Trinidad de Ardales. Color-wash was hardly ever used, or color-shading. Equally, neither clearly bichrome paintings are found, nor figures associating paint and engraving.

* It is difficult to attribute any compositions to the earlier phases of the Upper Paleolithic, which are poorly represented. Researchers in the area tend to distinguish only two successive styles, which they date in the Solutrean and Magdalenian periods.

In the first of these phases we can find animal figures fitting well into Leroi-Gourhan's Styles II and III, for example in the caves of La Pileta, Doña Trinidad and El Moro. These have animals with heavy bodies and short limbs, incorrect perspective, small heads, and conventionalized details in ears and manes. In caves like La Pileta the animals are accompanied by finger-marks in red.

In Magdalenian assemblages, here as in the rest of southwest Europe, it can be seen that greater efforts were made to express volume and occasionally movement, as in Cueva del Morrón. Using the same techniques as in earlier periods, it was possible to achieve a greater realism and better coordination of the different parts of many of the figures.

Chapter 2.
The Central Cantabrian Valleys.
Introduction to Paleolithic Cave Art in Cantabria.

1. A large human population during the Upper Paleolithic

The territory we now call Cantabria had a large human population during the Upper Paleolithic, due to its relatively good climate and the abundance of game, fish, seafood and plants available to those groups of hunter-gatherers. If we add the intense karstification of the area, it is easy to understand the reasons for large number of well-preserved archaeological deposits, and consequently of examples of mobiliary and rock art in the caves. The situation of the Autonomous Community of Cantabria, in the center of the long Cantabrian corridor, means that it provides a summary of many of the cultural characteristics of the region during the Upper Paleolithic, and even concentrates some of the changes in landscape which are found along the length of the Cantabrian region. In fact, in Cantabria we see the transition from the more orderly relief, with older lithology, in the West, to the predominance of Cretaceous limestone and more abrupt scenery in the East.

Cantabria holds some of the greatest names of European Paleolithic sites, such as Altamira, El Castillo, La Pasiega, El Pendo and La Garma, among many other less spectacular caves. After more than a century of research, nearly fifty caves with parietal art are known, while decorated objects have been recovered from nearly all the Upper Paleolithic deposits that have been dug. These human occupation sites include the caves of Castillo, Altamira, Hornos de la Peña, El Valle, El Pendo, Morín, Otero, Rascaño, Cualventi, La Pila and El Juyo. This sample must represent, however, an insignificant proportion of the works of art produced during such a long period, as many must have been destroyed or, perhaps, not yet discovered.

2. An important role in the beginnings of Paleolithic cave art research

Cantabria played an important role in the beginnings of Paleolithic cave art research, thanks to prehistorians like M. Sanz de Sautuola, H. Breuil, H. Alcalde del Río, and others. The controversy over the age of the paintings in Altamira, which took place in the years between 1880, when Sautuola' s publication pro-

Chapter2: Introduction to Paleolithic Cave Art in Cantabria

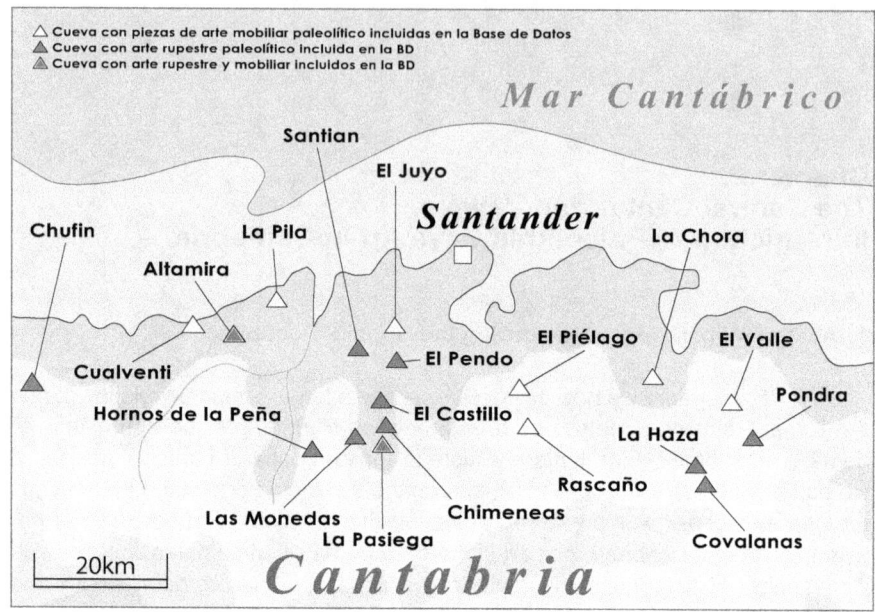
Palaeolithic caves in Cantabria

posed their Paleolithic chronology, and 1902, when this was generally accepted by prehistorians, was of extraordinary importance in the field of human sciences. In essence, the discussion was over the full artistic, intellectual and spiritual capacity of Paleolithic people (and also, indirectly, of materially primitive contemporary societies). It was difficult to accept and understand then that human groups, who lived on such a "primitive" material and technical level, could produce such excellent (and so well-preserved) paintings and engravings. At the end of the 19th Century, changes were analyzed from a too strict and simple evolutionary point of view, marking the apogee in the liberal belief in the human tendency to material and spiritual progress, considered as two sides of the same coin. This idea was imposed everywhere by Western European civilization, and was so well suited to its economic and political domination. On the other hand, after the long controversy about the evolution of the species, the arguments over Altamira helped to popularize Prehistory, and make it fully accepted socially as a period worthy to be studied, and as a scientific discipline capable of discovering greater knowledge about our past.

Years of feverish activity succeeded the recognition of the Paleolithic chronology of Altamira. Tireless explorers like Alcalde del Río and L. Sierra discovered many important parietal sites and deposits of Paleolithic occupation. Besides, they succeeded in establishing a fertile process of collaboration with prehistorians such as H. Breuil and H. Obermaier, who were based at the Institut de Paléontologie Humaine in Paris. This resulted in the excavation at Cueva del Castillo, and other less important caves, and the study of numerous cave art sites. In just twelve years, from 1902 to 1914, stratigraphic sequences were found which covered nearly all the Paleolithic, in Cueva del Castillo, and a first synthesis of Cantabrian parietal and mobiliary art was produced, in a volume of exceptional quality: Les cavernes de la region Cantabrique.

Cave art research languished after that date. This is shown by the fact that not a single new cave with art was discovered from 1911, when La Paisega was found, until the early 1950s, when renewed prospecting located the caves of Chimeneas, Monedas and Cullalvera. Investigation has speeded up since the end of the 1970s, and many new sites have been found, sometimes with quite important parietal assemblages. This has been thanks to the work of prospecting carried out by groups such as CAEAP, among others. The most important finds have been the caves of Chufín and Micolón, El Cuco and Cobrantes, Emboscados, La Fuente del Salín, El Linar and Sovilla, the caves of Arco and Pondra, Calero II, La Garma, the new paintings in El Pendo, and Cueva de Urdiales. The art in these caves has been studied by different scientists and groups; especially those linked to the University of Cantabria, which has had its own Department of Prehistory since 1978.

3. The distribution of caves with Palaeolithic Arts

The distribution of caves with art is almost the same as that of habitation sites. These caves are situated on the coastal strip and, less frequently, in inland valleys, always at low altitude, usually below 200m above sea level and only exceptionally as high as 600m. Some of them were major centers, occupied repeatedly during the Upper Paleolithic, with many figures in different styles and techniques. Examples of this kind of cave are El Castillo, La Pasiega, Altamira and La Garma. At the other end of the spectrum, some caves have only one or two figures, such as La Meaza, Sotarriza, Grande or El Otero. They are all important however in order to obtain a full view of the role played by art, and the rituals that went with it, in the life of those hunters.

The distribution of caves is relatively different when viewed from the North-South axis of the area. In the middle and inland valleys, the caves tend to be located close to the river-courses, which marked the main ways of communication, whereas they are more disperse on the coastal strip, and include locations between the valleys. Hence, the dispersion of sites is an important characteristic of the caves with art on the coastal strip, ranging from La Fuente del Salín in the lower Nansa valley to Cueva de Grande in Otañes, in the far east of the province. The recent important discovery of the Lower Passage in La Garma hill has filled the large gap which had existed in that part of the area, and which was due to the scarcity of limestone, and therefore of caves.

On the other hand, the concentration of sites is much greater in the middle valleys, just as happens in Asturias. Typical are the concentrations in the Nansa valley, which has the caves of Chufín, and Micolón, with another two nearby. Also in Puente Viesgo, by the River Pas, which has the four caves in Monte Castillo: El Castillo, Chimeneas, La Pasiega and Las Monedas; and in Ramales de la Victoria where as many as ten caves with Paleolithic art are concentrated by the rivers Calera and Carranza, tributaries of the River Asón. These caves include Covalanas, La Haza, Pondra and Arco.

The main areas and caves are the following:

* Near the mouth of the River Nansa there is a very interesting cave, La Fuente del Salín. It was sealed by the collapse of its entrance and now it can only be reached from a lower active level, through the quite large resurgence which gives the cave its name, in times of drought. A small parietal assemblage has been preserved inside the cave, and this is composed of negative and positive hand images, a few dots and finger-marks. The hearth corresponding to the Paleolithic occupation was dug, and a date of 22,340 +/- 510/480 years BP was obtained. This is probably the last human occupation of the cave, just before the entrance collapsed, as hardly any sediment has been deposited over this level. This late Gravettian date, or even an earlier one, would fit in well with the stylistic chronology given to the paintings.

Further inland along the Nansa valley, we come to a nucleus formed by the caves of Chufín, Micolón, Porquerizo and Los Marranos, all quite near together. The first has some of the oldest paintings and engravings in the province, probably of Gravettian and Solutrean age. Micolón has an exceptionally interesting group of engravings and paintings inside the cave, which is small and narrow, and quite difficult to visit. A number of engraved vulvar signs are unique in the region, and the style of the animal figures suggests a date for them within an early moment of Leroi-Gourhan's Style III. The other caves mentioned only contain a few dots and other smaller paintings in red.

* A large group of caves is situated in the coastal area in the west of Cantabria, in or near the drainage basins of the Saja and Besaya rivers. It is an area dominated in its center by the overwhelming presence of Cueva de Altamira, whose cave art tends to overshadow all the rest. Nevertheless, besides the polychromes and other paintings in Altamira, within a radius of a few kilometers other cave art is known of great interest. Thus, we find an assemblage of Magdalenian paintings, of bison and signs like a claviform and a grille, and also engravings, in Cueva de Las Aguas. Cueva de La Meaza has a sign made up of red dots, and

in Cueva del Linar a low, narrow passage has two impressive, oval-shaped constrictions, surrounded by engraved marks, as well as more conventional animal engravings on a flat roof. Another very interesting cave is Cueva de La Clotilde, which has engravings in clay, and figures with unusual representational conventions. Cueva de Cudón has some very old depictions, including a negative hand, dots and macaroni. The middle valley of the River Besaya has an important collection of engravings in Hornos de la Peña, located in the outer vestibule of the cave and in its interior rooms. In the same area is Cueva de Sovilla, with figures of hinds, reindeer, bison and horse, probably of late Magdalenian age. All the sites mentioned, except perhaps Cueva de La Clotilde, also contain important Paleolithic habitation deposits. This is also true of Cueva de Cualventi, in Oreña, with important objects of mobiliary art.

* The valley of the River Pas has an interesting group of enigmatic signs in Cueva de Santián, near the coast; and in the middle valley it has the exceptional group of caves in the hill Monte Castillo. This hill, and in particular the vestibule of its largest cave, was the main gathering point in the Cantabrian region during the Upper Paleolithic. Its strategic position in the regional landscape, and even the characteristic, unforgettable, conical shape of the hill are evidence of it. Its caves contain groups of depictions of all ages, starting in very old phases, probably Aurignacian and Gravettian in El Castillo, and possibly in an interior part of La Pasiega D. Art of Style III, dated in the Solutrean, was produced in Castillo, Chimeneas, and the Galleries A, C and D in La Pasiega. Finally, a large number of engravings and paintings correspond to the Magdalenian in Castillo, and Pasiega B, C, D (and also a few black paintings in Gallery A), as well as a smaller group in Cueva de Las Monedas, of a much later date. Throughout the different phases of decoration in the caves and passages inside the hill, not only were there changes in the stylistic conventions, and to a lesser extent, the techniques and thematic structure, but also the abstract signs associated with the figures and their relative frequency.

* The drainage basin of the River Miera widens considerably towards the coast. On its left bank it includes all of what is now the Bay of Santander, which has numerous Paleolithic sites in the surrounding area, such as the caves of El Juyo, El Pendo and La Llosa which have art, and the habitation site of Cueva de Morín. On its right bank it has the site of the Lower Passage in La Garma, with cave art still being studied. This is a complex cave, with many depictions on its walls corresponding to very different moments of the Upper Paleolithic, incredibly preserved intact until the present time. This is because the entrance was blocked by a natural collapse, and to reach the Lower Passage it is now necessary to descend several vertical shafts from higher levels of the same cave system. This gallery has an impressive habitation deposit intact on the floor of the cave, and cave art corresponding to at least three successive phases of decora-

Chapter2: Introduction to Paleolithic Cave Art in Cantabria

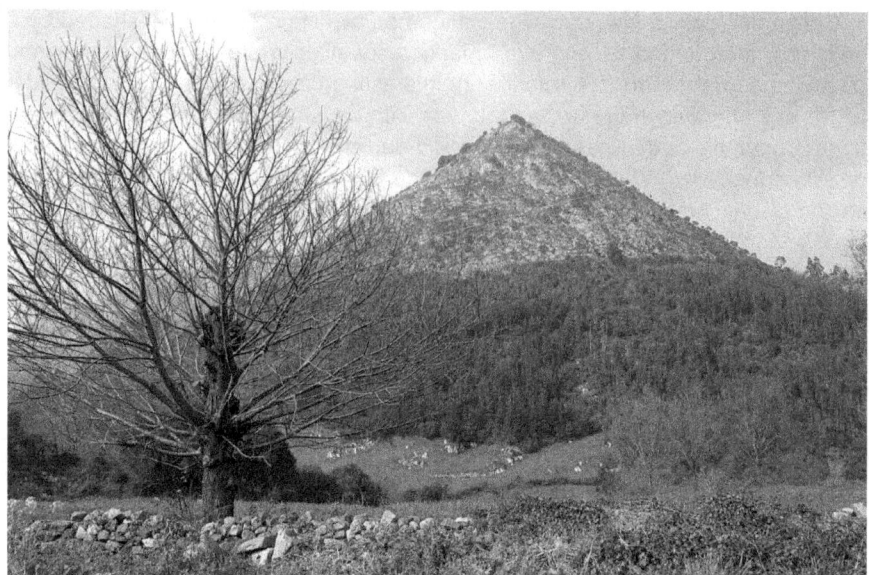
Mt.Castillo, Puente Viesgo, Cantabria

tion. The oldest one is probably Gravettian, and is represented by negative hand images, dots, paired marks and other finger-marks. A second group of paintings has animal figures painted in red with dotted lines, representing hinds, ibex, bison, giant deer and quadrilateral signs. Some of the animal engravings probably belong in the same phase. Finally, a large group of engravings and black paintings of Magdalenian age include bison, horses and ibex, and heads of hinds with striated engraved lines.

The inland part of the Miera valley is much narrower, with steep rocky slopes. Here we find sites where ibex was hunted and salmon were fished in the summer and fall, such as the caves of El Rascaño and El Piélago. There is only one cave with Paleolithic art, Cueva de Salitre, one of the highest caves in the region, and which has hinds in red in the Solutrean style, and other figures less well preserved.

* The River Asón and its tributaries form quite a large drainage basin. Right on the coastline, we find a couple of rockshelters in the hill at Santoña, which have Paleolithic deposits and some non-figurative engravings. A little further to the south, other sites do not have many more figures: Cueva del Otero has a single schematic representation of an ibex. This small figure, depicted from the front, is interesting as it reproduces a design which is often found on portable artifacts, such as perforated staffs, assegaies, or simple decorated bones, and so it is possible to date it in the late Magdalenian, which is the period when those mobiliary objects were made. Cueva de Cobrantes also has an assemblage of engravings in a Magdalenian style. Other caves in this area have important habitation deposits, where mobiliary art has been found, particularly in Magdalenian levels; e.g. the caves of Valle and La Chora.

Three groups of caves can be distinguished in the middle valleys. First of all, the caves of Emboscados, with important Magdalenian striated engravings of stags and a hind, and El Patatal, in the enclosed depression of Matienzo. Much better known is the group at Ramales de la Victoria, with the caves of Covalanas and La Haza, with red dotted paintings in Style III. They are near a large cave, El Mirón, which also has some non-figurative engravings, and thick archaeological sediments that are being dug at the present. Cueva de Cullalvera has the deepest known art in the region, as the last paintings are more than a kilometer from the entrance. Its most interesting art is found in two chambers. The first has signs such as vertical claviforms, lines and dots, while three horses painted in black in a quite late style are found in a further second chamber.

Finally, we come to a large series of generally quite small cave art assemblages, concentrated in less than a kilometer of the rocky slopes of the River Carranza, a tributary to the Asón. The western-most cave is Morro del Horidillo, and the furthest east is Venta de la Perra, which is located in the province of Vizcaya. Between these two, we find Pondra, the Arco B and C complex, and Cueva de Arco A. Cueva de Sotarriza is situated on the opposite side of the valley. Except for the engravings in the vestibule of Venta de la Perra, which are very old, or the black painting of a horse in Sotarriza, which is probably Magdalenian, most of the figures in the other caves can be attributed to Style III and the Solutrean period. This is shown by the appearance of the technique of dotted lines in red paint, and by the style of the figures, which represent bison and aurochs, horses, hinds and ibex, as well as quadrilateral signs. In some of the caves there are also very simple animal engravings, drawn with a single line, with very different conventions from those of the Magdalenian. The most interesting is the depiction of a mammoth, with an arched belly-line and other archaic conventions, in Cueva del Arco B.

* A few other smaller caves, with groups of engravings, are situated in the eastern coastal strip; either in Castro Urdiales, like Cueva del Cuco, or nearby, like the caves of La Lastrilla or Cueva Grande in Otañes, with a single panel of a stag facing an ibex. In this area, the most important cave is Cueva de Urdiales, which has only recently been discovered, and which has a splendid group of black paintings and engravings, doubtlessly of Magdalenian age.

4. Chronology of Arts

Chapter 2: Introduction to Paleolithic Cave Art in Cantabria

The main characteristics of parietal art in Cantabria will be described, following the chronological scheme which we currently believe to be the most accurate, and which distinguishes at least three long successive periods:

a) The beginnings are still not well known. Although the region was occupied, and several sites dated in the early Upper Paleolithic have been dug, such as Castillo, Morín and Pendo, we do not know any parietal art, or figurative mobiliary art, of a clear Aurignacian age. This is in contrast with the neighboring province of Asturias. In any case, the older age of the Aurignacian implies problems of conservation and discovery of parietal art and archaeological deposits which are much greater than happens with, for example, the Magdalenian. As a result, it is necessary to be careful when defining the art of this early period of the Upper Paleolithic. However, in the first half of the 20th Century, prehistorians such as H. Breuil proposed a chronology for the art of Cantabria which attributed a large number of figures to the very start of the Upper Paleolithic.

During the Gravettian, approximately between 27,000 and 21,000 BP, it was common to enter into caves in order to produce very simple parietal art. Red dots, finger-marks, paired lines and negative hand images were painted either using a technique for spraying paint, or by dabbing the paint on with a finger-tip. Whereas this type of figure is very scarce in Asturias, which has only one negative hand in Tito Bustillo, in Cantabria they are abundant in the Lower Passage in La Garma, Castillo, Fuente del Salín, Cudón, and Altamira where they are associated with animals in perhaps a slightly later style. In the same way, Chufín has animals and finger-marks painted in a very archaic style, which must correspond to the same period. Other examples are the engravings of animals in a similar style as well as painted finger-marks in Castillo and Pasiega D.

Regarding the assemblages of "exterior" engravings of animals, the situation is quite the opposite of that of the hand images: there are noticeably fewer sites in Cantabria than in Asturias. Just as in the western province, these must have been produced in the Gravettian, and possibly in the Solutrean. The daylight group of engravings in Cueva Chufín is practically interchangeable, in its identical ways of representing hinds and other characteristics, with those found in the Nalón valley, in Asturias. Hornos de la Peña has a much smaller group, while Venta de la Perra, by the River Carranza, is perhaps the most evolved of all the sites. An engraved figure in a nearby cave, the mammoth in El Arco B, could equally be of Gravettian age.

b) During the Solutrean, as in other parts of the region, the use of red pigment became even more common. It was applied with various procedures: as a more or less wide, single line; as dots dabbed on the wall; as a partial or full color-wash; or as lines varying in width as a first attempt at expressing volume.

Chapter2: Introduction to Paleolithic Cave Art in Cantabria

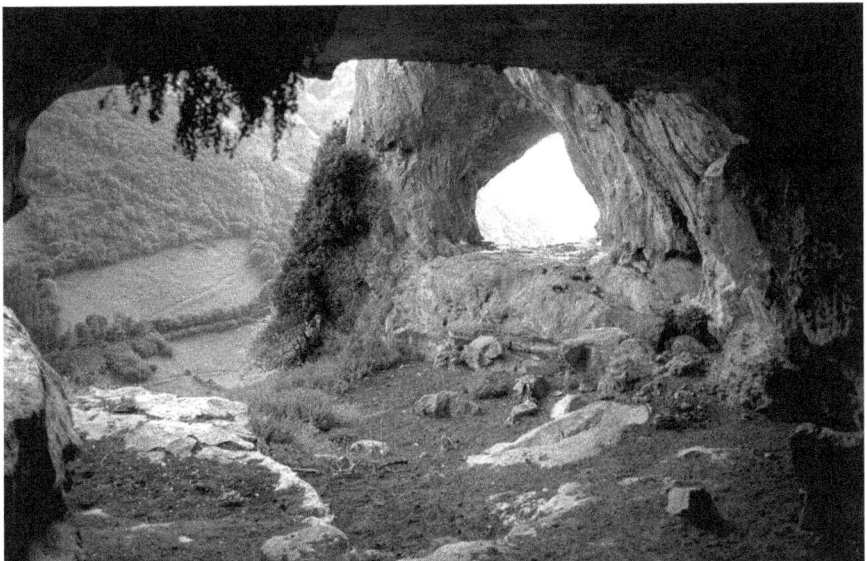

A natural rock shelter found near the cave of Pondra, Cantabria

This type of art is found in Covalanas and Haza, and is also represented in many of the figures in Pasiega, Arco, Pondra, Garma and Pendo. Black paintings are less common, but do exist in Micolón, Chimeneas and Altamira. In these cases the pigment was applied in a different way, with simple, narrower lines and usually dry, as charcoal. They are normally outline figures, without color-wash or variations in width of line, which were techniques developed in black pigment during the Magdalenian. The engravings found are essentially of simple lines in Micolón, Castillo and El Cuco, or associated with red dotted lines in Pondra, Arco A and Arco B-C. These are outline animal figures, with few interior details, and with more archaic conventions than we find in those figures with interior masses of striated lines, and often with repeated lines around their outline, which are of Magdalenian age. Engraving is occasionally associated with paint, especially in red figures of later phases, e.g. in Pasiega A.

Regarding the themes represented, a typical one consists of abstract signs in a quadrangular shape, often subdivided internally into three parts, and incorporating borders of short lines around their edges. They are found associated with lines of dots. Subdivided oval signs, and ladder-shaped signs or scaliforms, are also frequent. Some of the compositions made up of parallel rows of red dots must correspond to this period, as in Meaza, Arco A, Castillo and Pasiega C. At least the first of these signs, the quadrilaterals, are exclusively found in the Cantabrian region, and so far are only known in its central valleys, between Arco A, in the Carranza-Asón valley, and El Buxu, by the Piloña and Sella rivers. Within

57

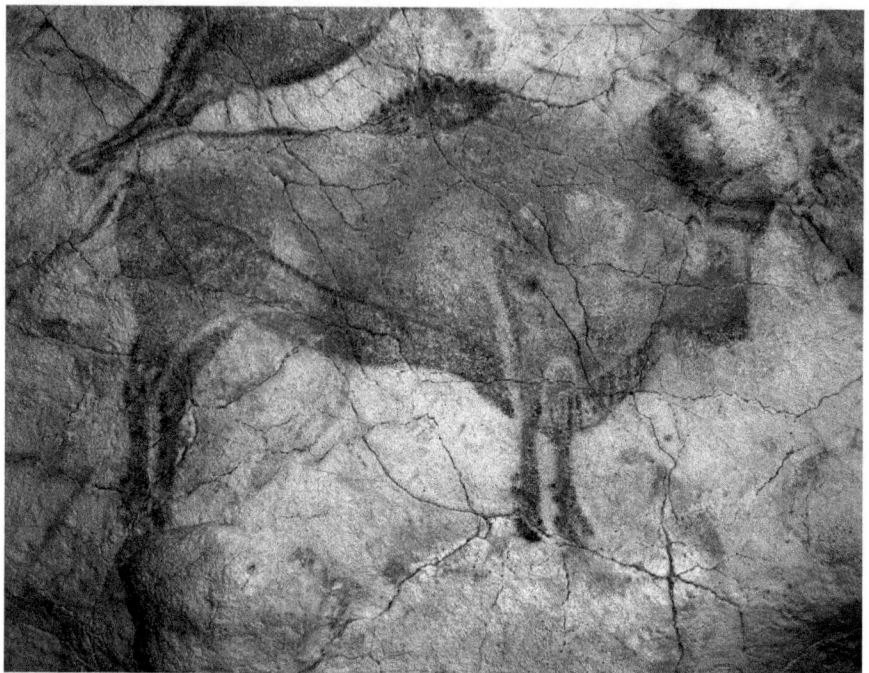

A bison of Altamira

this area, the relative frequency of the signs tends to increase towards the center, that is to say, in the valleys of the Pas, Besaya and Saja. In fact, Castillo, Chimeneas, Pasiega A, C and D, and Altamira contain most of the quadrilateral signs known to date.

The form of these signs tends to change slightly with time. At first, we find plain rectangular and oval signs, as in Covalanas, Arco B and La Garma, or signs subdivided transversely into three fields, as in Castillo or Chimeneas, where they are sometimes associated with series of red dots. Later, it is more common to find oval and quadrilateral signs with a pointed protuberance on their longest side, and sometimes subdivided longitudinally, as in Altamira, Pasiega C, A and D, Castillo and Arco B. Apparently by a process of morphological abbreviation, these signs led to the classic claviforms, now associated with animal figures in Style IV.

Among the animal figures, we still find a similar distribution to that of the exterior engravings of the previous stage, with large numbers of hinds and horses, of aurochs and bison, and other animals to a lesser degree. The more unusual species that can be found are bear, in Micolón, reindeer, in Pasiega A and

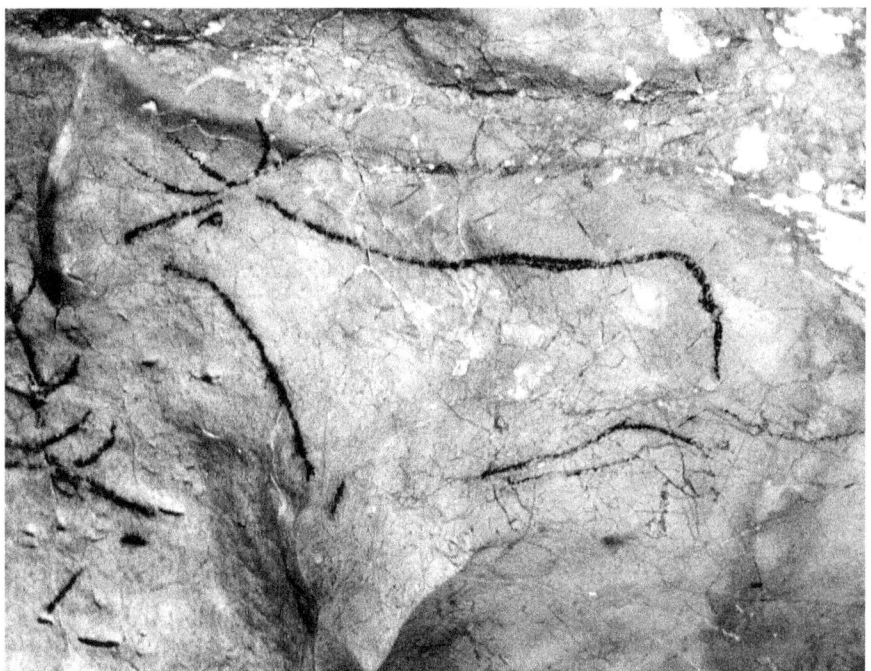

Stag in black, Chamber of the Stags, Cueva de Chimeneas

La Haza, mammoth in Castillo and Arco B, giant deer, in La Garma, and birds, in Pasiega B. The compositions that are known include of course the pairing of bison or auroch with horses, with hinds and goats in more marginal positions, that was so important in Leroi-Gourhan' s interpretations. This composition, which was already found in the previous stage in the daylight figures of Hornos de la Peña, as well as in the "Great Niche" in La Lluera, now appears in caves like La Pasiega, both at the end of Gallery A and in Zone D. However, other associations are much more frequent, mainly those based on hinds and horses, as in Cueva de Covalanas, Pasiega A, Pendo and Pondra. There are many forms of the composition, but some of the most significant seem to be pairs of animals occupying individualized spaces, such as small hollows in the wall, facing each other, or back-to-back, and also occupying superimposed planes. Examples are found in Covalanas, Arco A, Arco B, Pondra, Pasiega A, C and D, Pendo, Garma, and of course, Arenaza in the province of Vizcaya.

c) During the Magdalenian, or Leroi-Gourhan' s Style IV, approximately between 16,000 and 11,500 BP, we can find in Cantabria the same general tendencies that are appreciated in other areas of SW Europe: the preference for depicting usually static animals naturalistically, showing great progress in the representation of the third dimension. This was accompanied by a great variety of technical and expressive resources, used now with the aim precisely of reflecting reality more faithfully. Furthermore, this technical variability seems to spread to the purely artistic: in comparison with the relative homogeneity of earlier compositions, in fairly concise and tidy panels, in the Magdalenian the caves were filled with works of art of a very unequal technical and artistic quality, and of different sizes and degree of visibility. Together with this "democratization" of parietal art, perhaps produced by more kinds of people and with more variable purposes than in earlier stages, we can also appreciate a veritable explosion of decoration on artifacts, as tools or simple stone plaques are decorated much more often than before. Finally, another characteristic of the Magdalenian seems to be a greater degree of long-distance integration in the stylistic conventions and even in the abstract signs and iconographic structure. As we will see, this has a great effect on the Cantabrian region, which now interacts strongly with the area of the Pyrenees.

Despite this, the region is able to maintain its own personality, especially in the early Magdalenian. The classic claviforms are painted at this time, probably derived from an abbreviation of the previous quadrilaterals with pointed protuberance, and which are found in Pasiega B and C, Castillo, Altamira, Las Aguas and La Garma, as well as grille-shaped signs, in Altamira and Las Aguas. The typical animal figures are engravings of hind' s heads with striated lines in their chin and chest. This theme has played an important role in cave art research, as in Altamira and Castillo they appeared both on the cave walls and roofs and on deer scapulae recovered from early Magdalenian strata. This has made it possible to set a date of about 15,000 BP for the first figures of this type. Very similar engravings are known on the walls of Pasiega B and C, Emboscados, Cobrantes, Grande in Otañes, and La Garma.

The early part of the Magdalenian was also probably the time when large compositions were produced in Pasiega B and perhaps the front part of Pasiega C, the polychromes in Altamira (which have been dated to between 14,900 and 14,000 BP, except for a few smaller and later figures), the compositions in Las Aguas, and other slightly later ones in Castillo (where bison have been dated to about 13,000 BP), and La Garma. In several places in the latter cave, we can find many of the more typically Magdalenian motifs and techniques. Bison are painted in black and engraved around their outline, hind' s heads are striated, and "masks" were produced by adding an eye, nostril and mouth to the natural relief of the wall (these figures are also found in Altamira and Castillo). Other animals were painted in a partial color-wash of variable intensity, with abundant lines of interior organization.

Iconographic composition tends to change in the middle and late Magdalenian, as reindeer, ibex, and bears appear more often, while bison (as in the Pyrenees) and horses dominate the assemblages. The caves that can be included in this period are Cullalvera, Sovilla, El Otero and Las Monedas, where radiocarbon dates of about 12,000 BP have been obtained. Certain figures in other more complex sites, like El Castillo may also belong to the late Magdalenian. These caves have fewer conventionalized abstract signs, and the only characteristic ones are the late claviforms in La Cullalvera and El Pindal in Asturias, which are identical to those found in caves in Ariège, demonstrating the strong cultural integration which existed between both regions at that time. Shortly afterwards, the region suffered a complete cultural and economic reorganization, above all during the temperate climatic phase of the Alleröd (11,800 to 10,800 BP), which among other things brought an end to Paleolithic parietal art.

2-1. Cueva de Chufín

Cueva de Chufín, or Moro Chufín, is located on the banks of the River Lamasón, 100m from its confluence with the River Nansa. The nearest village is Riclones, in the municipal district of Rionansa (Cantabria).

The landscape around the cave is now very different from the one that existed when it was occupied by Paleolithic populations. Apart from the climatic and vegetation changes that have taken place everywhere since the glaciation, a reservoir was built here in the 1960s, and this has altered the natural environment, both outside and inside the cave. Palombera reservoir has flooded the confluence of the two rivers, and its average level is 30m above the original course of the rivers. In this way, the water has filled lower caves, some of which might have formed part of the Chufín cave system, and is very close to the Paleolithic entrance of the cave. Inside the cave, the passage descends until it reaches a flooded section in the form of a permanent lake, which is so near to Paleolithic paintings that it could affect their conservation.

Nowadays Cueva de Chufín can be reached, either by going down a steep hill from the village of Riclones, or by crossing the reservoir in a small boat, which takes you to a point only a few meters from the entrance.

The cave has long been known to the people of Riclones, and its name comes from a folk-tale describing how the Moor Chufín, a mythical character, had hidden treasure in the cave. This story, similar to many others told in different parts of the region, led to some especially credulous or optimistic people digging in the cave in search of the treasure, but instead partially destroying the archaeological deposits in the entrance.

In 1972, Don Manuel de Cos Borbolla, in the company of his sons and the reservoir guard, Don Primo González, noticed the paintings on the cave walls. He informed Martín Almagro Basch, who at that time was the director of the National Archaeological Museum in Madrid, of the discovery. Professor Almagro took charge of the study of the cave and found more paintings as well as a highly interesting panel of engravings in the entrance. His results were published quickly, the following year, and although it is now somewhat out of date, it remains the only full study of the art in the cave to have been published.

In 1974, Professors V. Cabrera Valdés and F. Bernaldo de Quirós began to dig the archaeological deposit in the entrance. In the course of their work

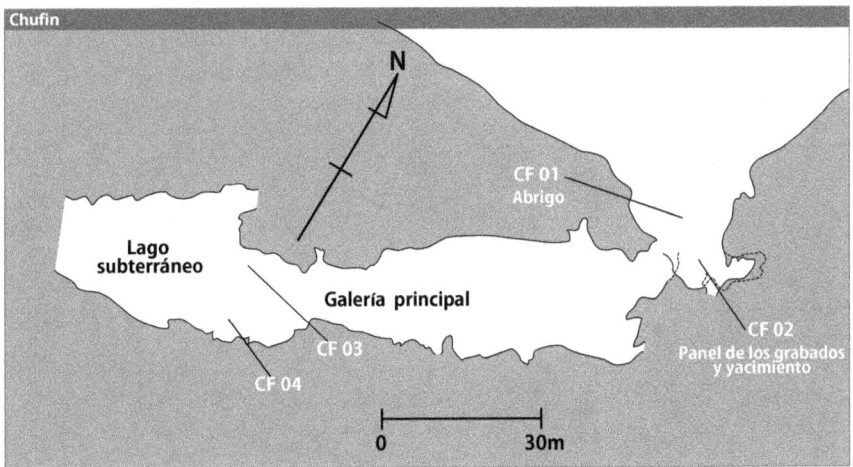
Cueva de Chufín, Ground Plan

they located more engravings and paintings in the inner passage, and these were published three years later. Two areas were dug in the vestibule: one below the main panel of engravings and one on the right of the vestibule, which gave different results. An area of seven square meters was opened near the engravings, and a fluvial level was reached, below which there was a thin layer with lithic tools. These were so little significant that no conclusions could be made about the age of the occupation. Eight square meters were dug on the right-hand side, and here a habitation structure was found in the form of a circular hollow, 2m in diameter and 40cm deep, supported by large limestone blocks. The lithic assemblage in this level included several hunting points with flat retouch, which could be attributed to the upper Solutrean, coinciding with the C-14 date obtained: 17,420 +/- 200 BP. Two lower layers were found below this level, but with assemblages that are not diagnostic.

The best-known cave art in Chufín was produced precisely in that exterior rock-shelter. On its left-hand side, a large block of limestone, about 5m long has a large number of animal figures: fourteen hinds, a few bovines, including a bison, and other non-figurative lines. All the figures were drawn with deeply engraved lines, and most of them follow a very simple compository scheme, reduced to three lines. One represents the head and forehead and is prolonged to the ear (usually only ear is drawn), a second line indicates the cervicals, back and croup, and is sometimes prolonged as far as the rump, and the third line represents the chest. None of the figures have interior details, apart from three of them which have a short line indicating the mouth. The representation of belly and limbs is equally very rare, and is only present in three figures.

2-1: Cueva de Chufín

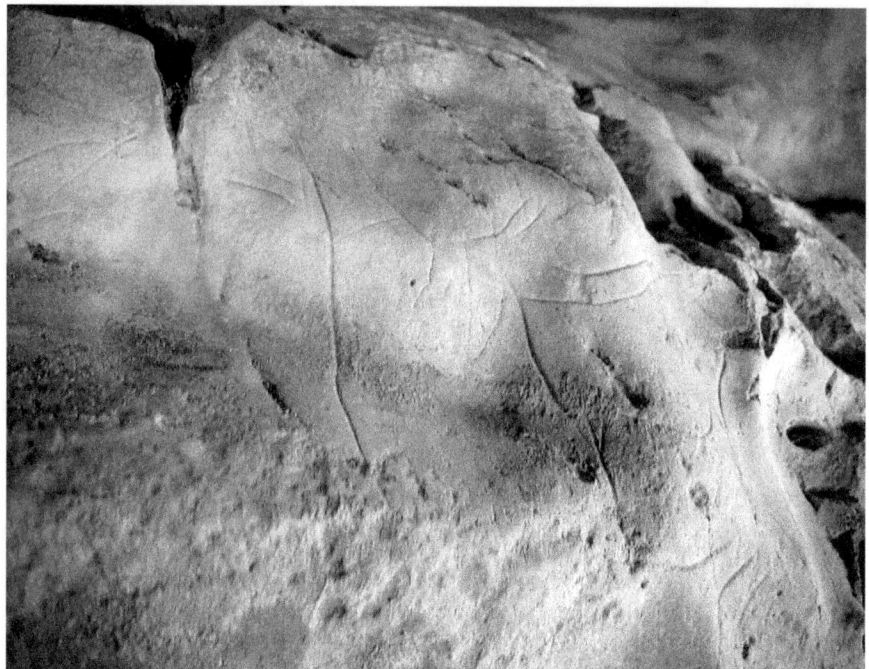

Engraved hinds

      Two groups of figures can be distinguished, with differences in the size and in the depth of the engraving. Those on the lower frieze are the largest, between 50 and 100cm long. The figures on the upper frieze are somewhat smaller, as none is longer than 40cm, and besides, the groove is shallower, and the figures were sometimes represented upside-down or vertically. These characteristics seem to be linked to the different working conditions. Thus, the large figures on the lower frieze could be drawn from a relatively comfortable standing position on the floor at the foot of the large block. As a result the figures are larger. But the higher they are on the block, the smaller the figures tend to become, and this is probably due to a reduced manual field for the artist. Finally, the fact that some of the figures are upside-down or vertical, as well as being smaller, suggests that they were drawn from a position on the upper surface of the block, where the artist' s manual field was even more limited.

      At the back of the rock-shelter, a narrow passage leads to a low crawl about twenty meters long, where numerous hollowed-out bear pits are visible on the cave floor. The floor gradually descends and the passage becomes easier, and it finally reaches a large chamber with Paleolithic art on both walls. On the right-hand side we can see a panel of paintings, with two figures of horses, a bovine, and an indeterminate quadruped. The abstract signs at the end of the

2-1: Cueva de Chufín

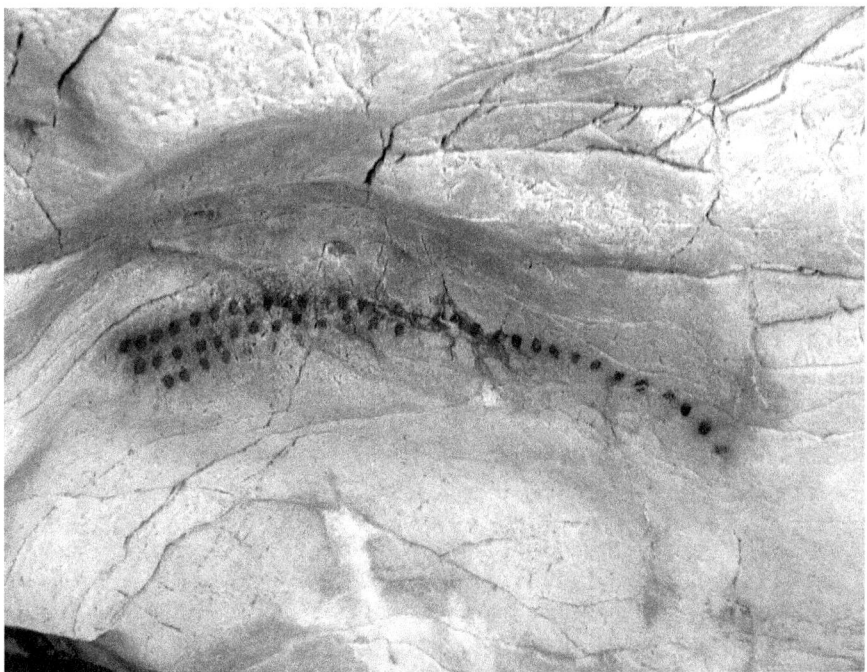

Series of dots

passage, just before the lake, are of greater interest. Here there are two groups of five vertical lines, and a group of short marks in pairs. All these figures were painted with red pigment, which can be very difficult to see in some cases.

The left-hand wall has a large ledge of limestone, above which the Paleolithic artists produced numerous depictions on the wall and around hollows in the roof. Here two groups of figures can be distinguished by the techniques used to produce them: engraving and red paint. The former includes three bison, two horses, a doubtful anthropomorph and other lines still being studied. These engravings, unlike the ones in daylight, are very fine. The signs painted in red consist of several groups of dots, which are composed in more or less complex structures based on parallel lines of dots, and which have rectangular or elliptical shapes, as well as a stag and other very faint figures in red. A feature common to all these signs is that they are usually associated with natural rock forms, such as flat surfaces, cornices, fissures or concavities.

The parietal art in Chufín shows two, or perhaps three, different moments of decoration. In fact, the two groups of engravings, the exterior ones and the finer ones on the left of the interior passage, are clearly different in style and technique. The chronology of the red paintings is more controversial, as we shall see.

So, the decorative phase of the exterior engravings, possibly at the end of the Gravettian or in the early Solutrean (22,000 - 19,000 BP), is well defined. They can be integrated technically, stylistically and iconographically, with other assemblages dated in this early time, such as La Lluera, La Viña, Santo Adriano and El Molín (all in Asturias), and less clearly with the exterior figures at Hornos de la Peña (in Cantabria) and at Cueva de Venta de la Perra (in Vizcaya), as these have their own special characteristics.

The fine engravings inside Cueva de Chufín are in a later style, although they are also likely to be pre-Magdalenian. Characteristic evidence of this is found in the lack of proportion, the small heads and large bodies of some of the figures. In our opinion, the date obtained in the dig at the entrance could correspond better with these engravings than with the rest of the paintings and engravings, which are older.

On the other hand, the animals painted in red have a very simple, scarcely naturalistic form, without interior details. Regarding their chronology, we consider that it is especially significant that they are associated spatially and technically with red finger-marks, vertical lines and dots. The first at least, paired lines painted with two fingertips, are associated in the region with animal figures in a very archaic style (in Pasiega C), or with negative hand-images (in Fuente del Salín and La Garma). That is, with themes that sometimes correspond to the Gravettian or even Aurignacian periods in the south-west of Europe. The red paintings in Chufín must have been produced at a similar time to the exterior engravings. We do not believe that they necessarily have to be later, simply because they were painted inside the cave, as was once thought. In our opinion, they probably form one of the oldest groups of figurative art located inside a cave in the Cantabrian region.

Finally, it should be noted that another exceptional decorated cave is situated on the shore of the Palombera reservoir, about 200m from Cueva de Chufín. This is Cueva de Micolón, with Paleolithic parietal paintings and engravings, which can be dated in Leroi-Gourhan's Style III, between 20,000 and 16,000 BP. It is, however, much more difficult to visit Micolón because the cave passages are extremely narrow. Some other caves located relatively close to Chufín have Upper Paleolithic sediments, or very simple cave art, such as Los Marranos and El Porquerizo.

Bibliography

Almagro Basch, M., 1973: Las pinturas y grabados rupestres de la cueva de Chufín. Riclones (Santander). *Trabajos de Prehistoria*, 30, pp 9-67.

Almagro Basch, M.; Cabrera, V.; Bernaldo de Quirós, F. 1977: Nuevos hallazgos de arte rupestre en Cueva Chufín. Riclones (Santander). *Trabajos de Prehistoria*, 34, pp 9-29.

2-2. Cueva de Altamira

This cave, without doubt the best known cave in the Cantabrian region, is situated about two and a half kilometers to the south-west of the town of Santillana del Mar. Its entrance is very near the top of a low limestone hill, just 161m above sea level, in a dominating position over the surrounding land. From this place, as its name indicates (Altamira could be translated as "high view"), there are wide panoramas over the regional territory, especially an area of karst to the west and the north, where the coastline is, about 5km away at the present time. Equally, towards the valley of the River Saja, hardly two kilometers to the south.

The archaeological site of Altamira, so stunning for the beauty of its paintings, is not, however, an isolated case. In a radius of ten kilometers around the cave there are several sites with Paleolithic art, even if they are much less spectacular. So, we can find the caves of Las Aguas and Linar to the west of Altamira, La Clotilde by the River Saja in the south, Cueva de Cudón in the east, across the River Saja after its confluence with the Besaya, and also Cueva de Sovilla up-river in the Besaya valley. Upper Paleolithic archaeological deposits, usually habitation sites, are even more common in the area, and include the caves of La Peña Caranceja, Cualventi, Gurugú and La Pila.

A hundred and twenty years after their discovery, the polychrome bison still stand out for their esthetic qualities among all the known decorated caves in the north of Spain, and are doubtlessly one of the most astonishing creations in western prehistory. The remainder of the cave' s archaeological register is, however, rather more conventional, and relatively similar to other decorated sites and archaeological deposits in the region. The walls and roofs inside Altamira, as well as the famous polychrome animals, have numerous engravings, black paintings, and some in red, yellow and violet, of animals, anthropomorphic beings, abstract signs and non-figurative motifs. Equally, a habitation deposit of Solutrean and early Magdalenian age has been studied in the entrance of the cave, within the daylight area. Human occupations became especially frequent between approximately 18,500 and 14,000 BP, and this lapse of time may correspond to the production of all, or nearly all, the art inside the cave. As will be explained later, scientists are not unanimous on this point.

It seems that the cave was known to the local people of Santillana and Vispieres since 1868. Don Marcelino Sanz de Sautuola, a restless scholar, naturalist and archaeologist, studied it between 1875 and 1879, and he discovered and correctly interpreted the Paleolithic deposit in the entrance. Here he found

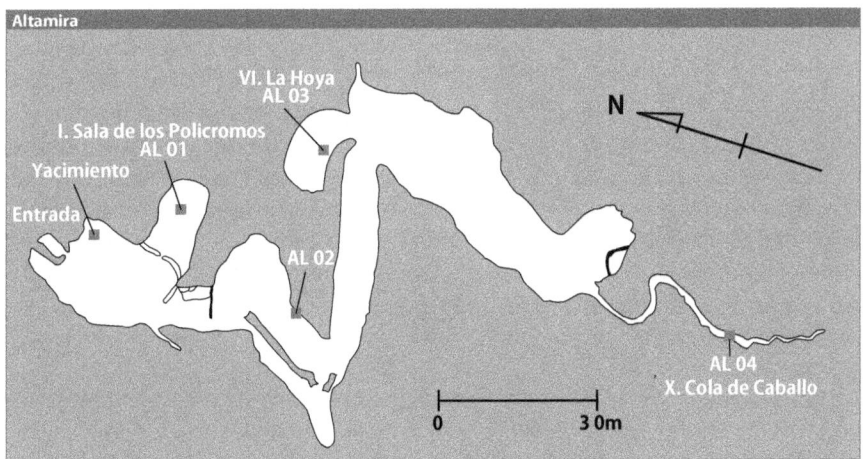
Cueva de Altamira, Ground Plan

abundant tools in stone, bone and antler, charcoal, and remains of the animals and shellfish consumed on the site, and which were similar to the kind of material recovered from French caves. He also spotted some black drawings on the cave walls, although he did not think much about them at first. In 1879, his daughter Maria accompanied him on one of his visits, and discovered the large bison painted in red and black on the roof at the back of the entrance vestibule, which was very low above the floor in this part of the cave. This discovery was the start of great events. Sautuola began the study of the art as quickly as possible, and soon published the results of his very correct analysis, proposing the Paleolithic age of the paintings and the deposit, in a memorable booklet printed in 1880. As is well known, this was in complete contradiction with the established concept people then had of primitive societies and evolution, and started a bitter controversy. This was only ended in the first years of the twentieth century, when the accumulation of evidence from sites in the Dordogne and French Pyrenees forced not only the acceptance of the Paleolithic chronology of the paintings in Altamira, but also the most transcendental point in the discussion: the full esthetic and intellectual capacity of populations that were "primitive" technically and economically, both in Prehistory and in modern times.

At the beginning of the century, the French prehistorians, E. Cartailhac and H. Breuil (the latter was just beginning his fascinating career in Prehistory), traveled to Santillana and made a full, detailed study of Altamira. Their documentation and analysis of the cave art, aimed at proving its Paleolithic age, and at comparing it with the art of modern primitive people, was completed in their 1906 publication. This also included the results of the digs carried out by Alcalde del Río, an important local researcher who was then beginning his collaborations with H. Breuil.

Despite this, the fundamental study of Altamira is the book published by H. Breuil and H. Obermaier three decades later, in 1935. It had a great deal of novelties in comparison with the previous work of 1906, for example in the drawings and measurements, which were a consequence of the improved facilities for copying and lighting, as the floor below the polychromes had been lowered. Together with more adequate financing, this allowed more exhaustive documentation and the correction of some errors in the first book, both in the stratigraphic order of the figures in certain panels, and in the copies made of some of the figures themselves. Furthermore, it added the results of new digs carried out in the vestibule by Obermaier in 1924 and 1925 to the earlier work of Alcalde del Río.

Opinions about Altamira, regarding chronology, nature and order of the cave art, were changed substantially by A. Leroi-Gourhan' s great publication. Although this prehistorian was not in possession of the specific documentation on the cave, and his study has striking omissions and great overall simplification, he proposed a modification in the age of the polychrome animals, taking it back several millennia. In this way, for Leroi-Gourhan, the bison on the famous ceiling, the technical and expressive apogee of the Upper Paleolithic, need not necessarily belong to its final stages, as Breuil had thought. Instead, based on analogies between rock art and mobiliary art, he proposed that they had been painted in the early or middle Magdalenian (or in his Styles III - IV). This change has since been ratified by the absolute radiocarbon dates obtained for the polychromes.

Since Leroi-Gourhan' s study, a large number of summaries of the fieldwork carried out in the first third of the century have been published. These include impressions, reinterpretations and modernizations (and to which the present essay might be added), but they contain hardly anything of a comparable standard to those first monographs. The most interesting contributions have been the studies of the last passage in the cave, the "Horse' s Tail" , made by L. G. Freeman and other prehistorians, the new digs carried out in the vestibule, the radiocarbon dating of the cave art and the deposit, and the splendid photographs of the art recently published by P. Saura. But, despite this large number of publications, we cannot disguise the present lack of knowledge we have about Altamira. Breuil' s fieldwork, excellent for its day, is simply not good enough at the present time. In fact, just limiting ourselves to the documentation of the art, we can point out that there are many figures in Altamira that have never been published, other animal figures that were described in publications were not reproduced in drawings, and even the documentation of the ceiling with the bison is limited to the more visible and spectacular figures, with partial reproductions of each figure.

The entrance of Cueva de Altamira faces north-northeast, at just over 160m above sea level. It leads to a relatively straightforward cave nearly 300m long. It is especially significant that it is formed in limestone strata of a regular thickness, about 1m, alternating with thin beds of clay. The formation of vertical fissures and the fracture and collapse of blocks of limestone are quite common features in the cave. This permanent structural instability has its implications in a very angular, broken, longitudinal development, in passages and chambers with rectangular cross-sections, with flat roofs and vertical walls, sometimes offering overhanging panels, whose vertical faces and horizontal steps were used by the artists. On the other hand, this regular shape has had consequences for the conservation of the cave, which was also affected by dynamiting at a nearby quarry (before the paintings had been discovered) and possibly by the work carried out to lower the floor in the chamber with the polychromes. As a result, in the 1920s it was necessary to build large pillars and supporting walls to prop up the roof in different parts of the cave. The most important supports, between the vestibule and the decorated chamber, artificially separated these two spaces which had originally been united. The effects of this building work include the reduction in the surface area of the chamber, the probable covering of cave art, particularly on the roof or on fallen blocks, and the alteration of the ventilation conditions in the chamber.

It has been possible to show the existence of different phases of collapse in the vestibule next to the original entrance, which have happened throughout the history of the cave. The most important episodes limit the Paleolithic human occupations stratigraphically, as they are situated below the Solutrean level, and on top of the later Magdalenian level. This last phase of collapse of blocks happened in the middle or late Magdalenian, and made the entrance smaller and more difficult, and possibly made the vestibule a less attractive place for a habitat. As time passed, the entrance was covered over more completely, and with it, Cueva de Altamira was slowly forgotten.

The large vestibule at Altamira has, therefore, remains of important human occupations during later moments of the Upper Paleolithic. The different digs made there have revealed the existence of successive occupations between the late Solutrean (about 19,000 - 16,500 BP) and the early Magdalenian (from about 16,000 to 14,000 or 13,500 BP). But the excavations have not been easy. Many of the large collapsed blocks have to be removed, so it has been difficult to dig down much further in the deposit. The use of more expeditious methods to clear the area and advance further cannot be recommended because of the cave's instability, and the danger of new collapses. For this reason, we still do not know today whether there really were pre-Solutrean occupations, or not. This, in turn, is the cause of different chronological theories about the paintings on the walls and roofs inside the cave.

Basically, two strata have been differentiated. The oldest, the Solutrean layer, contained a great deal of flint and quartzite tools; the hunting points made with flat retouch, and a concave or notched base, are especially characteristic. There were also deer antler spearheads; monobevelled, bi-pointed assegaies with central flattening, and other bone tools. Among these, the most interesting are four perforated pendants made from bone plaquettes and decorated with lateral engraved marks. A bone from this level has recently been dated to 18,540 +/- 320 BP, a date which fits in perfectly well with our knowledge of the Solutrean period.

The early Magdalenian layer had a much more abundant bone assemblage, as is usual in this period. The tools included assegaies with a quadrangular section and monobevelled base, perforated needles, spatulas, pendants made from horse and auroch teeth, and many stone scrapers, burins and backed bladelets. This layer has been dated by C14 several times, with results between 15,910 +/- 230 and 13,900 +/- 700 BP. A scapula with an engraved deer was dated by accelerator mass spectrometer to 14,480 +/- 250 BP. These scapulae, which often have striated hind' s heads, are very similar to some of the parietal engravings inside the cave. The date, therefore, means that these examples of mobiliary art can be attributed to the early Magdalenian, as in El Castillo or the Asturian cave of El Cierro, thus overcoming the doubts caused by their position in the area of contact between the Solutrean and Magdalenian layers in Altamira.

But just as the interior of the cave has parietal art, interesting artifacts have been found on the cave floor in different places inside. The most important was a fragment of a perforated staff, with several engraved figures of chamois, and which was found in the Hall of the Paintings, and probably of early Magdalenian age. A number of borers, a fragment of spatula, and a tube made from a cut bird' s bone, were found in the Main Gallery. Even more surprising was the discovery of three flat Pecten shells, i.e. the opposite of the concave shell used for drinking by medieval pilgrims. They were perforated by their hinge, and hidden under a block about half way along the cave passage.

The human groups who occupied Altamira lived from the hunting of red deer, and occasionally bison or auroch, or animals of rocky terrain such as ibex and chamois. Their diet was complemented by birds, fish, and very rarely, by seal, and the gathering of diverse products, which included marine shells. The gathering of sea food on the coast, which would then have been further away, and the return to the cave with limpets (Patella vulgata) and winkles (Littorina littorea) became more important in the early Magdalenian.

The best overall study of Altamira, published by Breuil and Obermaier in 1935, differentiated ten topographic areas along the 300m length of the cave. Cave art is found in all of them, from the back of the entrance vestibule to the final narrow passage. However, the artists did not distribute the decoration at random throughout those areas, but were particularly interested in closed areas, the chambers and side-passages with only one entrance and no way out. Thus, they worked most intensely at the back of the vestibule, which had a relatively independent chamber with a flat roof on its left-hand side (Zone I), as well as in a chamber on a lower level, on the left, half-way along the cave (Zone VI, or "Hoya", The Pit), or in other narrow side-passages. Finally, and again quite intensely, they decorated the final passage, where it is necessary to stoop and crawl (Zone X, or "Cola de Caballo" , The Horse' s Tail). In fact the zones I and X contain over 95% of the cave art in Altamira, which we shall now briefly summarize.

* The Hall of the Paintings, or Zone I. At the back of the vestibule, a large, low-roofed chamber on the left-hand side, out of the reach of daylight, is the location for the famous ceiling painted with polychrome animals and many other examples of cave art. Today, this hall is separated from the vestibule by a wide wall holding up the roof, built in 1922, and besides, the floor has been partially dug out so that the paintings can be seen more easily.

The hall is 18m long, and about 8 or 9m wide. The original height of the roof was between 2m at the entrance and 1.10m at the back. All the paintings and engravings known in this chamber were produced on the ceiling, which must have been difficult, especially considering the size of the polychrome animals, which in some cases are nearly two meters long.

These animals, painted in different tones of red and black, and often engraved too, are the best known figures in Altamira and we shall start our descriptions with them. There are well over twenty large figures of a type of bison that was the ancestor of the modern day European bison, situated mostly on the left of the ceiling, although a few poorly-conserved examples are found on the front and right, separated from the others. A smaller number of hinds and horses were represented with the same technique, but the wild boar that have sometimes been identified are rather doubtful (at least one of them is really a leaping bison, with the characteristic horns and beard).

The animals were painted in very different positions and postures: standing up and bellowing, resting and turning their heads back, trotting and jumping, or just standing still. They seem to be figures isolated from one another, without any obvious relationships among each other. However, numerous interpretations of the whole composition have been made, since that of Max Raphael, above all of later structuralist prehistorians, as well as more recent naturalistic interpretations. From these different points of view, they all consider the ceiling to be representing simply a herd of bison. But, in any case, we should remember that Paleolithic people never saw the ceiling as we see it today, as the lighting

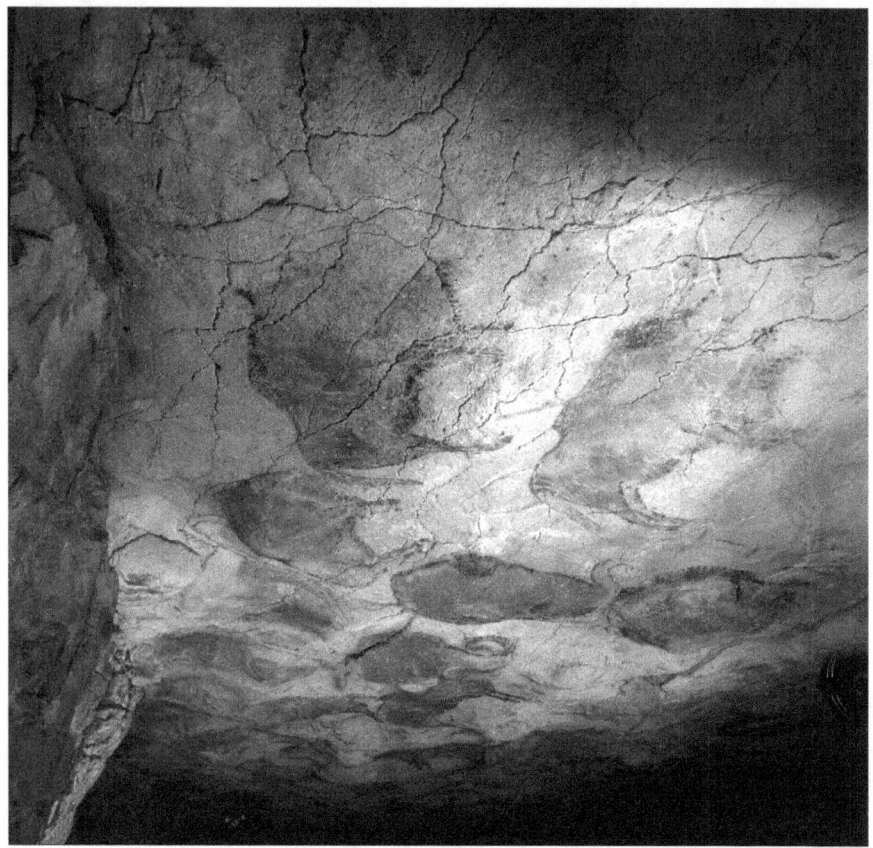

The Hall of Paintings

and distance from the floor has changed. Nor did they have a copy of the whole compostion as clear and illustrative as the one made at the start of the century, and systematically reproduced since then. They must have had great difficulty in obtaining a mental image of the relative positions of the larger bison, and the horses, hinds, acephalous animals and other supposedly complementary figures.

The techniques used were relatively more complex than was usual in Paleolithic art. First, the animals' outlines were drawn in black or with a burin, and then the colors were applied: reddish ochers combined or alternating with black, or in the case of some of the bison, only in black. The color was spread on directly by hand, with brushes or pieces of animal skin, or occasionally with coloring "pencils" . The outlines were improved and defined more precisely with multiple engraved lines, which were also used to indicate details like the eyes, horns, which were fine and systematically in correct perspective, the muzzle and

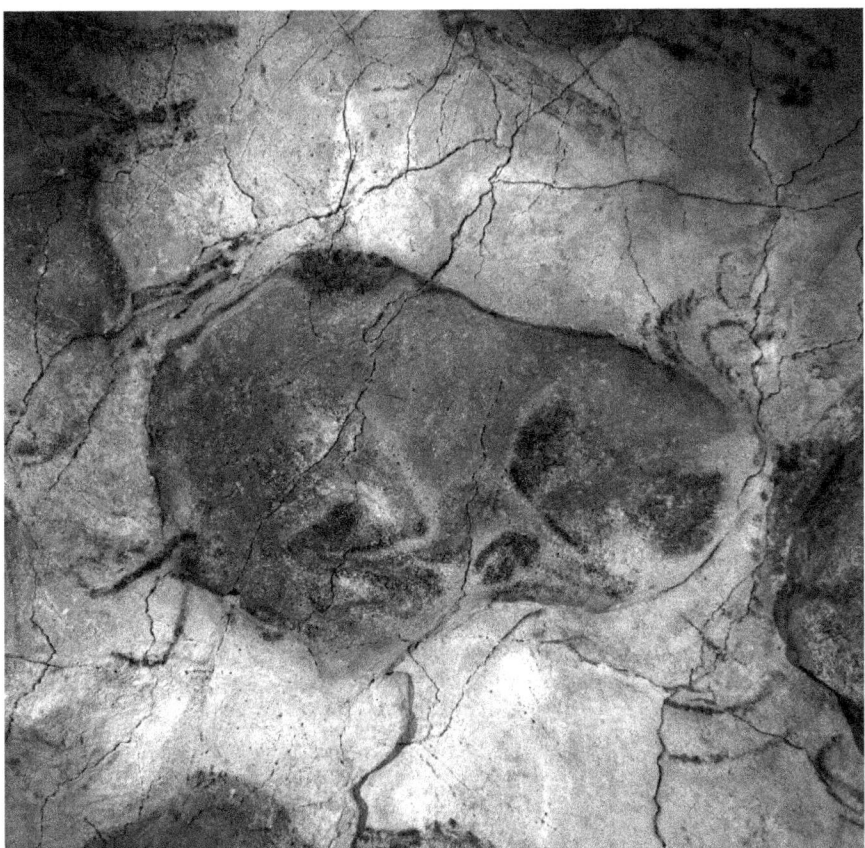
Polychrome bison lying down

hoofs. These engravings also defined the limbs, and separated planes at different depth. As well as the graded colors, and ordering of anatomical parts like horns, limbs and ears in different planes, the volume of the animals' bodies was shown by washing and scraping different areas inside the bodies. For the same reasons, prominences in the ceiling were used by adjusting the figures to these positive volumes, and lines of fissures or rock ledges were systematically used to support different parts of many figures. The result was a large group of animals in different tones of red, surrounded by black and engraved lines, standing out extraordinarily well from the yellowish color of the rock, and which amazes every spectator who enters the hall and turns a light towards the ceiling.

The homogeneity in technique, style, and to a certain extent size, of the polychrome paintings has led many researchers to believe in the existence of a single hand, or at least a single maestro or director of the artwork and this seems reasonable. Nevertheless, it is likely that not all the bison on the ceiling are synchronic, and therefore some of them need to be segregated. The recent radiocarbon dates, although they still have certain problems in their interpretation, show that most of the animals, including the truly polychrome ones, were produced some time between 14,900 and 14,100 BP, towards the end of the early Magdalenian period. But two smaller bison, shaped in black and engraved, and facing one another, may be later, and produced between 13,600 and 13,100 BP.

The polychrome bison, and these other monochrome figures possibly added later, which apparently occupy free spaces and form the main composition, are in fact just the last great art to be produced on the roof, which had been profusely decorated before. Below the bison, and in better view in lateral areas of the hall, we can see a large number of painted and engraved animal figures and signs, seemingly of quite diverse age. In brief, we can find a large number of animals in red, produced with wide linear outlines or in color-wash. They include a group of horses in a clearly pre-Magdalenian style, with small heads, short limbs and large bellies. Superimposed on the horses there are several negative hand images in violet and two positive hands in red. Above the red figures there are also black figures, in a Magdalenian style. Equally, red claviform signs are very common, as there are more than forty examples, similar to those in the Gallery B of La Pasiega, as well as "grilles" , and over seventy "comet" shaped signs, formed by series of converging engraved lines. The polychrome animals are superimposed on all these series of depictions. Finally the ceiling has great numbers of engravings of animals and anthropomorphs, which mix human and animal characteristics. These appear both above and below the different paintings, and the most interesting are hind' s heads with striated bands marking their chin and chest. There is also an exceptional figure of a stag bellowing, opposite the head of an ibex. Although the stag does not seem to be wounded, it reminds one immediately of similar animals in Peña Candamo, El Buxu and Gallery B in La Pasiega. Furthermore, the composition of stag and ibex is identical to the one in Cueva Grande in Otañes, a small Magdalenian site in the east of Cantabria.

The multiple superimpositions of figures observed by Breuil in different places in the hall, together with lesser examples in Castillo, La Pasiega and Peña Candamo, were one of the most important foundations for the chronological order that he proposed for Paleolithic parietal art in the Cantabrian region. Later, structuralist prehistorians have tended to believe in a not very convincing synchronism of nearly all the art in this great Hall in Altamira.

* Zones II to V. These sectors are located in more or less open and comfortable passages, occasionally with small side-passages. In Zone II, sections of wall covered with a layer of clay were used to draw in the clay with fingers or blunt-tipped objects, and a bovine' s head can be recognized among the lines

of a composition five meters long. These walls continue with abstract engravings of sinuous, intertwining lines, and some animals. A few black animal paintings are found too, with relatively different stylistic conventions.

A little further inside the cave, in Zone III, a corroded stalagmitic flowstone was used for two large, deeply-engraved figures, apparently horses. Beyond the flowstone, a few animals, which were engraved or painted in black, are normally isolated figures.

At the back of Zone III, on its left-hand side, a narrow side-passage has on its walls and roof all the red abstract signs which are known in the interior passages of Altamira. They are four oval signs, subdivided into three fields, and a band nearly two and a half meters long with scaliform designs, as well as other quite faded signs. This relative hiding-away of abstract signs is a well-known feature in Cantabrian Paleolithic art, with examples in Cueva del Castillo and La Pasiega.

The opposite wall has a series of cornices with good vertical sections of wall. These have a series of hinds and stags, engraved with fine lines, and occasionally with bands of striated lines.

In more open corridors, through Zones IV and V, we can find a few figures painted in black or engraved, but no important compositions. The most interesting at the start of Zone IV are blocks of limestone with simple engravings of animals, like horses and an anthropomorph, drawn before the blocks fell to the floor. Or a magnificent whole hind engraved on the left wall with repeated lines around its outline and striated bands in its head and chest. A black line below the hind was recently dated to 14,650 +/- 140 BP. A little further on, we come to more engravings of an auroch and a bison, and black paintings of a possible feline and other animals.

* Hall VI. This is a large side chamber, which is reached by descending a flowstone, hence its usual name, "The Pit" . At the bottom, both walls have panels of art. They include representations of two very stylized ibex, in a similar composition to figures at the back of Gallery C in La Pasiega, although the latter are technically rather more complex. A hind' s head is very simple but quite expressive, and a third ibex is badly deteriorated by calcite formations. At the start of this hall, there is a black outline of a bison. They are relatively coherent stylistically, and perhaps correspond to a very early Style IV rather than Style III. One of the figures has been dated by C14-AMS to about 15,000 BP.

* Zones VII to IX. After the Pit, we reach a couple of chambers with many collapsed blocks and stalagmitic reconstruction. There are few depictions

Quadrilateral signs in black

in this part of the cave. In fact, they tend to become rarer as we leave the sectors nearest to the entrance, until they become abundant again in the very last passage, Gallery X. In chambers VII-IX, we can only see non-figurative black marks, a few rare intercrossing engravings of horses, and at the end an indeterminate quadruped painted in black.

    * Gallery X, or "The Horse' s Tail" . In contrast, the narrow, winding final passage in Altamira, about 50m long, harbors a large number of black paintings and engravings and even a few remains of red paint. Five of the most important black paintings are quadrilateral signs of the Cantabrian type, some of which are divided into three parts, with lines ordered like steps inside the sign, while some also have an enlargement of their longest side. Another three, smaller, quadrilateral signs are associated with them, and these have series of lines radiating outwards from their perimeter, and so are of a less conventional type than the first.

2-2: Cueva de Altamira

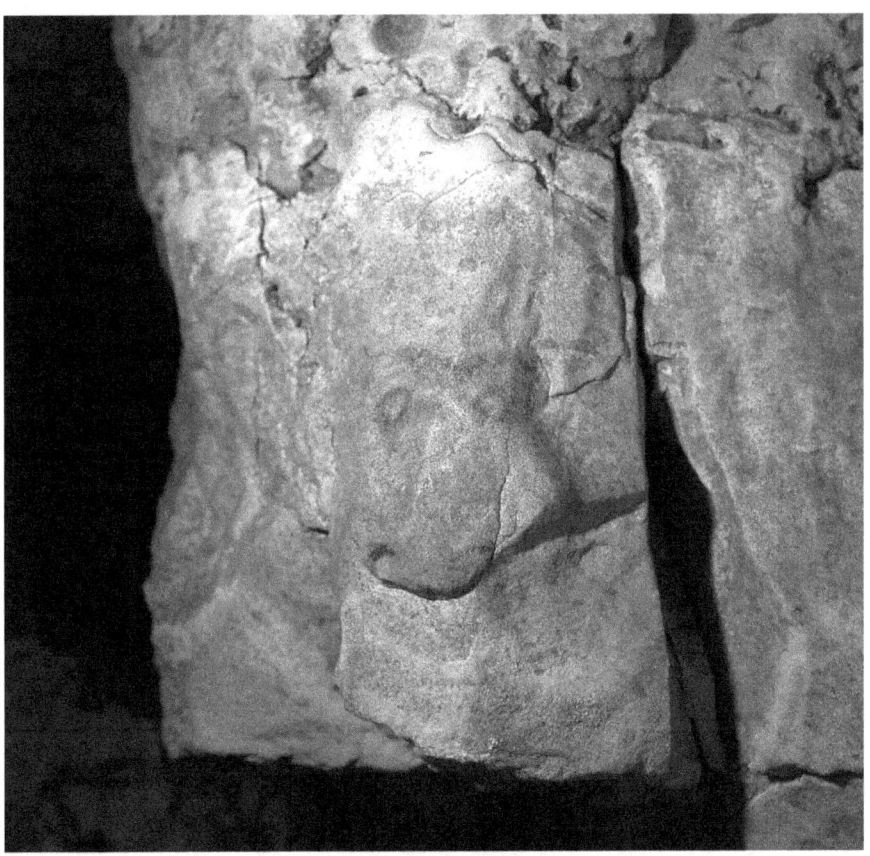

Mask painted in black

This composition of signs was dated by C14-AMS to 15,440 +/- 200 BP.

In the same way, at least two "masks" are surprising figures in this last passage. They are natural rock forms which were animated by the addition of eyes, nostril or mouth painted in black. Exactly the same idea has been recognized in other masks in Cueva del Castillo and in the Lower Passage in La Garma. Besides these, there are black paintings of animals, such as a horse in a rather archaic style, and non-figurative marks, and above all engravings of bisons and a horse, some ibex, and particularly hinds. Indeed, the end of the passage has perhaps the most important group of striated hind' s heads, and also stags, in the whole cave.

At present, it is very difficult to make an even remotely accurate inventory of the themes represented in Altamira, both because of the volume and

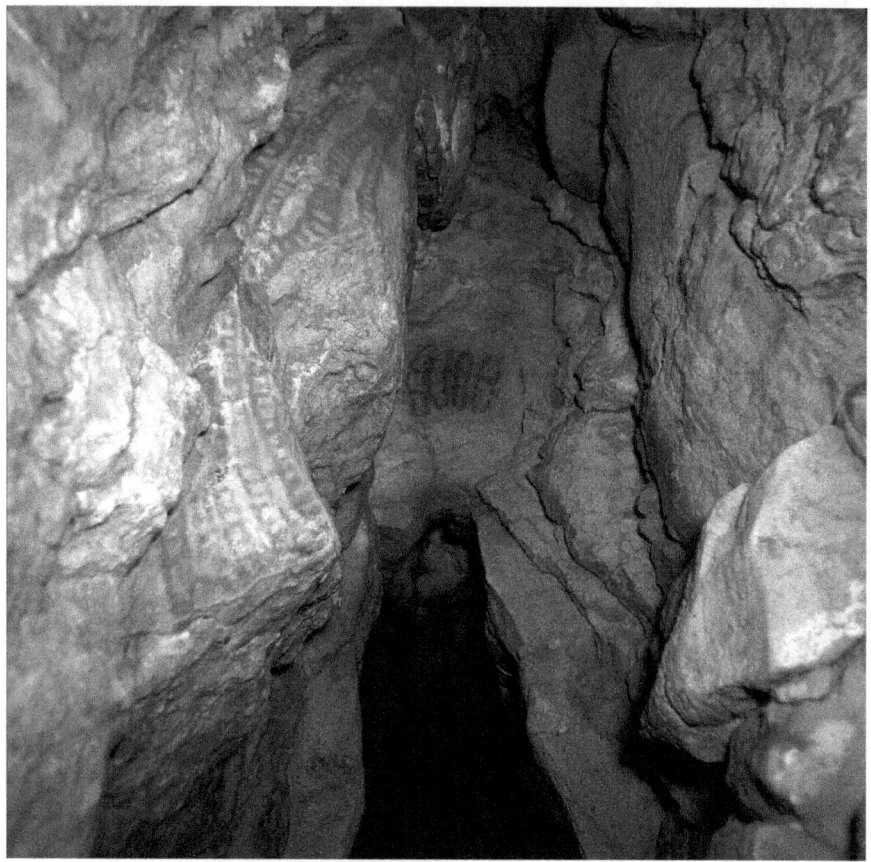
Painted abstract signs in the interior of Altamira

complexity of the art and because the studies published and available are by no means exhaustive. González Echegaray' s study of 1978 is still the most indicative, and this established a minimum of 141 clearly identifiable animals: 37 bison, 35 cervids, mostly hinds, 33 horses, 24 caprids (including a chamois), 7 aurochs, 2 or 3 possible carnivores (a highly dubious wolf and felines proposed by Breuil), possibly 2 mammoths, and a deer with wide antlers, which has sometimes been identified as an elk, although the presence of this animal in the Cantabrian region is merely hypothetical. There are also several negative and positive hand images, at least 9 engraved anthropomorphs, and several "masks" . Regarding the signs, of which there are well above a hundred, the most important are the claviforms and the comb or grille shaped signs, in red, and the "huts" or "comets" made up of converging striated lines. These are all found in the Hall of the Paintings, while the rest of the cave has the oval and scaliform signs in red, in the central passages, and the black quadrangular signs with a pointed protuberance or a fringe, in the "Horse' s Tail" . It is worth noting, and perhaps relevant chronologically, that these different types of signs only appear in certain areas of the cave, and are not repeated in different places. Their high relative abundance is, however, usual in the central part of the Cantabrian region during the Solutrean and early Magdalenian, as there is also a high proportion of abstract signs in the caves of La Pasiega, El Castillo, Chimeneas and Las Aguas.

As we have seen, Altamira has practically the whole range of cave art techniques, except sculpture and bas-relief. But they are not distributed regularly or uniformly throughout the cave. The Hall of the Polychromes is completely different from the rest of the cave, as here all the techniques are found (apart from engraving on soft clay), which probably shows how this part of the cave must have been reused systematically on many different occasions, and during millennia. Away from this hall, red paintings are very rare, as the only ones are the signs in the side-passage in Zone III, and a few remains of figures in the Horse' s Tail, and of course polychromes do not exist anywhere else in the cave. The animal paintings in black, of different stylistic conventions, and the engravings including those with striated lines, are dispersed more homogeneously throughout practically all the decorated areas.

Regarding the chronological attribution and order of all these figures, prehistorians are divided between those who believe that the cave art covers a longer time span than the known habitation deposit, and those who consider that it covers the same periods. In recent years, other researchers have proposed that nearly all the art was produced in a relatively short time during the early Magdalenian. The main supporter of the first theory was Breuil, who divided the figures between the Aurignacian and the final Magdalenian, when the polychromes would have been executed. Leroi-Gourhan paralleled the archaeological deposit and the art, although he thought that visits could have been made after the early or middle Magdalenian, in order to produce a few engravings in different parts of the cave, which are in a very advanced Style IV.

To be more exact, Leroi-Gourhan suggested that all the black figures were relatively synchronic, and corresponded to later moments of his Style III, which he believed could be dated at the start of the Magdalenian. He situated the art in the Hall of the Polychromes in the Magdalenian III-IV, which included the polychrome animals and the claviform signs, but without referring to the red horses, hands, lines of red dots and huts or comets, which certainly do not seem to be of the same period. The engravings, present throughout the cave, would have been done to fill spaces between the paintings, and would correspond to different moments of occupation of the site, and some of them in the Horse' s Tail might even belong to the late Magdalenian, especially the group of bison, horse and mammoth (which other writers interpret as a second bison).

Without wishing to position ourselves systematically in the middle of these different hypotheses, some ideas seem especially probable. Like Breuil, we think it is perfectly possible that Altamira contains pre-Solutrean decoration. Or rather, that the possibility of pre-Solutrean occupations and cave art cannot be totally excluded. Examples of older figures are the red paintings at the back of the main panel, hands, and the simple engravings on the collapsed blocks in Zone IV. And it is clear that there are figures later than the early Magdalenian. At least, the smaller bison on the main panel were produced about 13,600 or 13,100, according to the radiocarbon dates, which corresponds to the middle Magdalenian in the region. At the same time, it is true that most of the art known in Altamira was produced during the periods of occupation recorded in the vestibule deposit. Thus, the red paintings correspond to the Solutrean, that is if they were not done a little before, whereas the style and conventions of many figures, and the radiocarbon dates obtained, indicate that art was produced more abundantly and with greater assiduity during the early Magdalenian, and even middle Magdalenian, including part of the black figures, striated engravings and polychromes.

Therefore, we think that, with the available information, it is not impossible that some depictions are older than Style III. It is likely that the Style III figures, of Solutrean age, include at least the oval and scaliform signs inside the cave, while some of the black figures and signs may correspond to a later phase of Style III, and are probably of Magdalenian age. Some of the engraved animals, at least the striated ones which have been dated in their mobiliary variant to about 14,500 BP, a part of the black paintings, and of course, the polychromes, are in early Style IV.

Bibliography

Sanz de Sautuola, M. 1880. *Breves apuntes sobre algunos objetos prehistóricos de la provincia de Santander. Imp. y Lit. de Telesforo Martínez. Santander.* (Facsimil en Madariaga, B., 1976, pp. 67-96).

Cartailhac, E.; Breuil, H. 1906. *La caverne d'Altamira à Santillane près Santander (Espagne).* Imprimerie de Monaco. Monaco.

Alcalde del Río, H. 1906. "La Préhistoire aux environs de Santander. La station humaine d'Altamira". En Cartailhac, E.; Breuil, H. 1906.

Alcalde del Río, H.; Breuil, H.; Sierra, L. 1911. *Les cavernes de la région Cantabrique*. Imprimerie Vve. A. Chéne. Monaco.

Breuil, H.; Obermaier, H. 1935. *La Cueva de Altamira en Santillana del Mar*. Tipografía de Archivos, Madrid. (Reimpresión Ed. El Viso, Madrid, 1984).

Leroi-Gourhan, A. 1965. *Préhistoire de l'art occidental*. Lucien Mazenod, Paris (2nd ed: 1971).

Freeman, L.G.; González Echegaray, J.; Bernaldo de Quirós, F.; Ogden, J. 1987. *Altamira revisited, and other essays on early art*. Institute for Prehistoric Investigations and CIMA, Chicago-Santander.

Valladas, H.; Cachier, H.; Maurice, P.; Bernaldo de Quirós, F.; Cabrera Valdés, V.; Uzquiano, P.; Arnold, M. 1992. Direct radiocarbon dates for prehistoric paintings at the Altamira, El Castillo and Niaux caves. *Nature* 357, pp. 68-70.

Moure, A.; González Sainz, C.; Bernaldo de Quirós, F.; Cabrera Valdés, V. 1996 "Dataciones absolutas de pigmentos en cuevas cantábricas: Altamira, El Castillo, Chimeneas y Las Monedas". A. Moure (ed.), *"El Hombre fósil" 80 años después*. pp. 295-324, Universidad de Cantabria, Santander.

Saura, P. A. et al. 1998. *Altamira*. Caja Cantabria y Lundwerg. Barcelona.

2-3. Cueva de Hornos de la Peña

Cueva de Hornos de la Peña is situated in the hill known as "La Peña" , near the village of Tarriba, in the municipal district of San Felices de Buelna. The entrance is in the small, narrow valley of the River Tejas, 60m above the river-course, but this, only a few kilometers to the north, joins the wide, open plain of the Buelna valley.

The cave art in Hornos de la Peña was discovered in 1903 by the great explorer of the archaeology of the region Hermilio Alcalde del Río. It was, therefore, one of the first caves with parietal art to be known in Europe. Three years later, this researcher included the cave in a small book together with the studies he had made of other Paleolithic art sites: Altamira, El Castillo and Covalanas. In 1911 it formed part of a major publication on Cantabrian cave art: Les cavernes de la region Cantabrique, written by the discoverer of Hornos de la Peña in collaboration with the prehistorians H. Breuil and L. Sierra. This 1911 publication remains the main reference to the parietal art in the cave. During those early years of the century, in 1909 and 1910 to be precise, archaeological digs were carried out in the vestibule of Hornos. The scientists of the Institut de Paleontologie Humaine at Paris documented an important stratigraphic sequence, with Mousterian, Aurignacian, Solutrean, and Magdalenian industry, and also Neolithic artifacts. Among the objects recovered was a piece of mobiliary art: a fragment of a horse' s frontal bone, decorated with the rear-quarters of precisely a horse, and this enabled stylistic and chronological correlations to be made with the art on the walls inside the cave.

A few brief publications that have appeared in the last two decades have added new figures to the parietal inventory of Hornos de la Peña. But they have also expressed doubts about some of the interpretations made by the first researchers, and have shown how certain engraved animal figures have been badly deteriorated by human action. This has happened at different times, but particularly during the Spanish Civil War from 1936 to 1939, when the cave was used as a shelter. No complete modern revision of the cave art has been published.

The cave has a large arched entrance facing south, seven meters wide and four meters high. This is now closed by a stone wall and an iron gate, installed in order to protect the art inside the cave. The entrance leads into a vestibule (or Chamber A), 16m long, lit by natural light, where the oldest art in the cave was produced.

2-3: Cueva de Hornos de la Peña

The left-hand wall has a beautiful figure of a horse, executed with deep incisions, although the forequarters and chest of the horse are missing. Non-figurative lines can be seen next to this equid. The first archaeologists who worked in the cave also mention, on the right-hand side of the vestibule, a large block of limestone with numerous incised lines, among which there were a figure of a bison and the rear-quarters of another horse. Unfortunately, this block no longer exists, and it probably disappeared when the wall was built across the entrance.

Towards the back of the vestibule, the height of the roof gradually lowers until it reaches 1.5m above the floor. Here there is a narrow gap, which is the start of the inner passages of the cave. In 1903 this gap was blocked by a calcited mass of sediment which contained abundant skeletal remains, mostly of horses.

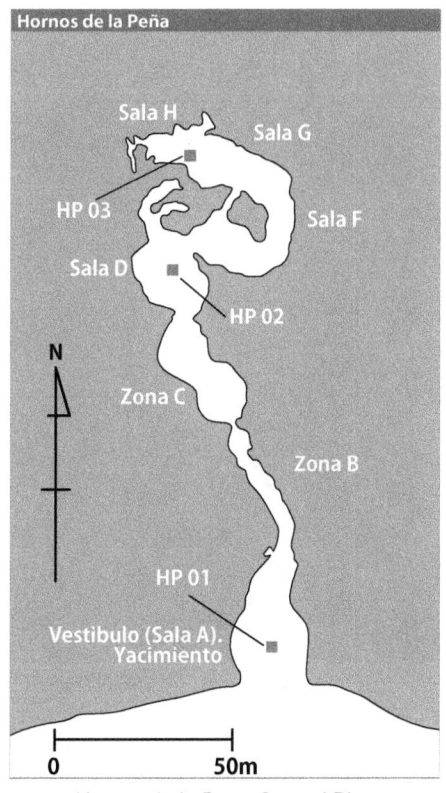

Hornos de la Pena Ground Plan

The passage starting at this point is still very low, although the original floor has been lowered about one meter in order to make visits more comfortable. After about 60m, in which the first two sectors of the cave are crossed (Zones B and C), a larger chamber is reached (Chamber D). This chamber, with a high roof, has two figures. On the right there is a whole figure of a stag, engraved with fine lines. On the left, a figure of an auroch fills a large hollow in the wall. This figure was engraved with a fingertip in a clay surface, and is represented by the head, the horns in twisted perspective, and the start of the chest and cervical lines.

Chamber D divides into two passages: the one on the right leads to the end of the cave, while the other finishes in two blind chambers. These small chambers on the left have a horse painted in black, the only painting in the cave, an auroch with a spear, again made with a finger in clay, and engraved figures of two ibex and a horse.

85

2-3: Cueva de Hornos de la Peña

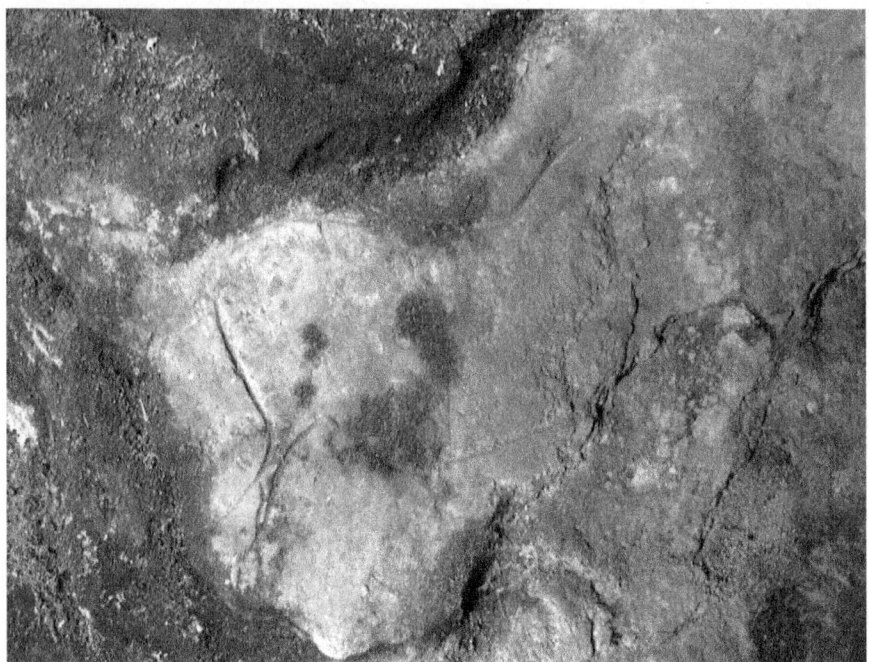

Engraved horse in the entrance

By returning to Chamber D, we can continue the route towards the end of the cave. Chamber E has a complete figure of a deer, and some remains of paint. A narrow passage connecting with Chamber G has engravings of an ibex and two horses.

But the greatest concentration of art is found in the last chambers, G and H. In the first we can find six bovines, a horse's head, and a doubtful figure of a reindeer, all engraved with fine incised lines. The bison were represented following different compository schemes, from whole animals to depictions the head alone. One of the best among the latter is a bison seemingly panting, with its tongue out of its mouth. Several details, like the hairs of its beard, eyes, and horns in correct perspective, were also represented.

Finally, Chamber H contains what are perhaps the most naturalistic figures in Hornos de la Peña, distributed in two areas. The first of these is a small chamber, at most about 6m wide, with a low roof, where the figures occupy all the back wall and part of the roof. Another passage leads off at the back of the chamber, in the form of a narrow rift only big enough for one person. The main part of Chamber H has a large composition of engravings, among which there are four horses, a bison, a possible snake and the antlers of a deer. Whole figures of an-

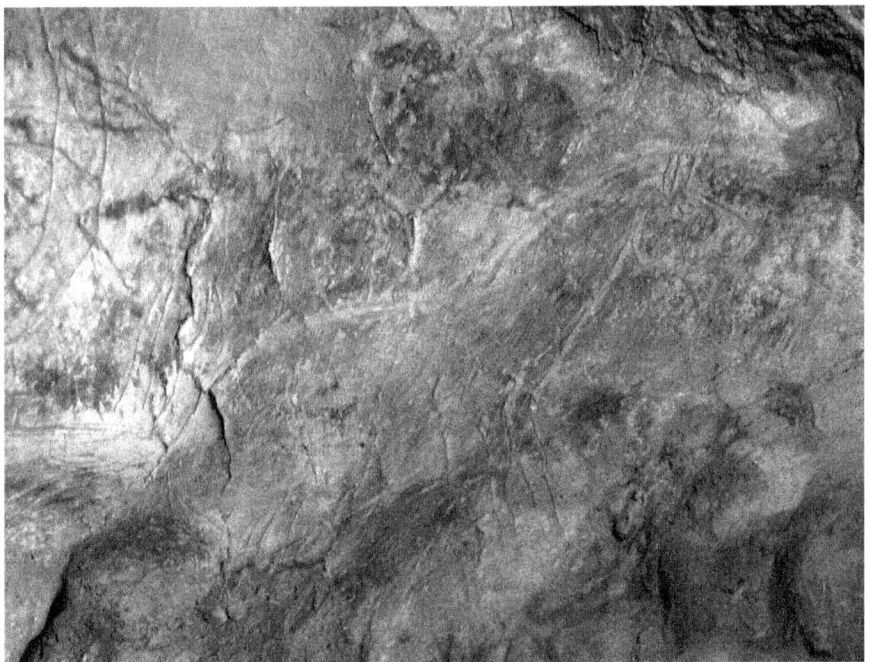
Engraved horse facing right

imals predominate in this chamber, although there is a possible bovine of which only the head was represented. Next, the small rift at the back of Chamber H has what is, without doubt, the most characteristic figure in the cave. It is an anthropomorphic figure, facing right, which has a very long head, the trunk, an arm and a leg. The posture in which it has been drawn is similar to other figures in Altamira: standing on both feet, leaning forwards slightly and with one arm raised in the air. An attempt was made to represent fingers and toes by short parallel lines on the hand and foot. At the back of the figure, next to its buttocks, a line is started which could be interpreted as a tail, and this, together with the shape of the head, gives the figure a rather animal appearance. The addition of tails to anthropomorphs is not unusual, and happens in some figures in Altamira, La Peña de Candamo, and Gallery C in La Pasiega. The engraving of the rear-quarters of a bison is found near this anthropomorph, but on the roof of the passage.

Several proposals have been made regarding the age of the figures in Hornos de la Peña. At first, H. Breuil established six stages of decoration, from the early Aurignacian, when the finger engravings would have been done, to the early Magdalenian, and the more naturalistic engravings near the end of the cave. This evolutionary scheme is perhaps too rigid.

2-3: Cueva de Hornos de la Peña

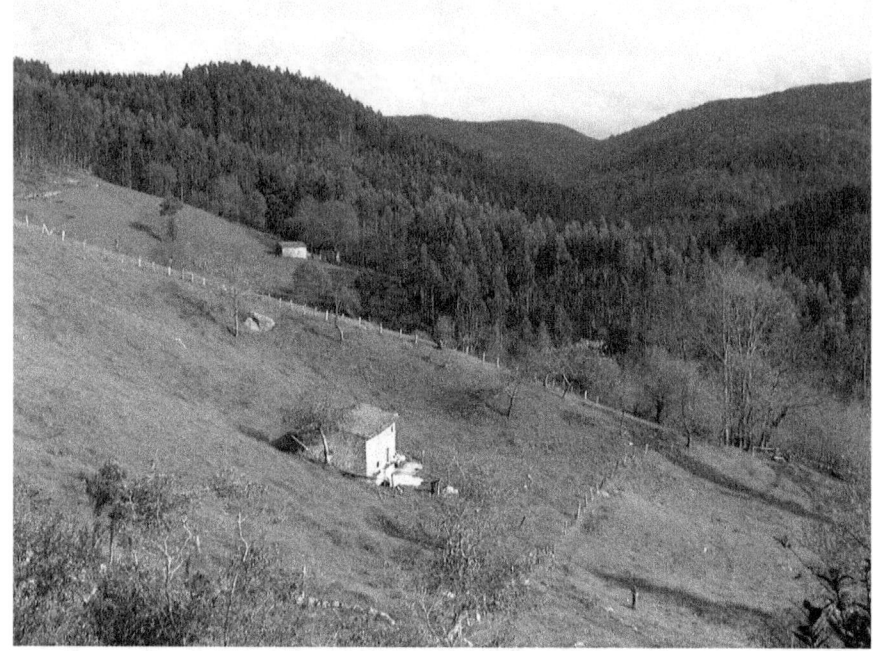

Mountains around Cueva de Hornos de la Peña

In the 1960s, A. Leroi-Gourhan proposed that just two stages of decoration existed in the cave, and the figures were produced in two different parts of the cave, and with a different style and technique. The engravings at the entrance would correspond to a very late Style II, or the start of Style III, i.e. to the early or middle Solutrean. In turn, the abundant engravings inside the cave were attributed to his early Style IV, corresponding in the Cantabrian to the early or middle Magdalenian (approximately between 15,500 and 13,000 BP). This proposal has been accepted widely since then, although the figures inside the cave are occasionally very heterogeneous in style and technique. Thus, the synchronism of all these interior figures can only be accepted in a very general sense, and with many reservations. In fact, there is no reason why some of the interior engravings, particularly those in soft clay surfaces, should not be as old as the horse and bison engraved in the outer vestibule.

Regarding the iconographic organization of the art, it is striking that there are no depictions of hinds, the most common theme in Cantabrian cave art, especially in several caves near Hornos de la Peña, like Sovilla, Castillo and Pasiega. It is equally noticeable that conventional abstract signs are practically absent. Nevertheless, the high frequency of horses and above all, of bison, agrees quite well with the predominant themes found in the region during the last phases of the Upper Paleolithic.

Bibliography

Alcalde del Río, H.; Breuil, H.; Sierra, L. 1911. *Les cavernes de la region Cantabrique.* Imp. A. Chene. Monaco.

Ucko, P.J. 1987. Débuts illusoires dans l'étude de la tradition artistique. *Bulletin de la Société Préhistorique Ariège-Pyrénées* 42, pp.15-81.

2-4. Cueva del Castillo

This cave takes its name from the hill where it is situated, overlooking the town of Puente Viesgo, in the center of Cantabria. In 1903, an important archaeological deposit was located in the entrance vestibule of the cave, and numerous paintings and engravings were discovered in its interior. Hermilio Alcalde del Río, a local teacher, was the discoverer, and he also undertook the first studies in the site. Later, at different times during the century, other caves were found in the same hill, whose entrances had been blocked and hidden by collapses. These are the caves, each with an archaeological deposit and cave art, of La Pasiega, Las Chimeneas and Las Monedas; as well as La Flecha, which only had an archaeological deposit in its entrance.

In the Upper Paleolithic, the large outer rock-shelter at El Castillo, 190m above sea level and facing east-northeast, was occupied much more often than the other caves which were then open. It was thus the main habitat in the hill and in all the immediate geographical area. These other smaller caves, despite being in the same intensely karstified limestone hill, seem to be mere satellites of the great habitat and decorative complex centered on El Castillo. They were occupied more occasionally as camps, for meetings and diverse activities, some of which would have involved the production of cave art.

After the first studies in the cave, the vestibule of Castillo was excavated by the Institut de Paleontologie Humaine at Paris, directed by H. Obermaier and H. Breuil, between 1910 and 1914. The cave art was studied at the same time, with the collaboration of Alcalde del Río and several foreign archaeologists. This work played a vital role in the definition of the Paleolithic cultural sequence in the Cantabrian region, due both to the good state of conservation of the archaeological deposit and to its great thickness. Layers corresponding to nearly all the periods of the Paleolithic were dug, reaching over 20m in depth. Furthermore, the documentation of the cave art inside the cave, where there are many complex panels with superimpositions of figures in different techniques and styles, was also important for the model of the chronology of cave art elaborated by Henri Breuil. This model, based on a succession of technical procedures and stylistic changes throughout the Upper Paleolithic, was the main one used in chronological studies until 1965, when Leroi-Gourhan published his major work. Nowadays, the panels of figures in El Castillo are still proof of the distribution of many assemblages of cave art through millennia of decoration, despite the interpretations of some structuralist prehistorians, who tend to consider that all these complex panels are synchronic, or that the superimpositions are a form of composition.

The excavation of the stratigraphy at El Castillo was restarted in the 1980s by V. Cabrera, an archaeologist who had previously studied the results obtained by the first digs, which had hardly been analyzed and were not well published. In summary, in the twenty meters of depth in the vestibule, nearly thirty archaeological layers could be differentiated. These go from the late Acheulian, about 150,000 years ago, to the end of the Upper Paleolithic, and even the Epipaleolithic and more recent prehistoric periods. This long sequence, as it is being dug and studied at present, is providing valuable information about the transition, or replacement, between the Neanderthal populations of the Mousterian period and the Homo sapiens sapiens of the Aurignacian and later Upper Paleolithic periods.

The multiple occupations found in the long stratigraphic sequence is probably a result of the good habitation conditions of the vestibule, and the excellent strategic position of the Castillo hill.

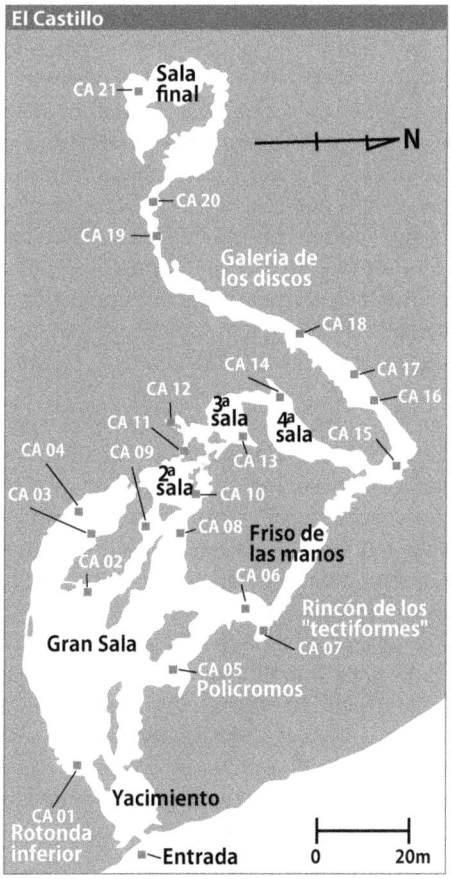

El Castillo Ground Plan

It is located in the center of the Cantabrian region, in the middle of the regional relief, and right in the area of contact between the open coastal zone and the interior valleys. The hill forms the eastern end of the Sierra del Dobra, a mountainous West-East ridge between the rivers Besaya and Pas. It dominates the route into the Toranzo valley up the River Pas, and also the nearby Pisueña valley, and it therefore controls the way to the high summer pastures, which must have been important for the herds of wild ungulates. On its other flank, the hill also controls the route to the Besaya valley, going round the Sierra del Dobra to the north.

The characteristic conical shape of the hill and its central position in the region landscape, between these two main types of territory: the coastal plains

2-4: Cueva del Castillo

and the inland valleys, indicate that the large vestibule of Cueva del Castillo must have been an essential camping place for the Paleolithic hunters of this central area of the Cantabrian region, on their movements between the coast and the valleys. Marine shells are frequent in the Upper Paleolithic deposit as far as the layers of the Magdalenian period. Furthermore, from the hill itself, different biotopes can quickly be reached, each with its own resources. Lithic raw material for the manufacture of tools is relatively abundant in the area, in the form of conglomerates on the hillside, and cobbles from the bed of the River Pas. The area also had good hunting and fishing, as the archaeological deposit so clearly shows; this was available both on the flatter ground in the valley and on the quite steep hillsides, which would have had partially different vegetation and resources, depending on their orientation.

The interior of the cave has a complex series of passages. The art tends to be distributed throughout practically the whole cave, with very unequal densities of figures. This, and the great variety in the techniques, styles and formats, the superimposition of figures in several panels, as well as the habitual occupations in the vestibule, show that the cave must have been visited and modified on numerous occasions. As a result, it contains art that can be attributed to nearly every period of the Upper Paleolithic. Partly because of this, and partly because the cave has been greatly altered to accommodate tourist visits (work has been done since the 1950s, without adequate archaeological control), it is now frankly quite difficult to obtain a precise idea of the spatial structure of the art. The alterations to the cave impede a correct evaluation of the difficulty of the routes taken through the different parts of the cave during the Paleolithic, or the original visibility of the panels. So, we have to reduce the description of this abundant art to the main areas and content, as follows:

* From the vestibule, we directly enter the first "Main Chamber" , a large hall which has different decorated passages leading off. But first, we should mention a lower passage, below the route into the Main Chamber. This is a semi-circular passage, or oxbow, which has the first group of noticeably homogeneous animal engravings. They are simple figures drawn with a single line, representing horses and stags, in a good composition of superimposed animals, and a few hinds and goats. The stylistic character, in terms of their proportions, perspective, degree of completeness in outline and interior, suggest they correspond to an early period in the Upper Paleolithic.

* The Main Chamber is nearly 70m long. The art is distributed on almost all its walls, including a final chamber or side-passage, and it contains nearly all the most typical themes and techniques to be found in Cueva del Castillo, except for the conventional abstract signs. Some of the more important figures are a large painting of a stag in red, now somewhat faded, a magnificent depiction of a

male auroch, facing right and painted in black in a quite late style, as well as other black paintings less spectacular or definable. There is also a group of horses painted in black, but badly faded, and this is perhaps the part of the cave where the art is worst conserved. In several places in the chamber, we can see a large number of generally small engravings, above all of hinds, sometimes with magnificent striated heads and chests.

This Main Chamber also has a few very schematic anthropomorphic figures. They are in a style which is common in the art of recent prehistoric periods, and may be associated with the Bronze Age deposits which are recorded in the Chamber.

* From the first part of the chamber, we can descend to the so-called "Polychrome Frieze" , in a passage which continues down to the "Gallery of the Hands" . This panel of "polychromes" , on successive sections of wall, is one of the most important accumulations of paintings in the region, and has figures belonging in very different moments of the Upper Paleolithic. Here we find the first hand images, painted as negatives by spraying diluted red pigment around a hand. They are superimposed by a number of red hinds, in a simple style. The panel also has some oval signs in red. On a higher part of the wall there is the front-quarters of a large bison outlined in red, which used the natural shape of the rock to suggest the rest of its body, a large horse similarly in red, and around them smaller figures of a horse' s head, a hind, and the front-quarters of a stag. Above and to the right of the large horse, the remains of a red claviform sign can be appreciated, similar to the ones in La Pasiega B and Altamira.

The lower part of the panel has four figures of bison, which are the most recent figures. Three of them have been dated by C14-AMS, with the result that they were painted on at least two different occasions. The oldest is the smallest one on the left, dated to about 13,500 BP, and another two in the center of the panel, superimposed on the hands, signs and hinds, had dates of about 13,000 BP. In fact, these bison are not polychromes although the effect of using and including the red color of the previous figures does evoke that type of figure. Instead, they are outlined with black paint and engraving, and only the fourth animal, on the right of the panel, had a reddish-brown color wash inside the bison' s body in addition to the black paint and engraving of its outline and the interior details.

* Going down a slope from the "polychromes" , we reach the "Gallery of the Hands" , an "L" -shaped passage, which has a small chamber called by the first explorers the "Tectiforms Corner" . The walls and even the roof of the passage are decorated by numerous negative hand images associated with red discs. They are nearly all left hands, and superimposed on some of them there

2-4: Cueva del Castillo

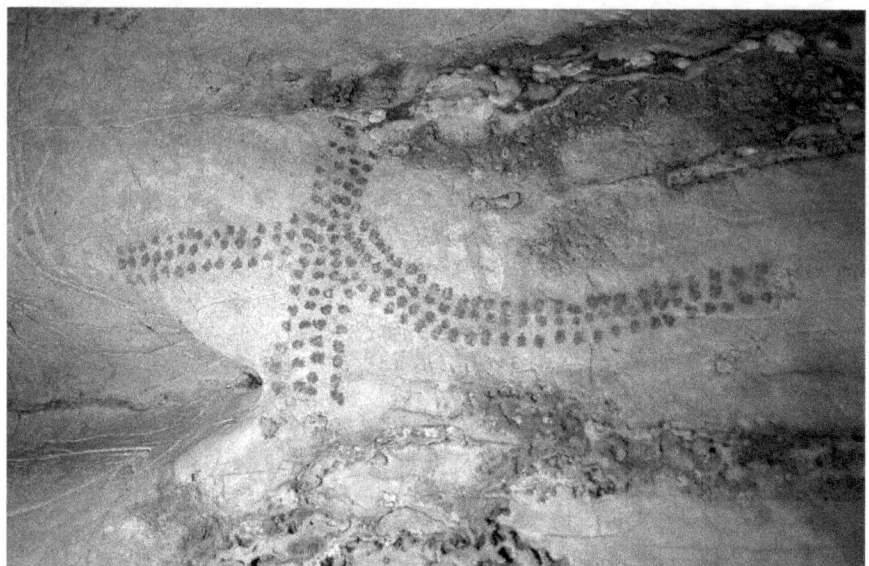

Lines of dots in the form of a cross, Tectiform Corner

are at least seven bison with a very simple outlined form in yellow. A large number of engravings are superimposed both on the bison and on red quadrilateral signs. These mostly represent hinds in a quite archaic style, but some of them have striated chins.

On a bend in the Gallery of the Hands, near the entry to the chamber with the signs, we can see other highly interesting figures: a large-bellied, long-eared horse, with arrows in its body, next to another horse and a hind also painted in a pre-Magdalenian style. There is also a large quadrilateral sign with a pointed protuberance midway along its top side, and smaller oval signs.

More complete hinds with striated engraving in their heads are superimposed on the quadrilaterals and other red signs on the end wall of the passage. Very near these, magnificent ibex are engraved with detail, together with red dots and quadrilateral signs, and more rarely, black figures. One of these, at the start of this passage, represents the front-quarters of a bison in a clearly Magdalenian style, very similar to figures in Pyrenean caves.

* The roof and one wall of a small side-chamber contain an exceptional group of abstract signs wrongly called "tectiforms" . In fact they are sub-rectangular signs, different from the true tectiforms in the caves in Perigord in France, and therefore very similar to the signs found in many caves in the center of the Cantabrian region, such as Arco B, La Haza, La Pasiega A, C and D, Chimene-

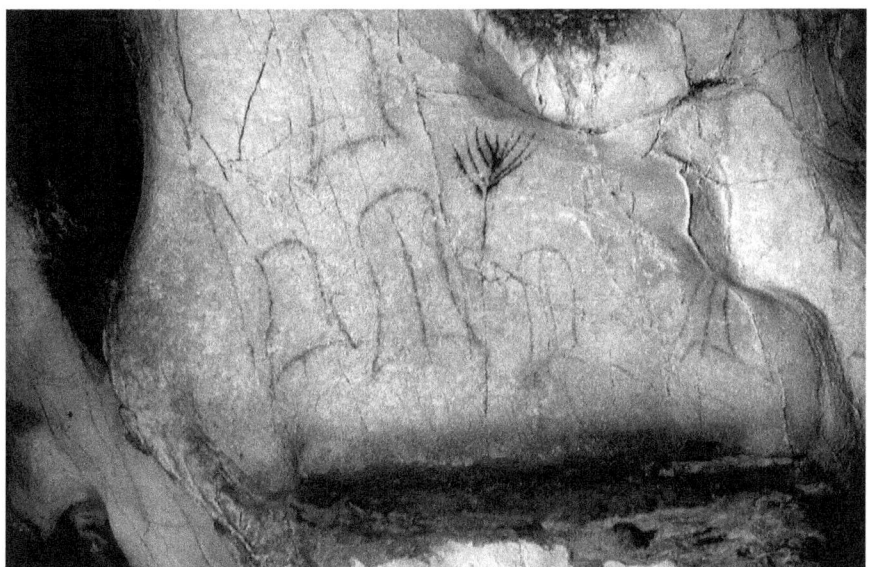
Bell-shaped signs in red and branching sign in black

as, Altamira, Mazaculos I or Llonín. This tiny chamber has ten rectangular and oval signs, subdivided transversely into three fields and frequently with borders filled with short lines. They are associated with parallel lines of red dots, usually painted directly with a finger on the rock. At the back of the chamber, a couple of engraved bison are not well known. One of their bodies is filled with lines, and these are apparently Magdalenian figures, of a much later date than the painted signs.

* The "Second Chamber" can be reached directly from the first, Main Chamber, by a difficult route between large boulders, or alternatively from the start of the Gallery of the Hands. Along the first route we find some of the best hind' s heads in the cave, striated in their chins and chests, identical to the figures drawn on flat bones (deer scapulae) during the occupations of the early Magdalenian in the vestibule, documented in layer 8, and dated between approximately 16,500 and 14,000 BP. Among the boulders there is also a pair of engraved horses, facing each other, in a simple but very beautiful composition. The passage from the Gallery of the Hands has a few more negative hand images, and a controversial animal' s head painted in red.

The more interesting compositions in the Second Chamber include a group of bell-shaped abstract signs, painted in red, with a superimposed branching sign in black. The same chamber has a few black animal paintings, above all well-executed figures of ibex. But the most important figure is a bison in a vertical position, using the natural shape of a stalagmite, painted in black and engraved. This chamber also has a large red quadrilateral sign, pointed in its top side.

* The Third Chamber, following the route towards the end of the cave, has a good, interesting group of black animal paintings, mostly in the passages leading into the chamber. They are figures of stags, horses, aurochs and other less easily defined animals, only painted around their outline, typical of Style III, which is not too common in black paintings in the Cantabrian region. A magnificent engraving of a whole auroch, with its horns in semi-twisted perspective, is of the same period. The passage between the second and third chambers, which has been altered completely, also contains two male bison in line and facing right, painted in black with very late conventions of representation. The same area of the cave has a large number of animal figures in black, usually quite small and depicting goats or deer. Nevertheless there is a whole horse using color wash in the area of its head. A side passage on the left near the entrance into the Third Chamber has a "mask" represented on a rock pendant, to which an eye and a line for the nose were added in black, in an identical procedure to other figures of "masks" in Altamira and the Lower Passage in La Garma. A good head of an ibex as a black linear drawing is nearby.

* Although the Fourth Chamber has fewer figures, there are some animals in black, and engravings of horses. A series of red-violet dots are grouped together.

* The "Gallery of the Discs" in the deepest part of the cave, is a long corridor with several figures, mainly in red, but with few engravings, unlike in the rest of the cave where they are abundant. At the start of the passage the head of an auroch is painted with horns in semi-twisted perspective and one ear. The most typical motifs in this passage are the lines of large dots or discs sprayed in red and organized in different compositions. There are also some negative hand images, diamond and cross shaped signs, non-figurative lines and the painting of a mammoth in red, as well as numerous bear scratches on the walls and floor.

Although excellent documentary work and analysis was carried out after the discovery of the cave, to which important studies have been added by prehistorians such as J. González Echegaray, E. Ripoll, A. Moure and others, it now seems that a detailed revision of the art in Cueva del Castillo is necessary, so that it can be analyzed on more modern bases. In present conditions, the inventory of the themes represented can only give us a general idea of the contents, and could be modified substantially. A critical view of the figures which have been published to date enables us to reach a total of 240: about 56 negative hands, 54 hinds, 26 horses, 24 bison, 18 stags, 10 ibex, 6 aurochs, 3 chamois, 2 masks, 1 anthropomorph and 1 mammoth, as well as 5 cervids, 13 bovine, 5 caprids, and another 22 unidentified quadrupeds. Among the non-figurative art, there are

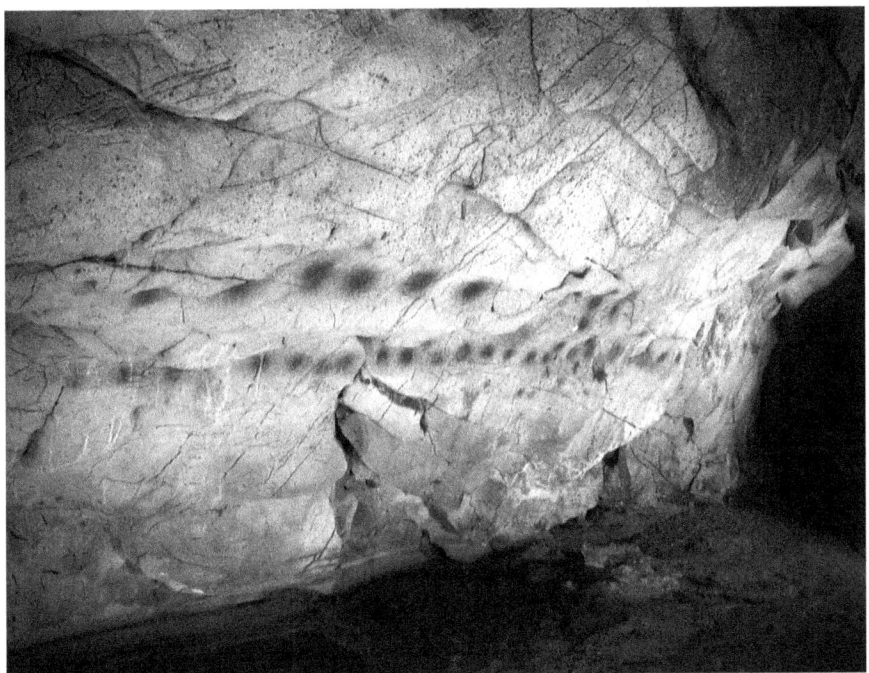
Gallery of the Discs

some 52 complex signs, mainly quadrangles, quadrilaterals with a pointed side, ovals or bell-shaped signs, and up to 27 dots, single, or as series of lines or in groups. The stains of color and series of simple lines, which are plentiful in the cave, have never been studied in detail, so they have never been counted nor is their distribution known.

The techniques used seem to be ordered in time in a similar way to those found in the nearby Cueva de La Pasiega. However, there are important differences in the distribution of the techniques in both caves, although they were both occupied at very different times throughout the Upper Paleolithic. In El Castillo negative hands and discs, painted by spraying the pigment, are very common, whereas this technique is hardly found in La Pasiega. Black paint is used more profusely, compared with the predominance of red in Pasiega, including the application of color wash in black, which does not exist in the second cave. Furthermore, discontinuous dotted lines, and red color wash, are unusual in El Castillo, but common in La Pasiega.

In the very general terms in which we can move, Breuil's proposals for the order of the techniques, based on the superimpositions, are relatively compatible with the chronology suggested by Leroi-Gourhan. The latter distinguished four basic occupations in his Styles III and Early IV, during the Solutrean and Magdalenian periods. At present, although much of the art in El Castillo must correspond to those periods, it is likely that at least the hands and simple series of red dots or discs are of an earlier age to Style III, and are probably Gravettian. The synchrony of all the figures of some of the panels is equally far from certain, because of the different radiocarbon dates that have been obtained, among other reasons.

The oldest paintings, of Style III and probably also of Style II, are the red sprayed paintings, the red and yellow linear outlined figures, which were applied in different ways, and the lines of red dots. The black paintings, sometimes with color wash, seem more common in the sub-groups of early Style IV than in Style III, although there are clearly animals in that style in El Castillo, just as there are in Las Chimeneas. Some of these black figures, and the "bichrome" bison, recently dated by radiocarbon, would have been the last paintings in the cave, defined in the Magdalenian period.

The types of engraving, whose association with painting seems to increase with time, are highly varied, and range from simple, single lines, or repeated lines, to partial striation (this is usually in hinds, with direct parallels with the scapulae from the early Magdalenian layers in the habitation deposit, or with the ones from Altamira, dated to about 14,500 BP), or even with lines filling the whole figure in the case of some ibex and bison. These varying styles of engraving must correspond to different periods, although they seem to be most abundant in the sub-groups of early Style IV than in previous styles, and there are even a few engravings superimposed on a "bichrome" figure. This relative abundance of engravings in early Style IV is also found in La Pasiega, and the distribution of the figures, nearer the entrance of the cave, and their generally small size, is equally similar to those in La Pasiega.

The distribution of motifs and techniques through El Castillo provides interesting information. It is clear that the oldest depictions, such as the hands and discs, are found in practically all the cave, including the parts nearest the end. In contrast, paintings and engravings of a more clearly Magdalenian style, or in Style IV, seem most common in the middle of the cave or nearer the entrance. This general distribution, in disagreement with certain interpretive schemes still in use, is nevertheless relatively similar to the one found, for example in La Pasiega, in both its eastern and western parts, and in the Lower Passage in La Garma.

Bibliography

Alcalde del Río, H. 1906. *Las pinturas y grabados de las cavernas prehistóricas de la provincia de Santander: Altamira, Covalanas, Hornos de la Peña, Castillo.* Impr. de Blanchard y Arce, Santander.

Alcalde del Río, H.; Breuil, H.; Sierra, L. 1911. *Les cavernes de la région Cantabrique.* Imprimerie Vve. A. Chéne. Monaco.

Cabrera Valdés, V. 1984. *El yacimiento de la cueva de "El Castillo" (Puente Viesgo, Santander).* Bibliotheca Praehistorica Hispana, XXII. Madrid.

Leroi-Gourhan, A. 1965. *Prehistoire de l'art occidental.* Mazenod, Paris.

Moure, A.; González Sainz, C.; Bernaldo de Quirós, F.; Cabrera Valdés, V. 1996. "Dataciones absolutas de pigmentos en cuevas cantábricas: Altamira, El Castillo, Chimeneas y Las Monedas". A. Moure (ed.), *"El Hombre fósil" 80 años después.* pp 295-324, Universidad de Cantabria, Santander.

2-5. Cueva de Las Chimeneas

Cueva de Las Chimeneas is situated in the hill Monte Castillo, in the town of Puente Viesgo in Cantabria. Together with its neighboring caves of El Castillo, La Flecha, La Pasiega and Las Monedas, it forms part of the most amazing Paleolithic site in the Iberian Peninsula, where a significant part of the cave art known in Spain is concentrated.

Las Chimeneas was discovered in the middle of the 20th Century, long after the discovery of another two important caves with Paleolithic art in the same hill: El Castillo in 1903 and La Pasiega in 1911. In 1950, construction work was under way to make it easier for tourists to visit these two caves, and this involved cutting a track round the side of the hill, from Cueva de El Castillo to La Pasiega. During this work two new caves were found, Las Monedas and La Flecha. Shortly after, in 1953, another cave was discovered, although its exploration revealed no evidence that it had ever been occupied during the Paleolithic. Then, some pits in the floor were descended to a lower passage, which gave positive and surprising results; the walls of this passage had been decorated with paintings and engravings, of animals and abstract signs, in the Upper Paleolithic. The high level passage had so many of these vertical pits that the cave was known as Cueva de Las Chimeneas (Cave of the Chimneys).

Although the archaeological deposit in Las Chimeneas has been examined twice, it is still not well known. After the cave was discovered, the few objects that were collected from the cave floor gave little chronological information. They included the jawbone of a deer, and flint tools consisting of three blades, a denticulate, and two endscrapers. In 1971 digs were carried out in the original entrance and in Chamber B, next to the panel of quadrangular signs, but they were both sterile. Despite these results, it seems likely that a Paleolithic deposit exists in the original vestibule in the Lower Passage, which is now covered by collapsed blocks and by flowstone and stalagmites, making any excavation extremely difficult.

The present layout of Cueva de Las Chimeneas is very different from how it appeared in the Paleolithic. It is now entered via the higher passage, which connects with the lower passage down a pit. This pit, which was descended during the exploration, was enlarged for tourist visits, and is now a long, winding stone staircase. In the Paleolithic, however, the Lower Passage was entered directly through an entrance, now blocked by a collapse that must have happened in the Pleistocene. The vestibule reached through this entrance is now filled by a

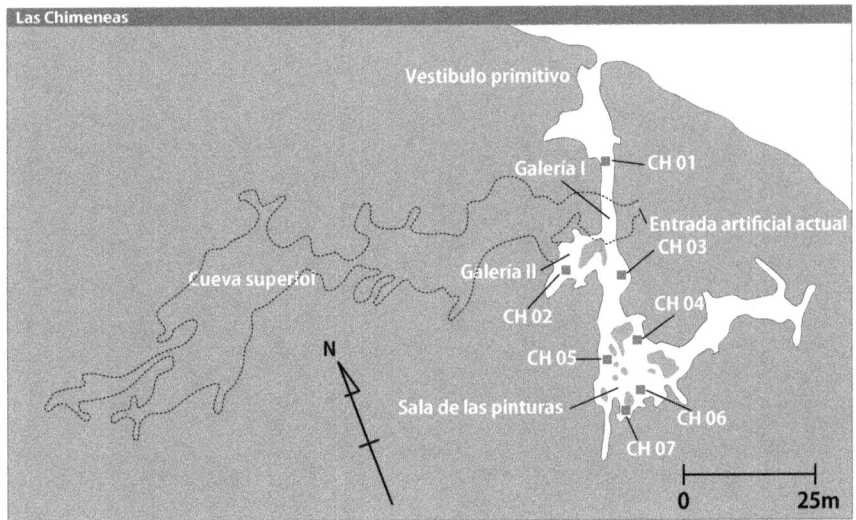

Las Chimeneas Ground Plan

forest of stalactites and stalagmites, so that it is now very difficult to move through this part of the cave. These calcite formations have grown since the entrance collapsed, and did not exist when the cave was decorated. In the Cantabrian region stalagmitic formations developed quickly in the temperate and wet climate of the early Holocene, and have sealed and hidden many archaeological deposits and also parietal art.

The former vestibule connects with a long passage (Gallery I), about 80m long and nowhere narrower than 4m in width. Its floor has a lot of gours, permanently filled with water. In the middle of the passage, a small natural hole in the floor is seen to open in a tiny chamber, which has bones of a deer on its floor. A few meters further on, a side-passage (Gallery II) is the location of the staircase now used to enter the cave, and has the first Paleolithic art in the cave: a figure of a goat engraved with a finger in a surface of soft calcite. This technique, one of the simplest and easiest, is found in other panels at the end of the cave, and is in fact one of the characteristics of the cave. This last section of Gallery I has several groups of non-figurative lines, macaroni, a deer and a doubtful figure of a quadruped, all produced with the same simple technique as the previous figure.

Gallery I ends in a circular chamber (Chamber B), about 17m wide and 20m long, which has the three main groups of art in the cave. The most visible of these panels was done on a section of wall hanging from the roof on the left-hand side of the chamber. It has several quadrangular signs painted in black, together with non-figurative lines, surprisingly well conserved. These signs, typical of the central area of the Cantabrian region, consist of rectangular figures sub-divided

2-5: Cueva de Las Chimeneas

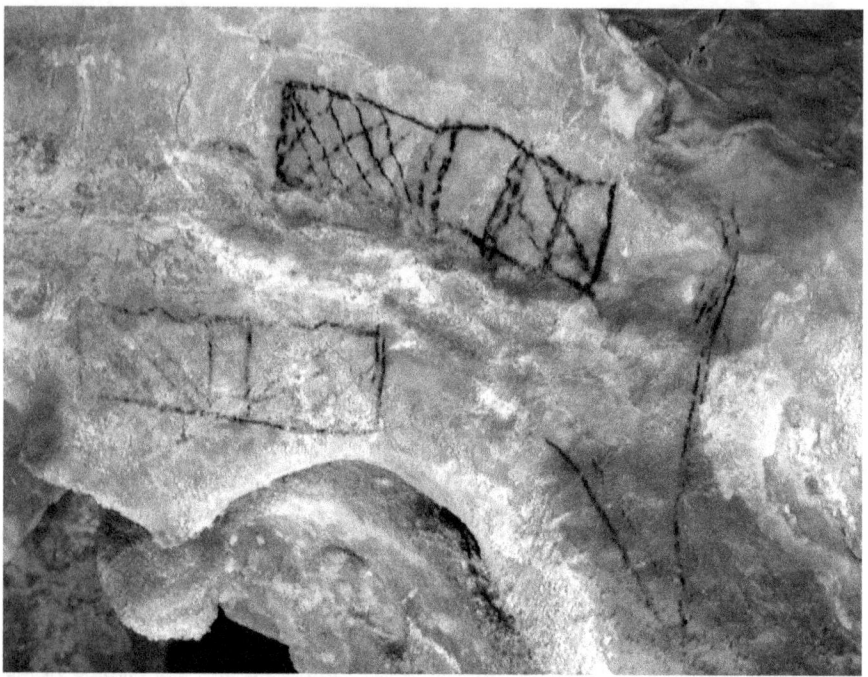

Cantabrian quadrilateral signs

internally, very often into three adjacent fields. In this case the interior sub-divisions are transversal, but similar signs exist in other caves which are sub-divided longitudinally to the long axis, e.g. in Altamira, El Castillo and La Pasiega A and C. On the left of this panel, another quadrangular sign was engraved, with its perimeter formed by two parallel lines filled with short transversal lines, as a kind of fringe. This sign is similar to some of those in group XII of the Asturian cave El Buxu.

To the right of the panel with these signs, a narrow gap leads to a short narrow passage (Gallery IV), only big enough for one person at a time, which contains the most spectacular figures in the cave. This passage is a kind of ox-bow which connects again with the chamber immediately next to the signs. The first figure we see in this passage is a complete stag facing right. The same passage has another five stags and the head, mane and start of the chest of a horse. The technique used in all these figures was as black outlines, drawn with a pencil of charcoal. They are all in a similar style, with small heads compared with voluminous bodies and chests. Regarding the compositary schemes, they are whole figures, except for the horse, and two of the stags, represented only by the head, antlers and the start of their backs and chests.

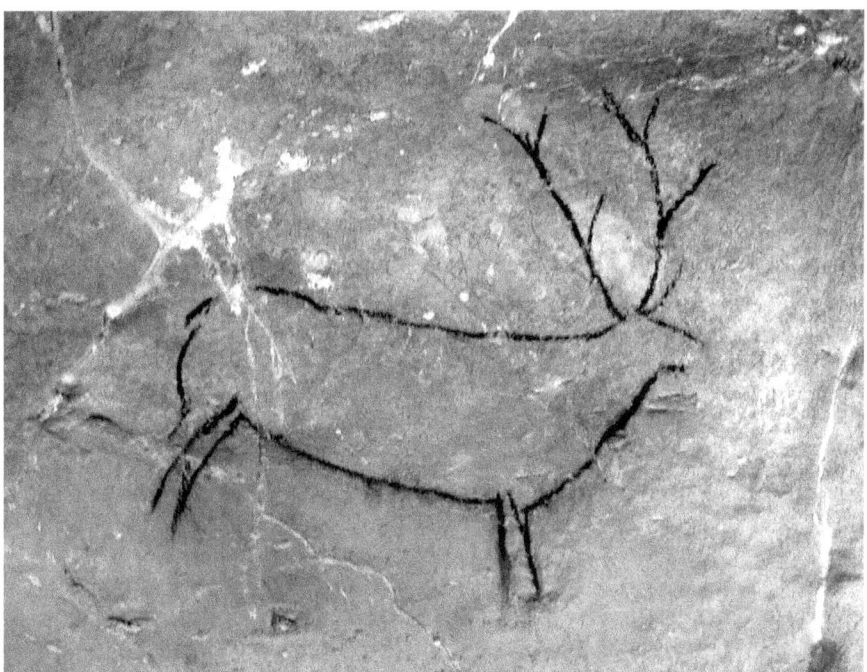

Stag in black, Chamber of the Stags

The third group in this decorated chamber is found on the roof of a small area on the right, separated from the main part of the chamber by several stalagmitic columns. The peculiar form of this roof, consisting of two successive longitudinal ridges, looking like fossilized sea-waves, was used by the artist to produce the figures in four panels, on both sides of the two ridges. Here there are a total of seven bovines, probably all aurochs, five stags, two hinds, two chamois, an ibex, and part of a probable horse. These figures have some characteristics in common. The compositive scheme is quite homogeneous, based on the representation of the head, back and start of the chest, although some heads are represented alone, but no figure has any limbs. This structure is a result of the narrow, long shape of the rock surface, just as happens on many decorated bone or antler objects. This has not allowed the animals to be represented whole, unlike the panels with the black paintings. The technique used in all cases was direct incision in the soft covering of the rock, with a finger or a blunt-ended instrument; two of the figures also have black paint over the engraved line.

The art of Cueva de Las Chimeneas has some special characteristics. In most Cantabrian caves, the artists produced the animal figures in more visible walls than the conventionalized signs, which do not usually occupy panels easily seen from the main route through the cave. Exactly the opposite occurs in Las

Chimeneas; the signs appear in the most visible parts of the cave, whereas few animal figures are found on the walls of the main passage, and mostly appear in the narrow Gallery IV, or are semi-hidden among the ridges of the roof. As for techniques, only two were used: black outline paint, and engraving on soft surfaces, either with a finger or a wooden instrument. Only two figures seem to combine engraving and black paint.

The iconographic organization is comparable with the structure of a pre-Magdalenian Cantabrian cave, although the greater number of stags than hinds is not usual in the region. In total, apart from the quadrangular signs and the non-figurative lines, there are 32 animal figures: eleven stags, nine bovines, three ibex, two chamois, two hinds, two horses and three indeterminate quadrupeds.

All the evidence of parietal decoration seems to have been done in a short length of time, and may be considered as more or less synchronic. As a result, all the art in Las Chimeneas has normally been attributed to Leroi-Gourhan's Style III, included in the late Solutrean or early Magdalenian. Similarly, J. González Echegaray considered that the figures, mainly species of ungulates corresponding to temperate climatic and ecological conditions, could be situated in the Lascaux oscillation (17,000 BP), also taking into account the style of the figures.

Many of the stylistic features of the animal figures do indeed agree with that chronology; figures out of proportion in their small heads and voluminous bodies, outlines not finished, open mouths represented by a gap between the forehead and jaw lines, and twisted perspective (especially in one of the chamois). But this stylistic chronology has been questioned recently by two absolute dates obtained: 15,070 +/- 140 BP for one of the stags, and 13,940 +/- 140 BP for a group of lines in the panel of quadrangular signs. There is now a division between supporters of these radiocarbon dates, even though the two results are contradictory, and those who still prefer an older chronology for Las Chimeneas. Among the reasons of the latter group of prehistorians there is the fact that if the dates were to be accepted, it would mean that nearly all the Cantabrian cave art might have been produced in just two millennia (between 15,000 and 13,000 BP), including such different assemblages in the concept of the animal figures as Altamira, El Castillo, Covaciella, as well as Chimeneas, or in the type of abstract sign included.

Bibliography

Moure Romanillo, A.; González Sainz, C.; Bernaldo de Quirós.; Cabrera Valdés, V. 1996. Dataciones absolutas de pigmentos en cuevas cantábricas: Altamira, El Castillo, Chimeneas, Las Monedas. En Moure, A. (ed.): *"El Hombre fósil" 80 anos después. Servicio de Publicaciones. Universidad de Cantabria. Santander,* pp 295-324.

González Echegaray, J. 1974. Pinturas y grabados de la cueva de Las Chimeneas (Puente Viesgo, Santander). Diputación Provincial de Barcelona. Instituto de Prehistoria y Arqueología. Wenner Gren Foundation for Anthropologicla Research. *Monografías de arte rupestre. Arte Paleolítico,* Nº 2. Barcelona.

3-6. Cueva de La Pasiega

The cave system of La Pasiega is situated on the steep hillside of Monte Castillo, half way between the decorated caves of Las Chimeneas and Las Monedas, and therefore also very near to Cueva de El Castillo. It was discovered in 1911 by the German archaeologists Hugo Obermaier and Paul Wernet, who were then taking part in the major excavations in the vestibule at El Castillo. The cave art inside La Pasiega, which turned out to be one of the most important decorated sites in the Cantabrian region, was then studied by the team of H. Breuil, H. Obermaier and H. Alcalde del Río, and magnificently published in 1913.

Rather than as a simple cave, it is better to describe La Pasiega as a cave system, not too big but very complex. It had several entrances during the Upper Paleolithic, and as many as three may have been used, which connected in a series of chambers and passages, sometimes on different levels. The building work done for tourist visits mainly in the 1950s and 60s, have complicated the topography even further by blocking up some passages with rubble, building interior walls, or by the successive opening up of new entrances at different times.

Four large general areas of the cave have been distinguished: Galleries A, B and C, and the Zone D which includes the intermediate sectors between the western area (Gallery C) and the eastern parts (Galleries B and A). This means that, from an iconographic point of view, during the Upper Paleolithic two or perhaps three different groups of art may have functioned independently. These could have been the eastern part (Galleries B, A and the eastern sectors of Zone D), the western (Gallery C), and a central group (the western sectors of Zone D) which could have been independent from the others, or have functioned as the last part of Gallery C. Solutrean industry and the usual remains of Paleolithic human occupation were found in the original entrances of Galleries C and B. A layer probably corresponding to the early Magdalenian was also found in the second of these entrances, during the digs carried out by J. Carballo, and by J. González Echegaray in 1951 and 1952 when the cave was being prepared for tourist visits. These two entrances to Galleries B and C were certainly the main ones, and perhaps the only ones, in the Upper Paleolithic.

The following summary of the available evidence, according to its position in the cave, includes the results of the project documenting the cave which has recently been developed by the Universities of Cantabria and Alcalá de Henares.

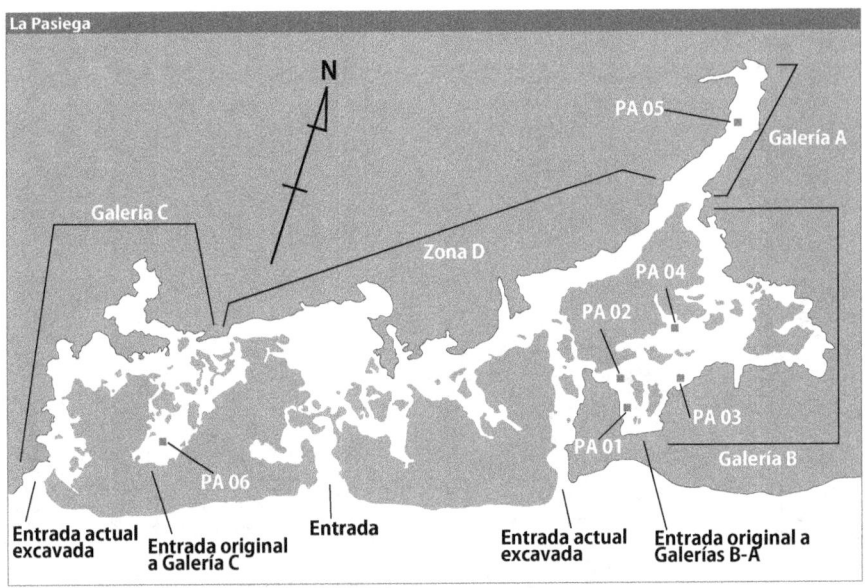

La Pasiega Ground Plan

1. Gallery B. Its original entrance was a habitation site in the Solutrean, and probably early Magdalenian periods, judging from the industry that has been found. Using this entrance, Gallery B was once on the route leading into deeper parts of La Pasiega cave system: Gallery A and parts of Zone D. Possibly for this reason, the art in Gallery B is more heterogeneous in technique and style than these more remote parts of the cave, which show greater unity. Equally, taking into account the most usual factors for both anthropic and natural alterations, the cave art is generally in a poorer state of conservation nearer the entrance of Gallery B, than further inside the cave.

The great diversity in type of cave passage, technique, and to a lesser extent style, in Gallery B makes it difficult to obtain a clear idea of the order of its cave art, which is quite abundant. Over two hundred Paleolithic graphic units, according to the latest calculations, include 24 horses, 20 ibex, 16 indeterminate quadrupeds, 11 hinds, and as many as 9 stags, 3 aurochs and 2 bison, and other unidentified figures of bovines, deer and carnivores, as well as a bird and a fish. There is also an engraving of an anthropomorphic figure. The signs consist mainly of classic red claviforms, as well as series of dots, and a couple of small quadrilaterals. Besides these figures, there are numerous shapeless stains of red pigment, the remains of figures that have now disappeared, and non-figurative lines and series.

The walls and roof nearest to the entrance, coinciding with the hab-

2-6: Cueva de La Pasiega

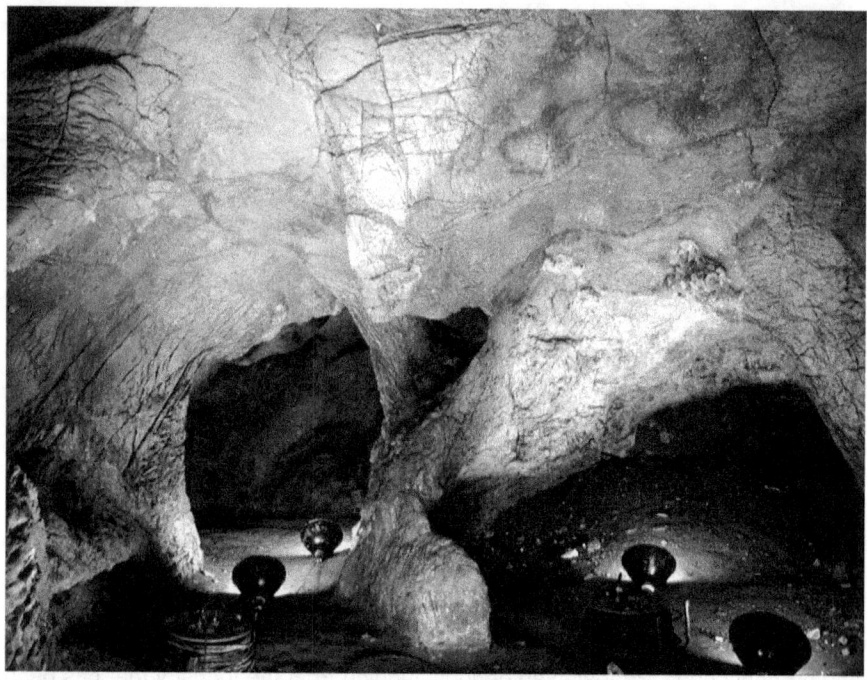

Ceiling at the entrance of Gallery B

itation deposit, contain the most complex groups and the apparently "central" panels, with large, "important" animals painted and engraved in the outline, and many smaller engraved figures, with much more diverse themes and apparently organized at random.

Here, in the first chambers of Gallery B, we find the association of bison or auroch with horses, represented by figures outlined in red and occasionally in partial color wash. Besides, there is another unusual animal in the Cantabrian region, the giant deer, the largest Pleistocene deer, now extinct. Around these large painted figures there is a large number of animal engravings, some of which are of a very high quality. The best of these are horses with repeated lines around their outline, masses of striated lines filling the ventral areas, and many details indicated with very fine engraving.

The next area, a little further into the cave, has the same thematic association in several panels, applied here with more complex techniques, such as color wash and engraved outlines, together with several types of abstract signs, including claviforms. We also find here animal engravings, many of which have never been published, sometimes superimposed on bovines and horses. One of the best of these is a hind superimposed on the largest painted horse.

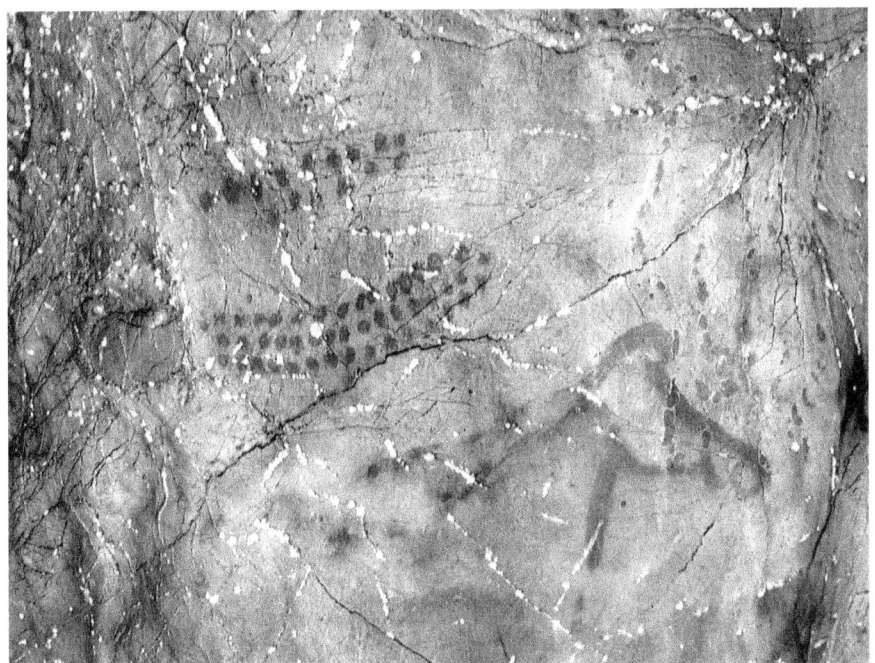
Sign, hind, horse, panel of paintings and engravings

In this entrance area, the pictorial techniques and some of the stylistic conventions are indicative of the transition between Styles III and IV in the first passage, and more clearly early Style IV further inside. The engravings in both zones, however, are more homogeneous, and are always above the paintings. In some cases they show bands of striated engraving.

As we mentioned, the panels at the back of this entrance area, in the middle sectors of Gallery B contain a large number of claviform signs painted in red, generally in panels easily seen from the route through the cave. These signs are similar to the ones known in Altamira, and are believed to be synchronic with the red animal paintings in the front part of Gallery B.

Further inside, there are more groups of signs, which can probably be associated with the above-mentioned animal figures too. One of these is the so-called "symbolic inscription" : a series of abstract signs along a line on the right-hand wall of the central chamber. It is as mysterious as other signs, but more suggestive for many people because of the complexity produced by such an orderly association of symbols.

Finally, in generally more isolated or marginal sectors of Gallery B, which are often difficult to reach because the passages are so narrow, we can find groups of animal figures, mainly engravings, of a different thematic structure from the paintings at the entrance. The most interesting of these sectors is a high-level passage, with some signs painted at its entrance, and also a few paintings of animals. Superimposed on these, we have recently found a series of animals: stags, hinds and a horse, engraved along the walls of the passage. They are simple or repeated engravings, which frequently include areas filled with striated lines. The passage becomes very narrow and difficult, before opening in a small chamber, where the Paleolithic artists drew a large number of animals, with technical conventions, and above all a thematic structure, very different from the other sub-groups in Gallery B. Here, horses are associated with ibex and a few deer on each side. The analysis of the distribution, position and size of the figures has made it possible to establish the interaction of these aspects with the limitations of space, size of manual field, and postures used. In this way, together with the technical and stylistic homogeneity of the figures, which correspond to early Style IV, we can suppose that the group is internally synchronic.

The last part of Gallery B, before the junction with Gallery A and Zone D, has fewer depictions, which are more heterogeneous in technique and style. In contrast with other zones of the Gallery, here we find an apparently haphazard accumulation of figures. They include black paintings, which may have parallels in the more recent paintings in Gallery A; some signs that are half way between the typical Cantabrian quadrangular signs and "grilles" ; groups of dots; some red figures; and above all several, rather isolated, animal engravings, in some cases similar to the ones at the start of Zone D.

2. Gallery A. In fact, this is the last twenty meters of the long passage connecting much of the central and eastern parts of La Pasiega. It is quite a small space, but with plenty of good limestone surfaces that are light-colored, empty and clean, available in domes and hollows in the wall and roof. Access from the end of Gallery B must have been worse than it is today, as the floor has been dug away in places, but it cannot have been too difficult.

Gallery A has a cave art assemblage in a final position, at the end of the cave, with an extraordinary concentration of animals and signs in red, as well as exceptions in yellow, brown, black and, sporadically, engraving. There is a great density of depictions of animals and signs, many of which are of a rare esthetic value. Furthermore, the parietal art of Gallery A is well conserved, and quite coherent from different points of view. Indeed, it is near to being the paradigm of Cantabrian cave art of the Solutrean-early Magdalenian period, when the region achieved an artistic personality differentiated from other surrounding areas. This was shown in many different ways.

One way was in the thematic structure, with abundant figures of hinds (some 34, or 18.1% of the total), horses (30 figures, or 16.0%), and complex signs (60, or 30.6%), mostly long quadrilaterals with a pointed protuberance or crescent-shaped. In other words, with the typical forms of the center of the Cantabrian region during the Solutrean and early Magdalenian periods. In total, about a hundred animal figures are known in Gallery A. As well as the hinds and horses, there are 14 stags, 5 aurochs and 4 bison, 3 ibex and 2 reindeer, and a deer and another 7 indeterminate quadrupeds. Regarding the non-figurative art, apart from the conventionalized signs, there are series of dots, lines and stains of color. Even so, the proportion of this type of shapeless motif is noticeably lower than in other galleries. It seems that this area, essentially pictorial, was much more reserved and restricted than previous parts of the cave, which have more heterogeneous depictions.

Studying the techniques that were applied has been quite complex, although they are characteristic of the chronology mentioned above. We have identified two areas where the wall was prepared before painting. Regarding the procedures, red paint predominates, although series of figures exist in variations of sepia and brown. Similarly, as many as eleven figures were painted in black, and are sometimes superimposed on the red paintings. The red paint was nearly always applied in simple lines, occasionally associated with lines made up of discontinuous or juxtaposed dots. Some of the lines were widened in order to give shape to parts of the animals' outlines, and color wash was used, affecting part or all of the figure. Engraving was used in addition, precisely in the same figures where color wash was applied. Finally, there are some separate engraved figures, which went unnoticed for many years: a possible oval-shaped sign, and two that are probably sketches of unrecognizable quadrupeds.

Concerning their distribution, the figures follow almost one after the other along the twenty meters of roof and walls. But some notes need to be made: the density of figures tends to increase towards the end of the passage, and some compositions can be differentiated in certain independent panels. The most interesting is the one at the end, where the passage finishes abruptly, turning in a right angle to the left. Here we find the largest group of signs in all the cave; rectangles distributed on the walls of this last passage, which is only 40cm wide, and surrounding large paintings of a bison and a horse facing each other, which seem to dominate over the whole Gallery. Smaller animal figures, painted with ocher pencils, are on the sides of this great composition. To the left, further inside the narrow passage, the animals tend to become less common, in comparison with the signs. To the right, above a small flowstone formation, smaller panels are found in hollows in the walls and roof, with more animals painted in red, including a magnificent reindeer, and further pointed quadrilateral signs.

2-6: Cueva de La Pasiega

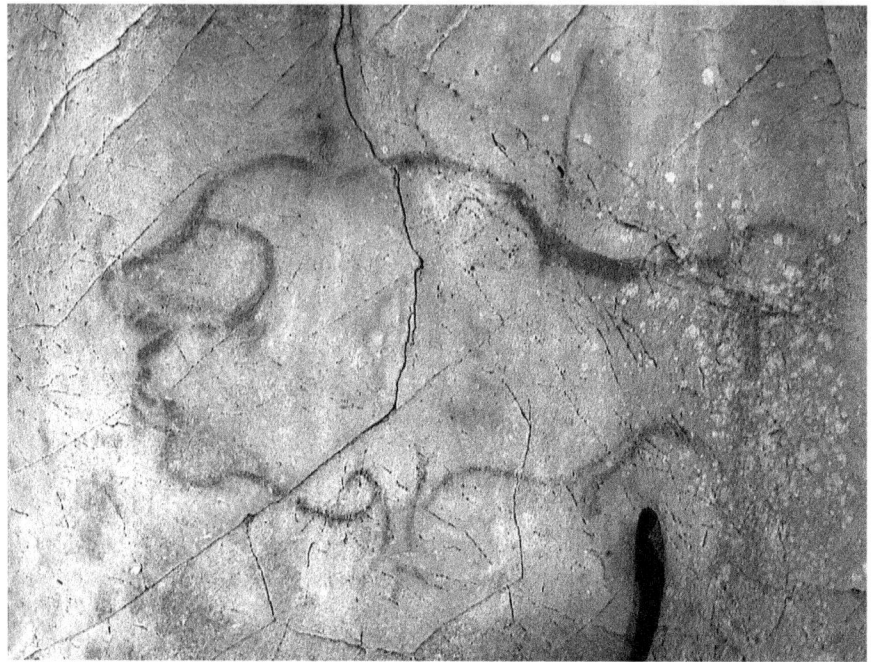
Violet bison repainted in black

Leroi-Gourhan's proposal regarding the style of the figures is acceptable. This art corresponds to a late, or second phase, of his Style III, with other figures in the transition to early Style IV. Some of the black figures could definitely be catalogued within early Style IV.

3. Zone D. This is a quite complex part of the cave, but one with less cave art, which is in any case very heterogeneous. During the Upper Paleolithic, the artists could have reached this zone from Gallery B, directly from the surface through a small entrance which has now been covered over, or through Gallery C, again through a complicated passage which has now been walled off.

The main cave art in Zone D will be described from the connection with Galleries A and B. Practically at the junction with these passages we can find the first group of engravings and red paintings, and the latter are probably of the same age as the nearby figures in Gallery A.

A little further on, we find another group of figures on a bend in the passage. This includes as many as seven painted signs: quadrangles, one with a pointed protuberance, or ovals, and an engraved horse, as well as several series

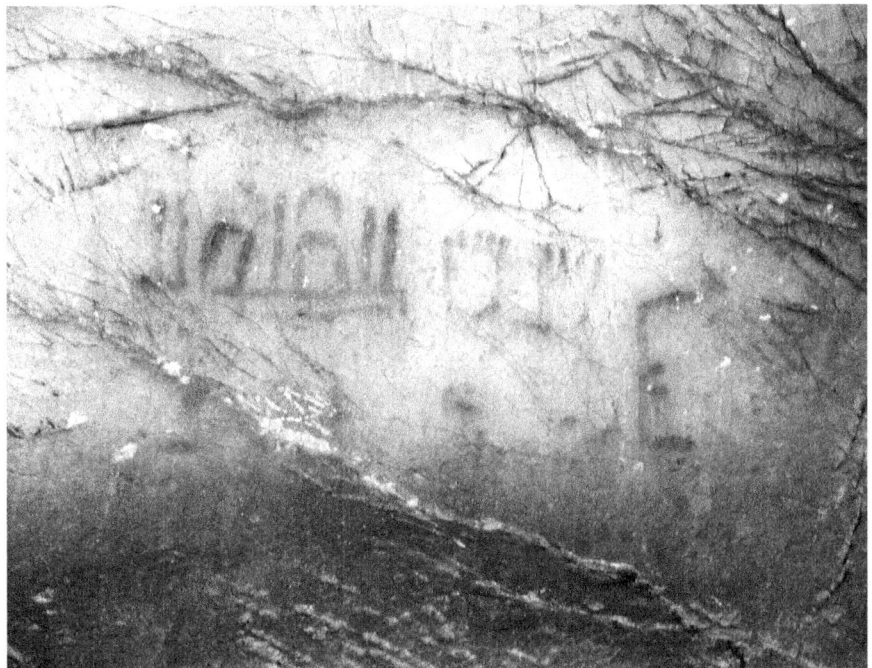

"Symbolic inscription" of La Pasiega

of non-figurative engraved lines. Another panel nearby has a hind in red, and other less important figures.

The middle areas of Zone D are very complicated; they were visited less in the Paleolithic, and consequently have a much lower density of art. The depictions that are found vary greatly in technique, style, and presumably, in their age. A small side-passage, only big enough for one person, contains a few engravings in a clearly Magdalenian style, and near these, in the roof there is an isolated hind in red, in Style III. Further on, in the western part of Zone D, we come to some of the most hidden groups, with the most difficult access, of all the cave art in La Pasiega. Here, in a small chamber, in the center of this maze, we find the most unusual figures, stylistically speaking, in the whole cave. Several engraved animals, and the cervical-dorsal line of a quadruped, are associated with pairs of red lines, painted by dragging the pigment vertically down the wall with two or three fingers. The type of engraving, a very clear, simple, single line, and the archaic style and conventions of the animals (four bovines and a hind), or their association with red fingermarks, which are not known in other parts of the cave, suggest that this is one of the oldest panels in La Pasiega, although the age cannot be determined more precisely.

2-6: Cueva de La Pasiega

A high-level chamber has two horses, discovered in the 1950s, which are painted in Style III. A little further on, in one of the most difficult parts of the cave, there is a panel with three engraved horses, one of which has never been published, and several black charcoal marks. A final passage, near to the junction with Gallery C, has painted figures, which were also engraved in part. A horse and a bison can be identified clearly, with the remains of other figures, one of which is probably a second bison, and a large number of red stains, and modern alterations.

The techniques and styles of the art in Zone D is, as we have said, very diverse. This is probably a result of the different ways of entering the zone, and of the highly varied chronology of the different panels.

4. Gallery C. Without doubt, this is the most complex part of La Pasiega, which originally had its own entrance, now covered over. It contains a large number of depictions, which are quite diverse from the technical, stylistic and probably chronological points of view. The phases which are doubtlessly best represented range from an intermediate stage of Style III to the central moments of Style IV. That is to say, between about 20,000 and 13,000 BP.

In general, two large areas can be distinguished in Gallery C, with quite different densities of figures. Just as happened in Gallery B, the art is much more abundant near the former entrance, in a space about 18m long. In contrast, deeper inside Gallery C several sectors are decorated with a much smaller number of figures.

The left-hand side near the entrance has animals and signs clearly corresponding to Style III. They are nearly all painted in yellow or red tones, and are together with a number of engravings, normally superimposed on the paintings, with technical and stylistic conventions that can easily be included in early Style IV. The series of engravings that can be seen is quite large, and includes several figures of hinds, a goat and an auroch that have never been published. The right-hand side has mainly animal figures, painted and engraved, in early Style IV. But it also has other animal figures in red or in yellow which are stylistically indistinguishable from the ones on the left that were attributed to Style III.

In contrast, the back of the chamber is the location for a fairly homogeneous group of animal figures, painted in black, engraved, or in some cases combining both procedures. Taking into account their conventions of representation, this group is somewhat later than the figures nearer the entrance, and probably dates from the middle phases of the Magdalenian. Nevertheless, some of the depictions here may be older; for example, a red quadrangular sign with a pointed protuberance, certainly comparable with the Style III figures in the first part of the chamber.

The group of black paintings and engravings at the back of the main chamber show a significant structure within Leroi-Gourhan' s proposed scheme. Panels situated on both sides of the passage, practically facing each other, contain several groups of figures which are apparently complementary. One panel has two bison (one in black and the other engraved), and a black bovine, to which an unfinished sketch of another bison around a corner from this frieze might be added. The opposite wall has three horses (two engraved and one painted in black and engraved), and an engraved hind' s head, which in fact has never been published, in one panel. In a second panel there are another two horses (one painted and one engraved) and a possible hind' s head. The low height of these three panels above the floor, in comparison with the other panels in this chamber, together with their uniformity in size and style, further confirms their synchronic and probably complementary nature. Another area close-by containing two ibex painted in black and engraved, as well as a third example only engraved, and which has not been published yet, seems to complete this group. It has a Magdalenian style, very similar to other caves in the region with a "Pyrenean" appearance, such as Covaciella, Urdiales or Altxerri.

Generally speaking, we are not sure if a chronological order can be proposed for the art in Gallery C, based strictly on the techniques employed, even though the superimpositions usually correspond to the same scheme (sienna, followed by red or violet, and then by black, and with animal engravings over both red and black). The issue is complicated by the use of two colors for the outlines of certain figures: black is used over violet-red in a bison on the right-hand side, and over red color-wash in the large bovine on the left.

At the moment, we believe that two phases with clearly different styles can be distinguished, and they correspond to the oldest and the most recent art in the chamber:

a) the group painted in Style III, with animal figures, and quadrangular and oval signs. They were produced with sienna or red lines (where red is normally superimposed on sienna). They are found on both sides of the main chamber, more abundantly on the left, but also on the right.

Other more isolated figures would correspond to this phase, situated further inside the cave, such as a red quadrangular sign, or a chamois in sienna with its horns in twisted perspective.

b) the group of animal figures in Style IV, which are painted in black, en-

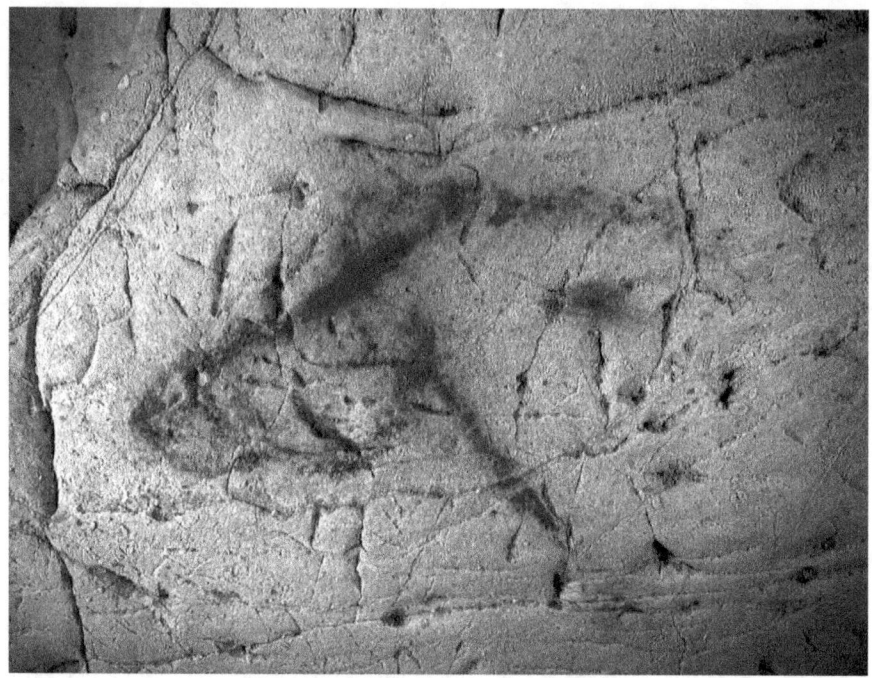
Horse's head in brown, Galeria A. Centro

graved, or combine both procedures. They are located on both side-walls at the back of the main chamber.

It is likely that a large number of the figures near the entrance were produced between these two stylistic and chronological phases, although we cannot form a precise idea of their age. The most probable order (taking into account the fact that the chronological difference might be a question of minutes) is as follows: claviforms and animal figures in red color-wash, or as violet linear drawings gone over in black; black outlined animal figures; and then animal engravings. The latter are superimposed on the claviforms and on the black figures on the right-hand side of the passage, and also on the red Style III figures on the left.

The art in Gallery C is not restricted to its main chamber. The gallery leads into a maze, with depictions painted in black, red, sienna and violet. Several ways on can be taken from the back of the chamber, and these have sporadic examples of cave art. Thus, a few engraved lines and non-figurative red stains are found in the passage leading to the present entrance, which was tunneled open in recent years. A secondary passage at a slightly higher level than the main chamber has a splendid engraved figure of a horse, and unpublished figures such as red stains and a large number of engravings with wide lines that

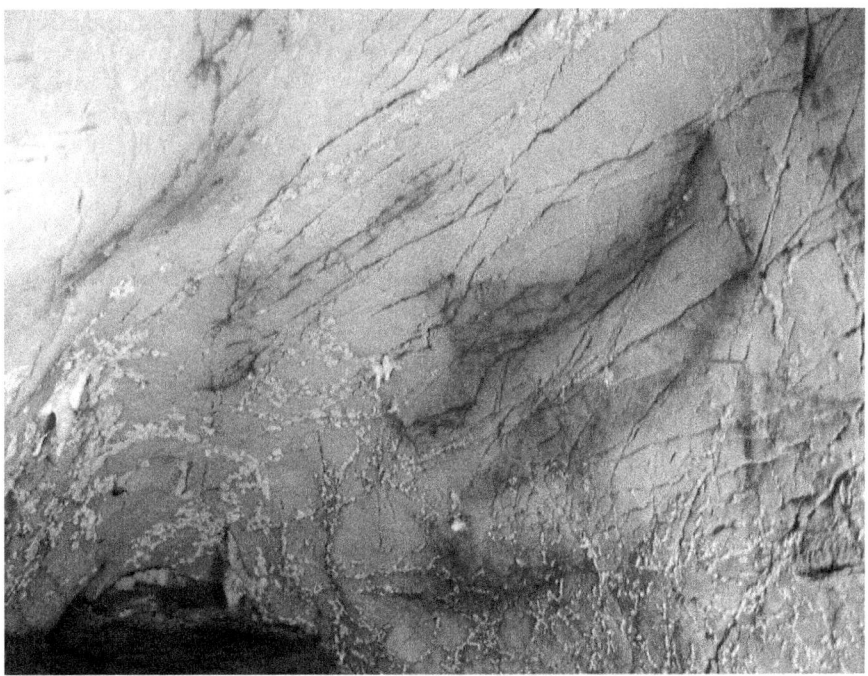
Group of claviform signs, Galeria B. Gran sala central.

include two quadrangular signs. Two of the ways lead finally to Zone D. The easiest of these has a few figures, engraved or painted in red or black. Lastly, a number of vertical pits in the floor of the maze can be descended to a large lower passage, although so far this has only be seen to contain modern human alterations, and marks scratched by animals.

La Pasiega cave system contains, therefore, a great deal of parietal art, with a highly irregular distribution. During the recent revision of the cave, nearly forty different decorated sectors have been recognized, with a variable number of panels and figures in each one. As we have seen, the greatest concentrations, and those with the greatest diversity in technique, size and iconography, are found in the chambers near the original entrances to Galleries C and B. These same parts of the cave have series of superimpositions which played an important role in the chronological scheme developed by Henri Breuil at the start of the century. We also find a very high density of figures in the area at the end of Gallery A, and even in the chamber in the small side-passage to Gallery B. But in these places the technical and stylistic homogeneity of the figures is much greater.

The thematic structure is equally very diverse. Certainly the theme of bison or auroch plus horse is found in the four main areas, and is significant due to the figures' position and greater visibility, or because more complex techniques were frequently applied, in a larger format. However, other formulae of thematic structure are often found, especially in isolated sub-groups. The latest inventory of the cave art in La Pasiega has 720 Paleolithic parietal units. Among the animals there are, at least, 80 horses, 69 hinds, 32 goats, 28 stags, 17 bison, 14 aurochs, 2 reindeer, 2 anthropomorphs, 2 bovines and 2 indeterminate deer, and one figure each of a carnivore, chamois, giant deer, possible mammoth, bird and fish, as well as 37 unidentified quadrupeds, and 55 remains of figures, either animals or signs, which are no longer recognizable. There are 134 complete signs, especially quadrangles, pointed quadrilaterals and claviforms, and 25 dots, in groups or organized in series. Finally, up to 215 red stains, series of black marks, and engraved lines have been catalogued, where it seems unlikely there was any figurative intention.

The different areas in La Pasiega bear witness to a long sequence of pictorial occupation which, to judge from the styles represented, lasted from a middle phase of Style III, as in different sectors in Gallery C and Zone D, and in almost all Gallery A, until the middle of Style IV, which is found in most of Gallery B and the central sectors of Gallery C. This main sequence of decoration, then, took place between 19,000 and 13,000 BP approximately. However, it is possible that at least the group of engravings with red fingermarks, in the interior of Zone D, may have been done before this period of time.

The techniques used during this length of time, in the different sectors of the cave, are extremely varied. In paint, they used dotted lines and simple lines; partial or whole color-wash, occasionally with the addition of engraving; and bichrome paintings, original or by being repainted later. The formulae for the application of red paint, which predominates absolutely in Style III sub-groups, are much more varied than for black, which was used in simple lines with very little shaping, compensated by the more common addition of interior lines and other conventions of representation. In turn, the engravings are equally highly varied, and more frequent in Style IV sub-groups. They were done in clay; with simple, single or repeated lines; and sometimes with striation or scraping. They include figures of hinds with striated areas in their chins and chests in Gallery C and in two different sectors of Gallery B.

Bibliography

Balbín Behrmann, R. de, y González Sainz, C. 1993. Nuevas investigaciones en la cueva de La Pasiega (Puente Viesgo, Cantabria). *Boletín del Seminario de Estudios de Arte y Arqueología,* LIX, pp 9-38.

Breuil, H.; Obermiaer, H. y Alcalde del Río, H. 1913. *La Pasiega à Puente Viesgo (Santander) (Espagne).* Institut de Paléontologie Humaine. Imp. Vve. A. Chêne, Monaco.

Leroi-Gourhan, A. 1965. *Prehistoire de l'Art occidental.* L. Mazenod, Paris (2nd ed. 1971).

2-7. Cueva de Las Monedas

Cueva de Las Monedas is located on the southwest-facing hillside of Monte Castillo, at 187m above sea level. Consequently, it is very near the other caves in the same hill: El Castillo, Las Chimeneas, La Flecha and La Pasiega.

Some time after the important research carried out in the caves of El Castillo and La Pasiega at the start of the century, new discoveries were made in the 1950s, at the same time as a track was cut round the side of the hill to La Pasiega. Cueva de Las Monedas was discovered in April 1952, when the land was being cleared for the plantation of eucalyptus trees. At first, the cave was called "Cueva de Los Osos" (Cave of the Bears) because of all the skeletal remains of this animal that were found on the cave floor. But as a result of the discovery of twenty-three coins, from the reign of Isabel and Ferdinand, the name was changed to "Cueva de Las Monedas" (Cave of the Coins), and it is still referred to in that way in scientific publications. This was not going to be the last discovery of cave art in Monte Castillo, as one year later, Cueva de Las Chimeneas was found, with another important group of Paleolithic paintings and engravings.

In the months following the discovery of Las Monedas, several prehistorians working in the region, namely J. Carballo, J. González Echegaray, and E. Ripoll, published the news of the find separately. Nevertheless, the only complete study of the parietal art in the cave was not published until 1972, by Ripoll. He had been in charge of the documentation of the art in 1952, when copies were made of the paintings and small digs were carried out in different parts of the cave. At the same time, the cave was prepared for tourist visits.

The first dig was in the passage situated to the north-east of the vestibule. Two levels were encountered with abundant remains of bear, and also of deer. Two trenches were dug in the vestibule, where again two levels were found. The first level contained bones, a few fragments of very coarse pottery, a bronze awl, and half of a second awl. The lower level only had very small bone fragments.

The most interesting finds were made during the work preparing the cave for tourism. Another bronze awl was found, a bronze ax, and three basalt axes. However, this work was performed without any kind of archaeological plan or support, and almost certainly destroyed an important Bronze Age deposit. In other parts of the cave a few quartzite flakes were found, but none of the different kinds of digs ever found a level with Upper Paleolithic industry.

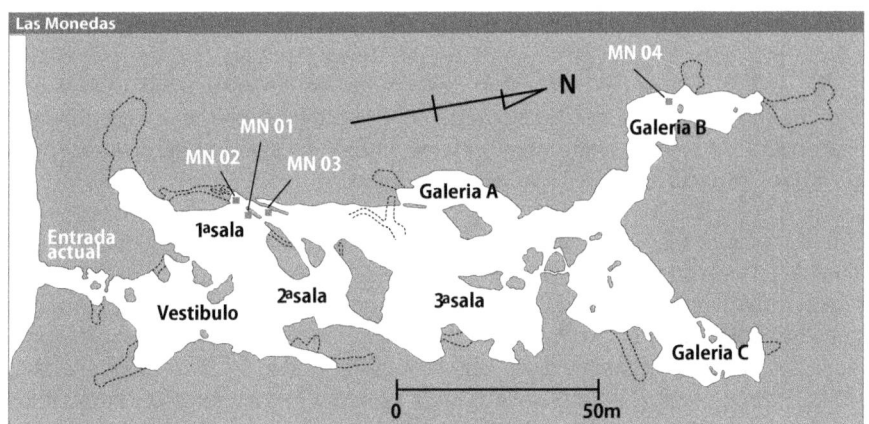
Las Monedas Ground Plan

The art in Cueva de Las Monedas forms a homogeneous group from the points of view of its location, the techniques used and the iconography. All the figures are located in a small passage about 13m long, which divides near the entrance into two narrow corridors separated by a vertical block of stone. Entering this passage at its southern end, the first panel we see is on the left-hand wall, and is composed of numerous lines in charcoal black, which do not form either animal figures or conventionalized signs. Further ahead the passage becomes narrower, and most of the cave art was painted on its right-hand wall.

Four meters from the previous panel, we find the two most characteristic figures in Las Monedas. They are a horse and a reindeer drawn on two faces of a projecting piece of the side wall, in the form of a sharp-edged limestone block. Both figures are in a vertical position, following the direction of the faces of the block, with their heads upwards and their backs towards the edge. The horse is the more complete figure, and includes some characteristic interior partitions marking the mane, muzzle and the typical "M" -shaped ventral line, which indicates the different colors of the horse' s coat, in its back and its belly. The reindeer, situated on the right-hand face of the block, is not so complete, as the fore limbs and belly are missing. Nevertheless, many details are included, such as the hairs under its chin.

Two meters further on, several figures are located in the narrowest part of the passage: three horses, two ibex, a reindeer and a possible mustelid. The three horses show quite different stylistic conventions. The first was drawn with a fairly wide line, and neither the head nor the belly were represented. Despite this, the proportions are correct. The second horse was drawn in a very similar way, with wide lines of black paint. Unlike the first, the head and belly are present, but not the rear-quarters which could not be drawn because of a layer of calcite on the wall. This figure is different in that it is not on the cave wall, but in a kind of dome formed by the stalagmitic formation. The third horse was also drawn in black paint, but with a lighter tone, and finer lines. The style is very different from the others too, and its proportions are not correct.

One of the most curious figures in the cave is a possible depiction of a mustelid. This figure is of an animal facing left, with a long, thin body, and with a round head which is very large in comparison with the body. Although neither limbs nor belly were represented, it is best classified as a mustelid, despite some reserves. These small animals are very rare in Paleolithic art. The clearest example is a black painting in the Clastres Gallery in the French cave of Niaux. If we admit the possibility that it is indeed a mustelid, the figure in Las Monedas could be a weasel, a stoat or a marten.

At the end of the passage, the roof is lower, and divides into two rifts separated by a large central flake of rock. This flake was used by the artists as the surface for the paintings of two reindeer in line, on the left-hand face. The opposite face, here at the head of this decorated passage, has more figures. They include a bison in a vertical position and a horse that uses a prominence in the wall to represent its eye.

Another passage, parallel to the one we have been following, contains more animal figures as well as numerous non-figurative lines. The animals include depictions of a bear, a stag, two ibex and a horse.

From the iconographic point of view, Las Monedas cannot be called a typical Cantabrian site, with the usual high frequency of deer, especially hinds, and abstract signs. Its most common theme is the horse, with 14 figures, as well as the figures of ibex (4), bison (2) and stag (1). However, the most striking fact is the presence of several very unusual themes in Cantabrian cave art, namely reindeer, with four figures, almost a fifth of all the figures of reindeer in the region. Equally, there is a painting of a cave bear, which is quite rare in the Cantabrian region. Lastly, we have already mentioned the presence of a painting of a possible mustelid. It is also noticeable that there are numerous unfinished outlines, and an even larger number of mere non-figurative lines. In contrast, conventionalized abstract signs, as found in other caves, are practically absent.

Regarding the technical procedures, all the figures were done with black paint, without any engraved parts. The paint was applied in lines, both around the outline and in the interior details. A few figures also have areas with partial color wash and different tones of color.

2-7: Cueva de Las Monedas

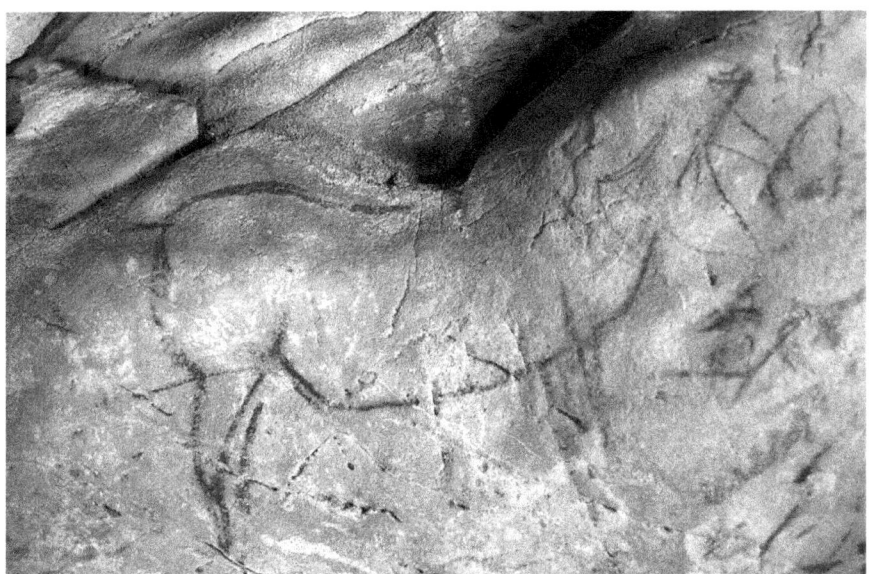
Horse and signs in black

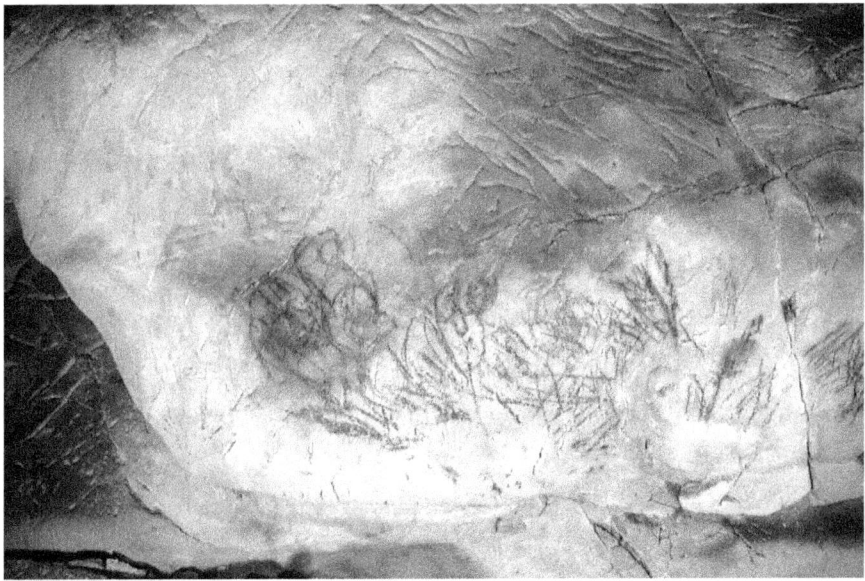
Non-figurative black lines

2-7: Cueva de Las Monedas

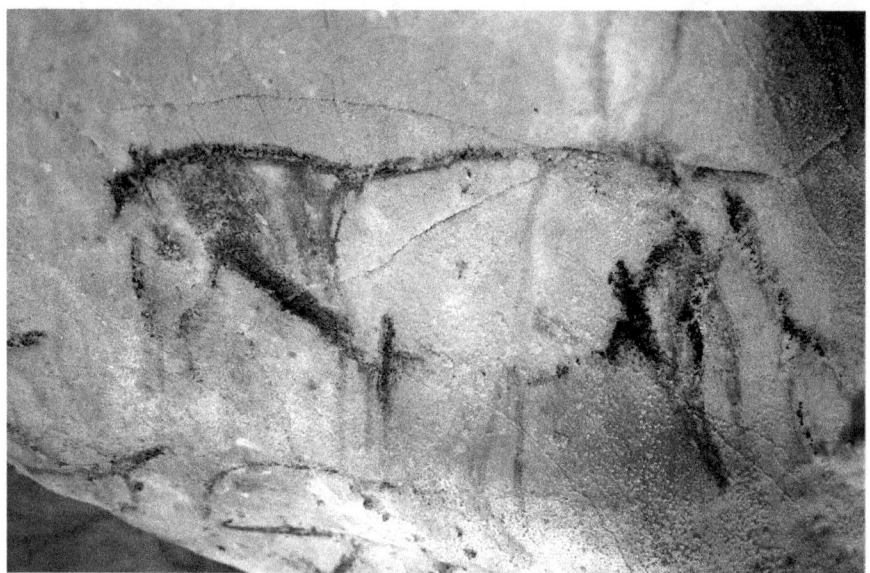

Horse in black, 1st chamber

From the chronological point of view, this is one of the clearest examples of a synchronic site in the Cantabrian region. It has been attributed to Leroi-Gourhan's Style IV, that is, in the Magdalenian period, between about 15,000 and 11,000 before the present. Some of the characteristics which support this age for the cave art in Las Monedas are the relative abundance of lines of interior partition in the animals' bodies (the ventral "M", the mane, muzzle, or scapular color), the representation of the limbs in two different planes, and the correct use of perspective. Equally, the proportions are correct in most of the figures, although a few have a voluminous body and small head, which are stylistic conventions corresponding (although not exclusively) to earlier periods. Nevertheless, these same relatively "deformed" figures have features that are typical of Style IV, such as the interior partition lines already mentioned. Finally, the presence of animals such as reindeer, bear and mustelid, suggest that the paintings were done in quite a late phase of the Upper Paleolithic. It is true that these animals were depicted throughout the Upper Paleolithic, but they become more common in later moments. And thus, they have supported the customary attribution of Las Monedas to a late phase of Style IV.

This age has been confirmed by C14-AMS dating. In 1996, several samples of pigment were taken from the vertical horse and an ibex. The date obtained for the horse was 11,950 +/- 120 BP, while the ibex gave two dates: 12,170 +/- 110 and 11,630 +/- 120. Although one of the two dates for the ibex does not seem coherent with the others, the cave art in Las Monedas can reasonably be situated between 12,390 and 11,710 BP, in a very late moment of the Magdalenian period.

Bibliography

Ripoll Perelló, E. 1972. La cueva de Las Monedas en Puente Viesgo (Santander). Diputación Provincial de Barcelona. *Monografías de Arte Rupestre*, 1.

Moure Romanillo, A.; González Sainz, C.; Bernaldo de Quirós, F.; Cabrera Valdés, V. 1996. Dataciones absolutas de pigmentos en cuevas cantábricas: Altamira, El Castillo, Chimeneas, Las Monedas. En Moure, A. (ed.): *"El Hombre fósil" 80 años después*. Servicio de Publicaciones. Universidad de Cantabria. Santander, pp. 295-324.

2-8. Cueva de Santián.

Cueva de Santián is located near the village of Velo, in the municipal district of Piélagos. Its geographical location shows certain characteristics which are repeated in other sites corresponding to the late Würm. The lower course of the River Pas flows quite close to the cave, about 1km away, and the estuary and present coast are just 5km away. The distance separating Cueva de Santián from the Bay of Santander is also relatively short, about 8km. However, during the Würm glaciation, sea level was about 100m lower than today, and the cave would have been 13km from the coastline then. Although the position of Santián, on the ridge between the valleys of the Pas and the Miera, was very good from the strategic point of view, the direction of the entrance, which faces north-east, and its narrowness and humidity, could not have encouraged its prolonged use as a habitat, especially in a region that is so rich in open, available caves.

The first news we have of Cueva de Santián dates from 1888, when the minutes of a meeting of the Comisión de Monumentos on May 14th reports the information given by Don Manuel Santillán about the discovery of a cave at a place called Peñas Negras in Piélagos. He does not, however, make any reference to the existence of paintings in the cave. The recent death of Don Marcelino Sanz de Sautuola, the discoverer of the paintings in Altamira, also reported at the same meeting, meant that the Comisión could not attend to Don Manuel Santillán's request that a study should be made of the cave. Nevertheless, this did not stop the discoverer preparing the cave to make it easier for visitors to see it, and gating the entrance with a wooden door.

In October 1905, the cave was "rediscovered" by Hermilio Alcalde del Río, who replaced the old, deteriorated, wooden door with a metal one, and also who mentioned for the first time that the cave contained Paleolithic art. His discovery was followed by the work documenting the depictions, which he published together with H. Breuil and L. Sierra six years later in Les Cavernes de la region Cantabrique.

No systematic study was ever made of the archaeological stratigraphy that might have existed in Cueva de Santián. The deposit was altered greatly by the different building work done in the cave for tourist visits at the end of the 19th Century and again in 1953. The known archaeological material from the cave is limited to a number of perforated sea shells, collected in the "Chamber of the Horse" by H. Alcalde del Río, and another small collection of material, which has hardly been studied, as well as a human skull, obtained when the entrance was widened in the middle of the century.

In contrast, the cave art is very well documented. Cueva de Santián consists of a narrow passage, which widens a little in a few places to form a few small chambers. The cave art is found in two of these chambers. The first is 75m from the entrance in the so-called "Chamber of the Horse" , where two signs were painted with red pigment on two faces of a stalactite. The first of these, visible from the center of the chamber, is a vertical line which divides into three shorter lines in its upper part. This motif, with certain variations, is the most common one in Santián. The figure is, however, incomplete now, as the stalactite has been broken, probably in the 20th Century. The other side of the same formation has remains of red paint which may have belonged to another similar sign, although it is now only possible to see a vertical line with very diffuse pigment.

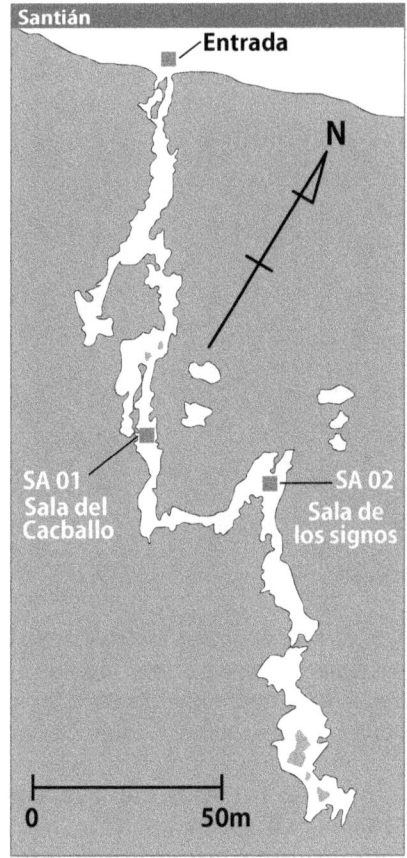

Santian Ground Plan

The right-hand wall of the same chamber, 3m from the red signs, has another red painting which looks rather like a horse in a rampant position. The question is whether this red stain is really a Paleolithic painting, or instead a natural stain of color which happens to have the shape of a horse. Its state of conservation, and the non-existence of a specific analysis of the pigment, makes it impossible to decide one way or the other. It could be added, if the painting is accepted as anthropic, that it shows a rather unusual technique and style. In the first place, if it is a painting, the technique applied was red color wash, without drawing a previous outline sketch of the figure. This is not very usual in Paleolithic art, although it has been recognized in figures of bison in the groups V and X of Tito Bustillo. However, these figures are poorly conserved, and it is possible that they originally had an outline. From a stylist point of view, the rampant posture of this "horse" in Santián would be unique in Paleolithic cave art. Animals are painted in vertical positions, although they are not too common, and form less than

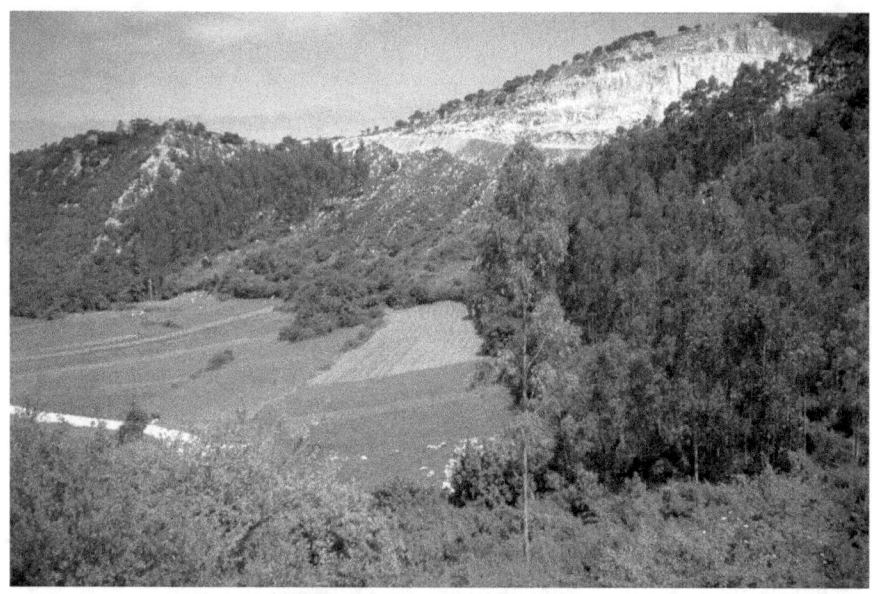
Limestone mountains near the cave

5 % of animal figures in Paleolithic cave art. But the direction of most of these figures is the result of their location on a long, vertical rock surface, and this is not the case of the "horse" in Santián, which could have been depicted in a normal horizontal position on the surface where it is situated.

Further inside the cave, we reach the second concentration of paintings 120m from the entrance. This chamber has three panels with Paleolithic art. A fourth panel has numerous engraved lines which appear to have been done recently. The main panel occupies a large section of the right-hand wall, slightly over 4.5m in length, and contains fifteen signs of a similar kind to the ones in the "Chamber of the Horse". The different variants of these signs have been defined as simple bars or lines; bars ending in the palm of a hand; toothed bars with transversal lines on one side; and bundles of lines united at the base and spread open at the top. These signs are distributed in two horizontal rows, with five in the top row and ten below. Their average height is 65cm, ranging from 35cm, the shortest, to nearly 100cm, the longest. The ones in the top row are more than two meters above the floor, so it is likely that the artists used some kind of structure to reach this part of the wall, or painted the signs, as the first researchers suggested, "climbing on a friend's shoulders". The opposite wall has the other two panels, which have two red dots and an "X"-shaped sign respectively, the latter being similar to a sign in the last passage in Cueva de El Castillo.

The themes depicted in Santián are quite rare in Paleolithic art, which

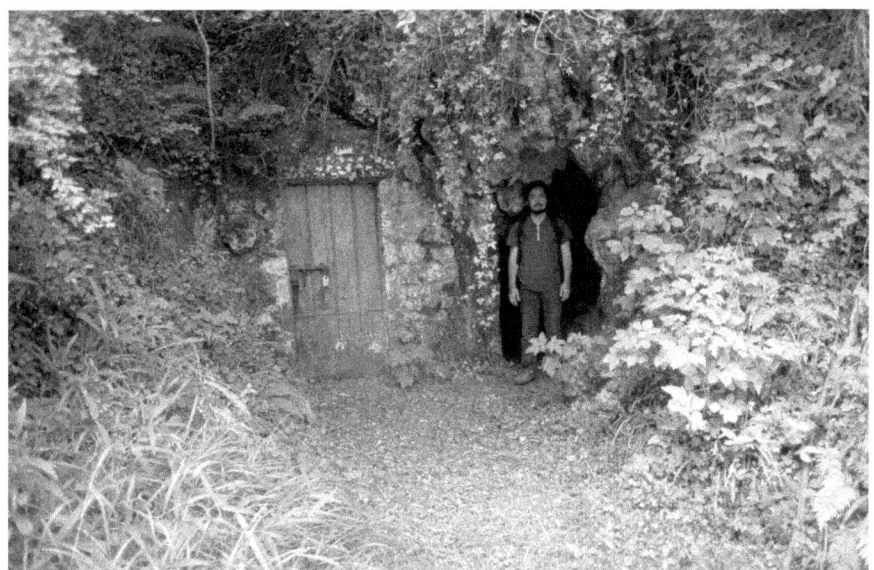
Entrance

makes the iconographic and chronological interpretation extremely difficult. The first study carried out in the cave related the signs with schematic representations of human arms, legs of herbivores and birds, and even projectile weapons (Australian boomerangs, which at the time were often used to interpret different Paleolithic signs). These kinds of interpretation were usual in the early years of research, when ethnographic comparisons played an important role in studies of cave art. In this context, the researchers working in Santián at the start of the century looked for parallels between these figures and projectile weapons used by primitive Australian and Eskimo people. However, it seems more reasonable to consider the figures in Santián as abstract signs, and reject the possibility that they represent either weapons or human and animal limbs.

The chronology of these signs is equally complicated. The use of inorganic pigment makes it impossible to date them directly by C14-AMS. At the same time, the lack of similar figures with a well defined chronology does not allow their age to be established with any precision. Because of this, since the paintings were discovered in 1905, the different chronological proposals have covered practically the entirety of the Upper Paleolithic. The first researchers suggested that they could belong to the initial Aurignacian period, although they commented that this was only a tentative, hypothetical proposal. In the 1980s, Professor Moure Romanillo proposed a new chronological hypothesis which dated the paintings of Santián in the middle Magdalenian or in the initial late Magdalenian, by establishing parallels with signs which are technically similar and which

2-8: Cueva de Santián

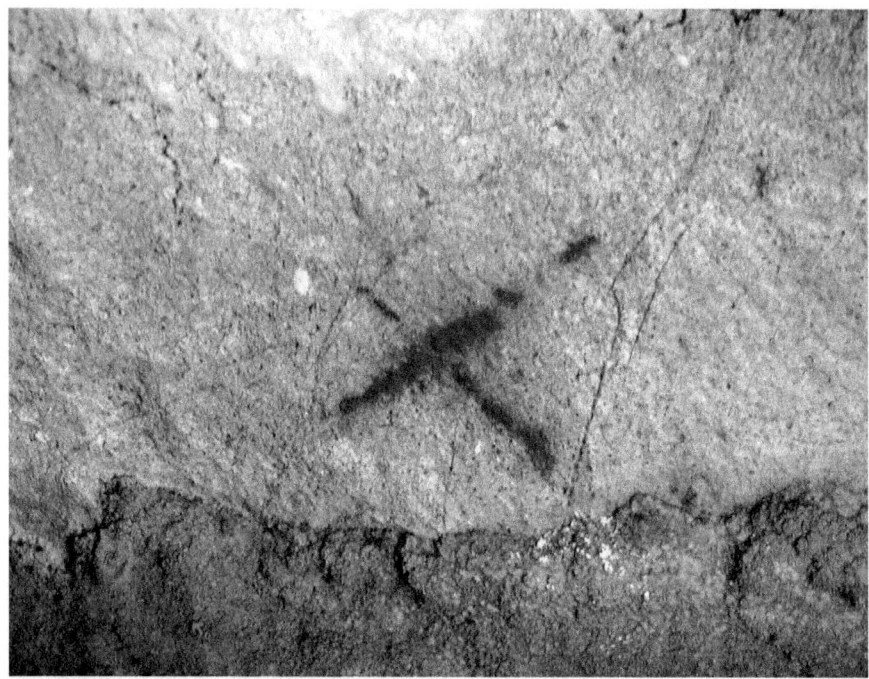

Red sign formed by two lines

are found in Style IV assemblages, corresponding to about 14,500 - 12,000 BP. In our opinion, it should be remembered that a similar sign exists in Gallery A of La Pasiega, superimposed on a red stag. As no more precise information is available, this suggests that a late phase of Style III is the most probable moment for these paintings in Santián. Regarding the "X" -shaped sign, the only known parallel is in the Gallery of the Discs in Cueva de El Castillo. This motif is not closely associated with any figure, although the red discs and the figure of a mammoth in the same passage in El Castillo can all be dated in a pre-Magdalenian time.

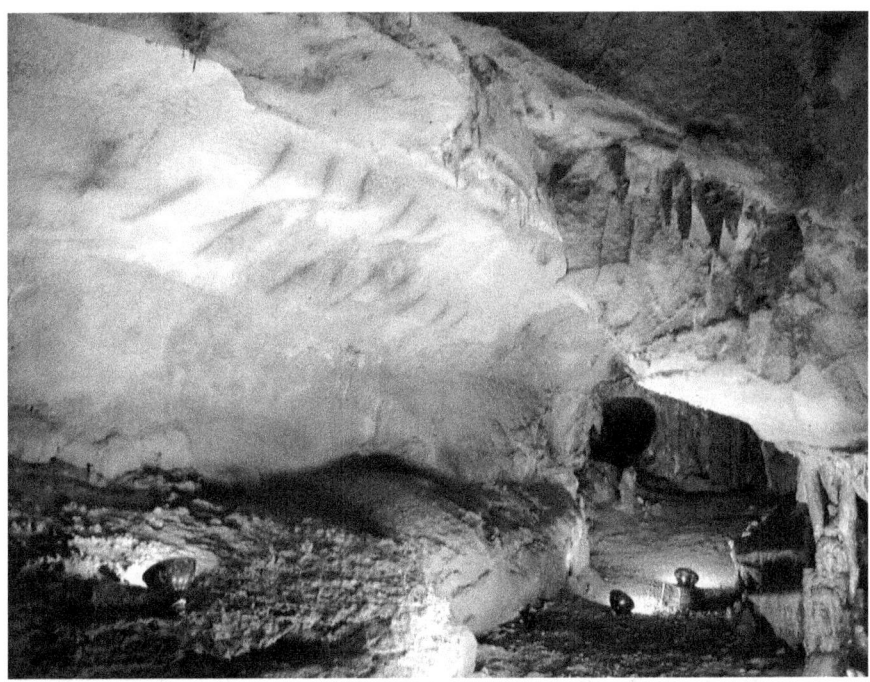
Red signs in the form of arms

Bibliography

Alcalde del Río, H.; Breuil, H.; Sierra, L. 1911. *Les cavernes de la region Cantabrique.* A. Chene, Monaco.

Moure, A. 1991-92. Documentación del arte rupeste cantábrico: la cueva de Santián (Piélagos, Cantabria). *Zephyrus* 44-45, pp 7 - 15.

2-9. Cueva de El Pendo

Situated in the village of Escobedo de Camargo, near the present-day Bay of Santander, Cueva del Pendo is one of the classic Upper Paleolithic sites in the Cantabrian region. Its impressive archaeological deposit was dug by Marcelino Sanz de Sautuola at the end of the 19th Century, and archaeological digs have succeeded since then until the present time. Some of the more important digs were carried out by Jesús Carballo in the 1920s and 30s, when a magnificent collection of decorated bone and antler artifacts were recovered. These were of Magdalenian age, above all of the late Magdalenian, between 14,000 and 11,500 BP. Other important digs were carried out in the 1950s, and published some time later by J. González Echegaray.

These and other excavations have uncovered a large deposit in the entrance area of the cave' s huge main chamber, containing remains of human occupation in the Middle Paleolithic and of almost all the periods of the Upper Paleolithic and Epipaleolithic. The evidence of prehistoric activity is distributed through a long stratigraphic sequence with more than twenty layers, only comparable in the Cantabrian region with the deposit in Cueva del Castillo. However, the most interesting areas in the deposit are partly covered by large limestone blocks that have collapsed from the roof at the entrance of the cave. As a result, the archaeological strata is only accessible at the base of the large boulder slope which descends from the present entrance to the center of the huge chamber, and logically, this is where most of the digs have been focused.

In recent years, R. Montes Barquín and collaborators have re-worked the stratigraphic sections cut by the first excavators in order to take samples for environmental and chronological analysis from the lower levels of the sequence. It was precisely during this work in Summer 1997, when unexpectedly they found an important frieze of paintings, doubtlessly Paleolithic in style. The paintings had previously gone unnoticed because the red pigment was very faint, and partly covered by dust and fungus. Despite their poor conservation, the paintings give a new dimension to the small group of figures which had been known in the cave since the early years of the century, and which consisted of only a couple of engravings, situated in a narrow passage at the end of the cave. These two engravings are also badly deteriorated now, and are hardly recognizable; they represent one or perhaps two rather indeterminate birds (possibly either a great auk or an anseriform). Whatever the case, they are very unusual animals in the cave art of the Cantabrian region.

The panel with the paintings occupies a long frieze of the cave wall, situated at the back of the large main chamber. It is within the dark zone of the cave, but it is still possible to see the light from outside lighting the boulder slope in the entrance. In the Paleolithic, the frieze was accessible in places from the boulders below it, but some kind of scaffolding or ladders must have been used to reach many of the figures, especially the ones on the left. Therefore, unlike the engravings at the end of the cave, this frieze of paintings would have been visible from practically all points in the main chamber, as long as it was lit up, of course.

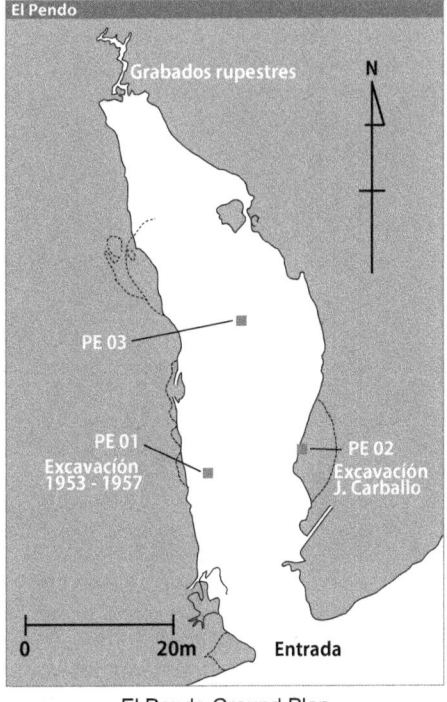

El Pendo Ground Plan

The figures were painted in red, except for one which is in yellow. The dissolved pigment was applied as areas of color wash, or as simple lines, or as dots, making either discontinuous lines or more often lines of large overlapping dots. The depictions are six definite hinds and another two more doubtful ones (one of them, in red color wash, could equally be an auroch), a hind's head, and a goat whose front-quarters were painted with overlapping dots while the relief and angles of the rock completed the figure. There is also a horse, whose mane is represented with parallel lines, an indeterminate figure, a few short non-figurative lines, at least one isolated red dot, and another two smaller ones away from the panel which are possibly splashes of pigment. There are also a few black marks on the right of the panel, which were perhaps left by torches being rubbed against the wall.

The composition seems to be dominated by figures of a large hind opposite a horse, which occupy the center of the panel. The other figures, mainly hinds as we have seen, are distributed around these central animals. It is surprising that there are no abstract signs, such as quadrilaterals, which accompany similar paintings in the caves of La Pasiega, Covalanas, or Arco B. But apart from that, taking into account the arrangement of figures within the panel, and the

2-9: Cueva de El Pendo

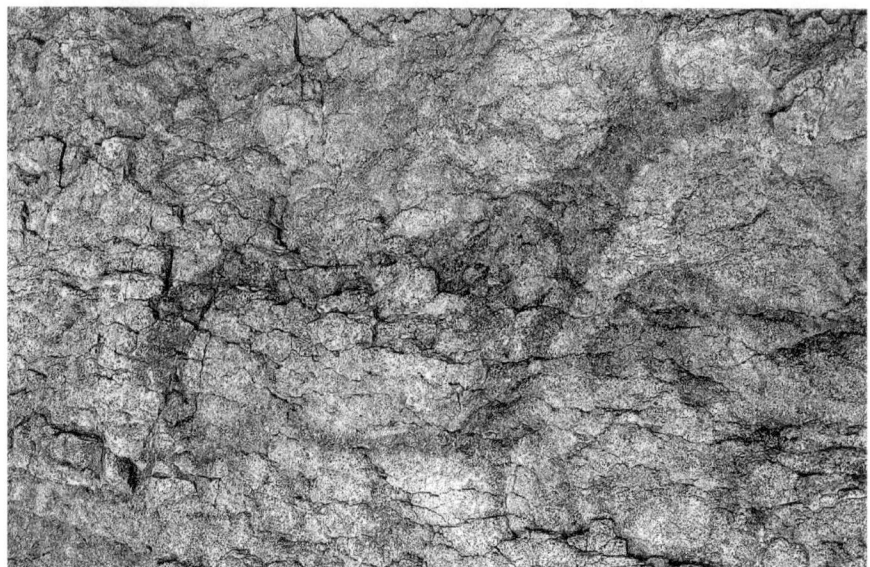

Hind and horse in red

technical and stylistic homogeneity, this seems to be a synchronic composition. The virtual absence of superimpositions, only the figure in yellow overlaps with the rear leg of the large hind, appears to support the same idea of the synchronism of the composition, or at least of all the red figures.

The red paintings in El Pendo immediately bring to mind a large number of cave art sites in Cantabria, particularly the caves of Arenaza, Arco A and B, Pondra, Covalanas and Haza, and part of more complex assemblages in Pasiega A and C, and Llonín. All these caves, corresponding to Leroi-Gourhan's Style III, show such a frequent characteristic of the Cantabrian region as the use of red pigment, the drawing of lines as a series of dots, or the application of color wash in all or part of the animals' interior. The hierarchy of techniques inside the animals' bodies, where the most time-consuming techniques were reserved for the most important or definitory parts, is similar in all these sites. So is the twisted perspective of the ears, the placing of the limbs, especially the rear ones, in two different planes, or the first lines of interior partition. The most common lines of this kind separate the neck from the body, or go from the withers to the front limbs, or fill the horses' manes.

The same iconographic composition as this panel in El Pendo, based on hinds and a horse in the central position, is found in such caves as Covalanas and Pasiega A, or in the animal themes developed in Pondra and Arenaza, always in cave art of the same style and chronology. Concerning this last question, the age of the paintings, we have no definite information. But if we consider the series of superimpositions in which this type of figure is found, in Pasiega A, B and C, and Llonín; the archaeological materials in those sites or others like the caves of Trescalabres, La Meaza and La Haza; or the type of engravings used in figures nearby, in Arco A and B, and Pondra; or other arguments based on the fauna represented, it seems highly probable that they cannot be younger than the Solutrean period, between 21,000 and 16,500 BP in the Cantabrian region.

Bibliography

Alcalde del Río, H.; Breuil. H.; Sierra, L. 1911. *Les cavernes de la region Cantabrique*. Imprimerie Vve. A. Chéne, Monaco.

González Echegaray, J. et alii. 1980. *El yacimiento de la cueva de "El Pendo" (Excavaciones 1953-57)*. Bibliotheca Praehistorica Hispana XVII, Madrid.

Montes Barquín, R. *et alii*. 1998. Cueva de El Pendo. Nuevas manifestaciones rupestres paleolíticas. *Revista de Arqueología* 201, pp. 10 - 15.

2-10. Cueva de La Haza

Cueva de La Haza is located at the foot of the hill Monte Pando, 160m above sea level, on the right-hand bank of the River Calera, very near the Cantabrian town of Ramales de la Victoria. This hill has numerous caves, especially Covalanas, with an important group of Paleolithic paintings, and El Mirón, where an archaeological dig is examining levels that go from at least the Mousterian to the Bronze Age, in a cave which must have been the main habitation site in the area during the Upper Paleolithic.

The caves of Monte Pando are in a strategic geographical position. Apart from being a place with plentiful hunting and fishing, this area controls a natural gap for communication between the coastal strip and the high summer pastures, and beyond those, the Meseta. This route must have often been traveled, at least as far as the glaciers allowed, and not only by the Paleolithic human populations, but also by herds of ungulates. Cueva de La Haza is positioned precisely next to an old road which, in historical times, was the traditional way of communication between the Cantabrian coast and the Meseta in the south. During the Upper Paleolithic, it could have been used in the same way, at least in more temperate phases, uniting the Paleolithic sites in the Asón valley with a number of caves in the province of Burgos, like La Palomera in the Ojo Güareña cave system, Penches and even Atapuerca, all of which have Paleolithic cave art.

Cueva de La Haza was discovered by Hermilio Alcalde del Río and Lorenzo Sierra on September 13th 1903, two days after the same explorers had found Cueva de Covalanas. Despite the fact that they both took part in the discovery, they did not collaborate in the first fieldwork documenting its art. Thus, on January 4th 1904, Lorenzo Sierra visited the cave, apparently alone, in order to make the first copies of the paintings. In turn, H. Alcalde del Río published a small book in 1906, with some of the caves then known to have art, including Covalanas. However, he surprisingly only mentioned the existence of La Haza, without even giving its name, and did not include further details of the cave in his book because of "the lack of a previous study of the same".

It was not until 1911 when both discoverers, together with abbé H. Breuil, published the study of the cave art in La Haza, in their book *Les cavernes de la region Cantabrique*. Since this time, the cave has formed part of the catalogue of caves with art in the Cantabrian region. Eighty years later, in 1991, a team of researchers from the University of Cantabria published a new study of the cave and its neighbor Covalanas, adding new information and bringing its study up to date.

When visiting La Haza, we find one of the smallest decorated caves in the north of Spain. A large exterior rockshelter leads into the cave itself, where originally one had to crawl on hands and knees through an entrance slightly more than 2m in width. The interior of the cave is limited to a single small chamber, 4.5m wide and 8m long, which is partially divided up by stalagmites and columns. But when the cave was occupied in the Paleolithic, it must have had a quite different appearance. Since then the cave has been transformed by natural and anthropic factor.

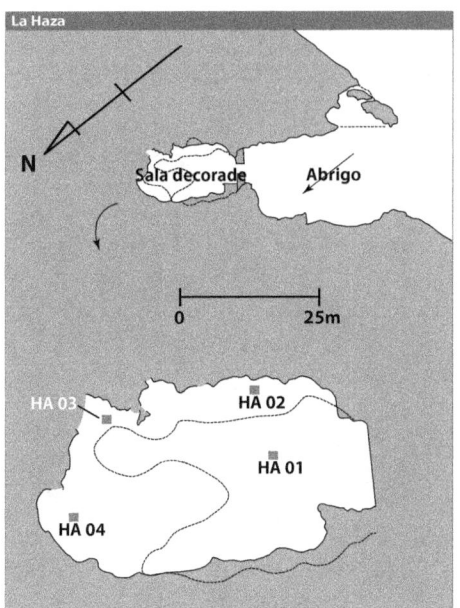

La Haza Ground Plan

The columns in the center of the chamber formed some time after the occupation, as their position on top of the archaeological deposit shows. The level of the floor was somewhat higher than it is now, and it was lowered for tourist visits in the middle of the 20th Century, when the wall and metallic door which now protect the entrance were installed.

The archaeological deposit in the cave was practically destroyed, just as in so many Cantabrian caves, by this work to accommodate visits, and we only have a little isolated information about a few artifacts. Lorenzo Sierra had collected various ungulate bones, and two tools in flint and three in quartzite, which do not allow any kind of chronological attribution. Later, a few researchers have mentioned the presence of lithic tools with Solutrean retouch, which appeared during the building work in the cave in 1959.

The art inside the cave is distributed in three groups of figures, two on the right-hand wall and one on the left. The most striking figures in the first panel are two animals representing a hind and an ibex, both facing left. The ibex is the more complete figure, and its outline was drawn in full, apart from the forehead, which might have faded, with two fore limbs and one rear limb. Its interior is articulated by three lines converging on the top of the fore limbs. The head and back of a hind was painted, also in red, on top of this figure. As well as these two animals, there is an unidentified quadruped, an inverted "D" -shaped sign, and other non-figurative lines.

137

2-10: Cueva de La Haza

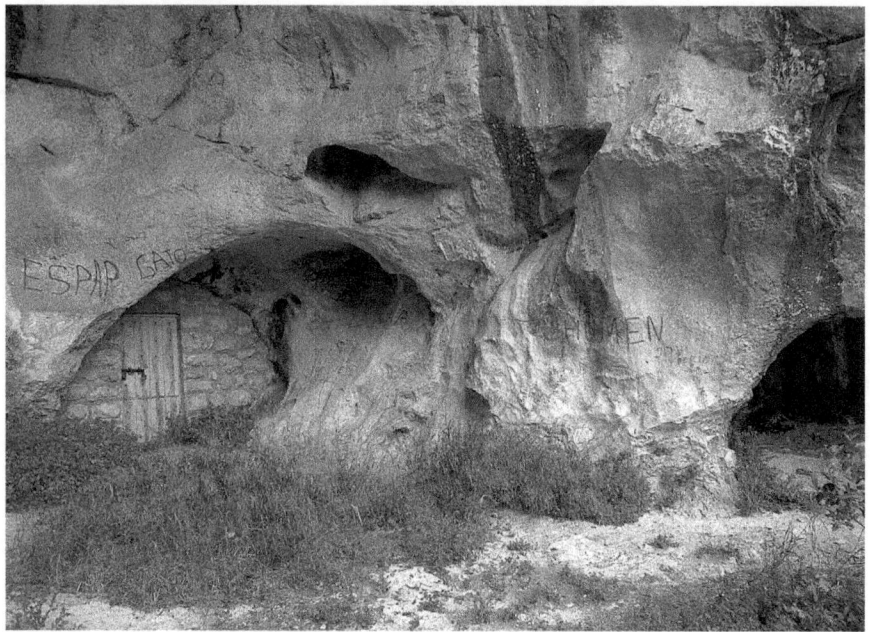

Entrance of La Haza

The second group is on the same right-hand wall, less than three meters from the first. An animal identified as a horse is depicted in the lower part of the panel. For the first researchers, this was a "dapple-gray" horse, because it had dots of red paint inside its body. The upper part of the panel has a further two animals. The one on the right is the best-conserved painting in the cave. It is clearly a horse, depicted whole, apart from the fore quarters. On its left we find the largest figure in the cave: a practically whole reindeer, where the artist used the natural shape of the wall to represent part of its back and head, as well as to give more volume and life to the figure.

The back wall of the cave, at right angles with the panels just mentioned, contains abundant remains of red paint, possibly belonging to animals that have now almost completely disappeared. It is only possible to imagine, with reserves, an animal facing right in the middle of the wall. This animal would therefore be facing the three better-conserved animals, described in the previous panel.

The third group of depictions is on the left-hand wall, in the deepest part of the cave. As well as a quadrangular sign, and other remains of red paint, the only figurative art represents an almost whole horse, also in red, with a line crossing its muzzle, at the end of a long narrow head.

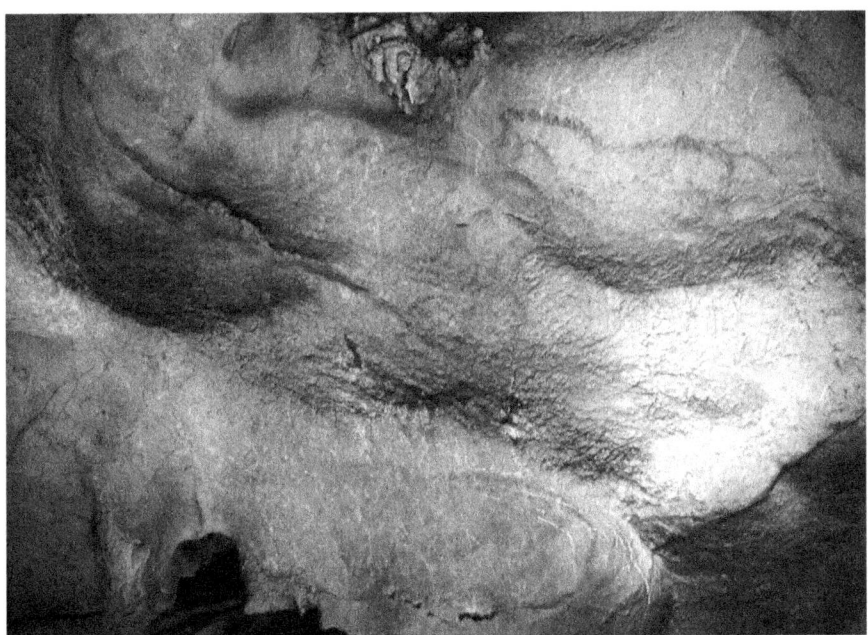
View of the interior of the cave with the figures of two horses and a reindeer

Some of the characteristics of this art give Cueva de La Haza its own personality, and allow it to be differentiated from the nearby cave of Covalanas. The iconographic organization is one of these characteristic elements. Compared with the massive depiction of hinds in Covalanas, the most frequent theme in La Haza is the horse, of which there are three figures. There are also figures of a reindeer, ibex and hind, one each, as well as one or two unidentified quadrupeds.

The techniques used in the figures are based, just as in Covalanas, on the application of red paint. Nevertheless, the predominant procedure in the neighboring cave, the discontinuous dotted lines, is less common in La Haza, where it is only clearly seen in the scapular partition line in the reindeer. The artists in La Haza preferred to apply the paint in lines or occasionally in overlapping dots. Engraving was not used in any of the figures.

Regarding the spatial organization, the first thing to be stressed is the sheer existence of the paintings, which are located in the zone of semi-darkness. This contradicts the traditional idea that the outer areas of caves were only used for art during the oldest phases of the Upper Paleolithic, and for deeply engraved figures. The fact that this engraving technique was used in outer areas, with natural light, can be explained by the greater time that was required to produce this kind of figure. However, that does not exclude the

2-10: Cueva de La Haza

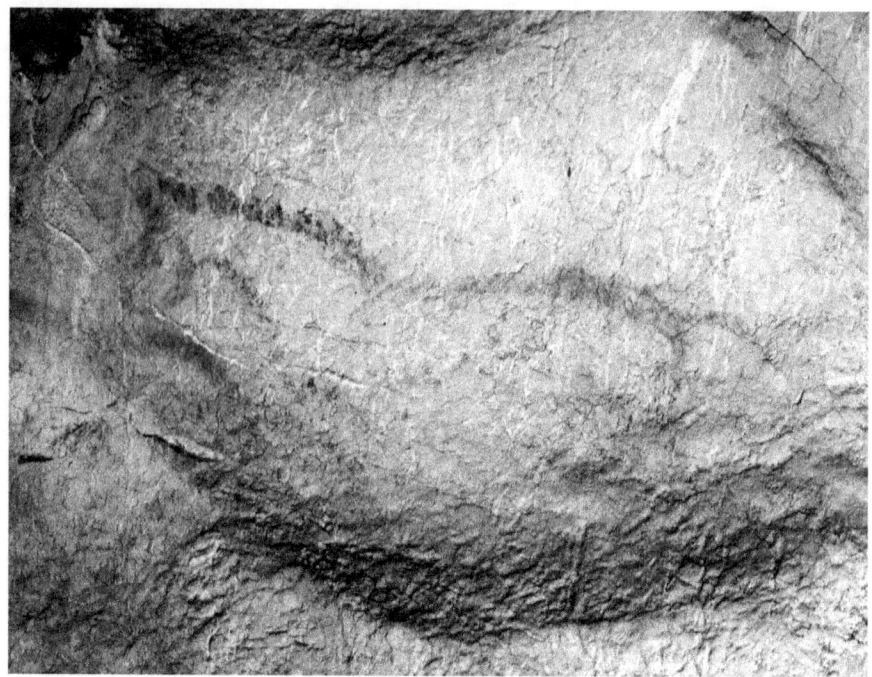

A more or less complete figure of a horse facing left and painted in red

production of paintings in the same zone, and these exist not only in La Haza, but also in the entrances of other Cantabrian caves such as Galleries B and C of La Pasiega, La Fuente del Salín and La Loja. The relative scarcity of exterior paintings is therefore due to the greater difficulty for their preservation.

The stylistic character of the figures seems to correspond to a very similar period to the neighboring cave of Covalanas. The only hind represented repeats some of the conventions of the hinds in Covalanas: its mouth open by a separation of lines, "V"-shaped ears painted as prolongations of the forehead and cervical-dorsal lines, which do not meet up. The reindeer also has numerous coincidences with the one in Covalanas. Both show the same interior details: a partition line in the scapular zone formed by two lines starting on both sides of the withers and which converge at the top of the fore limb, as well as a double line representing the belly. The way the natural form of the rock was used is also similar in both figures. In the same way, the horses were represented with highly characteristic conventions: manes in echelon, with a series of parallel lines, or the "duck-beak" or "spatula" muzzle, rounded and turned downwards, as in the horse depicted in the deepest part of the cave.

As we can see, this small group of animal figures shows a homogeneous style, in which the quadrilateral sign fits perfectly. Its character corresponds to Leroi-Gourhan' s Style III, probably developed in the Solutrean period, between 21,000 and 16,500 BP. We know that the cave was occupied by human populations at the time, as a few points with Solutrean flat retouch were found there.

Bibliography

Moure Romanillo, A.; González Sainz, C.; González Morales, M. 1991. *Las cuevas de Ramales de la Victoria*, Cantabria. Universidad de Cantabria, Santander.

2-11. Cueva de Covalanas

Covalanas is situated on the N.E. side of the hill known as Monte Haza or Pando, at 320 above sea level, overlooking the steep-sided inland valley of a tributary of the River Asón. It is, without doubt, the most interesting of the caves with Paleolithic cave art in Ramales de la Victoria; a group which also includes the caves of La Cullalvera, La Haza and El Mirón. These four caves can be added to other caves in the near vicinity, with which they sometimes show a close artistic and chronological relationship, namely Morro, Pondra, Arco B-C, Arco A, Sotarriza and Venta de la Perra. This second cluster of sites is found in the gorge of the River Carranza, another tributary of the Asón, and all except the last one, which lies within the province of Vizcaya, belong to the same municipal district of Ramales, in Cantabria.

This great accumulation of sites shows how important the inland valleys of the region were in the lives of the Upper Paleolithic hunters, complementary to their activities and resources in the rich coastal strip. It must have been important for those human populations to control the natural gaps from the small valley around Ramales to the valleys further inland and the high summer pastures. In fact, the density of cave art sites and depictions in the Ramales area is one of the highest in the Cantabrian region, together with the caves of Puente Viesgo, Llanes, or the middle course of the Nalón, and the Cares valley.

The art in Cueva de Covalanas was discovered in 1903 by H. Alcalde del Río and L. Sierra, who, together with Marcelino Sanz de Sautuola, were the two main local pioneers in the exploration and discovery of cave art. Some years later, in 1911, the site was published by the two finders and H. Breuil, as one of a select group of caves located and studied in the early years of the century. Later, in the second half of the century, interesting new information has been supplied by A. Leroi-Gourhan, regarding the chronology of the art, and J. M. Apellániz, in technical and stylistic aspects, and more recently a full revision of the site has been published by a team from the University of Cantabria.

The entrance area of the cave was dug out in the middle of the century, in a rather unfortunate incident. The aim was simply to lower the floor level and make it easier for tourists to reach the paintings at the end of the cave, and as a result, no special care was taken in the work, nor were any results ever published. Apparently faunal and industrial remains were found, and although these were limited and gave little information about their chronology, they are all we know of the small archaeological deposit which must have existed at the en-

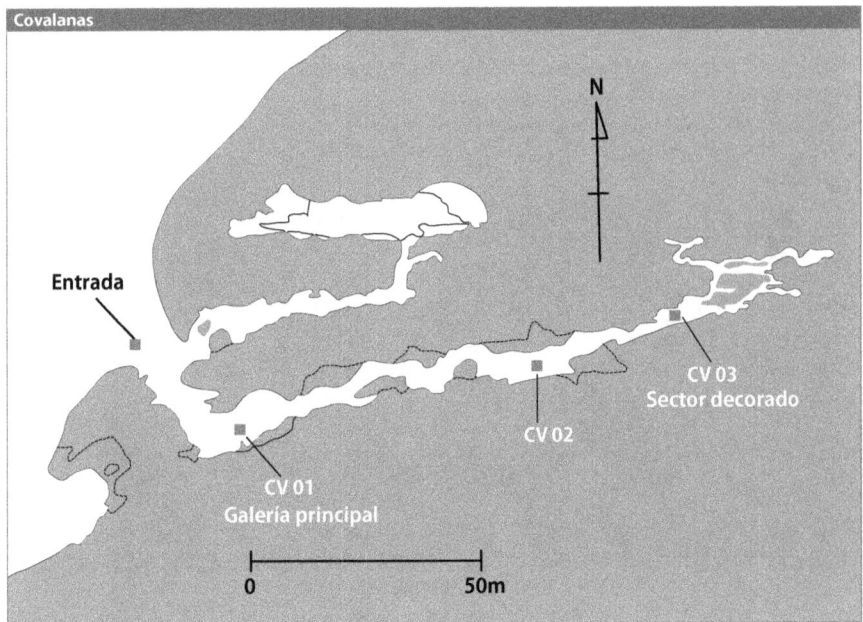

Covalanas Ground Plan

trance.

Cueva de Covalanas is located a short distance vertically above Cueva de Mirón, an impressive cave whose vestibule is much more appropriate for human occupation, due to its greater size, and better living conditions and access. The archaeological digs which are being carried out there at present have documented a long stratigraphic sequence including Solutrean layers (presumably the period when the figures in Covalanas were painted) and other periods of the Upper Paleolithic. Although we do not know exactly what was the size of the deposit that was destroyed in Covalanas, it cannot have been too important, and it may be supposed that the cave was usually, or nearly always, the ceremonial and artistic center complementing the habitational site in El Mirón.

Covalanas is not an especially long cave, and it consists of two passages which diverge from the rock-shelter at the entrance. Almost all the Paleolithic art is found in the last section of the right-hand passage, about 65m from the entrance, and distributed in seven panels on both walls of the passage, and in a small side-passage. Outside this area, a few remains of violet paint can be seen; they possibly correspond to at least one animal figure, located in the earlier part of the same passage, on the left-hand wall. There are also a few small remains of red paint, of a more clearly Paleolithic appearance, in the left-hand passage.

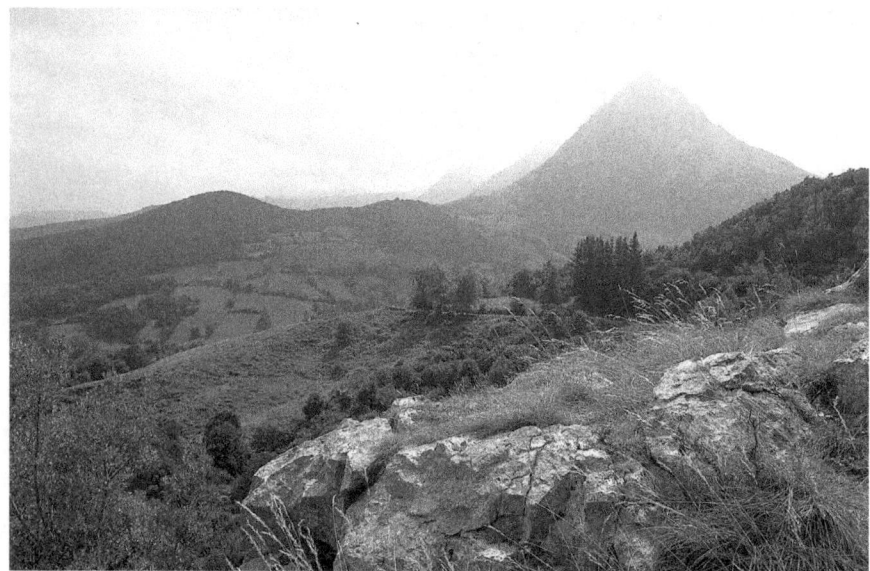
View from the entrance of Covalanas

Besides these, the cave has many black marks, of charcoal; most of these must have been left by torches rubbing against the walls, and are probably of a very long chronology, maybe from the Paleolithic occupations to practically the present time.

The predominant animal among the depictions is the hind, with eighteen figures in different degrees of completeness: there are whole figures, others reduced to the cervical-dorsal line and the head, and some of only the head. They are accompanied by a horse, a possible reindeer (sometimes interpreted as an auroch, and it is not easy to reach a definite conclusion), a doubtful figure of the fore-quarters of a bovine, and a possible cervical-dorsal line. Added to these, we have four rectangular signs in red color wash, another two oval-shaped signs, several isolated dots, a line of dots in association with the possible reindeer, and a few other lines.

All the figures are painted in red, applied in various ways, from color wash to dotted lines, which is the commonest and most characteristic formula in the cave. The dots were painted with a piece of animal skin, or directly with the fingers. They are either overlapping, especially in or about the animal' s head, or separated, usually in the parts furthest from the head. Engraving was only used in part of the outlines of two hinds' heads, and in fact we doubt if these lines are really of Paleolithic age, and not recent marks.

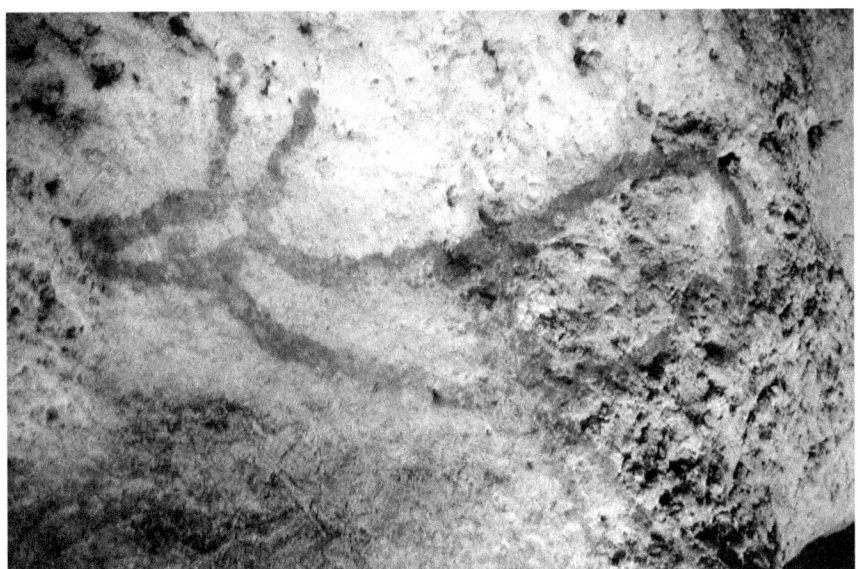

Hind with long ears

he organization of the figures within the panels in Covalanas is quite interesting. The same simple grouping of pairs of animals, almost always hinds, is repeated several times, in two superimposed planes, both facing in the same direction, or with other variations. One of the most complex panels has several hinds lifting or turning their heads towards the same point located outside the panel, to the right. For some prehistorians this represents a narrative scene, which is quite unusual in Paleolithic art.

The technical and stylistic homogeneity of the figures, their concentration in a small area, or their limited number, all suggest that the depictions are synchronic, just as in Cueva de La Haza, which is near Covalanas and has relatively similar stylistic and technical characteristics. This latter cave had Solutrean industry, which fits in well with the style of the figures in both caves, probably painted between 20,000 and 17,000 years ago.

The techniques used in Covalanas, such as the dotted lines and color wash, as well as the stylistic conventions of many figures, or the type of quadrilateral signs, are all fully coherent with the character of Leroi-Gourhan' s Style III in the Cantabrian region. The conventions most often repeated are the triangular shape of the hinds' heads, the depiction of two ears, open in a "V" -shape, the indication of the Adam' s apple in some figures, the partition lines in the withers or the neck, and the correct perspective in the two rear limbs. Because of these characteristics, Covalanas is now attributed to a central phase of Style III, and

145

2-11: Cueva de Covalanas

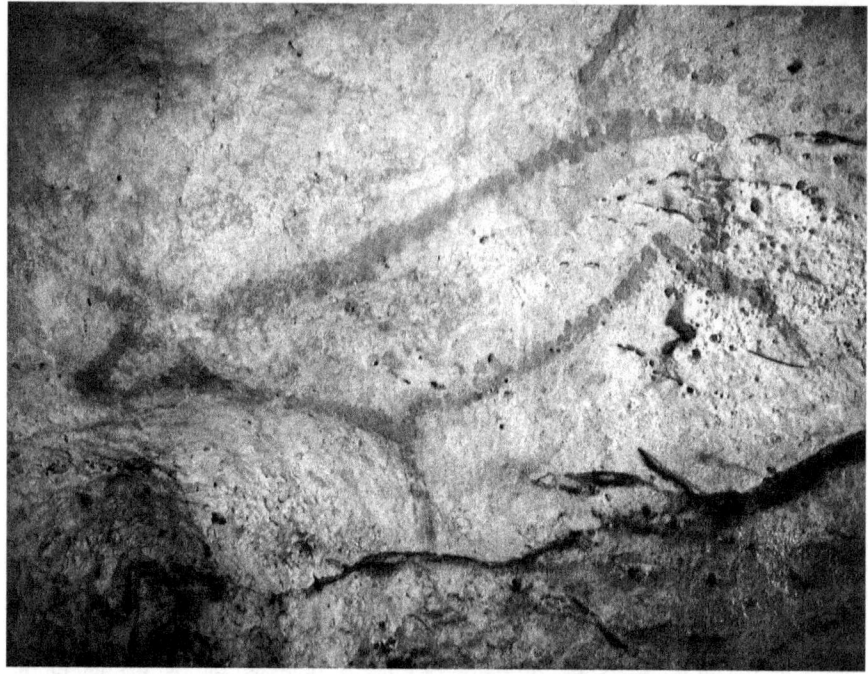

Hind in red

not to the end of the period, and its chronology is therefore Solutrean rather than early Magdalenian.

Cueva de Covalanas can therefore be included in a group of caves which covers its near neighbor, La Haza, and El Arco B-C, Arco A and Pondra, and further to the east, Cueva de Arenaza. Its relationship with other caves to the west is not so close, but they include Salitre, the Lower Gallery of La Garma, El Pendo and Pasiega A and C, above all. As well as the technical, thematic and stylistic similarities, the grouping of hinds in pairs, as we have noticed in some of the panels in Covalanas, reflects an idea also expressed in certain panels in Arenaza, Pondra, Pendo, and Pasiega A and C, and with other animals in the caves of Arco (A and B-C), La Haza and La Garma.

Some of the paintings in Covalanas have been affected by natural processes, and above all by the paintings and scratches done in the middle of the century, when the cave did not have the regular service of a guide. These alterations were later cleaned up, unfortunately rather too drastically, despite the good intentions. Even so, some the paintings in Covalanas are among the best preserved in the region due to the freshness of the dotted lines and the brightness of the red pigment, which stands out against the light-colored limestone walls.

Bibliography

Alcalde del Río, H.; Breuil, H.; Sierra, L. 1911. *Les cavernes de la region Cantabrique (Espagne)*. Imp. Vve. A. Chene, Monaco.

Leroi-Gourhan, A. 1965. *Prehistoire de l'art occidental*. Mazenod, Paris.

Moure Romanillo, A.; González Sainz, C.; González Morales, M.R. 1991. *Las cuevas de Ramales de la Victoria (Cantabria)*. Arte rupestre paleolítico en las cuevas de Covalanas y La Haza. Universidad de Cantabria, Santander.

2-12. Cueva de Pondra

This cave is located on the northern side of the gorge formed by the River Carranza, a tributary of the Asón, very near the boundary between the Autonomous Community of Cantabria and the Basque Country. The same gorge has other caves with Paleolithic cave art: from east to west they are, Venta de la Perra, Arco A. Arco B-C and El Morro del Horidillo, as well as Cueva de Sotarriza on the opposite side of the gorge. Furthermore, several caves are known, like Cuevas del Polvorín and Chiquita, which only have human occupation deposits, with lithic and bone assemblages and faunal remains, corresponding to the Middle and Upper Paleolithic. All these sites are found in a stretch of the gorge little more than one kilometer long, coinciding with its narrowest part, between the hills of Pico del Carlista to the north and Peña de Rebuño in the south.

This cluster of habitation and cave art sites, despite each one being relatively small, is probably a result of the existence of numerous caves suitable for use by groups of Paleolithic hunters, and the good living conditions they have, especially the ones whose entrances face south. Furthermore, the accumulation of sites is due to the advantages of their position for bands of Paleolithic hunters in order to control the movements of herds of ungulates, as they went from the lower valley of the Asón to the high summer pastures, on the wide slopes of the Carranza Valley. The hunting of caprids must have been possible all year round on the steep sides of the gorge.

Cueva de Pondra, and the caves of Arco and Morro, were discovered recently by members of C.A.E.A.P., an archaeological society based in Cantabria. They are still being studied by specialists from the University of Cantabria.

Pondra has a large vestibule with two entrances, facing west and south. Between the two, a wide space has excellent conditions for a habitat, and in recent times it was used as a shelter for the flocks of sheep and goats from nearby farms.

The cave art begins at the back of the vestibule, in the zone of semi-darkness. The left-hand wall of the main passage has a large panel almost nine meters long, with abundant red lines and marks, which are now very faded and partly covered by calcite. Nevertheless, as many as seven different groupings of remains of pigment have been distinguished on this wall, and these can be considered as a "minimum number of depictions" , all that is left of a composition now almost completely disappeared. The only figures that can be recognized

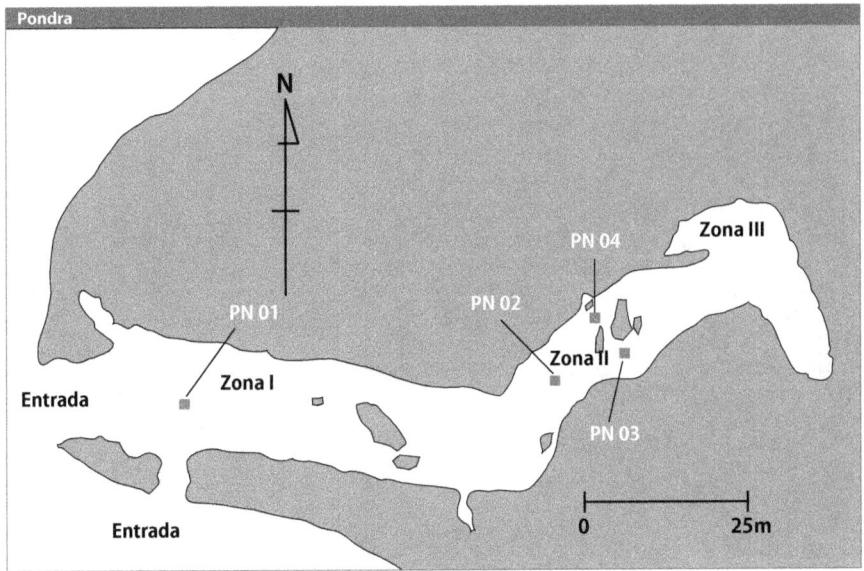

Pondra Ground Plan

are a few red dotted lines, sometimes in an almost circular shape.

Further sectors inside the cave have better preserved figures. In the completely dark zone, we find a small chamber on the left-hand side of the passage. A panel which has been badly altered by natural processes has two figures of hinds, in a close relationship, back to back. They were drawn as outlines, filled-in with color wash in a slightly lighter shade, in tones of yellow and light brown. Other lines in the same color can be seen on the same wall, and two series of simple, non-figurative engravings. The roof next to this chamber has the remains of a red line, beneath strips of calcite that formed after the line had been painted. This calcite, however, was cut in several places by the engravings of two horses, in a very basic Paleolithic style, and the engraved lines now have patina. The formation of the calcite deposit at some time between the execution of the painted line and the engraving of the horses shows that the different figures in this panel could not be strictly synchronic.

The other side of the main passage has the depiction of the head, neck and start of the chest of a young stag, painted in red with a wide line which becomes a discontinuous dotted line at the end of the neck and chest lines. The figure is almost completely covered by calcite, which forms a kind of mesh over the painting.

Lastly, at the end of the cave, dispersed on the roof of a low passage which is difficult to reach, we can see a few stains of red paint, the remains of

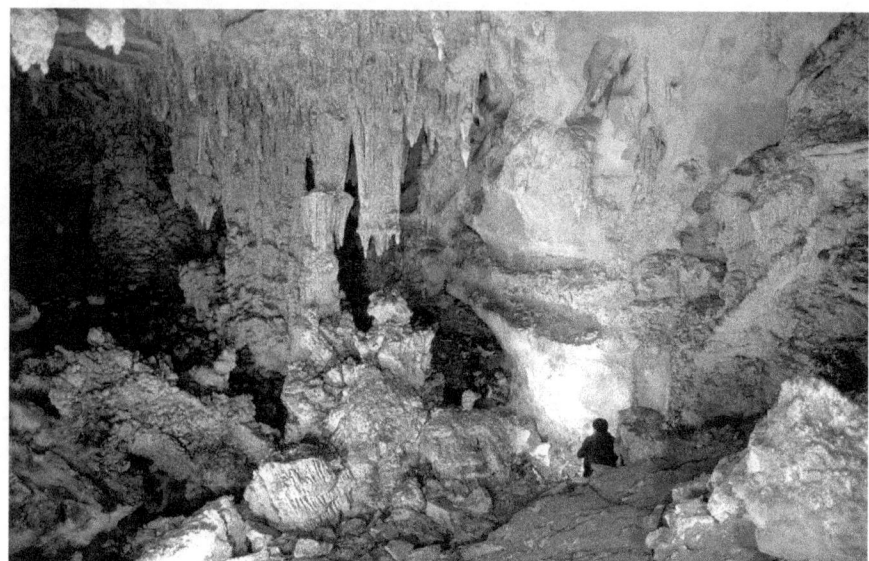

Galer'a principal, Sector II

a line in the same color, an unfinished sketch of a quadrangular sign, and a horse's head in yellow or light brown, as well as two series of simple, wide and shallow non-figurative engravings.

This is, therefore, quite a small group of cave art, whose technical and stylistic character is not too different from that of other sites a short distance away, such as the caves of Arco A and B-C, or even Covalanas and La Haza. All the figures in these caves can be included in Leroi-Gourhan's Style III, and consequently dated in the Solutrean period.

Bibliography

González Sainz, C.; San Miguel Llamosas, C. 1997. Avance al estudio de los conjuntos rupestres paleolíticos del desfiladero del río Carranza (Ramales de la Victoria, Cantabria): las cuevas del Arco, Pondra y Morro del Horidillo. *Actas del II° Congreso de Arqueología Peninsular (Zamora, 1996)*, pp. 163-172.

2-12: Cueva de Pondra

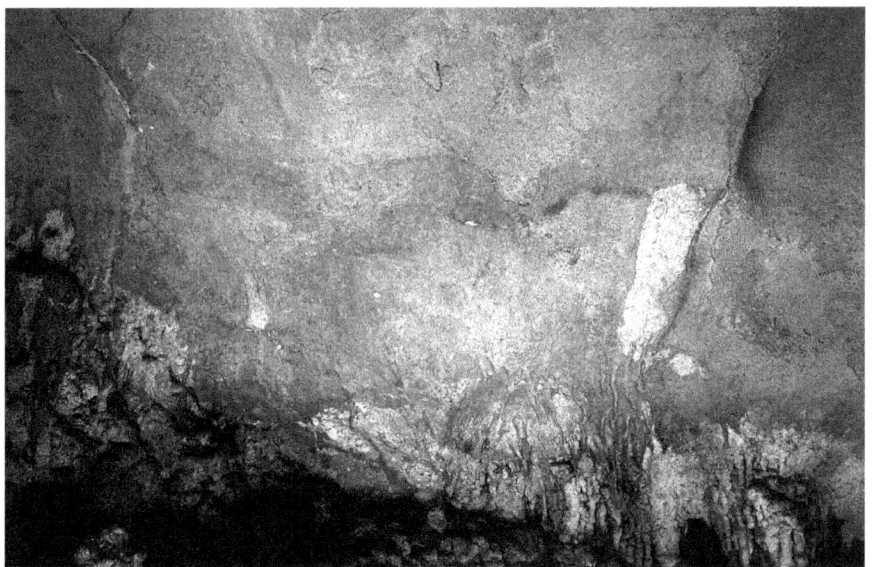
Hind painted in yellow shown in the Sector II

2-13. Cueva de La Garma

La Garma cave is located in the mountain with that same name in the Cantabrian village of Omoño, about 30km east of Santander. The mountain is covered by ever green oak trees today and along the top of the mountain can be seen a various kind of remains that covers a long term period from the end of the Lower Palaeolithic to the Middle Ages including bronze age settlements.

In this area of karstic topography were known a couple of other Palaeolithic caves such as El Truchiro, but it was in November the 2nd, 1995 that La Garma cave was found by a team of the University of Cantabria leaded by Pablo Arias Cabal and Roberto Ontañon Peredo.

La Garma cave consists of two caves, La Garma A and B. La Garma A consists of 3 passages (Upper, Middle and Lower) and these 3 passages are communicated between them by vertical chasms of about 10 m each.

La Garma cave is regarded as one of the most interesting ruins in this area now, but the reason is that this cave had been completely closed by a cave-in that occurred at the original entrance area about 13,000 years ago and the trace of people' s lives at that time had been left untouched as it was in this cave.

In the Lower Passage can be seen a couple of remarkable wall paintings and engravings, but according to the latest research, the cave paintings of La Garma were created in 3 different periods. The oldest ones are negative hands and non-figurative patterns and these are estimated to be created in Gravettian period (26,000~21,000 B.P.). The next was those of red animals and they are estimated to be created in Solutrean period (21,000~17,000 years B.P.). The last were those of black horse and engravings and those are estimated to be created in Magdalenian period (17,000 ~ 11,000 years B.P.).

On the walls that surround the main habitation deposit in the first 70 meters of the Lower Passage, numerous examples of art, in many different styles and varying age such as the red sign painted with dotted red lines and other paintings in red can be seen below a horse in black, depicted with conventions that are especially frequent in the east of the Cantabrian Region and the French Pyrenees.

A splendid example of Magdalenian mobile art was found among

2-13: Cueva de La Garma

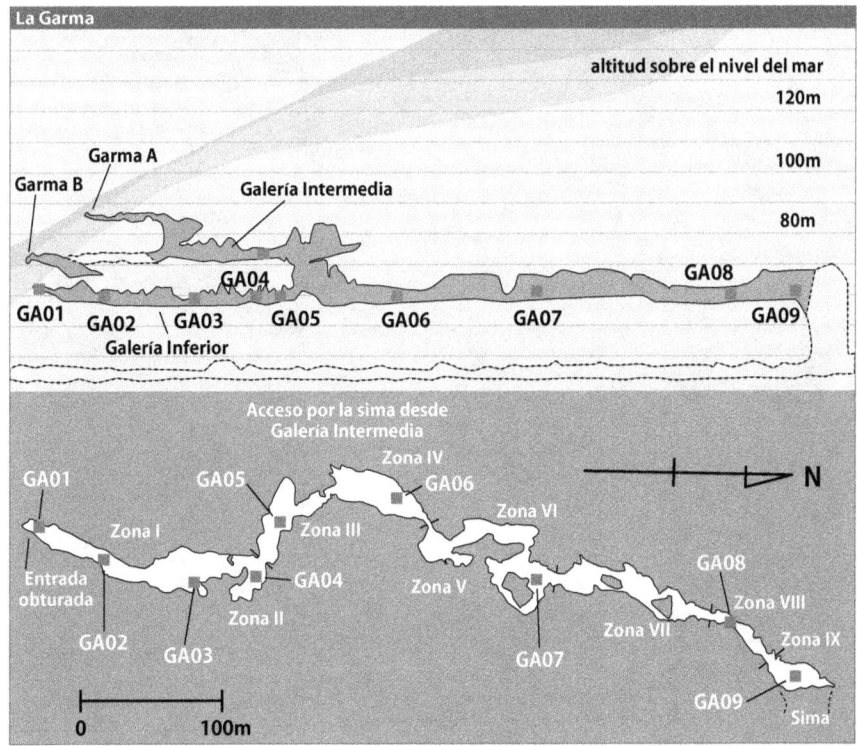

La Garma Ground Plan

the limestone blocks in the area of Zone Ic, quite near the cave entrance. It is a bovine' s phalanx, which has been decorated with a whole figure of an auroch surrounding the circular surface of the bone. The figure of the animal has been shaped in bas relief, especially carefully in its fore quarters, and there is an arrow in its side. In addition, the bone is perforated from top to bottom.

A horse in a vertical position can be seen on one of the walls next to the activity area associated with the structures in Zone III of the Lower Passage. The work surface was prepared before painting the horse. Its outline is drawn with charcoal, and this has also been spread out to fill the interior of its body. Color has not been applied in the belly area, in order to form the conventional M-shaped internal division. Some red finger marks can be seen on the same wall.

A large number of archeological artifacts have been found at an activity area located 120 m from the Palaeolithic entrance to the Lower Passage such as stone tools, decorated bones, associated with three areas marked out by large boulders, next to the left-hand wall of the passage.

2-13: Cueva de La Garma

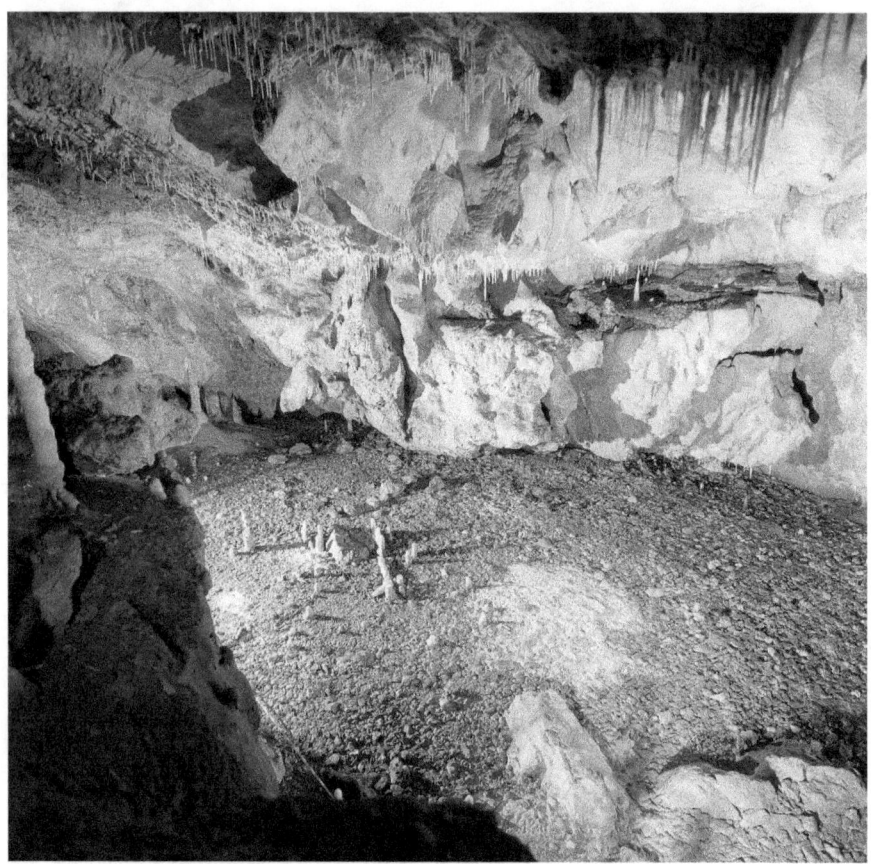

View of Zone Ic in the Lower Passage, near the entrance

On the wall of Zone IV can be seen a number of paintings of different times in the Upper Paleolithic. The first composition grouped the head of an auroch with two animals - probably ibex - placed one above the other on the right of the composition. Later, some non figurative lines were engraved, and then new figures of a giant deer or megaceros and an unidentifiable animal were painted with finer red lines, on top of the first paintings. Finally, lines were engraved to emphasize the outlines of the older figures. Calcite covering these paintings has been dated by Uranium and Thermoluminescence series and the dates obtained suggest that the art is over 23,000 years old.

Negative hand prints also characterizes this cave. There is a small side chamber at the end of Zone IX and on the wall can be seen a composition of five negative adult hands, painted in red by spraying the pigment over the back

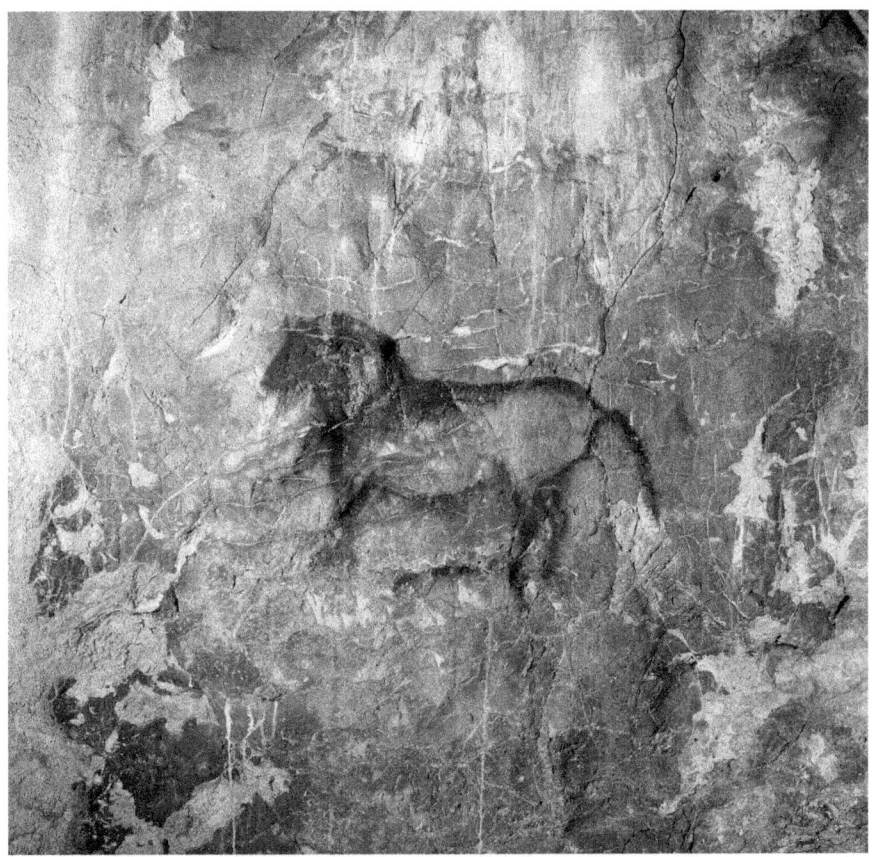

Complete figure of a horse in black

of the right hand while it was held against the cave wall. At this chamber, the Paleolithic artists had to stoop, and work sitting or kneeling down. The arched roof at the entrance to this chamber was highlighted with numerous red dots.

La Garma cave is a very precious ruins in terms of that Cro-Magnons living space of 13,000 years ago has been left intact. Consideration to the ruins preservation and further research is expected now.

2-13: Cueva de La Garma

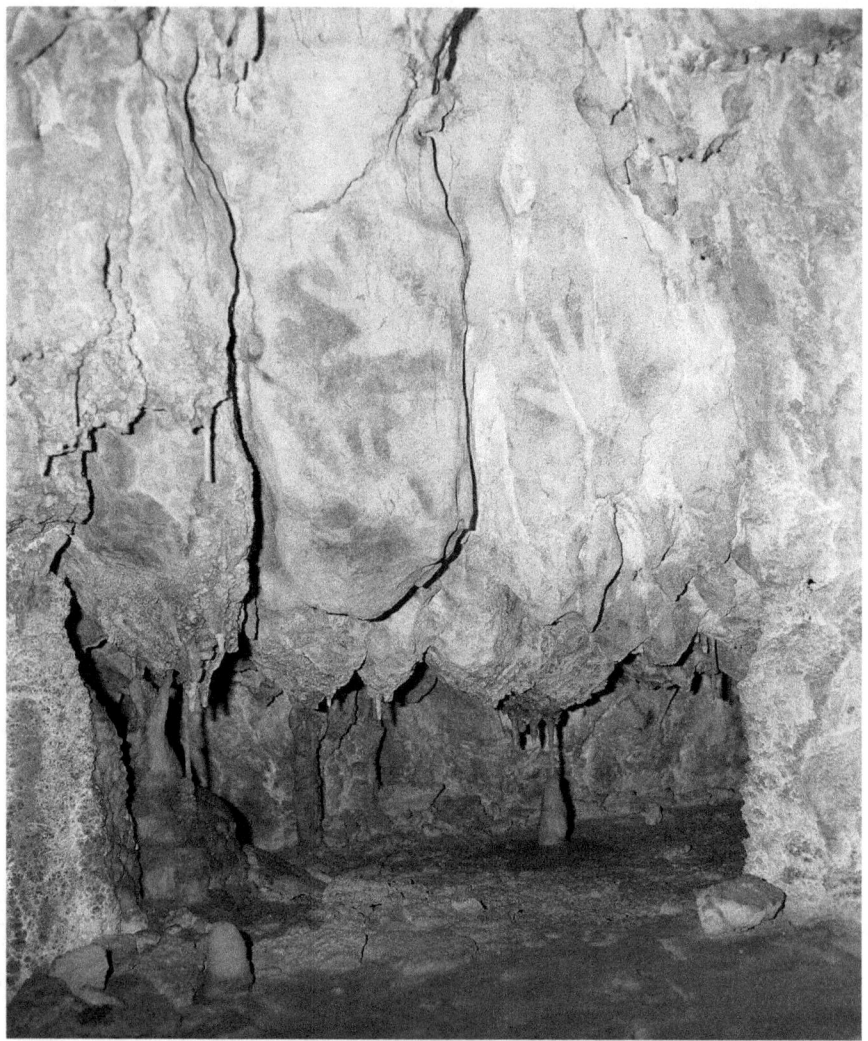

Negative hand prints found at the end of Zone IX

Bibliography

Arias Cabal, P.; Gonzáez Sainz, C.; Moure Romanillo, A.; Ontañon Peredo, R. 1999. La Garma. Un descenso al pasado. *Catálogo de la exposición*. Gobierno de Cantabria y Universidad de Cantabria, Santander.

Gonzáez Sainz, C.; Moure Romanillo, A. 2002. *"La Garma". In: Las cuevas con Arte Paleolítico en Cantabria,* pp. 209-218. Asociaci ón Cántabra para la Defensa del Patrimonio Subterráneo, Santander.

Gonzáez Sainz, C. 2003. "El conjunto parietal de la galería inferior de La Garma (Omoño, Cantabria). Avance a su organización interna" In: R. de Balbín y P. Bueno Ramílez (eds.), El Arte Prehistórico desde los inicios del siglo XXI. *Primer Symposium Internacional de Arte Prehistórico de Ribadesella. (Octubre, 2002),* pp.201-222.

Chapter 3.
The Western Cantabrian Region.
Introduction to Paleolithic cave art in Asturias

1. Introduction

The Principality of Asturias, at the western end of the Cantabrian corridor, was occupied and trekked assiduously by groups of hunter-gatherers throughout the Upper Paleolithic. They left multiple evidence of their activity in the caves of the region, and this includes examples of rock art and mobiliary art. Asturias, therefore, concentrates a very significant part of the total cave art known today in the Cantabrian region. Forty-five caves, from a total of a hundred and three in the region, are located in the central and eastern part of this autonomous community. Its western sector, beyond the valley of the River Nalón, has a very different geological structure, with older lithologies and less karst, and so there are fewer caves with archaeological deposits or remains of Paleolithic human activity.

The center and east of Asturias has a very complete cultural sequence of the Upper Paleolithic (38,000 to 11,500 BP). The main stratigraphies have been found in a few key sites such as Abrigo de la Viña, and caves of La Paloma and Las Caldas in the Nalón Valley; or the caves of Cova Rosa, Tito Bustillo and Los Azules in the Sella Valley. Equally, in the East the most important sites that have been dug are La Riera and Cueto de la Mina, in the Llanes area, and Llonín in the Cares Valley. Many of these sites also have magnificent assemblages of paintings and engravings. Furthermore, series of mobiliary art from La Viña, Las Caldas, La Paloma, Tito Bustillo and Llonín, among others, are of exceptional quality.

The Upper Paleolithic of Asturias has characteristics fully integrated with those of the rest of the Cantabrian region, but with a few distinctive features of its own. The main one is the abundant use made of a lithic material which is common in Asturias: quartzite, whereas flint is generally rarer and of poorer quality than in other parts of the Cantabrian. This implies a greater apparent crudeness in their lithic industries, and some differences in the tool composition. Thus, it is more frequent than in other areas to find tools of varied use, manufactured out of simple materials, such as side-scrapers, endscrapers on flakes, carenated end-

Chapter3: Introduction to Paleolithic cave art in Asturias

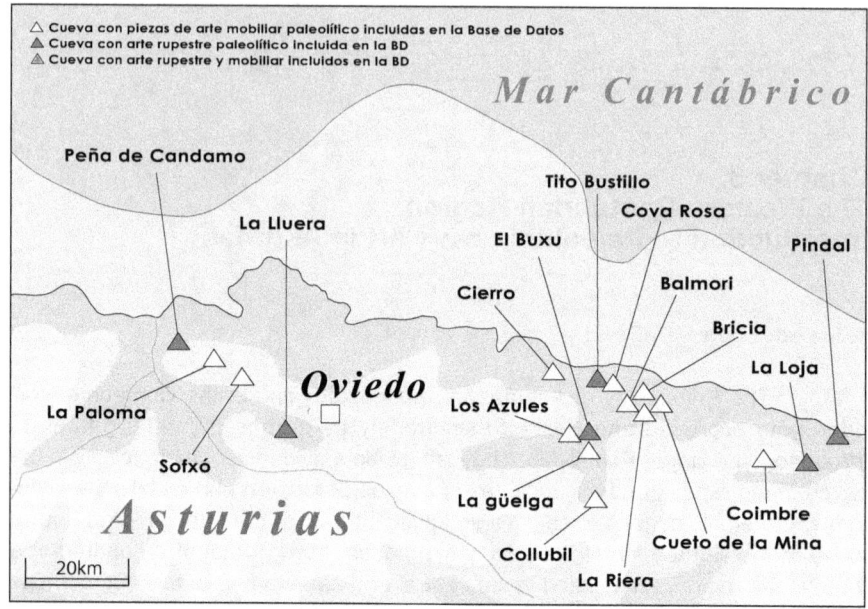

Palaeolithic Caves in Asturias

scrapers or denticulate pieces. Less frequent are those lithic tools that required large, long, parallel-sided blades (e.g. some kinds of burin). At the same time, certain types of tools, which are very common in Asturias and western Cantabria, seem to be linked to the possibilities for knapping and retouch allowed by quartzite, for example the lithic hunting points with a concave base of the Solutrean period (21,000-16,500 BP).

The economic organization of human groups here must have been similar to other parts of the Cantabrian region, with seasonal movements among different habitats, which were nearly always in caves. The subsistence strategy was to exploit varied resources: hunting herds of red deer, horses, bison and sometimes aurochs in open areas of the coast or lower valleys; or ibex and chamois on rocky, steeper slopes; or fishing salmon and trout in the rivers, or sea trout and plaice in estuaries; and also collecting shellfish along the shore (relatively frequent after 17,000 BP).

2. The documentation and research

The documentation and research of Paleolithic art in Asturias took place in a series of stages, similar to those of other Cantabrian areas, although the people involved are occasionally different. In the first stage we find researchers coming from the center of the Cantabrian region, and who included a number of

Chapter3: Introduction to Paleolithic cave art in Asturias

Asturian caves in their first studies of the region, especially the one published in 1911 by Alcalde del Río, Breuil and Sierra. This publication includes the Asturian cave art sites of La Loja, Pindal, Quintanal and Mazaculos II, all logically within the eastern part of the Principality. Other researchers like Hernández Pacheco and Conde de la Vega del Sella began their work soon afterwards, and carried out excellent studies of the caves of Peña Candamo and El Buxu respectively, as well as others with only a few cave art figures, such as Cueva de San Antonio.

Of the post-war period the only fact worth mentioning, perhaps, is the falsification of paintings in a cave which is still open to the public today. Later, between the 1950s and 1970s, Francisco Jordá, professor at the University of Salamanca, became the main authority on cave art in Asturias, and he carried out studies in El Pindal and Pedroses, and in Tito Bustillo together with other archaeologists. The more important researchers at that time also included Magín Berenguer, who made magnificent reproductions of the art in Tito Bustillo and Llonín, two excellent cave art assemblages discovered in those years.

Since the mid 1970s, the number of studies on specific caves has multiplied considerably, focusing on more exhaustive research and with more sophisticated tools of documentation. At the present time, a number of general summaries of Asturian art are in preparation. The team formed by R. de Balbín and A. Moure to study Tito Bustillo was important for the renewal they brought about in the procedures of analysis in the Cantabrian region, and equally significant is the research of J. Fortea in the caves and rock-shelters of the middle Nalón valley, e.g. La Viña, La Lluera and Santo Adriano, or in the caves of the inland valleys of eastern Asturias, e.g. Llonín, or the recent discoveries, still being studied, of Covaciella and El Bosque. Furthermore, a long list of archaeologists have carried out occasional studies, revising known caves, like La Loja or El Buxu, or publishing new discoveries, as in Coimbre, Tebellín, Covarón and Trescalabres.

3. The distribution of caves with arts

The more than forty caves with Paleolithic art which are known in Asturias tend to be concentrated in certain zones, forming four dense and discontinuous clusters of sites, with some gaps in between. The most characteristic areas are the Nalón Valley, with thirteen or fourteen sites above all in the middle valley, the caves of the Sella Valley, and finally two East-West corridors, one situated to the north of a line of hills known as Sierra del Cuera and the other to the south, following the course of the River Cares.

This distribution of sites, noticeably polarized in a few concentrations, is different from the distribution found in the rest of the Cantabrian region, where the degree of dispersion is much greater, although clustering does exist, such as

Chapter3: Introduction to Paleolithic cave art in Asturias

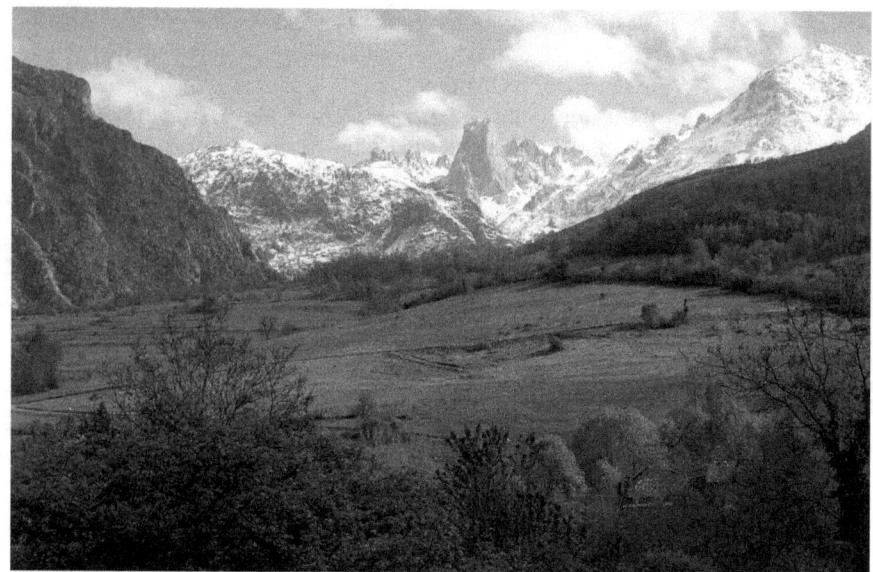

Pico de Europa, Asturias

in the middle valleys of the Rivers Nansa, Pas and Asón in Cantabria.

The four clusters we have distinguished in Asturias have their own peculiarities which need to be mentioned, with variations in the size of the art assemblages, their age, and the techniques applied and themes developed.

* The Nalón group. This is doubtlessly the area with the greatest difference in personality of the whole Cantabrian region. This is due to two factors; first because it is separated from other areas by a wide gap of about 50km (from the Sella valley), and second because of the great homogeneity in technique, age and style of most of the sites. Except for two of the caves, Peña Candamo and Entrecueves, the rest are all caves and rock-shelters with exterior engravings, that is to say, with art produced in the entrances of the caves, within daylight. These correspond to the first periods of the Upper Paleolithic, from the Aurignacian to the start of the Solutrean. These simple, strongly marked engravings were produced between approximately 33,000 and 20,000 BP, and are being studied by Professor Fortea, of the University of Oviedo.

The rock-shelters of La Viña form the most important assemblage, with an impressive sequence of occupations throughout practically the whole of the upper Paleolithic, and with two series of prehistoric engravings which can be differentiated by their style and their height above the floor, and which are partly covered by layers of archaeological sediments. The figures of the first stage

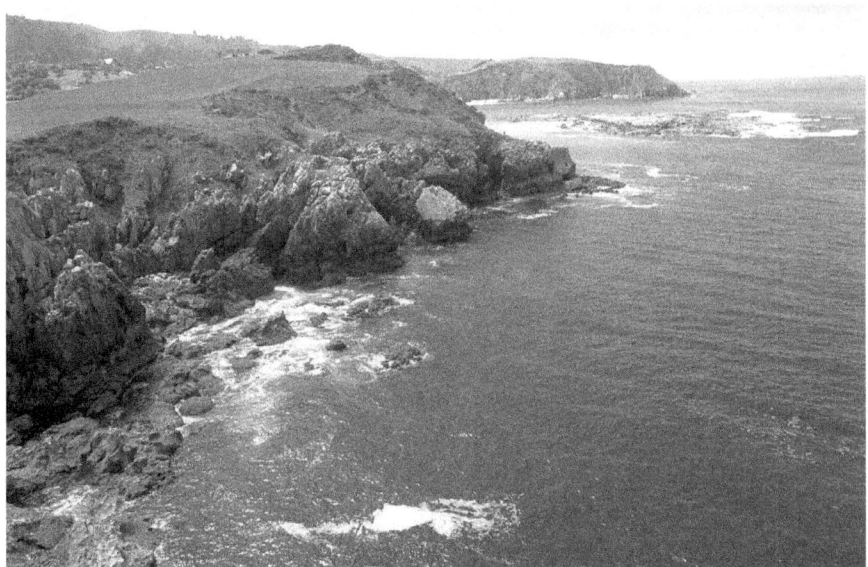

View of coast, Asturias

must have been produced while standing on the Aurignacian floors, taking into account the age of the layers that cover the figures, and the height and normal dimensions of the manual field. These are series of deep, vertical and parallel incisions. They are simple motifs, similar to those of Cueva del Conde, which have traditionally been attributed to the Aurignacian, and which are also located in the Nalón valley.

The second stage of engravings in the Nalón area corresponds to a much larger number of sites. As well as La Viña, these include La Lluera I and II, Godulfo, Los Murciélagos, Las Mestas, Molín, and two recent discoveries: Santo Adriano and Torneiros. These engravings are now figurative animal images, simple representations but where the species are clearly recognizable. The engraving technique and the positions are very similar to the figures of the first stage, but some caves and rock-shelters have complex panels, such as Viña and Lluera I, whereas others have a single animal, e.g. an acephalous bison positioned vertically in Cueva de los Murciélagos, or a hind in Cueva de Godulfo. The character of this decorative stage is particularly clear in sites like La Lluera, probably the most interesting of all. The rock-shelter of La Viña is one of the sites where the height of these figures, and the presence of engraved pieces of rock fallen from the wall and recovered during the archaeological dig, allows the art to be dated. This second stage, therefore, began in the Gravettian and its last stage of development took place in the Solutrean.

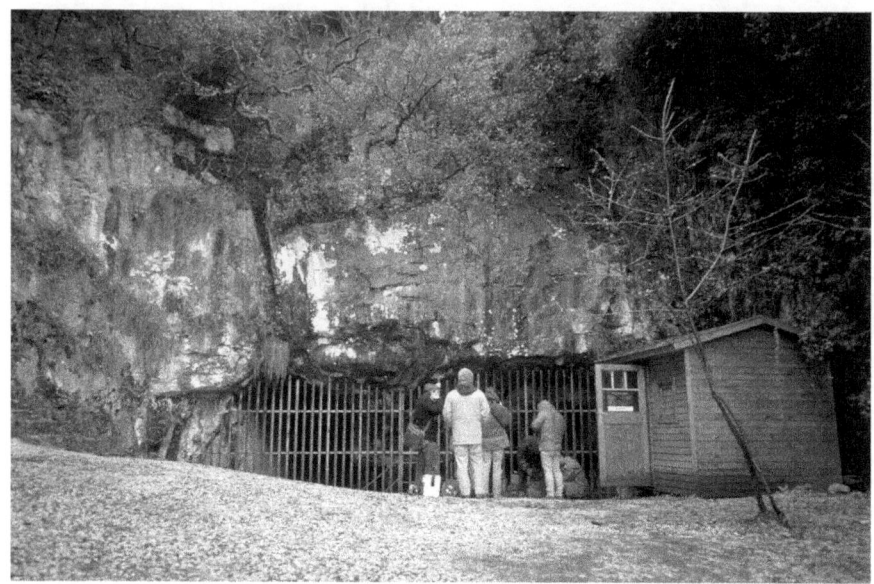
Entrance of El Pindal

The art in Cueva de Entrecueves contrasts noticeably with these exterior assemblages. Not only is it situated deep in a cave with quite difficult access, but it is also formed apparently by a few abstract signs painted in red. They include some ladder-shaped signs or scaliforms, an angle, and also quadrangular signs, different to the more typical Cantabrian quadrangular paintings, but possibly of the same age, Solutrean basically. The northern-most site in the Nalón valley is Peña Candamo. It is also the most complex of the area, with art of different styles and phases of the Upper Paleolithic, produced using a wide variety of paint and engraving techniques.

To the east of the Nalón valley, at the moment we find a large gap without sites which is difficult to explain. This covers all the coastal zone around Cabo de Peñas, and the smaller valleys between the Nalón and the Sella, i.e. of the Rivers Aboño and Piles, as well as to the south, the depression between Oviedo and Cangas de Onís, following the courses of the tributaries; the Nora and Piloña.

* The valley of the River Sella has an important group of sites around the mouth of the river and the immediate coastal areas. The main one is Tito Bustillo, with paintings and engravings produced probably during a long timespan, although the most spectacular are the polychrome animals, above all horses and reindeer, of Magdalenian age. The same karstified hill has Cueva de La Lloseta and La Cuevona, two caves with small groups of art. And close-by,

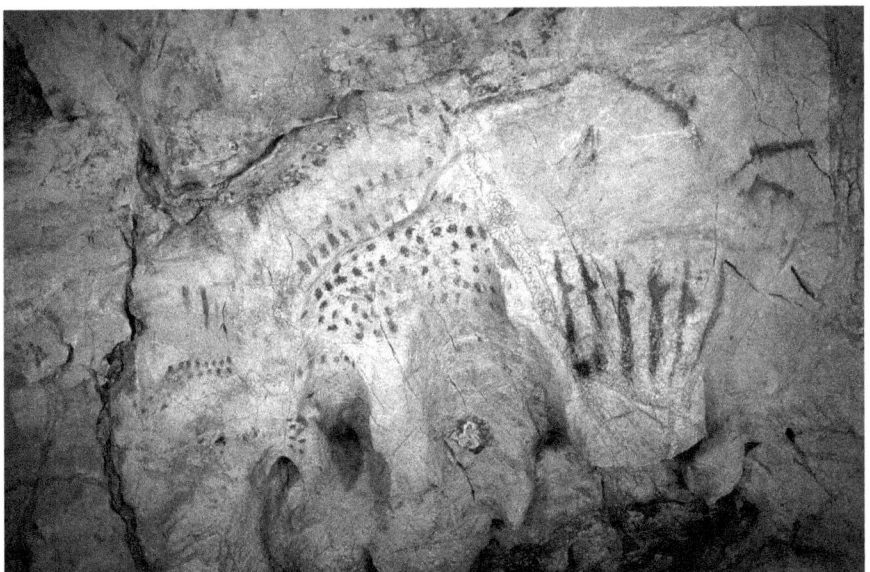

Figurative and non-figurative depictions in red, El Pindal

we find the assemblage at Les Pedroses, with red paintings and engravings of various animals, as well as Cueva de San Antonio, with just one horse painted in black. Located on tributaries in the interior of the Sella basin, another two caves have art. One is Cueva de El Sidrón, on the River Piloña, which has hardly been studied, and Cueva del Buxu, with excellent engravings and paintings of animals and signs, unfortunately not very well preserved.

In the east of Asturias, and in continuity with the coastal and interior sites of the Sella area, another two groups of caves are arranged in two parallel lines: one is in the coastal strip, and the other follows the valley of the River Cares, south of Sierra del Cuera, to its confluence with the River Deva.

* The eastern coastal strip, to the north of Sierra del Cuera, has a large number of caves with art, although this is generally not too spectacular, with few paintings and with an unusually high proportion of abstract signs, mainly in red (e.g. the caves of Balmori, Tebellín and Herrerías). Nevertheless, there also are sites with small groups of animal figures, such as Cueva de Trescalabres, which has depictions of several animals and a circular red sign, attributed to Style III, or the interior assemblage in El Coverón, with black paintings superimposed over other red ones. These are probably of Magdalenian age, but regrettably very faint.

A little further to the East, almost on the boundary with Cantabria, more

Chapter 3: Introduction to Paleolithic cave art in Asturias

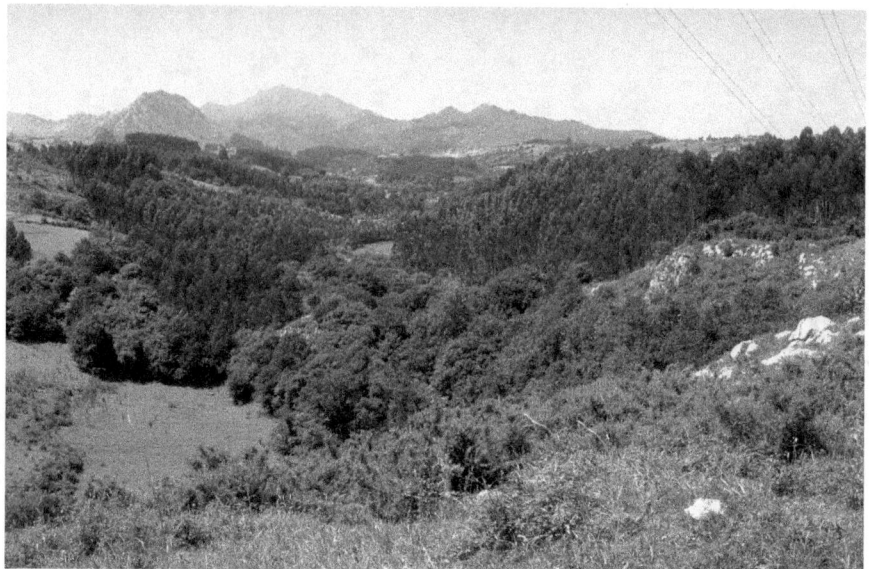
View from the limestone hill of Tito Bustillo

decorated caves are found, especially Cueva de El Pindal, with a large number of paintings and engravings, mainly of the Magdalenian period. Another two caves are Mazaculos I, which has a quadrangular sign, and Mazaculos II, with dots and a zigzagging line.

* Finally, between Sierra del Cuera and the massif of Picos de Europa, a natural corridor follows the course of the River Cares, where many sites of great interest have been discovered in the last few decades. Besides, this corridor connects to the west with the valley of the River Güeña, a tributary of the Sella, where the caves of Molín and Buxu are located.

Beginning in the west, the first small group of paintings is found in Covaciella, a new discovery. The main figures are situated in one panel, with several superbly executed and well-preserved bison, painted in black and engraved, as well as a painted horse' s head. They are complemented by a stag and an ibex engraved at either end of this well-ordered panel. These figures show all the most typical graphic conventions of the Magdalenian period and two C14-AMS dates have been obtained, situated about 14,000 BP. This date corresponds to the start of the middle Magdalenian in the region, and is wholly coherent with the style of the assemblage.

Cueva de El Bosque is located very near Covaciella, and has a good group of black paintings, mainly goats, and equally of Magdalenian style. Follow-

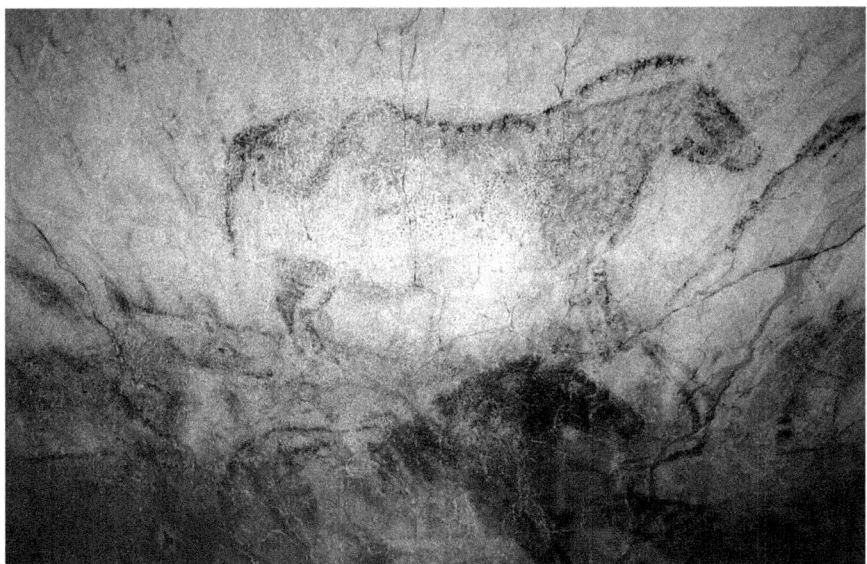

Two horses facing right, Tito Bustillo

ing the course of the River Cares to the east, the next important caves are Coimbre, with a large group of engravings, not well studied but also Magdalenian, and above all Cueva de Llonín.

Archaeological deposits are being dug in this cave, which has layers corresponding to the start of the Upper Paleolithic, Solutrean, middle and late-final Magdalenian, and more recent periods. The cave art is distributed in several parts of the cave, especially in a frieze 13m long containing many figures often superimposed upon each other. The different styles and techniques make it possible to distinguish several stages of decoration. The first figures were painted in red, in the Gravettian and above all Solutrean, the most important being an anthropomorph and a series of non-figurative marks as well as some animals. Later, a group of black figures were painted, including a typically Cantabrian quadrilateral sign. Then in the Magdalenian period, in early Style IV, a good number of animals were engraved with striated lines, while a few more complex figures, painted in black and engraved, may correspond to an immediately later moment, together with fine, realistic engravings of animals, mostly goats.

This inland corridor finishes at the confluence of the Cares and Deva rivers. The last site is situated here; Cueva de La Loja, with an interesting group of finely-engraved wild aurochs.

4. Characteristics of the arts in western part

Cave art in the western part of the Cantabrian region has certain characteristics of its own, which are as follows. First, it has a large number of abstract images. The frequency of signs, compared with animals for example, seems to increase along the Cantabrian corridor, at least as far as the east of Asturias, where they are most common. As mentioned above, this area has caves in which the art consists solely of conventionalized signs. These are the caves of Mazaculos, Herrerías, Balmori, Tebellín, possibly Sidrón, and even Entrecueves in the Nalón area. Others have only non-figurative lines, ranging from series of engravings in clay (caves of Los Canes and Subores), to non-figurative linear marks (Trauno, Samoreli and Cueto de la Mina). Nevertheless, the same area has sites where animal themes predominate, such as Trescalabres and Covarón.

The signs found in eastern Asturias are of the same types as those in the center of the Cantabrian region, for example classical quadrilaterals and quadrilaterals with a pointed protuberance in the middle of one side in Llonín, Buxu and Mazaculos I, or types intermediate between these and claviforms in Tebellín, and late-style claviforms in Pindal. Besides, loop-shaped signs have been recorded in Balmori, Pindal and Tito Bustillo, bastonets in Pindal, "grilles" in Herrerías and Covarón, as well as signs in the form of ladders, circles and ovals. These signs are generally painted in red, similar to the signs found in the caves of Monte Castillo, Altamira, or other sites in Cantabria. However, in the Sella valley and to the west, different kinds of signs become more common, with other forms and often engraved rather than painted (e.g. in Tito Bustillo, El Sidrón and El Buxu).

The animal themes are more difficult to differentiate from those in most of the Cantabrian region, with high frequencies of deer, especially hinds in the periods from the Gravettian to the Solutrean and early Magdalenian (27,000 to 14,000 BP). Bison, horses and goats are also common. The most usual techniques are also the same as in the rest of the Cantabrian. Just two observations can be made. One is that the technique of dabbing red paint to form dotted lines, used in the Solutrean, is less common than in other parts of the Cantabrian; and the second is that animals engraved with simple, deep lines are extraordinarily abundant in the Nalón area.

"Complex" assemblages, with multiple panels corresponding to different periods, and therefore with superimpositions, and varied techniques and styles, are spread out across Asturias. There is at least one such site in each of the four areas that we have described above. Thus, we have Peña Candamo in the Nalón area, Tito Bustillo in the Sella, Llonín in the Cares valley, and Pindal and even El Covarón in the eastern coastal strip. Together with these, a much larger number of caves have art apparently produced at a single time, and which therefore vary greatly from each other in techniques, and above all in the stylistic conventions used.

5. Chronology

Regarding the chronological stages of development that can now be recognized in Asturias, we find a very similar organization to that of other Cantabrian areas, especially its central sector. These can be described briefly as:

a) Early stages, corresponding to a long lapse of time, from the early phases of the Aurignacian to the start of the Solutrean, i.e. between 35,000 and 20,000 BP. The Styles I and II defined by Leroi-Gourhan developed during these stages. They are represented by the art in daylight areas of cave entrances and rock-shelters, starting with the non-figurative linear marks, in El Conde and La Viña, and continuing with animal figures, also as simple, deep engravings. A large number of sites correspond to this second phase, but the most typical could be La Lluera I. This figurative phase is not only present in the Nalón valley, but also in the center of the region, in the groups of art in the daylight zone of the caves Chufín, Hornos de la Peña and Venta de la Perra. These are always deep engravings, although red ocher has been noted on the wall at La Viña, and perhaps this was used as an abrasive. Equally they are always within the reach of daylight, with very simple animals, drawn strictly in profile, and developed from the cervical and dorsal lines. Normally they have one limb for each pair, with horns in twisted perspective, and no interior details of the body. Certain ways of drawing are particularly characteristic, and just three lines are often used to represent the whole forequarters of the animal. These engravings, and occasionally abstract signs, in the shape of triangles and sometimes ovals, correspond to the Gravettian period and the early Solutrean.

The hypothesis of Leroi-Gourhan, that the interior of caves was slowly conquered for areas of decoration, cannot be maintained today. It is now clear that at the same time, or even before, these exterior engravings were produced in the Nalón, other caves were being decorated in their interiors with simple paintings. These were positive and negative hand images, a few series of dots, finger-marks, and other paired marks. Well before 20,000 BP, paintings were being produced in Asturias, inside caves such as Tito Bustillo, with a negative hand, finger-marks and the lines in sector II, and also in Llonín and Peña Candamo.

b) The Solutrean period and the start of the Magdalenian, approximately between 20,000 and 16,000 BP is a stage when the Cantabrian region shows its own personality compared with the rest of SW Europe. One of the main characteristics is the great use of red paint, in simple outline figures, or dabbed-on as dotted lines, and then at the end of the stage, as color-wash affecting part or all of the figure, sometimes associated with engraving around the outline. At this time a large number of abstract signs appear, many of them typical of central areas of the Cantabrian region, with rectangular shapes, or ovals, with a pointed protuberance or crescents. Animal themes, in continuity with the second Nalón stage, are dominated by the hinds, together with horses and aurochs. In their design, it is more common for both limbs to be represented per pair, as well as some details of interior articulation, such as an eye, or partition lines, indicating the manes and the muzzles of horses, or as lines from the withers to the front limbs of hinds.

Many Asturian caves can be attributed to this period. These include the red paintings in Candamo and Entrecueves, and of different colors, although red predominates, in Llonín. Also some of the first phases of production of the main panel in Tito Bustillo, and perhaps in its chamber with vulvae. And paintings which are mostly red in Covarón, Trescalabres, Mazaculos I, and possibly part of the iconographic record in Pindal.

c) The last stage corresponds to the art produced during much of the Magdalenian, from approximately 16,000 to the end of this artistic cycle about 11,500 BP, during the temperate climatic oscillation of the Alleröd. This is, therefore, Leroi-Gourhan's Style IV. Asturian art shows at first a relative continuity in some abstract signs, like the quadrilaterals almost turned into claviforms in Cueva de El Tebellín, and in the animal iconography, still dominated by hinds. Soon, however, tendencies are seen towards naturalism in the style, and to the expression of volume and depth in the depictions, as the art becomes more clearly linked with areas beyond the Cantabrian, showing particularly strong ties with the Pyrenees. This is noticeable in mobiliary art from Asturian sites, like La Viña, Las Caldas and Tito Bustillo, especially in middle and late Magdalenian deposits (c. 14,000 - 12,000 BP), which have pendants and other pieces identical to the Pyrenees; but also in rock art, as will be explained.

During the Magdalenian, in contrast with earlier periods, we find a greater diversity in the technical procedures applied. Especially characteristic are black paintings, the association of engraving with paint, and sometimes polychrome figures. Assemblages only with engravings are very common now, often with the typical striated lines forming bands in the jaw and chests of some animal depictions, mainly heads of hinds, as found in Tito Bustillo and Llonín, or in other animals in Peña Candamo. Besides, many figures are of outstandingly naturalistic, with correct proportions, generally good perspective, including details in the interior of the animals, articulating the different parts of their bodies, and a more frequent use of volume and other natural forms and shapes of the rock surface.

Many of the engravings and black paintings in El Buxu, the group of signs in Tebellín, and the striated engravings and some of the paintings in Candamo, Tito Bustillo and Llonín probably correspond to the early phases of the Magdalenian. In the middle and late Magdalenian, some of the more classic assemblages were produced, such as in Covaciella, the polychromes in Tito Bustillo, and the black paintings and more recent engravings in Llonín. Equally corresponding to the late-final Magdalenian, we have some of the painted and engraved animal figures, and the series of claviforms, in Pindal, the group of engravings in La Loja, or the group of black paintings, mainly of goats, in El Covarón and El Bosque.

3-1. Cueva de La Peña de Candamo

The cave art in Cueva de La Peña de Candamo, in the village of San Román de Candamo, is the westernmost assemblage in the whole of the long corridor forming the Cantabrian region. Its position therefore marks the end of the area of limestone hills and well-developed karst landforms. The entrance of the cave is on the right-hand bank of the Nalón river but, whereas the other cave art sites in the middle valley are just above the present-day river course, this cave is located at the top of a steep hillside, called "Peña de Candamo", 200m above sea level. In this way, the entrance overlooks a wide area, and several natural communication routes, such as the access to the middle valley of the River Nalón. The great strategic value of the location has, in consequence, often been stressed, as it could have been used to control the animal herds moving along the valley and, perhaps, human groups too.

The cave was studied in 1914 by E. Hernández Pacheco, assisted by J. Cabré and Benítez Mellado, who carried out a magnificent work of documentation and analysis of its art. No artifacts or other remains of human occupation were found in the cave, but they were in another small cave near-by. This had a single, thick layer, with abundant industry of Solutrean age (21,000-16,500 BP), probably belonging to periodic human occupation of the site.

The cave is short, and generally rather small, but despite that, it is quite spectacular. It has many large calcite formations, like columns, flowstone and gour floors, which noticeably conditioned the organization of the art, especially regarding the choice of panels and even the techniques applied in the Upper Paleolithic. In fact, this profusion of calcite limited the production of art to a few accessible, clean walls, in three or four different locations. Besides, the growth of the flowstone separated a few small high-level chambers, like the so-called "Camerín" . In this space, after climbing a stalagmitic flowstone, Paleolithic people drew animal depictions visible from all points of the main central chamber in the interior of the cave.

The art begins on an inclined roof in an earlier chamber, easily reached from a sloping floor. This is the "Gallery of the Signs" , with three abstract motifs painted in red, composed of various concave lines in the shape of three-pointed stars, and next to other simple, non-figurative marks, also in red. Most of the designs are, however, concentrated in the main chamber, especially on a wall nearly eight meters long and over two meters high on its left-hand side. The use of scaffolding or some other form of ladders must have been necessary, therefore,

3-1: Cueva de La Peña de Candamo.

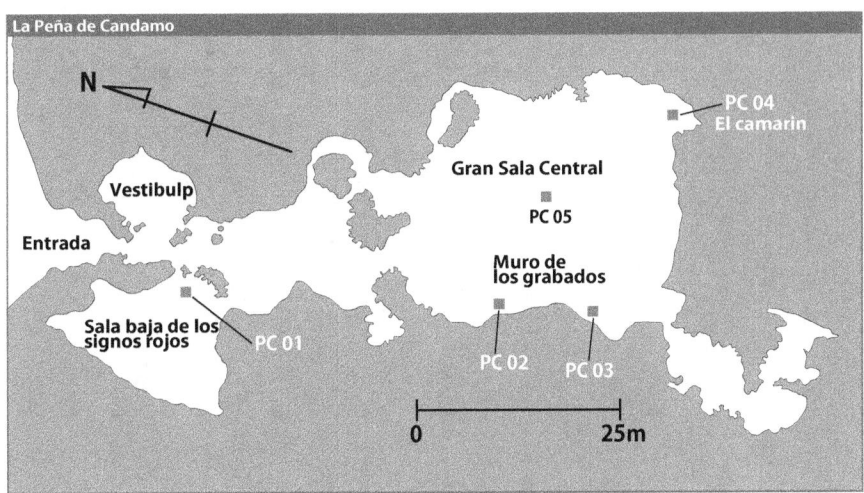

La Pena de Candamo Ground Plan

here and in other parts of the cave, as will be explained later. This central chamber is 25m long, 20m wide and 15m high, and very spectacular because of the large calcite formations that have grown on all sides, especially on the left.

The "Wall of the Engravings" , located on the right-hand side of the chamber, has one of the most complex and most interesting groups of cave art in the Cantabrian region. Unfortunately, it has suffered from the effect of natural processes, and even worse, from direct human action during the 20th Century. Because of this, some of the figures copied by Benítez Mellado at the start of the century, and by Magín Berenguer in the 1950s, have been lost for ever. But despite this degree of destruction, the higher figures are relatively well preserved, particularly on the left-hand side of the wall. In this way, it is still possible to see and enjoy a large number of figures painted in sienna and sometimes in red, black dots, figures engraved with simple or striated lines, and figures both painted in black and engraved.

The superimpositions among these figures on the "Wall of the Engravings" were studied carefully, and used by H. Breuil, together with superimpositions observed in Altamira, Castillo and La Pasiega, to devise the chronological structure of Cantabrian parietal art. It is striking that the oldest paintings, aurochs painted in sienna as simple outlines, with horns represented with twisted perspective, and associated with several series of parallel lines of black dots, should be hidden on the right of the panel, its least visible part from the center of the chamber. It is possible that at first only this more hidden part of the wall was used, or that only this group of paintings has been conserved, whereas others could have been obliterated by the great number of engravings and paintings carried out on

173

3-1: Cueva de La Peña de Candamo.

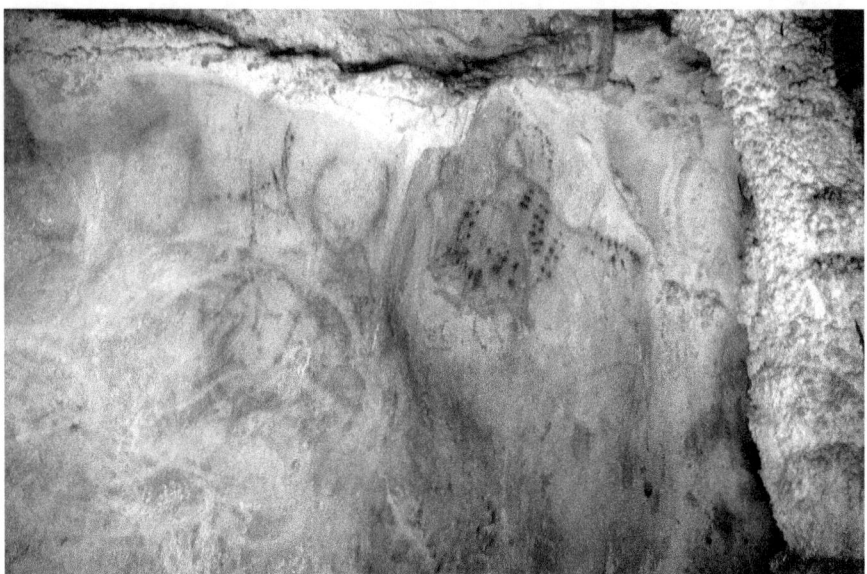
Right hand side of the Wall of the Engravings

the central part of the wall in later Paleolithic phases.

From the iconographic point of view, the most interesting figures on this wall include two large bulls facing each other (the one on the left is nearly two and a half meters long, one of the largest figures in Cantabrian art), two anthropomorphic figures, and above all, several stags with large, branching antlers, wounded with spears and roaring. This theme is repeated in several Cantabrian caves and, from the style of the figures, it can by dated in more recent moments of the Upper Paleolithic, mainly Magdalenian. Examples of caves with this type of figure are Altamira, El Buxu, and the Gallery B of La Pasiega. It is also noticeable that, unlike in the center of the Cantabrian region, in the caves situated between Tito Bustillo and La Garma, striated engraving is used here mainly to represent chamois, horses and stags, and not the almost inevitable hinds' heads found in the center of the region.

On the left of the wall, beyond a vertical separating edge of rock, another high panel contains further depictions. The most important of these is a horse painted in very dark red.

The art is completed with a couple of high panels located on the left of the main chamber, especially the famous "Camarín" , which dominates the chamber from above. Here, in a small space, we find two practically complete paintings of horses, heads of bovines, and another one or two horses. A previous

3-1: Cueva de La Peña de Candamo.

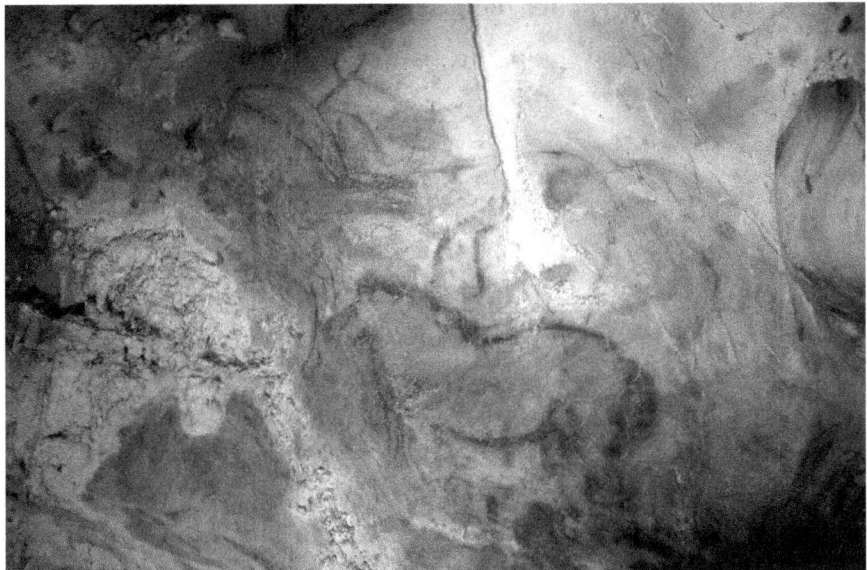
Horse in sienna

wall, high above the floor of the main chamber, has the black painting of an ibex, and like the figures in the "Camarín" , this faces, or opposes, the "Wall of the Engravings" .

The techniques applied in Candamo are therefore quite varied. The succession observed in some of its panels begins with red or sienna linear figures first, followed by black paintings, and finally engraved, striated or scraped figures, which are sometimes associated with black outline representations of stags and chamois. The distribution of the techniques appears to be linked to the accessibility and visibility of the panels. Thus, paint predominates in high, difficult to reach places; and detailed engravings in lower, more accessible panels.

Summing up, La Peña de Candamo is believed to contain 15 aurochs, 11 horses, 5 bison, 7 stags, 3 hinds, 4 ibex, 2 chamois, a doubtful wild boar and 2 doubtful seals, and 2 anthropomorphs. A critical examination of available documentation might increase the numbers of chamois and stags in detriment to ibex and aurochs respectively. However, the poor state of conservation especially in the lower parts of the panels, which have most of the fine engravings that are so complicated to interpret, does not allow any definite conclusions. In addition, the chamber nearer the cave entrance has signs in red, and there are series of parallel lines also in red, lines of black dots, and other non-figurative themes.

La Peña de Candamo is therefore a complex assemblage, formed by

3-1: Cueva de La Peña de Candamo.

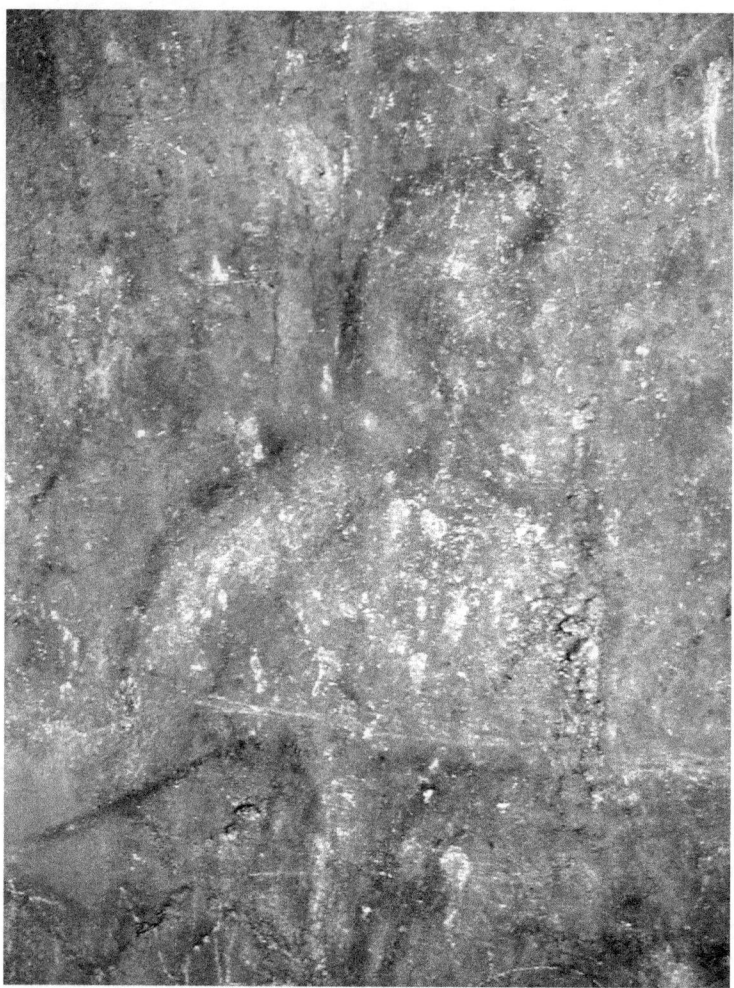

Figure of an anthropomorph facing right

successive additions of paintings and engravings, mainly in Style III and early Style IV of Leroi-Gourhan's series, corresponding to the Solutrean and early and middle Magdalenian (between 21,000 and 13,000 BP approximately). Most of the signs and animals in sienna, red or black, in the first chamber, on the big wall or in the "Camerín", were probably produced in the first of these periods, although an earlier age cannot be excluded for some of the figures, especially the outlines in sienna. Other black figures, and the abundant, excellent engravings on the "Wall of the Engravings", which are occasionally associated with black paintings, belong to early Style IV.

References.

Hernández Pacheco, E. 1919. La caverna de la Peña de Candamo (Asturias). CIPP, no. 24. Madrid.

Moure, J.A. 1981. Algunas consideraciones sobre el "Muro de los grabados" de San Román de Candamo (Asturias). Altamira Symposium (Madrid 1979), pp. 339-352. Madrid.

3-2. Cueva de La Lluera I

The caves of La Lluera are located in the village of San Juan de Priorio, just a few kilometers from Oviedo. They are therefore in the middle valley of the River Nalón, only five meters above the present-day river level. La Lluera I is a short cave, made up of two short passages with separate entrances, which unite inside the cave. La Lluera II is situated fifty meters upstream, and is an even smaller cave. The art at La Lluera was discovered in 1979 by the Polifemo caving club of Oviedo, and its study began immediately under J. Fortea Pérez, who concentrated on the cave art, and J.A. Rodríguez Asensio, who took charge of the archaeological dig at the site. These professors have published important reports about the site.

The excavation of the archaeological deposit at La Lluera I, in the eastern passage, revealed evidence of human occupation at different moments during the Solutrean, developed in the region between 21,000 and 16,500 BP approximately. Materials from the much later Azilian period were also found (between 11,500 and 9000 BP in the Cantabrian), and a bone taken from this layer was dated by radiocarbon to 10,280 +/- 230 BP.

The cave of La Lluera II also contained Solutrean material in a single level of human origin. It is likely that the parietal engravings found at both sites belong to this period, and to be more precise, their style seems to indicate a time in the early Solutrean.

Regarding cave art, La Lluera I is doubtlessly the clearest example of what Professor Fortea has called the second artistic type in the Nalón valley, including other nearby caves in the same area, such as Abrigo de la Viña, and caves of Molín, Adriano, Godulfo and Murciélagos, as well as in the westernmost parts of Cantabria (e.g. Cueva de Chufín on the River Nansa, and less clearly related, the caves of Hornos de la Peña and Venta de la Perra), which were discovered some time ago. The technical and stylistic similarities among the figures in all these sites are accentuated by the fact that they are all "exterior" assemblages. The work of engraving was carried out in them within daylight, or at most within semi-shade a little further inside the caves.

All the cave art at La Lluera I was engraved with simple, deep and quite clear lines, achieved by repeatedly cutting the same grooves. It has also been noticed that the groove's profile was sometimes cut back on the inner part of the animal figure, and other times on the outer side, in a very early attempt to ex-

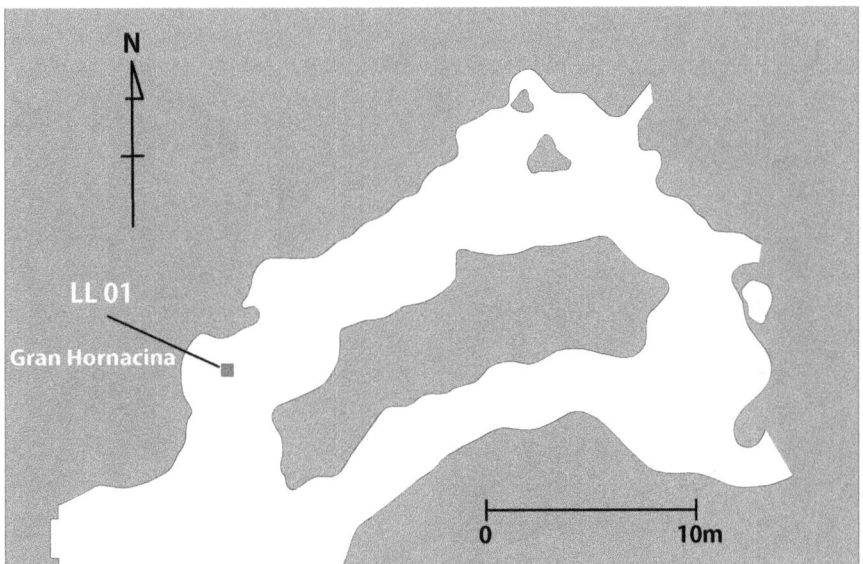

La Lluera I Ground Plan

press the volume of some of the animals represented.

The themes are the usual ones: depictions of the more or less typical wild animals in the Cantabrian region during the Full Glacial period, and which were thus very well known to the artists. Hinds, aurochs and horses were the main animals represented, together with an occasional ibex, and a possible mammoth. Conventionalized abstract designs (or "signs") are rare at La Lluera I, which has just a few fringed signs and crosses.

The stylistic conventions observed in these animals are relatively simple. They are figures defined by their outline, with hardly any of the interior details which were so common in styles of a later age. Besides, their profile is incomplete in many cases, apparently reduced to the parts which best allow the animal to be identified: the head, cervical-dorsal line and croup. In the cases when limbs are shown, above all in aurochs, horses, and less frequently in hinds, only one limb is drawn for each pair, and they are short, finishing in a point, normally without indicating the hoof, and open. For similar reasons, perspective is defined even less, apart from the attempts to show volume mentioned above, and there are hardly any elements indicating depth. So, normally only one of the hinds' ears is shown, or only one of the bovines' horns.

Some of the most common compository formats at La Lluera I are quite conventional and well known in the region. A significant one is the hind' s head

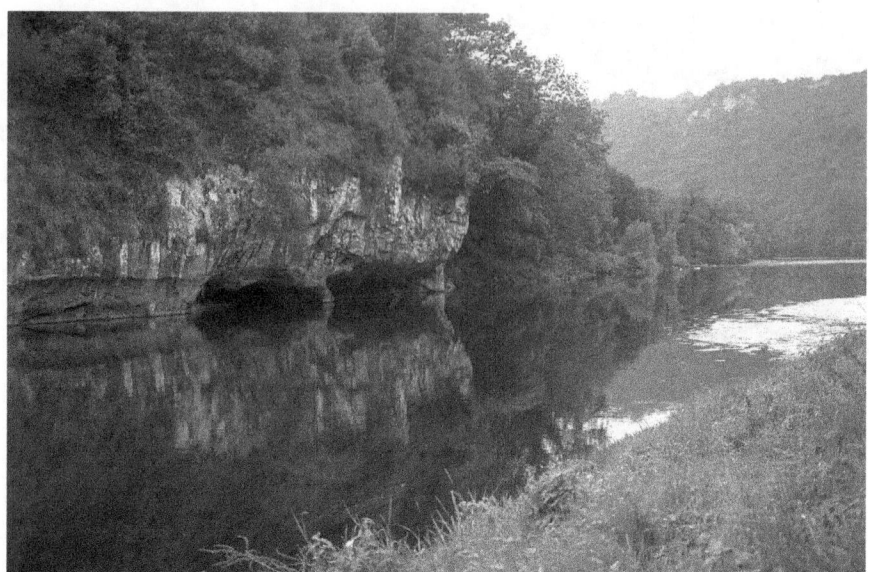
River Nalón

constructed with few lines: a straight line indicates the forehead and is prolonged to the ear, a concave line shows the neck, and below that a third, less curved line represents the chin and front part of the neck. Therefore, in this structure we already find some of the key conventions repeated in later periods in hind's heads which are technically and stylistically more complex: the long, pointed and triangular-shaped head, and the mouth open by a separation of lines.

The engravings at La Lluera I form a roughly synchronic composition, divided in different panels along the western passage. The study of its organization has proved to be very interesting. The engravings were produced from the exterior zone with full visibility, as far as the area where the shade begins to darken, and there the decoration stops. Throughout this decorated zone, between daylight zones and semi-shade, there is considerable variety in the iconographic compositions, density of figures, and degree of imbrication and superimposition. Similarly, it has been seen that the size of the figures tends to decrease the further the artists went from natural light, at least along the eastern wall.

Among these different panels, the most obvious and important one, which appeared to play a central role in the articulation of the assemblage, is known as the "Great Niche" , and it is the part of the cave art published in detail so far. This hollow in the wall has a surprisingly clear composition based on six or seven bulls and a horse, positioned over oblique parallel lines in the rock surface, and flanked by a dozen hinds, which are smaller and less complete. The central

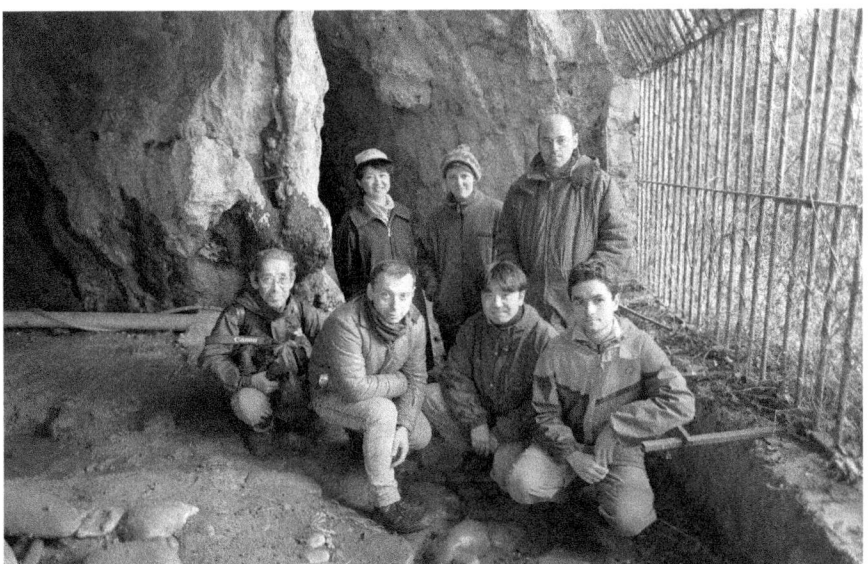
PhotoVR shooting team at the entrance of La Lluera I

figures of this panel seem the best finished and clearest of all the art at La Lluera I. Other panels are dominated by hinds and unfinished outlines which are difficult to identify, as well as containing examples of the species already mentioned, and ibex, a possible mammoth and abundant non-figurative marks. La Lluera I therefore displays an assemblage with quite homogeneous, more or less synchronic, designs, whose style is attributed by Professor Fortea to intermediate phases between Leroi-Gourhan' s Styles II and III.

Regarding the small cave of La Lluera II, it has a very restricted group of parietal art. Here, about fifteen closed signs, feminine sexual triangles, surround the forequarters of a hind, in a single composition. The engravings, which were produced in the exterior zone and thus are easily visible, have deep lines which were cut back in a clear attempt to represent volume as at La Lluera I. According to Professor Fortea, both sites would have been synchronic, and probably produced in an early moment of the Solutrean. Besides, they are complementary from an iconographic and symbolic point of view: the ideal sanctuary would have been divided here into two different but nearby locations; just as in many Cantabrian caves the large panels in the main passages are complemented by groups of abstract signs in small side chambers (e.g. in Tito Bustillo, Peña Candamo, Altamira, La Pasiega, Castillo or Cullalvera).

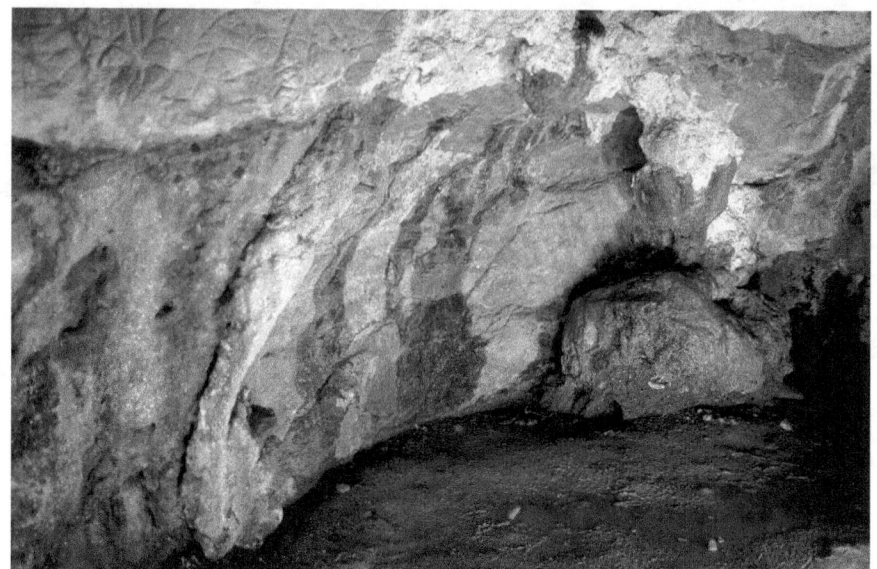
Great niche of La Lluera I

References

Fortea Pérez, J. 1989. Cuevas de La Lluera. Avance al estudio de sus artes parietales. Cien años después de Sautuola, pp. 187-202. Santander.

Rodríguez Asensio, A. 1990. Excavaciones arqueológicas realizadas en la cueva de "La Lluera" (San Juan de Priorio, Oviedo). Excavaciones Arqueológicas en Asturias 1983-86, pp. 15-17. Oviedo.

3-2: Cueva de La Lluera I

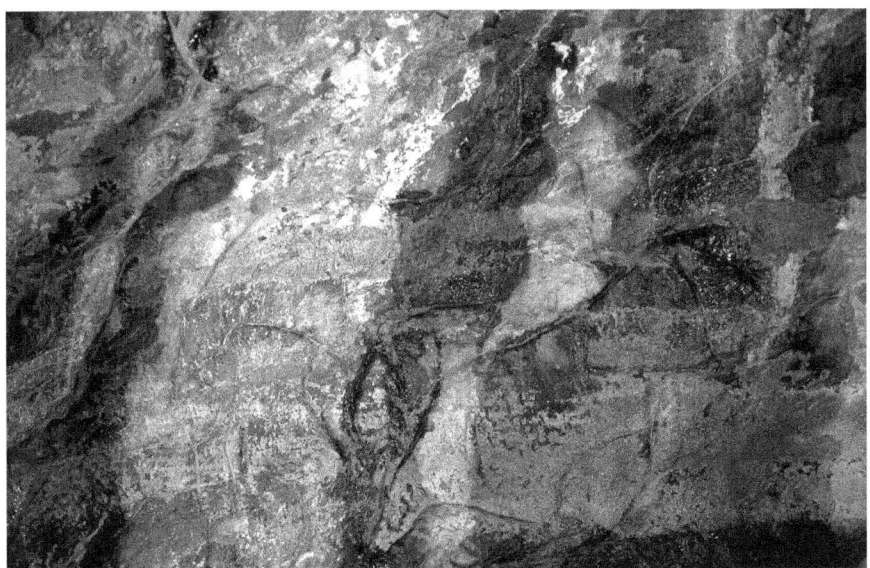
Two aurochs can be seen here, parallel to each other

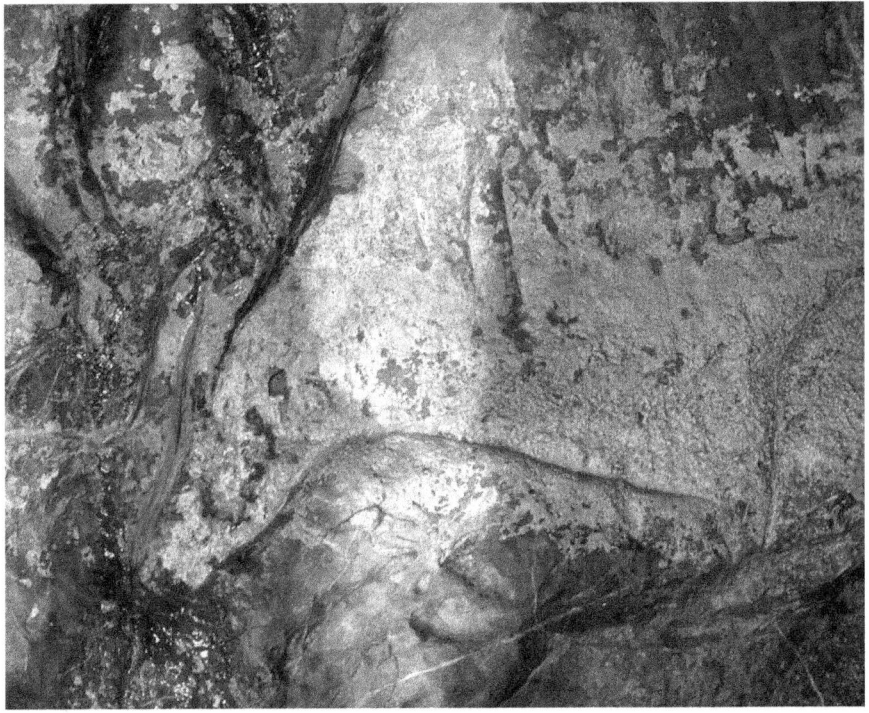
Engraved auroch

3-3. Cueva de Tito Bustillo

Cueva de Tito Bustillo is one of the five or six most important caves with Paleolithic art in the Cantabrian region, both because of the number of figures decorating its walls and for their stylistic and technical quality, and of course, for the esthetic quality of many of the figures.

The cave is located in the limestone hill of Ardines, a small hill overlooking the present-day estuary of the River Sella from its left bank. Nevertheless, during the Upper Paleolithic the coastline was further away, six or seven kilometers to the north at the time of maximum marine regression. At that time, Ardines hill controlled the natural route entering the inland Sella valley, as well as a wide, open coastal strip, which allowed easy communication between the different Cantabrian valleys, as it united them along a major East-West axis.

Ardines hill has well developed karst features, which helps to explain the large number of sites it contains with remains of Paleolithic occupation, and occasionally with cave art in the depths of the caves. This density of sites is comparable with Monte Castillo, La Garma, or other locations in the Cantabrian region that were frequently used in the Upper Paleolithic. In this way, Cueva de Tito Bustillo connects by a vertical chimney with Cueva de La Lloseta, which has its own Paleolithic habitat and a few paintings, and it must once have connected with the entrance of La Cuevona through a blocked passage at the eastern end of the "Long Gallery" . The same hill has the caves of Viesca, Pedroses and El Cierro, and slightly further away, Cova Rosa. The right-hand bank of the estuary has Cueva de San Antonio, which also has an archaeological deposit, in this case a single Paleolithic painting of a horse.

The cave we now know as Cueva de Tito Bustillo is in fact a long passage several hundred meters long, reached today through an artificial tunnel. The two original entrances are blocked by collapses of large boulders and other material. A narrower section, which forms an obstacle part way along the "Long Gallery" , and certain differences in the parietal art along the passage, have meant that two large sectors are differentiated in Tito Bustillo: the eastern and the western. Each sector had its own entrance in the Upper Paleolithic, and have an archaeological deposit.

In the Paleolithic, the eastern sector was probably accessible from the site of La Cuevona, which has a deposit of Magdalenian age. The former entrance to the western sector also has important archaeological stratigraphy, dug by Professor A. Moure Romanillo. Although the chronological interpretation of this

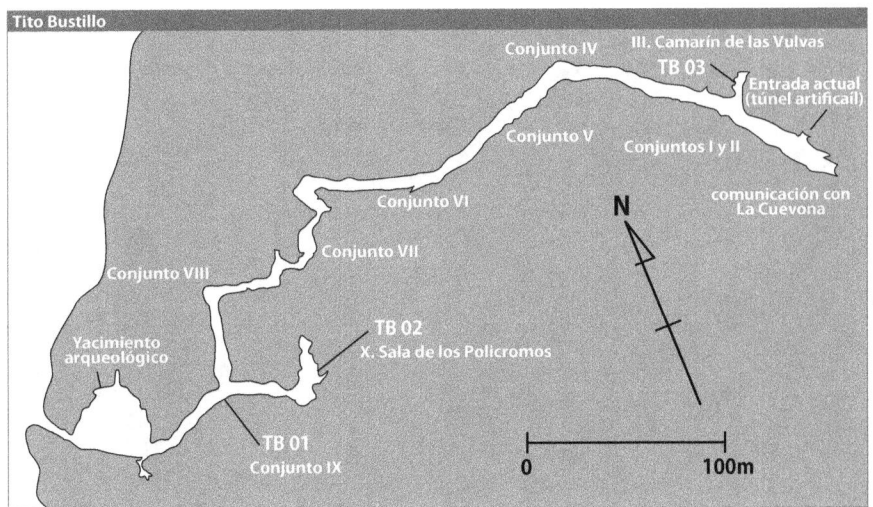

Tito Bustillo Ground Plan

site was not without its problems and discussion, there are sufficient arguments to believe that the levels excavated so far correspond to a series of occupations during the middle and late Magdalenian. The last layer (1a-b) was probably deposited about 12,700 BP, just before the cave was blocked by the collapse at its entrance. It is not impossible that the cave has levels of occupation older than the middle Magdalenian, not only because of some old dates obtained from the lowest layers, but also because the excavation has not reached the base of the deposit. In any case, the layers that are known must be synchronic with the more recent parietal art in the cave. It is also interesting that the harder organic material in the habitation deposit is extremely well preserved, so that, besides the usual hearths, lithic assemblages and remains of ungulates and shells, it has provided a magnificent collection of Magdalenian decorated artifacts, including contours découpés, spatulas, staffs, harpoons, spear-heads and plano-convex rods, as well as decorated stone plaquettes.

Regarding the cave art, the recent studies carried out by Professors R. de Balbín and A. Moure have allowed up to eleven decorated areas to be differentiated along the "Long Gallery" ; I to VII in the eastern sector and VIII to XI in the western. These often coincide with more or less narrow branches and side chambers opening along the axis of the main passage, the "Long Gallery" . These sub-groups are noticeably homogeneous internally in their techniques and styles, except for Chamber X, which has very complex panels, and as will be seen, abundant superimpositions of figures. The main groups of art will now be described following their topographical order.

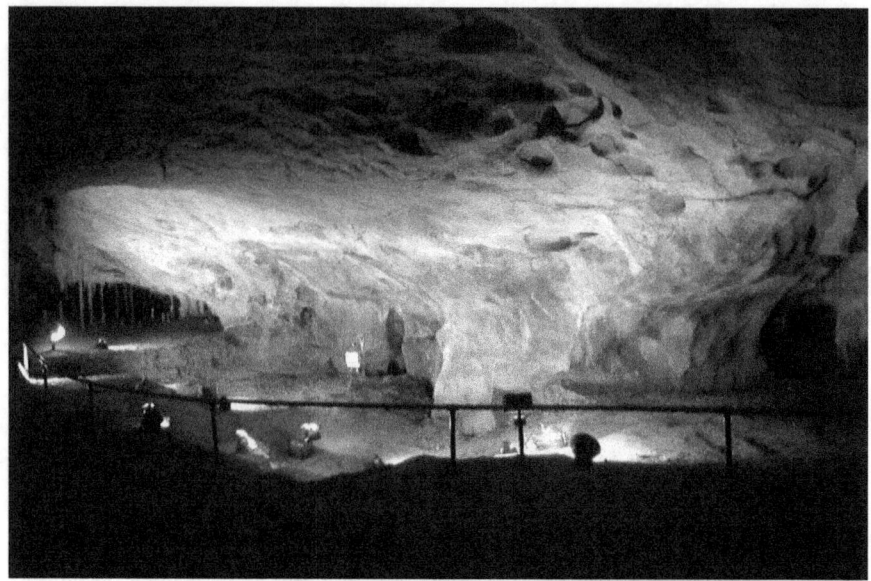

View of Sectors B, C and D of Zone X

The eastern sector. Zone I has a good group of animal engravings, especially hinds and stags, as well as a few abstract signs, whereas zone II has a group of red pairs of lines, with other marks and stains in the same color. The "Chamber of the Vulvae", or zone III, is located nearby, in a small side-chamber, some meters above the axis of "Long Gallery", and this is one of the most interesting groups in the cave. It has red paintings in the shape of vulvae, or circles and sometimes "Y" -shaped, interpreted as possibly representing feminine genitals. It also contains a headless female profile, equally in red, and large numbers of red dots. Further on, zone IV has a number of signs, such as loop-shaped signs, vertical lines and doubtful claviforms, painted in red. Zone V covers several rather disperse panels; among these the most interesting is the negative image of a left hand, in red. The next zone again contains engraved signs, with rectangular shapes. Finally, zone VII, in another side-chamber, contains the engraving of a cetacean (although this is a very rare figure in the Cantabrian region, it is not the only known representation; an even more explicit drawing exists on a pendant from the Asturian cave of Las Caldas), an ibex, a deer' s head, and other black marks.

The western sector. Four groups of art of very different size and entity have been identified here. The first, VIII, is known as the "Gallery of the Horses", and is a small side-chamber, whose access is hidden, where the Magdalenian artists drew some ten figures of horses, a large bovine, and three or four indeterminate animals, all executed in very fine engraving. This is a synchronic group in

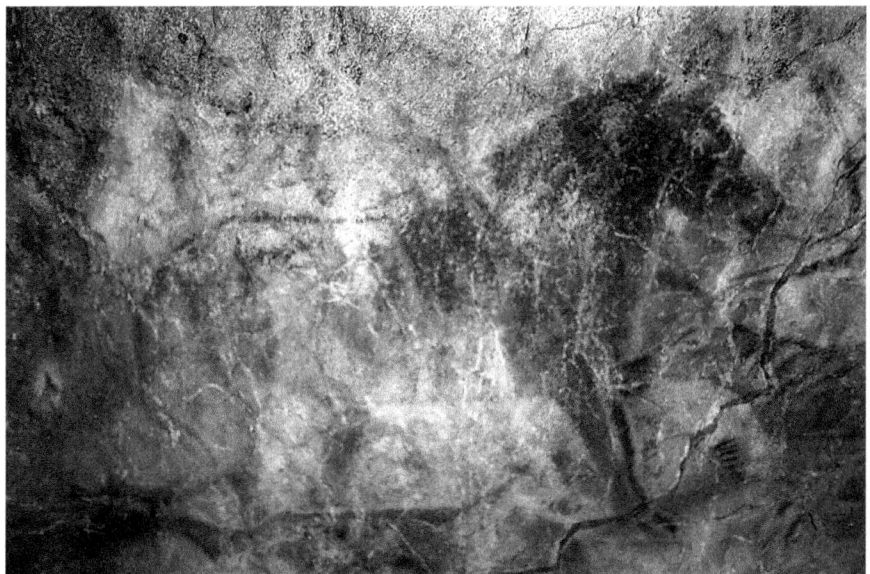

A horse facing right and the head of a reindeer facing left

Magdalenian style, with magnificent effects achieved by spreading a film of clay over the wall, and by scraping, as well as conventional engraving. In turn, zone IX only has a rectangular sign and a large horse similar to those in the main panel in Chamber X.

This Chamber X is the true center of the cave in quantity and variety of depictions, where several panels on the walls and start of the roof of this large room are decorated. A large number of animals, signs, and other less clearly defined motifs were represented, and accumulated here, during different moments of the Upper Paleolithic. In the more complex panels, Professors Balbín and Moure have been able to distinguish a sequence of up to nine phases of decoration, in which changes took place in the techniques and many of the themes represented. In summary, in these panels the different techniques applied were: red paintings, black paintings and engravings, both before and after the application of a large red stain which occupies a large part of the main panel. Among the engravings, some figures have striated lines, and other figures combine engraving with black paint. Finally, above all the previous art, large bichrome figures were painted in black and violet. These figures, representing horses and reindeer, were engraved and scraped as well as painted in the two colors. Other animals were depicted with engravings. The sequence is therefore complex, but quite similar to the one in Altamira, or to briefer sequences found in other Cantabrian caves with works of art produced at different moments of the Upper Paleolithic, such as Llonín, Candamo, Pasiega or Castillo.

3-3: Cueva de Tito Bustillo

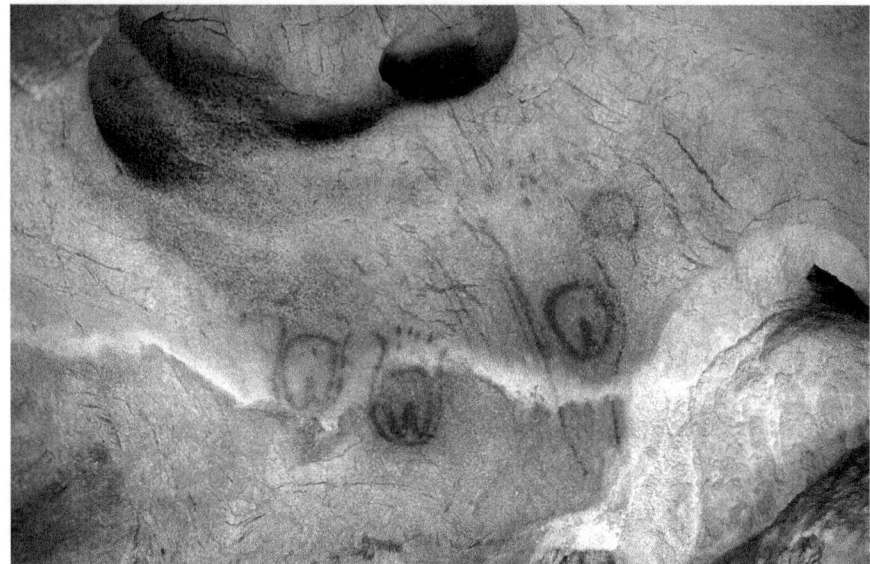

Panel of vulvae

The most interesting figures, because of their size and in some cases because of the sense of volume achieved, are those large horses, reindeer and bison produced in the latter phases of the panel. The iconographic composition, essentially based on horses and reindeer is certainly similar to the one in Cueva de Las Monedas, but very different to other, more classic sites, equally of Magdalenian age, such as Altamira, Gallery B in La Pasiega, Covaciella, Lower Passage in La Garma, Santimamiñe or Altxerri, where bison play a much more important role in the composition.

A small archaeological deposit at the foot of the main panel has been dug. This is associated with the production of the art, and was found to contain a hearth to give light, a few remains of food, or artifacts made of bone or stone, and coloring material.

Tito Bustillo is perhaps the cave with the most varied technical resources in the whole of the Cantabrian region. The wide range of techniques used, especially in Chamber X, should also be multiplied by their variable and versatile ways of application, which always tried to make the greatest use of the characteristics of the cave wall. The themes represented are unequally divided among the two sectors and different zones. The eastern sector contains fifteen animals, mostly engraved in zones I and VII. These are three aurochs, three hinds, two ibex, a stag, an indeterminate deer, a horse and a whale, and another three in-

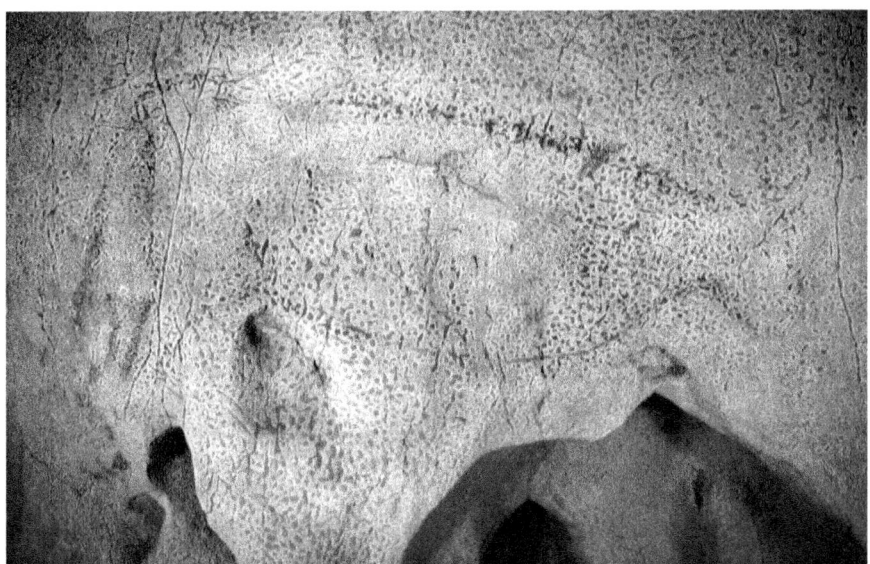
A bovine facing right, outlined in black

determinate animals. However, other types of design, more than a hundred are known, are much more abundant, especially in red paint. These include a negative hand image, a female profile, four vulvae, three circular or oval signs, up to thirteen rectangular signs of different types (mostly engraved), or simply series of dots, vertical lines or bars, loop-shaped signs, paired marks, together with numerous color stains and series of imprecise marks.

The western sector, on the other hand, is known to have as many as ninety-two animals, and those definitely identified are, at least, twenty-two horses, fourteen hinds, seven stags, five reindeer, five goats, four aurochs, two bison and six indeterminate quadrupeds. Nearly all the signs are painted in red, like ovals, series of parallel marks and stains, but they also exist in black, like a grille or in the shape of a shield, and engraved. These last signs, quadrangular in shape, are found in different zones of the cave (at least in zones I, VI and IX), and are different in form and technique from the "Cantabrian" quadrilaterals produced between the Asón and the Cares valleys, or as far as the Sella valley if we include an example in Cueva de El Buxu.

The great complexity in Tito Bustillo is reflected in a number of problems that are raised. It is not easy to decide if it should be considered as one or two art assemblages, especially taking into account that it is not necessarily a closed alternative, as the way along the Long Gallery must have been possible, but difficult, for the Paleolithic explorers. Regarding the chronology, recent studies have reasonably proposed that the last phases of decoration on the main panel, and also in the "Gallery of the Horses" were contemporary with the Upper Magdalenian habitation deposit. But at the same time they have tended to favor a "short" chronology for the rest of the main panel and for the whole cave, whose designs would have been produced between the Early, and the start of the Late, Magdalenian. They support this proposal, and its consideration as a single assemblage, on the presence of similar rectangular signs in both sectors, and the more precarious similarity in the engravings of hinds in zones X and I.

Nevertheless, we believe that there are good reasons to argue in favor of a "long" chronology for the decoration of Tito Bustillo. This could have begun long before the Magdalenian, despite the fact that the more familiar and spectacular animal figures would correspond to that period. The proportion of signs and animals is completely different in each sector, as signs predominate in the eastern sector, which is the only one with such archaic themes as negative hand images, paired marks and series of dots, all in red. The different proportion in signs and animals is repeated in the main panel in Chamber X, whose first three phases (again in red) include oval signs, series of parallel marks and other non-figurative designs, in comparison with just two animals, in a more archaic style than the later black or bichrome paintings. Phases 4 to 9, in contrast, show a greater abundance of animals, clearly belonging to Leroi-Gourhan' s Style IV. Thus the main panel in Chamber X tends to summarize in order similar contents to what is found dispersed among the different zones of the cave and in both sectors.

In coherence with the stylistic systems in use, and with the information recently obtained from other cave art assemblages being studied, we prefer a longer chronology for the two sectors of Tito Bustillo. It is clear that older figures predominate in the eastern sector, with the negative hand image, finger-marks and paired lines, groups of dots, loop-shapes, vulvae and circular signs, which could be included in Styles II, III or even early Style IV in Leroi-Gourhan' s system. As regards the western sector, phases 4 to 9 in Chamber X clearly belong to Style IV, in the Magdalenian period, but in our opinion it is probable that the earlier phases 1 to 3 are of pre-Magdalenian age. The discussion therefore suggests that the phases of human occupation and decoration of the cave ended about 12,700 or 12,500 BP. Human activity would have been particularly intense in Tito Bustillo from 15,000 or 14,500 BP, but may have continued from much earlier dates, probably before 20,000 BP in the case of the negative hand image or the paired lines in red.

References

Balbín, R, 1989. L' art de la grotte de Tito Bustillo (Ribadesella, Espagne). Une vision de synthese. L' Anthropologie 93/2, pp. 435-462.

Balbín, R; Moure, J.A., 1982. El panel principal de la cueva de Tito Bustillo (Ribadesella, Asturias). Ars Praehistorica I, pp. 47-97.

3-4. Cueva de El Buxu

This cave is situated in a limestone outcrop, in a small valley occupied by the Entrepeñas stream. This is a tributary of the River Güeña, which in turn flows into the River Sella at Cangas de Onís, a town a few kilometers away from Cueva del Buxu.

The cave was discovered by chance in December 1916 by one Cesáreo Cardín, an habitual collaborator in the archaeological digs of Hugo Obermaier and Conde de la Vega del Sella. These had asked him to visit Cueva de Las Inxanas, located in the same hill as Cueva de Buxu. C. Cardín, mistaking El Buxu for that cave, entered and found its examples of parietal art. He immediately informed Obermaier and Vega del Sella of his discovery, and they began the study of its contents, publishing their results two years later.

The cave has been modified drastically since then, mainly due to the work carried out to accommodate tourist visits. These changes not only substantially altered the aspect of the cave but also destroyed much of the its archaeological deposit.

The entrance is formed by an outer vestibule six meters wide and five meters deep, facing south-west. The original rock-shelter, however, was much larger, as is shown by the presence of numerous blocks of limestone which have collapsed from the roof, and the remains of a former floor, partially eroded away. This former rock-shelter would have faced south, situated 300 meters above present-day sea level, and 25 meters above the valley floor. Most of the archaeological deposit must have been in this outer area, and as we have mentioned it was practically destroyed by the work carried out in the cave in the 1950s.

The right-hand wall of this rock-shelter has a very low entrance (now covered over) leading to passages without any apparent archaeological interest. At the back of the rock-shelter, a hole 45 centimeters wide led into the interior of the cave. Nowadays the cave is entered through a metal gate, installed next to the original entrance. When this was discovered, it was so low that it was necessary to crawl on the floor towards the inner part of the cave. In order to make the visits easier, a trench nearly one and a half meters deep was dug in the rock-shelter and the first part of the cave passage.

The first strictly scientific archaeological dig was carried out in 1970, by E. Olávarri. As the exterior deposit had been destroyed, this excavation was

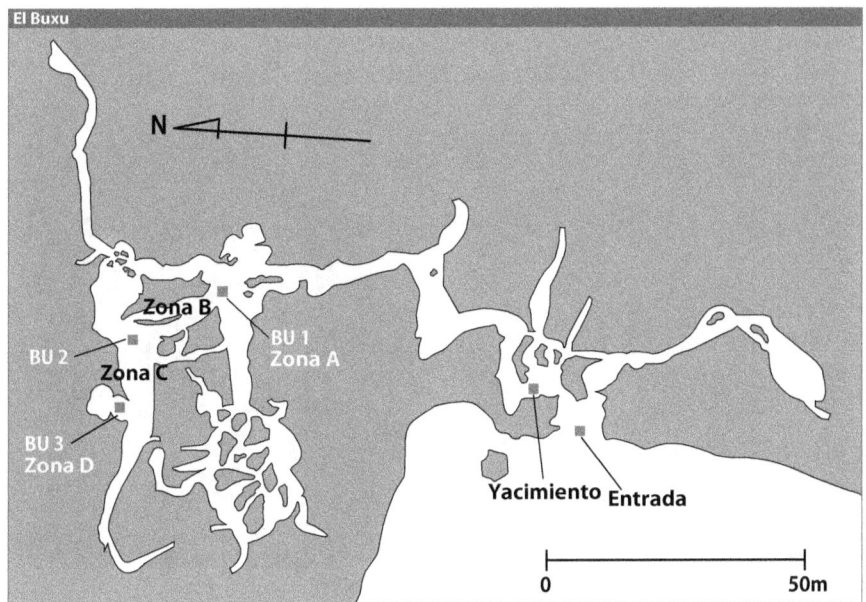

El Buxu Ground Plan

limited to several small trial digs in the first chamber of the cave. Despite being in only a marginal area of the deposit, this dig and the ones by M. Menéndez between 1986 and 1989 succeeded in finding stratigraphy which could be dated in the late Solutrean. Some of the more interesting artifacts found were two stone plaquettes decorated with engravings and, above all, the tooth of a cave bear which had been carved into the figure of a bird.

From the entrance gate, there is a distance of 60m to reach the first panel with parietal art: the so-called "Sector A" . In this area, a limestone arch marks the start of the roof of a canyon six meters long. When it was discovered, this arch was one meter above the floor. It had a complete figure of a horse (which has not been conserved), two small hinds, one painted in black and the other engraved and painted, and three stags painted in black, as well as a series of short vertical lines in the same color.

Continuing towards the end of the cave, Sector B is reached at the exit of the previous passage. This has an assemblage formed by several signs on the right-hand wall; three quadrilaterals and a ladder-shape or scaliform, all engraved. Of the three quadrilateral signs, only one is still conserved; it is a sign divided longitudinally into three bands, with short lines inside and outside. Its morphology is therefore similar to signs found in a number of caves in the center of Cantabria. On the left-hand wall, the first researchers found two magnificent engraved representations of horses which have unfortunately been destroyed by

3-4: Cueva de El Buxu

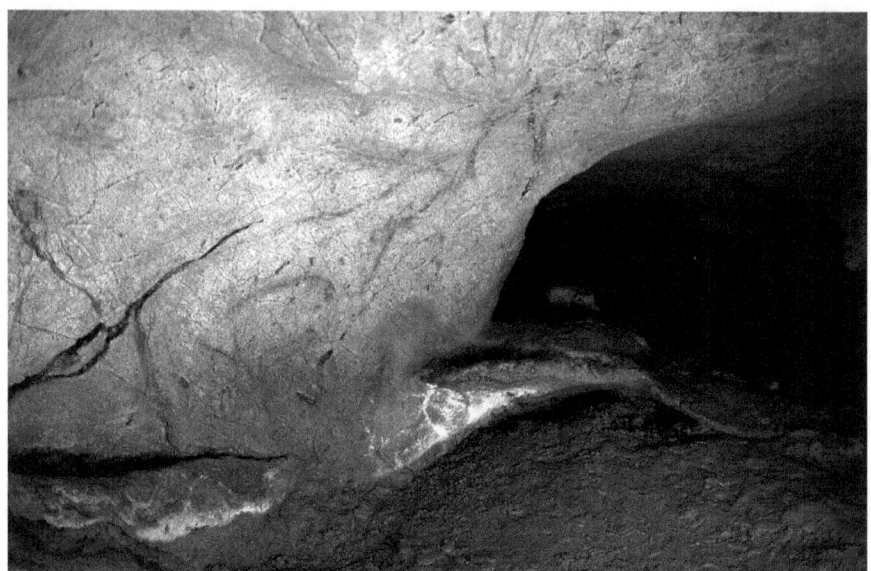

Panel with the fallow deer

modern inscriptions, and which we can only know today thanks to the photograph published in 1918.

At the end of Sector B, the passage turns ninety degrees to the left, and this is the start of Sector C. The densest panel in Cueva del Buxu is found opposite the exit from Sector B, on the right-hand wall. This is 2.3 meters wide, and has several signs and animal figures. The front third of an ibex, facing left, and painted in black is found on the far left of the panel. Another, complete, ibex was engraved on the panel's right. Between these two figures there are as many as ten quadrangular signs, all engraved, as well as a stag's antlers painted in black. Another two quadrangular signs were engraved to the right of the second ibex, and below there is an "E" -shaped sign painted in red. This is a very rare type of sign in Paleolithic art, with its only parallel in the "symbolic inscription" in Gallery B of Cueva de La Pasiega. It is equally worth mentioning that this is the only figure in the cave in which red paint was used. The right-hand wall of this passage has another three groups of engravings, which could represent the same number of animals, although the poor execution of the figures makes it impossible to identify the species.

Continuing along this passage for another seven meters, we find, on the right-hand wall, an alcove with the representations of several animal figures, both engraved and painted in black. On the left, three complete figures of horses were engraved, and a bison was represented by combining the techniques of en-

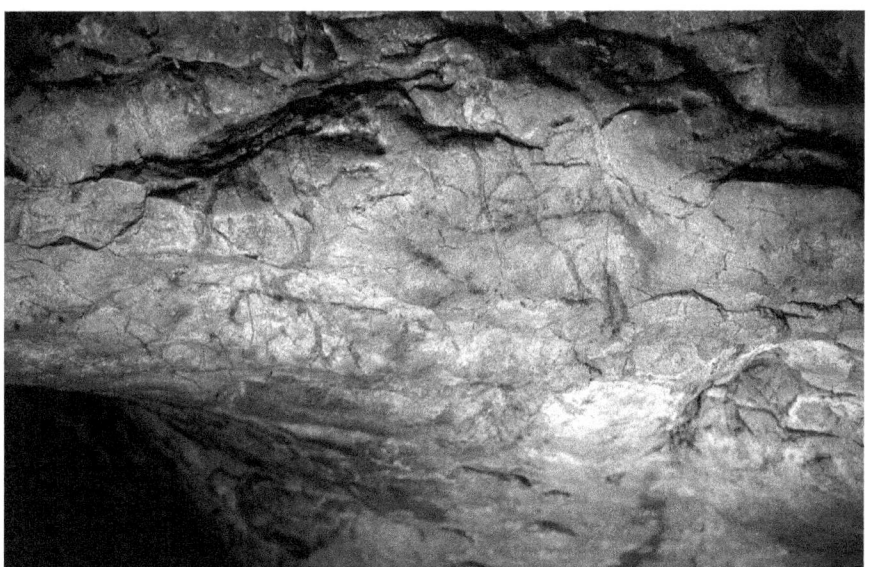

Engraved and painted stag and hind

graving and painting in black. Doubtlessly the most significant figures in El Buxu are depicted on the right. The central figure in this composition is a stag in black paint. Although the pigment is badly faded, the head, antlers, chest and back are clearly seen. The broad shape of the antlers seem to suggest this is a fallow deer, although some reticences could be made about this identification, mainly because so far no skeletal remains definitely of this species have been found in Cantabrian Upper Paleolithic sites. It must also be mentioned that the animal is depicted as roaring, with an open mouth, a slightly raised head and a swollen chest. A horse is engraved in the interior of this figure, and below it a stag is engraved and painted in black, and an ibex engraved. The largest figure in the cave is located in the upper part of this panel: the representation of a stag, engraved and painted in black. This figure has almost completely disappeared, and nowadays it is only possible to see the lower part of the front limbs. A small engraved ibex is found in the interior of this animal's body.

Opposite the alcove where the above figures are located, the left-hand wall of Sector C has an engraved figure of a horse. A few meters further on, we come to the last works of art in the cave: a black oval sign, an animal figure which may not be of Paleolithic age, the engraving of a bison and other engraved lines, some of which could form part of a quadrangular sign.

The question of the age of the cave art in El Buxu has not been settled definitively. The few cases of superimpositions in the cave suggest that the engravings were produced before the black paintings. Thus the deer's antlers are on top of an engraved quadrangular sign, and the small engraved horse is below the supposed fallow deer painted in black, and the engraved ibex is below the large stag in Sector D. In Sector C there is a small "parietal stratigraphy", where an engraved quadrangular sign was superimposed by an engraved ibex, and then by lines of black paint. These black lines could belong, however, to the first quadrangle, which would mean that the succession of figures were produced in a short period of time, and might be considered synchronic.

If criteria of stylistic dating are applied, the engraved animal figures appear somewhat older than the paintings. Thus, the horse (I) has a sinuous back, and a small head in comparison with a relatively large body. The two horses which are now lost (VI) had a mane which suggested a moment in the transition between Styles III and IV, and a failed attempt to express perspective in their limbs, besides which were represented in a very schematic way, as two lines that meet in the hoof. The same can be said of the engraved ibex (XIIg). Three engraved horses (XIII) have incorrect proportions, although in at least one of them the limbs were represented with greater realism. Finally, the recently discovered engravings, representing a bison and four unidentified quadrupeds, are represented in a very rough style, so that if they are effectively of Paleolithic age, they could correspond to an early period, perhaps the Solutrean.

Regarding the black paintings, they seem to show characteristics of a more recent period, yet not too distant from the age of the engravings. The clearest evidence lies in the superimposition over the engravings. Although some of the figures continue to show rather archaic characteristics, others seem more clearly Magdalenian, such as one of the bison (XIV). The stag (XVa) situated below the possible fallow deer shows an attempt at expressing perspective in its fore-quarters, as well as certain interior details, such as a ventral partition, and the representation of the muscles at the top of the fore-leg.

It therefore seems possible to propose that the parietal art of El Buxu was produced in two quite close periods of time. First to be done were the engravings: quadrangular signs and animal figures, which could be included in the latter phase of Leroi-Gourhan's Style III (final Solutrean or start of the Magdalenian). The black paintings, often associated with engraving, were done later, in early Style IV, in the early Magdalenian. Still unknown is the age of the E-shaped red sign, and other stains in the same color in other parts of the cave and which cannot be identified at all due to their poor state of conservation.

References

Menéndez, M. 1984: La cueva del Buxu. El arte parietal. Boletín del Instituto de Estudios Asturianos, 112: 755-801

Obermaier, H., Vega del Sella, C. de la, 1918: La cueva del Buxu. CIPP, Memoria no. 20. Madrid.

3-5 Cueva de El Pindal

Cueva de El Pindal is situated by the San Emeterio Headland, near the village of Pimiango, in the eastern limits of the Principality of Asturias. The cave entrance, facing east, has a magnificent view of cliffs hanging over the Cantabrian Sea. However, the Paleolithic artists had a very different view from this same place, as the coast line was then several kilometers further north, due to the marine regression which took place in the last glaciation.

The topography of Cueva de El Pindal is quite simple. The cave is basically a single large gallery, with no side-passages, 360m long. This tube was once a natural resurgence for a stream, and a small stream still flows in the lowest part of the cave in wet weather conditions.

The cave art was discovered by H. Alcalde del Río, one of the pioneers in the region, in April 1908, and so it was the first cave with Paleolithic art to be known in Asturias. The depictions are distributed in five parts of the cave. The first is nearly 120m from the entrance, on the left-hand wall of the passage. This is a horse's head, painted as an outline in red, and facing right. It shows certain conventions typical of Solutrean art (of between 21,000 and 16,500 BP), such as the lines indicating the limits of the mane.

Further inside the cave, about 240m from the entrance, we find a large panel nearly twenty meters long. This has about fifty figures, practically all the figures known in the cave, They are animals and abstract signs executed with a small number of technical procedures. The signs are the most homogeneous, as they are all painted in red. The animals are generally painted in the same color, but they sometimes include engraved lines, of great precision and quality in some cases. Some figures were represented solely with fine incised lines. Finally, recent research has discovered the existence of animal figures painted with yellow lines, which are now very faded, and occasionally situated below the red paintings and the engravings.

The signs take different forms. The simplest are groups of dots and short vertical lines which are usually associated with natural forms of the rock, such as hollows in the case of some groups of dots, or cornices and rock ledges, like the fingermarks situated over the figure of a hind. Several closed signs were painted on the far right of the panel. These are interpreted indistinctly as shield-shaped signs or vulvae, although morphologically related more with the latter because of their triangular shape. There is also a sign in the shape of a loop,

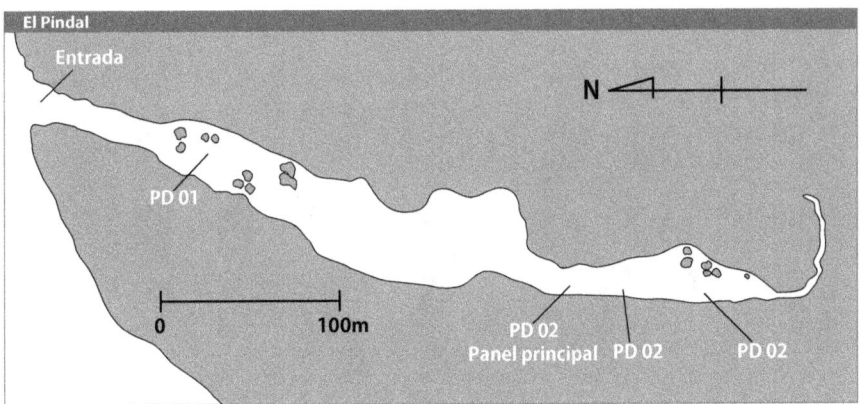

El Pindal Ground Plan

consisting of a vertical line finishing at the top in a large ring, which some researchers interpret as the head and trunk of a proboscidian. Some red marks to the right of the loop-shaped sign have recently been interpreted as the remains of the painting of a mammoth; in our opinion after reviewing this panel, this new interpretation is almost certainly correct. It is a very simple figure, outlined in red and with a high, arched belly line. Also present in this area are claviform signs: vertical lines with a protuberance to the right in the upper third of the line. A series of six of these signs is associated with some of the most important figures of bison, in the center of the panel.

The animal iconography of this large panel is dominated by the association of bison and horses, with twelve bison and five horses. In a more marginal position there are also a few deer, represented by a hind in red, and engraved antlers.

Bison therefore seem to occupy a dominant position in the composition, not only because of the number of figures, but also for technical aspects. These animals are on average larger than the horses, and besides they are depicted in the center of the panel, which makes them more visible. Neither does it seem that bison and horses were treated equally in the composition, as the former are usually represented complete, whereas only one of the horses is complete, and the others are reduced either to the head, or the head and cervical-dorsal line.

The same right-hand wall of the passage, a few meters further on, has another two panels quite close together. The first of these contains a horse' s head, a large figure of an acephalous bison, about one and a half meters long, and a fish. This last figure is one of the most characteristic in El Pindal, and was drawn with a very fine engraved line, which is superimposed on three red fin-

3-5: Cueva de El Pindal

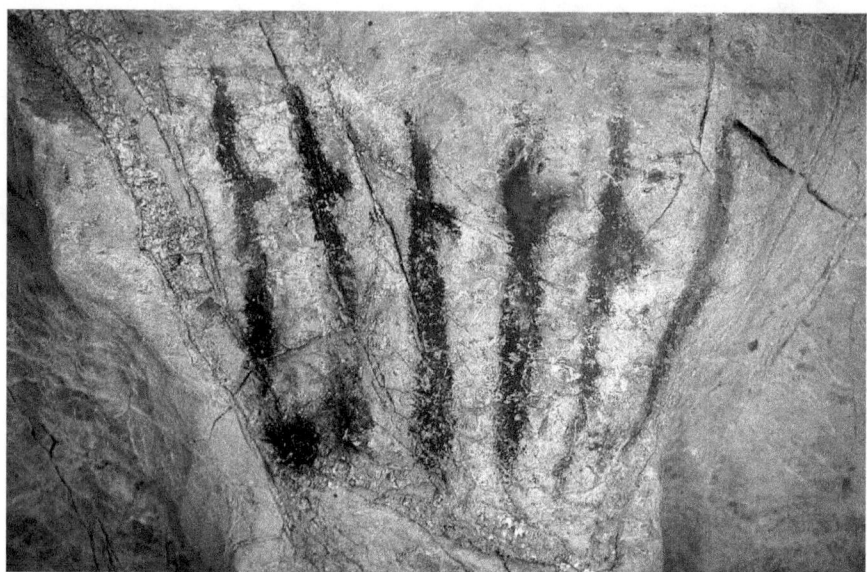
A group of six vertical red claviform signs

ger-marks, occasionally interpreted as part of the figure. The fish is represented complete, with a large concave caudal fin, two dorsal fins, and the pectoral, anal and pelvic fins. The rear dorsal fin is somewhat smaller than the front one, and could represent the characteristic adipose fin of salmonids. An eye and a longitudinal line separating the dorsal and ventral fins, of a different color and brightness, are depicted in the interior of the fish, which is not easily identified, despite the abundance of anatomical details. While the shape and size of the rear fin is characteristic of some sea fish, tunids to be precise, the rest of the fins and the general shape of the body seem to correspond to a salmonid.

El Pindal' s famous figure of a mammoth is found just a few meters on, towards the end of the cave. This is one of the few known representations of this animal in the Cantabrian region, and is depicted as a complete outline, with typical details of this extinct species, such as the convex form of the skull, the cervical depression and the short tail, but without indicating the coat. The interior of the figure has a large stain of red paint, which was once described as representing the mammoth' s heart. Despite the appeal of this interpretation, it must be totally discarded. The absence of marks depicting its coat, or the tusks, the representation of only one leg for each pair, and the pointed, arched belly, means that this mammoth can be compared with other examples in the Cantabrian region, which are in an archaic style, such as the figures in Cueva del Castillo and, above all, in Cueva del Arco B. These characteristics also appear in some early French assemblages, like Jovelle, Le Figuier, Chabot and Chauvet. Therefore,

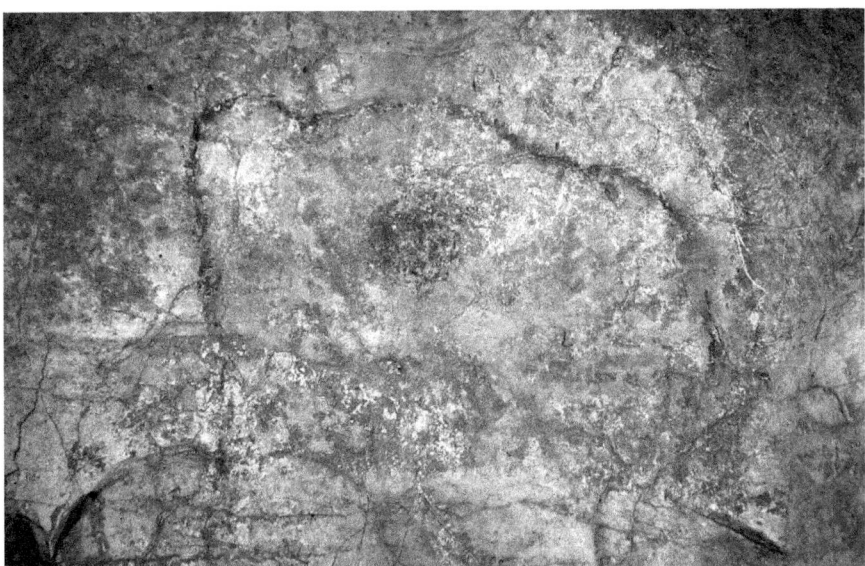

A figure of a mammoth facing left,

they seem to be stylistic conventions belonging to an early period, Solutrean or before, and not just anatomical characteristics of the animal represented, as has been suggested occasionally when identifying the figure in El Pindal as an elephant because it has not a woolly coat. Two series of parallel vertical red lines are seen near this mammoth.

The furthest panel is found 300m from the entrance, in a small chamber situated above the main passage, and which is reached by going up a small ramp. The wall and roof have black paintings of a stag, a horse' s head and another two figures which are now very faded and of which only a few lines remain. Some signs are also present: several dots, a branching shape and a sinuous line with a few transversal marks.

The assessment of the cave art in Pindal, from an iconographic point of view, seems to link it more with the caves in the eastern Cantabrian and the Pyrenees than with the much nearer caves of Asturias and Cantabria. This is shown by the abundance of bison (thirteen are represented) and horses (eight figures), the presence of rare animals like the mammoth and, above all, the fish (fish are relatively common in the caves of the eastern Cantabrian region), and the scarcity of deer, especially hinds. Among the signs, the series of late claviforms are identical to those in Cueva de La Cullalvera (in the east of Cantabria) and in several sites in the French Pyrenees, especially Fontanet

The question of the age of the art in Cueva del Pindal is rather more complicated. Several very different proposals have been made since the discovery of the cave. The first, devised by Breuil in 1911, differentiated four phases of decoration. This proposal was slightly altered by the same prehistorian in 1952, when he changed the order of some of the phases. According to this chronological scheme, the first figures to be produced were the outlines in red: the mammoth, a horse, and the signs on the left of the main panel. The second phase consisted of the figures made up of dotted lines, occasionally associated with engraved lines, and which would belong to the early Magdalenian. The black paintings formed the third phase, and the fourth corresponded to some possibly polychrome bison and the fish.

A. Leroi-Gourhan took a contrary view, considering the assemblage as synchronic, and dated it within his Style IV, corresponding to much of the Magdalenian period. He based his opinion on the presence of claviform signs, which in other caves are associated with highly realistic figures, and on the style of many of the animals.

More recent chronological proposals maintain this alternative between considering the art as corresponding to several phases throughout the Upper Paleolithic, or to a single decorative moment in the late Magdalenian. Thus, Professor Fortea suggests there were two phases of decoration. In the first some of the red figures were produced: the horse's head on the left-hand wall, and the hind and most of the signs in the main panel, particularly the vulvae and red dots and marks. The mammoth and black figures on the left-hand wall would also be included in this phase, which he attributed to Style III. Secondly, all the figures which included engraving, sometimes associated with red paint, were produced; this covers most of the bison and horses in the main panel, and the three engraved figures in the panel with the fish. Fortea placed the style of these figures in the middle or late Magdalenian, i.e. between 14,000 and 12,500 BP. In addition, Professors Balbín and Alcolea have recently published a revision of this parietal assemblage, with new reproductions, some previously unknown figures, and a significant reinterpretation of some motifs. Regarding the chronology, they follow Leroi-Gourhan's proposal that the art was relatively synchronic, and would have been produced between 14,500 and 12,000 BP, in middle and late phases of the Magdalenian.

References

Alcalde del Río, H., Breuil, H., Sierra, L. 1911: Les cavernes de la region Cantabrique. Imp. A. Chene. Monaco.

Balbín Behrmann, R. de, Alcolea González, J.J., González Pereda, M.A. 1999: Une visión nouvelle de la grotte de El Pindal, Pimiango, Ribadedeva, Asturias. L' Anthropologie 103, pp. 51-92.

Fortea,J. 1992: Pindal (El). In: El Nacimiento del Arte en Europa. Unión Latina. pp.246-248.

Jordá Cerdá, F., Berenguer Alonso, M. 1954: La cueva de El Pindal (Asturias). Nuevas aportaciones. Boletín del Instituto de Estudios Asturianos, 23, pp 3-30.

3-6. Cueva de La Loja

Cueva de La Loja is situated in the village of El Mazo, (Council of Peñamellera Baja) in the very east of Asturias, very near to the boundary with Cantabria. The cave entrance is just a few meters from the River Deva, on its left bank, in the natural gap between the coastal fringe, and the two inland valleys of the River Cares, coming from the south of Sierra del Cuera, and the River Deva, descending from the mountains of Picos de Europa. The cave is now only ten kilometers from the coast, but it must have been further away when the prehistoric engravings were executed, due to marine regression in the last glaciation.

As in the case of many caves with prehistoric artifacts, Cueva de La Loja was already known to the villagers when, on August 23rd 1908, H. Alcalde del Río, H. Breuil and L. Mengaud discovered the Paleolithic engravings and paintings. After the discovery, the parietal art was studied in a brief season of fieldwork, and the results were published three years later in Les cavernes de la region cantabrique. This included studies made in another sixteen Cantabrian caves with Paleolithic cave art, and was the first synthesis of Paleolithic Art in the North of Spain. Since then, Cueva de La Loja has been referred to in numerous books on history of art, and in works summarizing certain aspects of Paleolithic art, such as chronology, animal iconography or signs.

In recent decades a few details and comments have been added to the study carried out in 1911. One of these was published in 1978, by J. M. Gómez Tabanera, who revised the art and proposed new interpretations of two of the figures.

Cueva de La Loja is formed in Carboniferous limestone. The entrance faces east, and leads to an almost straight main passage, 98m long. It has just one side-passage, on the right-hand side of the main gallery, 28m from the entrance, and this is a narrow rift which returns to the surface. The last part of the cave has two siphons, on the left-hand side of the passage, 76m and 90m from the entrance. The cave floor used to be formed by a layer of clay. Recently this has been covered with gravel in order to accommodate tourist visits, but the original floor can still be seen in areas near the walls, and beneath low rock overhangs in the wall.

The natural conditions for habitation in the cave are not too good, and even today the cave sometimes acts as a resurgence. So it could not have been very suitable as a shelter for long periods in the Paleolithic. The rather limited ar-

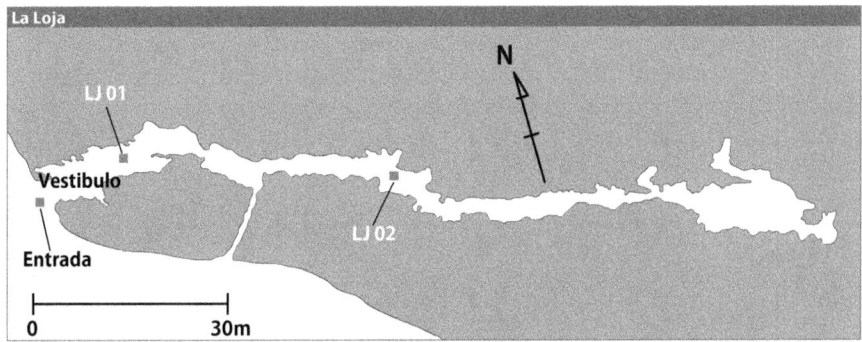
La Loja Ground Plan

chaeological digs that have been carried out seem to prove this. First, the material on the cave floor was gathered up by H. Alcalde del Río and J. Carballo at the start of the century. In 1929, Conde de la Vega del Sella made a dig that detected a level with Magdalenian artifacts. The last work was carried out by Gómez Tabanera in 1977, and by studying the material recovered in all the excavations during the century, he proposed a date for the occupation in the middle and late Magdalenian (i.e. between 14,000 and 11,500 BP).

The cave art of Cueva de La Loja is distributed in two panels. The first is under a cornice on the right-hand wall of the entrance vestibule, a few meters from the exterior. This consists of a few remains of red paint, which already in 1908 were in a poor state of conservation, and which might be part of a ladder-shaped sign or scaliform, made up of several short parallel lines. The fact that this appears in the first part of the cave, within daylight, is not such an exceptional circumstance in Cantabrian Paleolithic art as was once thought. Instead, what is really unusual is the conservation of paint in these conditions, here just three meters from the entrance. The evidence of La Haza, and La Pasiega C and B, among other sites, shows clearly enough that groups of cave art were painted in exterior areas. Another interesting point, and one which fits in well with our knowledge of abstract signs in the Cantabrian region, is that this sign was scarcely visible, hidden below the cornice. Signs in the form of ladders are found in somewhat similar positions in the caves of Altamira and El Covarón, among other sites.

The second panel is located 44m from the entrance, on the right-hand wall, and 4.3m above the cave floor. To produce these figures the artist needed to climb to the top of a stalagmitic flowstone, where it is frankly quite difficult to keep one's balance. This panel consists of six animal figures, engraved with very fine lines, and all facing the end of the cave. The question of exactly what animals are represented in La Loja has been the subject of debate among prehistorians. Four of the figures can be identified without difficulty, as they evidently

3-6: Cueva de La Loja

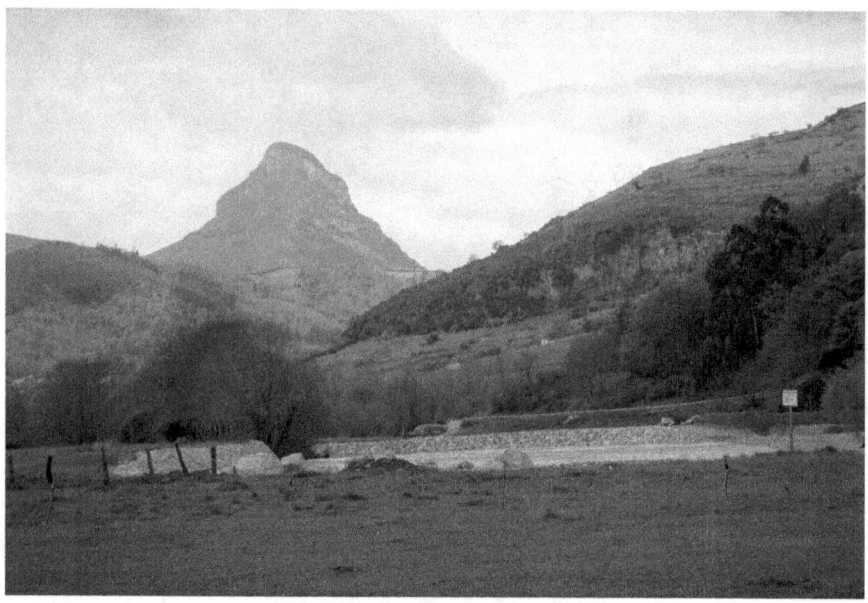

View from the entrance of La Loja

represent aurochs. Three different ways were used to draw the horns, all of them rather conventional: two figures have horns in correct perspective, while a third figure has horns seen from the front, in the shape of a lyre. The fourth figure, the least complete in the panel, has a less common way of representing horns; as a kind of arch around the head.

The other two figures, in the top left and top right, have been classified in different ways. In the first study of the cave, H. Alcalde del Río, H. Breuil and L. Sierra interpreted five of the figures as bovines, and classed the figure on the right as a carnivore, possibly a wolf. In 1952, H. Breuil corrects his first interpretation, and refers to four cows and a calf, and fails to mention the figure on the left. In 1965, Leroi-Gourhan only mentions the four clearest figures, which he classes as bovines, and avoids the two more controversial depictions. Later, Gómez Tabanera classified the two figures in the corners as horses. In more recent publications, it has been proposed that this is a scene, with a herd of six aurochs facing in the same direction, and as such this is one of the few scenes that can be taken as a narrative in the whole of Cantabrian cave art.

These figures were drawn with the technique of fine engraving. Despite this, and the considerable height of the panel above the cave floor, the animals are clearly visible due to the blackish color of the wall, with which the engraved lines contrast noticeably. This dark color of the wall seems to be the result of nat-

3-6: Cueva de La Loja

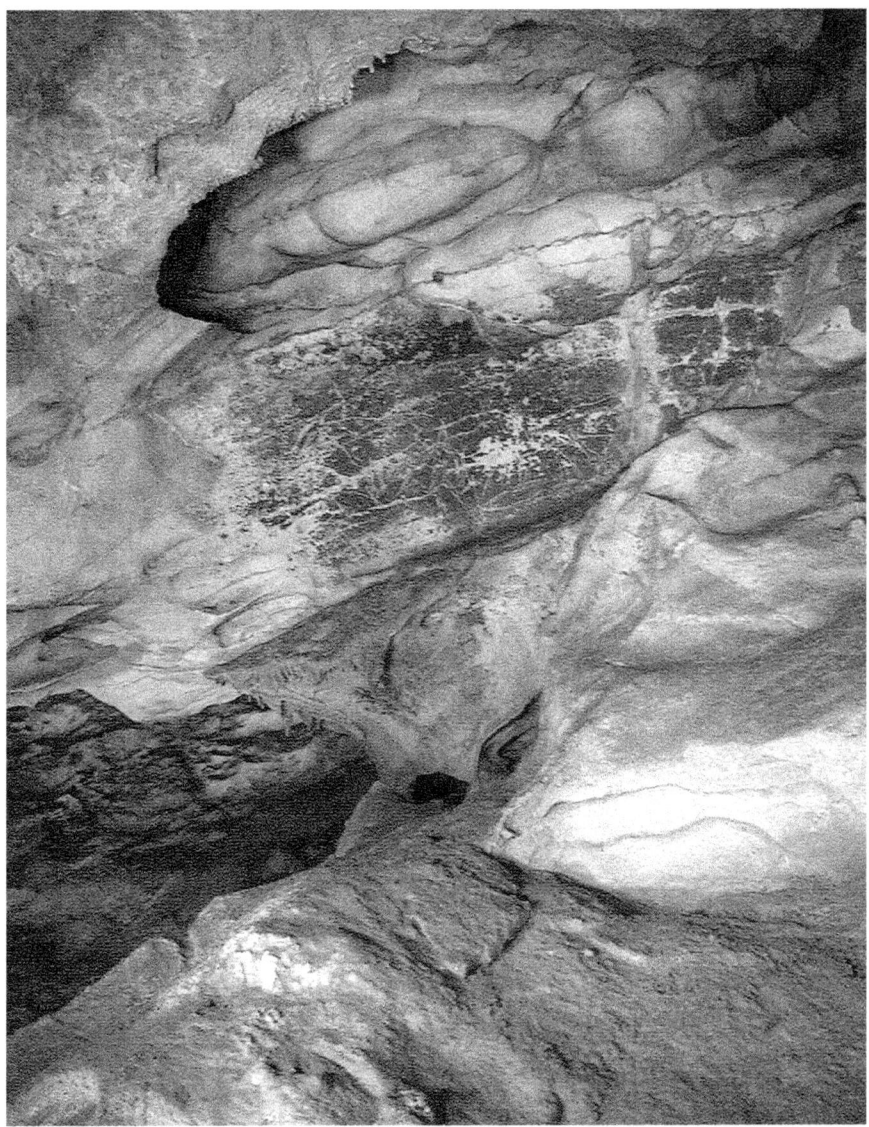

Black wall with engravings of a herd of auroch

ural processes of sedimentation, as it is found in other parts of the cave, in relation with rock overhangs and the edges of hollows in high areas of the passage.

    The group of animals, drawn with great realism, has the characteristics of a late style. The profusion of details in the heads, the full representation of the limbs, including hoofs, and their configuration in two different planes, all allow the

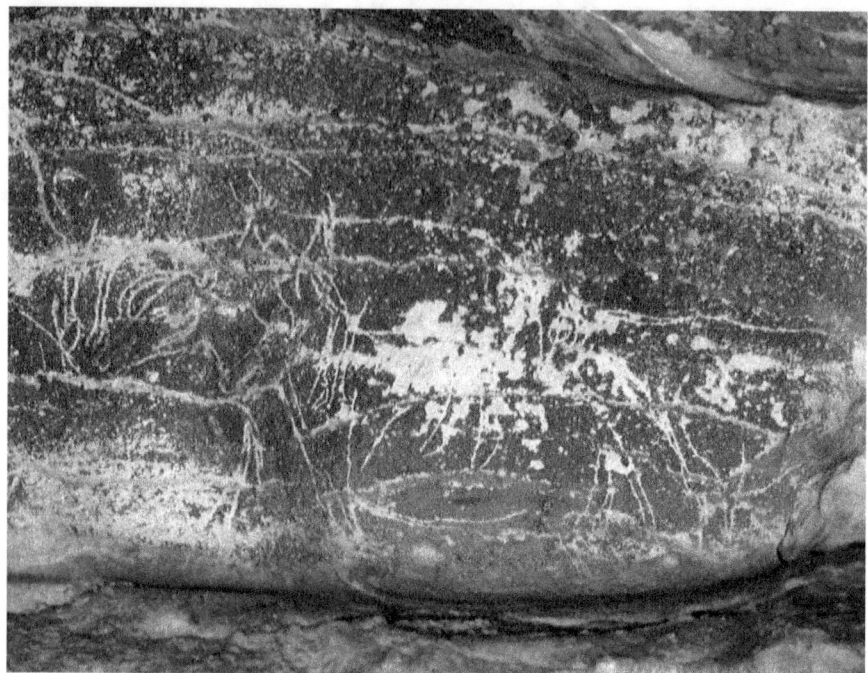

View of the center and right of the panel of engravings

figures to be included chronologically in Leroi-Gourhan's Style IV, and quite likely in a later moment of that style.

References

Alcalde del Río, H., Breuil, H., Sierra, L. 1911: Les cavernes de la region cantabrique. Imp. A. Chene. Monaco.

González Echegaray, J., González Sainz, C. 1994: Conjuntos rupestres paleolíticos de la Cornisa Cantábrica. Complutum, 5, pp. 21-43.

Gómez Tabanera, J. M. 1978: Para una revisión del arte rupestre de la cueva de La Loja. Boletín del Instituto de Estudios Asturianos, 93-94, pp 385-449.

Chapter 4
The End of the Cantabrian Corridor.
Paleolithic Art assemblages in the Basque Country

1. Introduction

The coast of the Basque Country, at the eastern end of the Cantabrian region, had certain special characteristics during the Upper Paleolithic (c. 38,000 - 11,000 BP), which need to be described, but it must be understood that they are still within the overall geographical, ecological and cultural unity shown throughout this natural corridor in the north of the Iberian Peninsula: the Cantabrian region, between the high mountains and the sea. One peculiarity is that the geological structure and the lithology of the Basque Country is somewhat different. In contrast with the western part of the Cantabrian region, in the Basque Country the predominant rocks are Mesozoic, with younger and softer limestone types. After the last major uplift of landmasses in the Tertiary period, the result was a very high-energy relief, divided and disarticulated. The landscape is even more broken on the coast, where the coastal plains are much narrower than in the center and west of the Cantabrian, and this is particularly true in Guipúzcoa, the province in the east of the Basque Country.

These differences in relief are linked with variations in the relative frequency of some of the ungulate species which were fundamental for Paleolithic subsistence. Consequently, caprids, both chamois and ibex, were hunted and consumed more often in the Basque Country sites. Especially in Guipúzcoa we find Upper Paleolithic habitats with high frequencies of caprid hunting very near to the present day coast line, such as Cueva de Ermittia and certain layers in Cueva de Ekain. They are of course also found in inland areas, in the caves of Erralla or Aitzbitarte, or Silibranka and Bolinkoba in the province of Vizcaya. In contrast, in the western part of the Cantabrian region high frequencies of ibex and chamois are only found in sites in the steep, rocky valleys of the interior, whereas red deer, horse and bovines are more important in sites in the coastal strip, with a more open, undulating landscape. This difference in the fauna documented in habitation sites is reflected to a certain extent, depending on the existence of other factors, in the themes depicted in mobiliary and cave art.

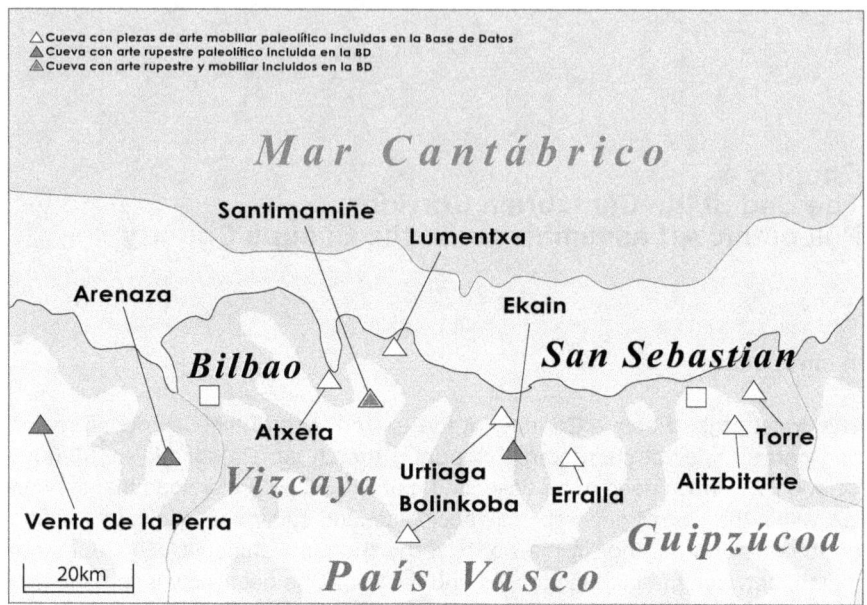

Palaeolithic caves in Basque Country

In the same way, lithological differences along the Cantabrian corridor are also the cause for variations in the prehistoric lithic assemblages. Flint is most common in the east, where it is associated with Cretaceous limestone, in comparison with the quartzite linked to the Paleozoic rocks in the west. This allowed a greater choice in the quality of the raw material, and higher frequencies of blade tools in the lithic assemblages of all the Upper Paleolithic periods in the Basque Country. Indirectly, this explains the higher frequencies of those tools especially associated with blades, such as burins, truncated pieces or straight backed points.

The geographical location of the Basque Country, situated between the rest of the Cantabrian region, the Dordogne in France, and the northern Pyrenees, all of which were densely populated, explains further differences it had, of a purely stylistic nature, with other areas in the Cantabrian. These are seen in the manufacture and decoration of certain tools, such as the antler harpoons of between 14,000 and 11,500 BP, or the hunting points with flat retouch produced between 21,000 and 17,000 BP, in the themes depicted in parietal art, or in certain conventions of decoration, to be described later. This same situation of the Basque Country, the ante-chamber of the Cantabrian region, also explains the greater presence of some of the animal species that were hunted and which correspond to a colder, drier, continental climate, as these penetrated into the peninsula from Europe at certain times of the year during long periods of the Upper

Pleistocene. For example, reindeer, which in general were rarely hunted in most of the Cantabrian region, are found rather more often in the Basque Country, during the Magdalenian, especially between 14,000 and 11,800 BP. In the same way, the only known example of saiga antelope in the Iberian Peninsula was recovered in the cave of Abauntz, in Navarra, on the natural route from the western Pyrenees to the Ebro Valley.

2. Distribution of caves with art

The Basque Country has a quite small number of caves with Upper Paleolithic cave art, and just seven sites are known. The density of decorated caves is therefore much lower than in Cantabria, or in the center and east of Asturias. However, the proportion of Upper Paleolithic habitation caves seems to be similar to that in the other parts of the Cantabrian region, or at least there is not such an obvious difference as there is in the number of caves with art. Furthermore, the archaeological deposits in the Basque Country have given important collections of mobiliary art, in caves like Bolinkoba, Santimamiñe, Lumentxa, Ekain, Urtiaga or Aitzbitarte IV, which seem similar to the ones from central and western parts of the region. Consequently, it is not possible to explain this lower density of parietal decoration as the result of any specific behavior in symbolic matters in this area, different not only from the rest of the Cantabrian region, but also from the areas of France to the north of the Pyrenees. Indeed, such a possibility is difficult to imagine in the open, mobile, societies of hunters. It appears, therefore, that the difference is due to a problem in the exploration of cave art, which has probably been less intense here, and to the lack of teams with the tradition, or certain specific skill, at locating engravings and remains of paint which may be very difficult to see.

3. Research.

The above comments are based on our viewpoint about partially different research traditions, even within the same Cantabrian region. The discovery of Paleolithic art received a great impetus in the center of the region at the start of the 20th Century. In this way, cave art caught the public' s imagination and acquired an important level of prestige. Because of this, since the 1940s and 50s, "Archaeology" and "Speleology" have been strongly linked, and developed together by youth groups of all kinds. This situation, supported scientifically by J. Carballo, an influential prehistorian in Santander, has caused important problems, but has had the advantage of the discovery of a large number of caves with art. In the Basque Country, on the other hand, archaeological prospecting has been linked much less with speleology, and more with mountaineering. As a result, there is greater tradition of exploring mountain areas, especially in search of megalithic monuments, or cave entrances and surface deposits, but it has been less customary to

Chapter 4 : Paleolithic Art assemblages in the Basque Country

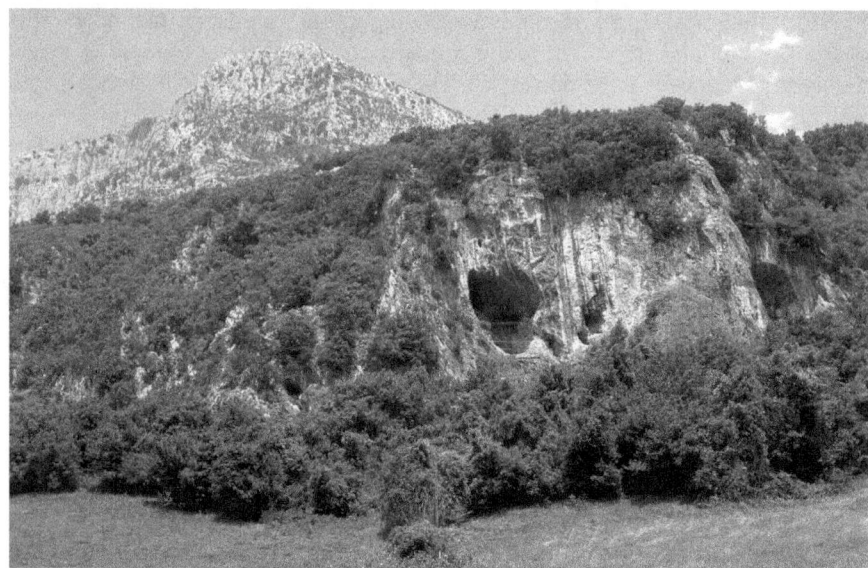

Entrance of Venta de La Perra cave

prospect inside the caves.

This is also related with the reigning idea of Prehistory as a way of seeking and documenting the origins of Basque traditional culture, which was a perspective led by J. M. de Barandiaran, the most important and influential Basque researcher in ethnography and archaeology until about twenty years ago. This search for connections found certain support in physical anthropology and above all studying the material culture of the builders of the megaliths and later societies, which were the aspects that received most effort in prospecting. The interior of Paleolithic caves were studied less, although J. M. Barandiaran suggested on several occasions that there was no break between the artistic-religious paintings of Paleolithic groups in SW Europe and the images of traditional Basque mythology, which he wanted to convert into the heir of Upper Paleolithic society. It is interesting to compare how these kinds of reasons explain how in the center of the Cantabrian region, in Cantabria, very few megalithic monuments were discovered until the 1980s, seventy years behind its neighboring communities of Asturias and the Basque Country, and then in certain cases by amateur archaeologists who thought they had discovered the homes of the ancient Cantabrians.

Our impression is that the differences in the orientation of research, and in the interest of the youth groups and amateur prospectors, is the main reason for the low number of cave art sites that have been discovered in the Basque Country. The most spectacular and noticeable sites seem to have been located,

Chapter 4 : Paleolithic Art assemblages in the Basque Country

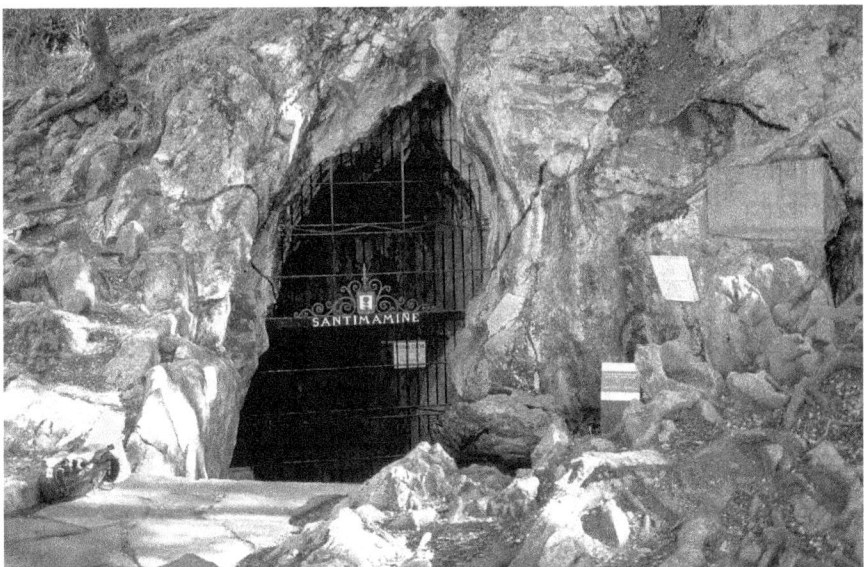
Entrance of Santimamiñe Cave

above all in Guipúzcoa, where the only two known caves are of an exceptional quality In contrast, the smaller caves, with just a few, faded paintings, or engravings, or dots, have not been located yet, but we hope they may start to appear in the next few years.

Research in cave art has therefore been somewhat less intense than in the other parts of the Cantabrian region, where it began earlier. The work carried out in the first decades in the center of the region included the exterior group of engravings at Venta de La Perra, situated on the western boundary of the Basque Country, and the cave was in the 1911 publication. In the same way, the only known cave with art in Navarra, Cueva de Alkerdi, was published in the early 1920s by N. Casteret, a French explorer of caves. But by this time, local research had an important team working in the field, and they had made their first major discovery, Cueva de Santimamiñe, whose parietal art was published by T. Aranzadi, J. M. Barandiaran and E. Eguren in 1925.

After the Spanish Civil War, and the difficult post-war period, archaeological research began to recover in the 1960s. At that time, the two caves in Guipúzcoa were discovered and studied, Cueva de Altxerri and Ekain. They were published by J. M. Barandiaran, in one case jointly with J. Altuna, following the methodological and interpretive line of H. Breuil. It was precisely Don José Miguel de Barandiaran' s students, J. M. Apellániz and J. Altuna, who brought out fuller, more modern studies of these caves in the 1970s. In their publications they gave

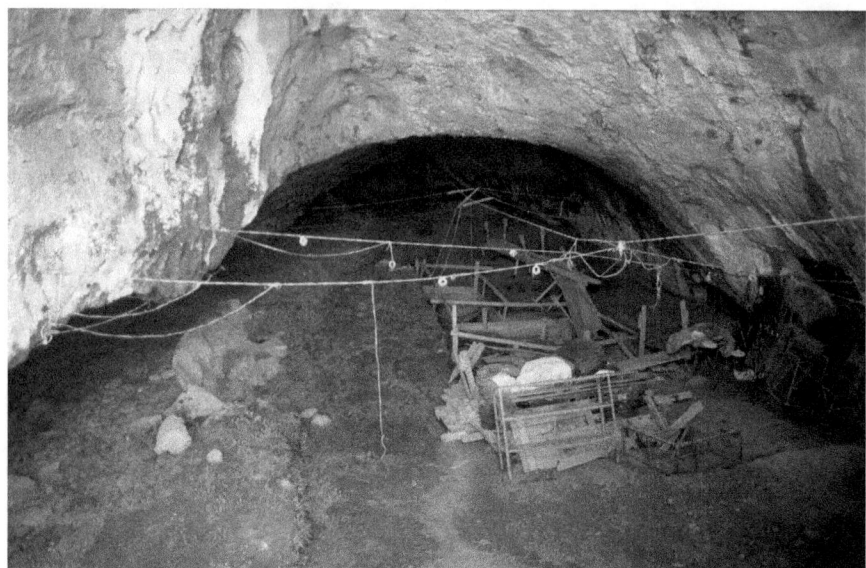

Entrance of Cueva de la Arenaza

special attention to their own interests: respectively, analysis of form and author, and comparison between the species depicted and Pleistocene fauna. Another of his students, I. Barandiaran, published in the early 1970s a new study of Alkerdi, and above all an important catalogue and evaluation of Paleolithic mobiliary art in the whole of the Cantabrian region. As happened in the rest of the region, and in this decade, these studies mentioned above referred to Leroi-Gourhan' s proposals almost exclusively as regards to chronology, comparing it with Breuil' s scheme, which was not abandoned altogether.

In the last twenty years, research in cave art appears to have slowed down, at least in comparison with several splendid studies on habitats and material culture of the Paleolithic groups. The most important publications have been the analysis of variation in forms and methods of determining the author developed by J. M. Apellániz, and the studies of mobiliary art, and synthesis of Paleolithic art in the Basque Country, by I. Barandiaran.

4. Artistic centers.

All the Paleolithic cave art known in the Basque Country and Navarra is located in caves on the coastal side of the mountain chains. Nevertheless, a magnificent collection of Magdalenian mobiliary art was found in Cueva de Abauntz, in Navarra, in a tributary valley of the River Ebro. Thus it is not impossible that cave art could be found in the southern part of the Basque Country, corresponding to the

Chapter 4 : Paleolithic Art assemblages in the Basque Country

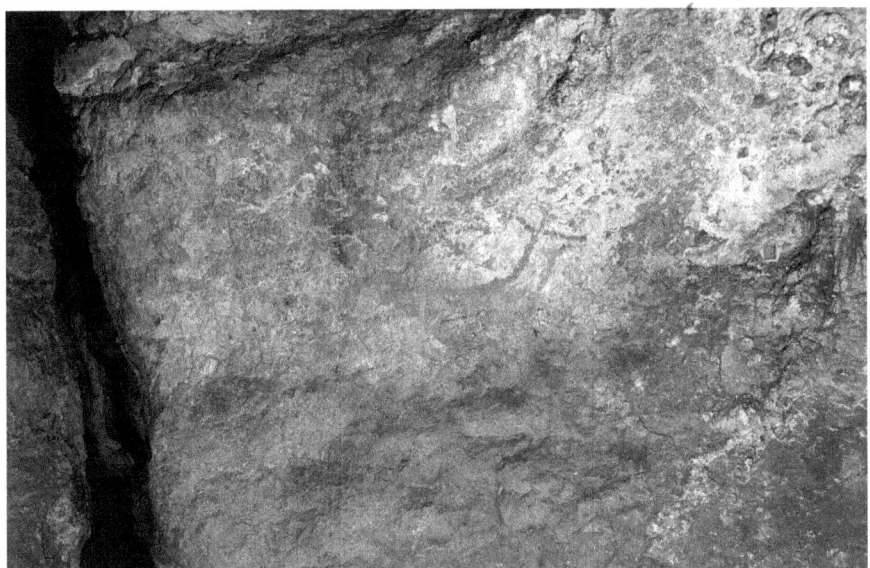

Hinds painted with red dotted lines

Ebro Valley, as in fact happens in surrounding areas, either in Burgos (Cueva de Penches and Ojo Guareña) or in Huesca (Cueva de la Fuente del Trucho).

The few known caves are distributed along the coastal flank of the mountain chain, without forming the clusters we have seen in the center and west of the region. Only the cave in the west, Venta de la Perra, in the gorge of the River Carranza, is by another five caves with art, all together in the narrowest part of the natural gap, of enormous strategic value. These are the caves of Sotarriza, El Morro, Pondra, Arco A and Arco B-C, all across the provincial boundary in Cantabria. Further west, we find Cueva de Arenaza, with an important group of figures, painted with red dots. The most spectacular site in Vizcaya, because of the large number of black paintings and engravings it contains, is without doubt Cueva de Santimamiñe, on the Guernica Estuary. It is apparently a more or less synchronic group of paintings, of Magdalenian age. Also in Vizcaya, we have groups of depictions rather more doubtfully of Paleolithic chronology in Cueva de Goikolau, near the coast in the east of the province, and Cueva de Atxuri further inland. The latter cave, which has the painting of the belly and limbs of an animal in red, also had, like Goikolau, a habitation deposit with layers of Upper Paleolithic and later ages.

As mentioned above, only two caves are known in Guipúzcoa: Cueva de Ekain and Cueva de Altxerri, which are zealously and perfectly conserved by the members of the Aranzadi Science Society at San Sebastián. The former, a

Chapter 4 : Paleolithic Art assemblages in the Basque Country

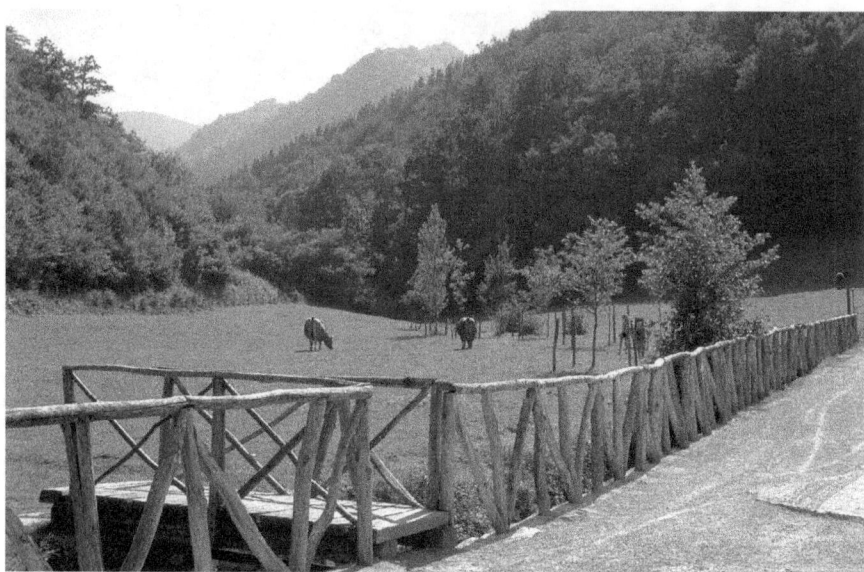

Pasture at the foot of Ekain Montain

Magdalenian site, has bichrome and polychrome paintings of horses, some of which are of exceptionally high artistic quality. These animals are accompanied by a few bison, deer, goats, and other less common species in cave art like fish and bears.

Altxerri is located in the lower valley of the River Oria, very near the present coastline. It is, like Ekain, one of the best groups of cave art in the Cantabrian region, and together with Santimamiñe, Covaciella and Cueva de Urdiales, one of the main examples of the "Pyrenean" style, and thematic structure, in the region. It is worthy of a fuller description. The cave has over ninety animal figures, mostly engravings done with various techniques, which are occasionally quite complex and include different ways of scraping clay surfaces. Black paint was used in association with some of the engravings, and other times independently, in the central and most visible panels in the cave. An upper gallery of quite difficult access has a panel with remains of several red figures, principally a large bison. Bison is the most common animal represented in the cave, but there other animals such as reindeer, red deer, ibex, horse and auroch. But, even more surprising than the beauty of some of these figures, is the appearance of such unusual themes as fish, including two examples of flat-fish, hare, fox, a bird, an anthropomorph, and an imaginary animal. It has also been proposed, although with doubts that are difficult to resolve, that the figures also include two saiga antelopes and a glutton.

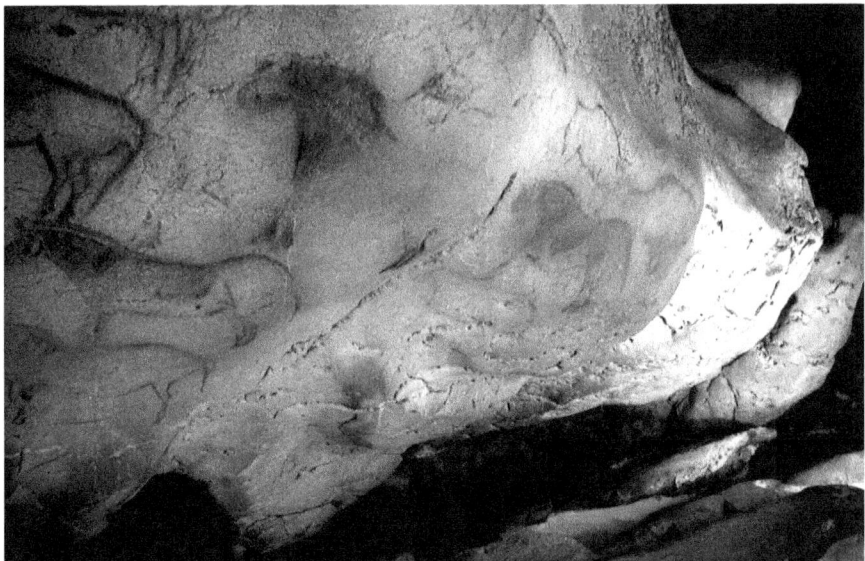
Large panel of horses and bison

The paintings and engravings in Altxerri are quite homogeneous, and their naturalistic style, their technique and the conventions used correspond to Style IV, in the Middle or Late Magdalenian. The cave is rather difficult to explore, and the panels could easily be damaged by non-qualified visitors.

Finally, in the Atlantic zone of the province of Navarra, we find Cueva de Alkerdi, in Urdax, which is a kind of connection between the Cantabrian region and the Pyrenees. Alkerdi is a very small cave, situated next to the site of Berroberría, which has an important habitation deposit with several Magdalenian strata, as well as Azilian and more modern layers. It has a small group of engravings, including the rear-quarters of a horse, a bison, a stag, and the remains of other unidentified motifs. A second panel has the profile of a horse' s head, and another head which may represent a wolf. All these figures are attributed to the phases of Magdalenian III-IV.

5. Summary

To summarize some of the points mentioned above, the eastern part of the Cantabrian region has a lower density of caves with art, which do not form clusters of sites. The lower density may be partly due to the prospecting carried out, which has been focused on the most spectacular and visible assemblages. The caves known to date are more or less synchronic internally, and none of them contain large accumulations of figures produced in different moments of the Upper Paleolithic. These major centers, occupied repeatedly and in different periods, are relatively common in the western half of the region, in caves like La Peña de Candamo, Tito Bustillo, Llonín, Altamira, Pasiega, Castillo and La Garma, but none have been found east of the Miera Valley.

Chronologically speaking, nearly all the caves can be attributed to quite late phases, in the Magdalenian. The only exceptions, the oldest caves, are those in the west of the Basque Country: Venta de la Perra and Arenaza. The daylight engravings in the first cave are usually situated in the Gravettian or early Solutrean periods, i.e. between 27,000 and 21,000 BP. Cueva de Arenaza corresponds to a slightly later time, and clearly belongs within Leroi-Gourhan' s Style III, together with the other caves in the center of the Cantabrian region where red dotted lines are common, often to paint hinds or other animals, which are frequently arranged in pairs. This group of caves is formed basically by Pasiega A and C, Pendo, Garma, Covalanas and Haza, Arco A, Arco B-C and Pondra. Other, more doubtful caves of this kind are Llonín and Trescalabres, Meaza, Castillo and Salitre.

The Magdalenian period (16,500 to 11,500 BP), and Leroi-Gourhan' s Style IV, are much better represented in the Basque Country. The caves of Alkerdi, Santimamiñe, Ekain and Altxerri certainly correspond to this period, as their style and technique show. Nevertheless, it could be quite complicated to date each of these caves with greater precision, based on the style of their figures or the iconographic composition.

Because of their geographical position, in the middle of the densely populated areas of SW France, and the center and west of the Cantabrian region, the caves of the Basque Country show fewer of the stylistic characters which are considered more typically "Cantabrian" . Furthermore, as the cordillera is less high here, there was greater contact between the coastal strip and the interior of the peninsula, such as the Ebro Valley. Because of this, the "Cantabrian" characteristics became more diffuse. For example, conventionalized signs are much rarer here, in comparison with their abundance in the rest of the region, where the different kinds of quadrilateral and divided oval signs are especially characteristic. In the same way, the thematic distribution of animals is quite peculiar, at least in the case of the complementary animals. Except in Arenaza, hinds and even stags are quite rare, compared with other parts of the Cantabrian region. Basque caves are polarized much more in the depiction of bison and horses, accompanied by ibex, and have higher frequencies of unusual species such as reindeer, fish, bears and foxes. This characteristic is partly the result of their more recent chronology, in the Magdalenian period, when these animals tend to become more common in all regions.

In the same way, the caves of the Basque Country have certain Magdalenian conventions of representation, specific to areas of the western Pyrenees and the east of the Cantabrian region. One example is the depiction of horses with a prominent, large rump (hypertrophy). This is very clear in a number of horses in Ekain, and even in the horse occupying the center of the main composition in Santimamiñe. Further to the east, this convention is known in caves to the north of the Pyrenees, like Sinhikole and Etxeberri, and also in some of the horses in Niaux, in the region of Ariege. In fact, Ekain and Sinhikole (112km away in a straight line) show clear parallels in the composition and style of the horses and even in the techniques employed. This proves that, not only the herds of reindeer moved from region to region, but also ideas and images traveled with the hunters who followed them. In contrast, horses of Magdalenian age in the center and west of the Cantabrian, as in the caves of Cullalvera, Monedas, Castillo, Pasiega, Tito Bustillo and Candamo, do not have this convention. There is just one example in the Lower Passage in La Garma, in the valley of the River Miera. At the moment, the latter cave marks the western boundary of this way of painting horses, which is so characteristic of the Basque Country. Furthermore, it is also the eastern boundary of a theme and technique, namely, the heads of hinds with striated bands in their chin and chest, which is so characteristic of Magdalenian sites in the center and west of the Cantabrian region, but which is unknown further east and in the Basque Country.

4-1 Cueva de Venta de la Perra

Cueva de Venta de la Perra is situated in the gorge of the River Carranza, opposite the village of the same name, and right on the boundary between the provinces of Cantabria and Vizcaya. The wide Carranza valley joins the main valley of the River Asón through a narrow gap, containing in the distance of a kilometer, numerous Paleolithic sites located in the steep limestone slopes of both sides of the valley. The northern slope, where Venta de la Perra is located, has the greater number of sites, as the cave entrances face south and are more suitable for habitation. This is the explanation for the high proportion of sites with archaeological deposits or cave art, especially the caves of Arco A, Arco B-C and Pondra.

The engravings in Venta de la Perra were discovered in 1904 by Lorenzo Sierra, making this the first cave with Paleolithic art to be found in the Basque Country. In his first visit, as well as finding a few flint artifacts, he also discovered the engraving of a bear. He returned in 1906, accompanied by the prehistorians Henri Breuil and Hermilio Alcalde del Río, and they saw more figures then. The three of them published their first study of the cave in their book Les cavernes de la region Cantabrique in 1911. Afterwards, other visitors have seen further examples of figures that had previously gone unnoticed. In this way, another bison was located on the left-hand wall in 1950, and in 1981 J. M. Apellániz added a group of lines to the catalogue of art in the cave. At the same time, several studies have been made of the cave art in Venta de la Perra, especially by A. Beltrán, and recently, by X. Gorrochategui and R. Ruiz Idarraga.

The entrance of the cave can easily be seen from the village of Venta de la Perra. It is within an impressive rock-shelter, which leads to the first passage, where the engravings are found. The cave does not end here; rather it divides into two passages, one of which is nearly 200 meters long. However, the Paleolithic artists chose the first part of the cave for their depictions, which are therefore in the daylight zone, and above the habitation space.

The archaeological deposit helped to situate the cave art in early phases of the Upper Paleolithic. The only dig was performed in 1931 by Telesforo Aranzadi and José Miguel de Barandiaran. At the base of the deposit they found levels with artifacts of Mousterian aspect, and of the early Upper Paleolithic, which were covered by a post-Paleolithic layer containing pottery. In the Paleolithic, the cave was used mainly for the processing of ibex hunted on the steep slopes around the cave, and the remains of large bovines are much rarer, despite these

4-1: Cueva de Venta de la Perra.

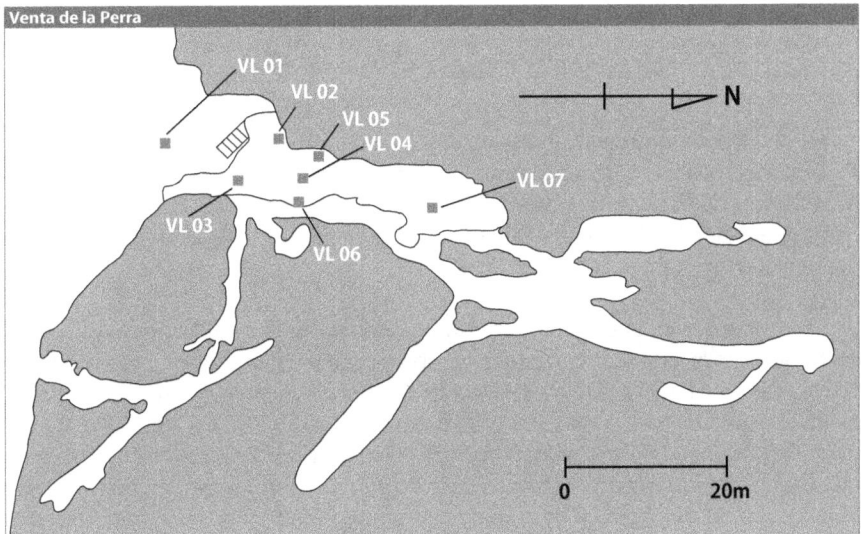

Venta de la Perra Ground Plan

being the principal theme depicted on the walls of the cave.

The first examples of graphic representations are found on both sides of the entrance. On the right-hand side, numerous lines were engraved in a flat limestone floor: they form parallel and converging lines and reticules, and were described merely as geometrical lines by the first explorers of the cave. The opposite wall has another group of deep incisions, consisting of parallel lines, this time on a vertical face of rock. Recently they have been interpreted as possible marks left when instruments were "sharpened" on the wall.

The animal figures are found very near at hand, but inside the first passage of the cave. Starting on the left-hand wall, two meters from the entrance, we see the rear-quarters of a bison facing right, represented by the croup, part of the tail raised up, the rump and a rear leg, where the hock has been shown. Facing this bison there is a second image of the same animal, with the back, the tail (again raised), the rump, start of the rear leg, and part of the belly line. Four meters away other engraved lines are apparently non-figurative, although some prehistorians have interpreted them as the remains of a third bison.

Turning to the right-hand wall, opposite the last figure mentioned above, we find one of the few depictions of a bear in Cantabrian Paleolithic art. The figure is almost one meter long, and is whole, apart from the belly. It is hard to say if it represents a brown bear, a species still living in certain places in the Cantabrian Mountains, or a cave bear, which became extinct at the end of the Pleistocene.

221

4-1: Cueva de Venta de la Perra.

The clearest difference between the two species is that the cave bear had a large prominent forehead, as in fact this figure seems to have, so it can probably be identified in this way.

Several engraved lines zigzag over the bear's croup. Although they have sometimes been interpreted as another bison, they do not seem to be more than simple non-figurative lines. Further engravings are seen to the right of the bear, again identified as a possible bovine, and next to this figure there is another acephalous bison facing right.

The art in Cueva de Venta de la Perra forms a homogeneous group, both technically and iconographically, showing the figures were produced in a short space of time, in other words that they are synchronic. From a technical point of view, engraving was the only procedure used. The incisions are always deep, although with some variations. The bison on the left-hand wall were executed with several deep lines which connected up to form a single outline shape. The figures on the right have a shallower groove, and the lines around the outline are not connected. It has recently been shown that, when these engravings were done, the normal technique was alternated with indirect percussion to chip off small pieces of rock. The predominant theme amongst those depicted is the bison, with at least three examples, as well as the figure of a bear, a very rare animal in Cantabrian cave art.

The single concept of this art assemblage, reflected in the technique, style and great visibility of the figures, has meant that there has been a general agreement as to their age. The first proposals situated the figures in quite early periods of the Upper Paleolithic. Thus, in 1911, Breuil considered that they had all been produced in a moment between the Aurignacian and the Gravettian, a date which he gave more precisely as the middle Aurignacian, in his 1952 book. Leroi-Gourhan made no direct reference to the cave, but he would doubtlessly have included it within his Style II, that is to say, between the Gravettian and the early Solutrean. Indeed, certain stylistic elements seem to correspond to this time: the absolute profile of the figures, without any indication of perspective, the unfinished limbs, and the exaggerated curve of their backs, particularly clear in the second bison on the left. Recently, an experimental method of dating by thermoluminescence has been used to find the age of calcite that covers two of the engravings. The results show that this calcite formed about 22,000 years ago, which tells us that the engravings must have been done before that time, before the start of the Solutrean period.

Other arguments that have often been used to support this early chronology are based on the presence of vertical non-figurative incisions, similar to those in the Asturian rock-shelter of La Viña, or the position of the figures,

4-1: Cueva de Venta de la Perra.

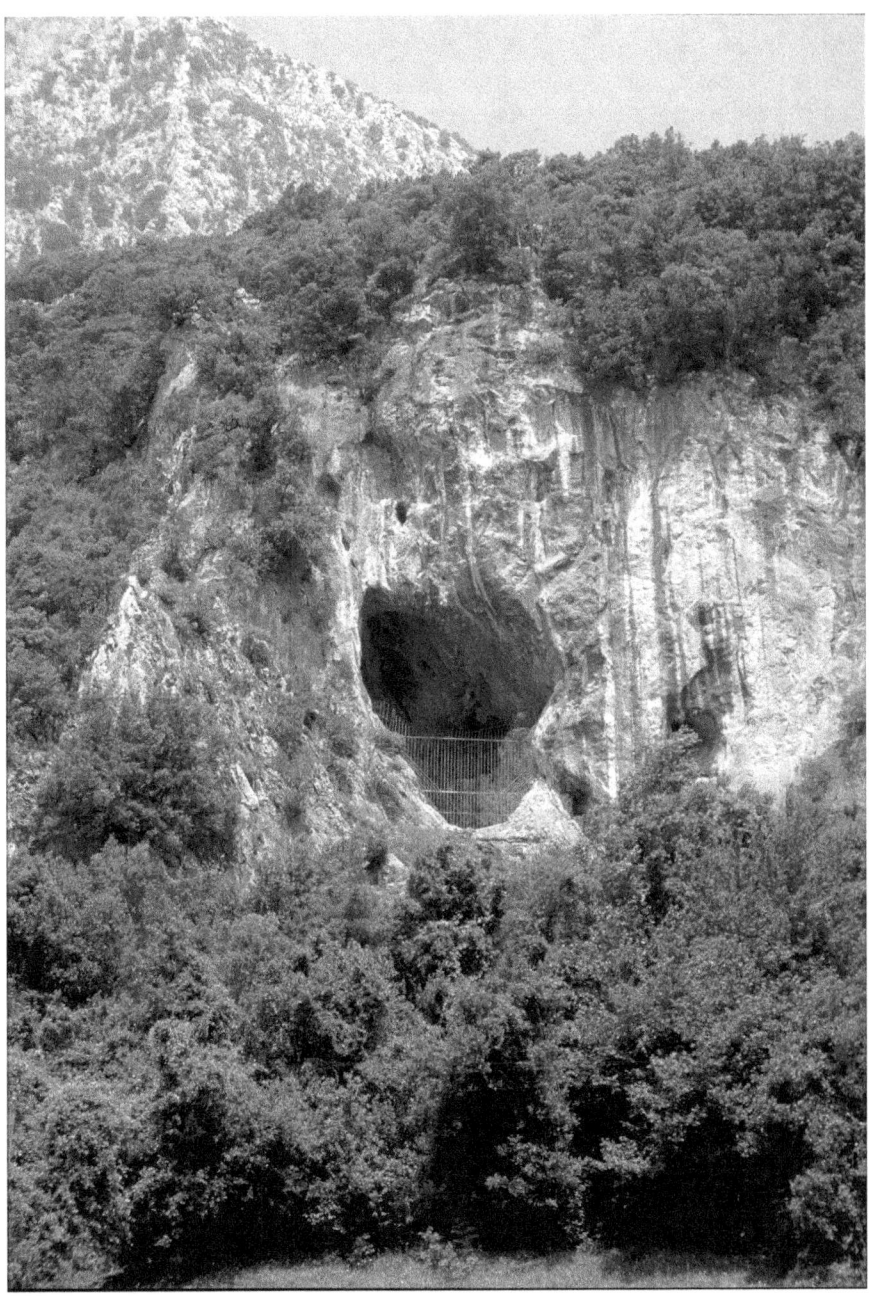

Entrance of Cueva de Venta de la Perra

4-1: Cueva de Venta de la Perra.

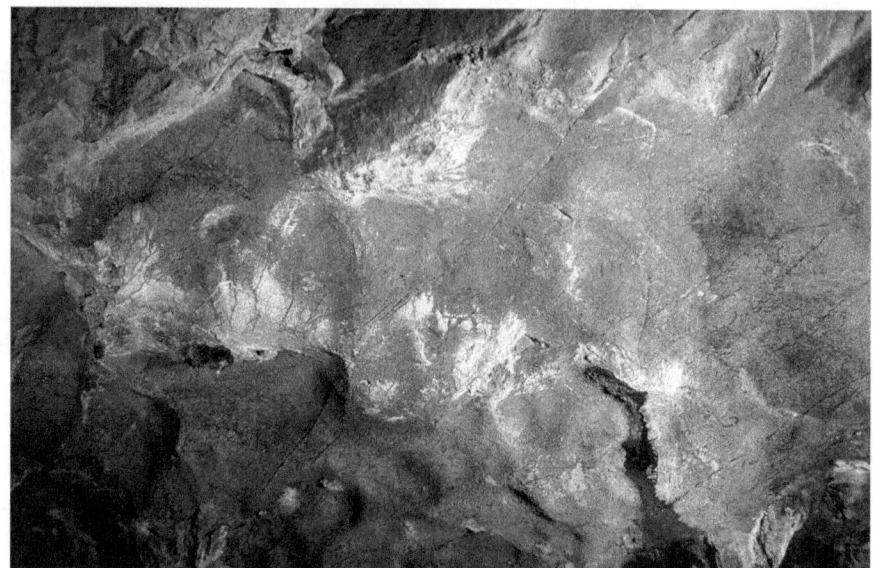

A bear facing left was engraved with a single quite deep line

within the daylight zone. Although we no longer accept, at least in its strictest, simplest terms, A. Leroi-Gourhan' s theory that the inside of caves was a slow progressive conquest, it is clear that most of the exterior groups of deep engravings correspond to early periods of the Upper Paleolithic. Good examples of old daylight assemblages can be found in the caves of Chufín, Hornos de la Peña, La Lluera and La Viña, where the figures are always engravings, and in La Viña they have been related with the stratigraphy of the archaeological deposit in the cave entrance.

The iconography of the art in Venta de la Perra is, however, somewhat different from that of other Cantabrian sites with exterior assemblages. These usually have a large number of hinds, as in Chufín or Lluera I, and smaller proportions of horses and aurochs, as in Hornos de la Peña and Lluera I, although bison is not completely unknown. The most striking figure in Venta de la Perra is the bear, which is quite rare in the Cantabrian region, and normally appears in Magdalenian sites, like Las Monedas, Ekain and Santimamiñe.

References.

Apellániz, J. M. 1982. El arte prehistórico del Pais Vasco y sus vecinos. Desclée de Brouwer. Bilbao.

4-1: Cueva de Venta de la Perra.

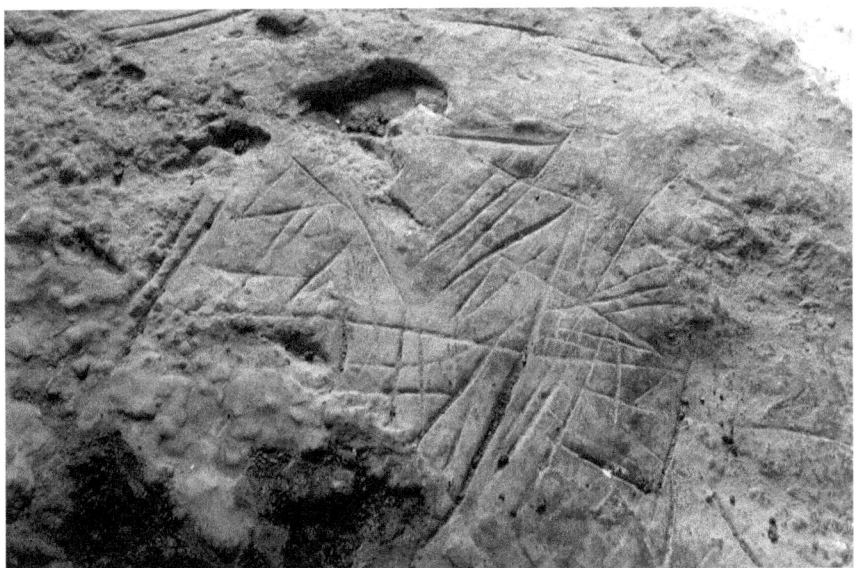

Non-figurative engraved lines

Beltrán, A. 1971. Los grabados de la cueva de Venta de la Perra y sus problemas. Munibe 23, 2/3, pp 387-398.

Ruiz Idarraga, R.; Apellániz, J. M. 1998-1999. Análisis de la forma y de la ejecución de las figuras grabadas de la cueva de Venta Laperra (Carranza, Bizkaia). Kobie XXV, pp 93-140.

4-2 Cueva de Arenaza

Cueva de Arenaza is situated on the side of the hill Pico de la Arena, 400m away from the village of San Pedro de Galdames, in Vizcaya. The geographical position of the cave, and the natural conditions of its surroundings, would have been highly suitable for settlements during long periods of time in the Upper Paleolithic. Its low altitude above sea level, about 150m, and its south-facing entrance, must have helped to ameliorate the harsh climatic conditions of the glaciations. At the same time, a steady supply of food by hunting and gathering was practically guaranteed during the Paleolithic. The cave is located near two areas where hunting gregarious animals must have been especially easy: the cliffs of the hills Monte Ganerán and Pico de la Cruz, in an area where the valley is narrower, near the present-day village of Garay. The River Galdames occupies the valley floor, about 80m below the cave, and this was doubtlessly fished by the prehistoric populations.

Cueva de Arenaza was known and often visited by the villagers of Galdames, as is shown by the names written on the walls, with dates between 1935 and 1965. It was also used to store the explosives for the mines that are in the vicinity of the cave, and it was therefore also known as Cueva del Polvorín (Cave of the Explosives Store). Nevertheless, the cave paintings were not found until 1973, when they were discovered by several members of the Gorrochategui family.

Arenaza is part of a cave system which is developed under Pico de la Arena, and which is connected with other caves. Its entrance is formed by a large arch divided in two by a column. It now looks very different from how it did in the Paleolithic, among other reasons, because a stone slope was built in its western half to slide down the wagons coming from the mines, and which were unloaded at the foot of the hill.

By crossing the arch of the entrance, we reach a large vestibule about 20m long and 10m wide, which becomes narrower towards the back. Archaeological digs have been carried out here since 1972, first under J. M. Apellániz and J. Altuna, and more recently by J. M. Fernández Lombrera. During this time, a large area of about thirty square meters has been dug against the eastern wall, and layers have been discovered that go from the late-final Magdalenian to the Roman period. The size and divisions of the sequence have made Arenaza one of the most important deposits in the region to study different processes of cultural and economic change, whether it is the study of the end of the Upper Paleolithic

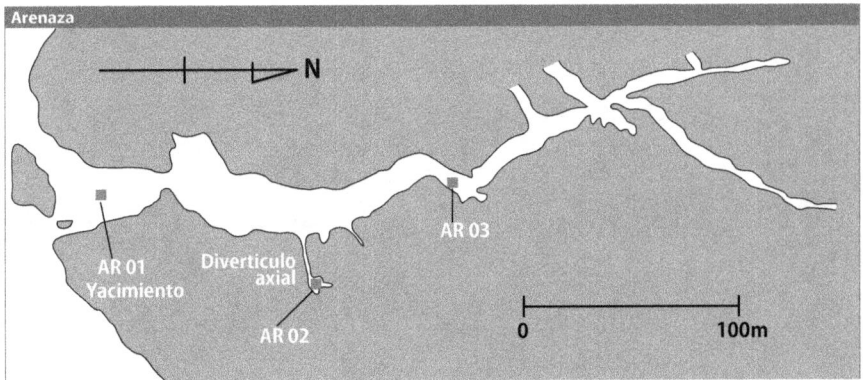

Arenaza Ground Plan

and the start of the Azilian period, or the transition from the Mesolithic societies which are well represented in the deposit to the first Neolithic in the region: a period with little known stratigraphy in the Cantabrian. In turn, the most important studies on the cave art have been carried out by J. M. Apellániz and by X. Gorrochategui, and the latest papers are still in press.

About 108m from the cave entrance, and the Paleolithic habitation deposit, on the right of the passage we come to the start of the so-called "Axial Side-passage" , a narrow passage about 15m long and in places only about 70cm wide. This ends in a small elliptical chamber, about 4m wide, with a short ramp on the left which climbs about 3m in its length of 6m. It is here, in this remote part of the cave, where we find almost all the parietal art in Cueva de Arenaza.

The cave art shows a great iconographic and technical unity. The only theme represented, or the only one recognizable in the present state of conservation, is that of hinds, of which there are ten figures. The techniques employed are based in all cases on the use of red paint, which was applied to the wall in different ways. The most frequent was as lines made up of a series of dots which were dabbed on the wall with a fingertip or some kind of pad. In some of the figures the paint was applied as a simple continuous line, or in masses of color wash.

The hinds in this "Axial Side-passage" are usually painted in pairs, although in no case do they represent a narrative scene. The compository schemes these figures show can be quite varied, from almost whole outlines, to figures of hinds only represented by their forehead and back. Nevertheless, it is not easy to draw definitive conclusions about the compository schemes present in the cave, due to the poor conservation of the pigment, and because in places the surface of the cave wall has broken off, which has partially destroyed some of the figures,

4-2: Cueva de Arenasa

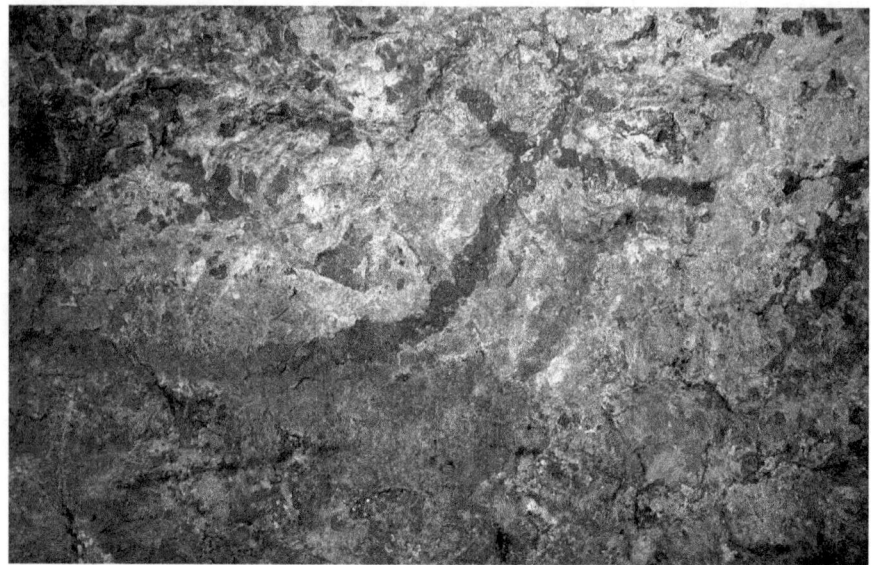

Hinds painted with red dotted lines

making it impossible to reconstruct the original schemes.

Returning to the main passage, and continuing inwards, we find a new panel about 50m away from the start of the Axial Side-passage. This has an auroch, and other lines that could be interpreted, with reserves, as the head of a second auroch. The former is a complete representation of a primitive bull, painted with red lines and engraved. Engraving was used to represent the whole animal, apart from the fore-limbs, and red paint was applied only in the upper part of the figure, i.e. in the forehead, horns, back, tail and start of the rump. The interior of the figure preserves some remains of red paint in the body, and the eye was also painted. The engraved lines have little patina, like other non-figurative lines engraved to the right. It has been mentioned that, a hundred meters from this panel, there are further remains of red paint, which have been interpreted as possibly representing the ears of a hind that has now almost completely disappeared.

As we have seen, the cave art of Arenaza is quite homogeneous. From the icongraphic point of view only two themes appear, which are hinds and aurochs, and no clear signs have been documented. The role that each of these species play in the thematic structure is quite different, as the cave has eleven hinds and only two aurochs (including the doubtful figures).

The technical procedures employed are equally homogeneous. All the

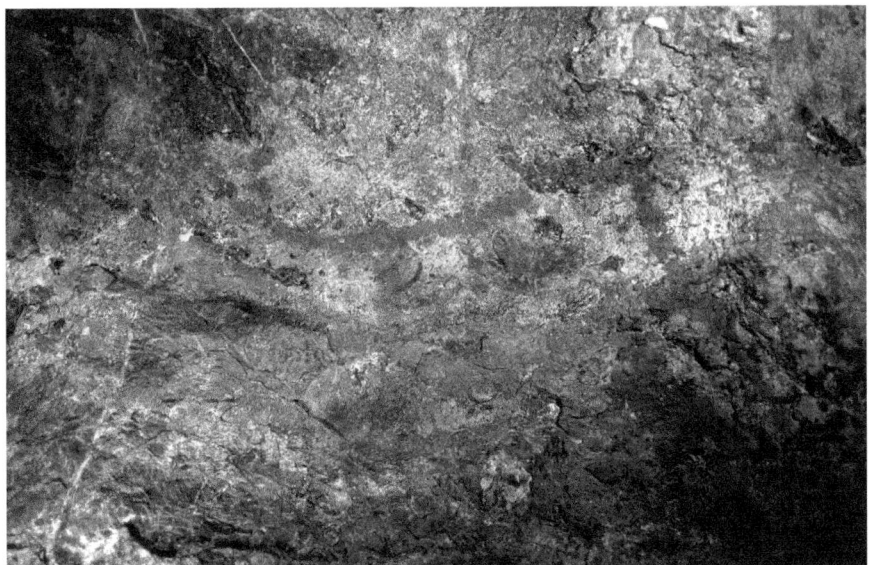
A figure of a hind facing right

figures were painted in red, applied in three basic ways: dotted lines, continuous lines and color wash. The only engraved lines are those in the two figures of bovines.

Despite having such a small parietal assemblage, Cueva de Arenaza occupies a very important position within Cantabrian Paleolithic art. In fact, the cave marks the eastern boundary of many of the characteristics of pre-Magdalenian Cantabrian art, which is so common in the communities of Cantabria and Asturias. We are referring to such aspects as: the iconographic character (the high frequency of hinds, although Arenaza does not have the typical quadrilateral signs); the pictorial techniques (dotted lines, either as overlapping or discontinuous dots); and the composition of the panels, pairing animals of the same species.

The cave art in Arenaza is normally included in the so-called "Ramales School", as defined by Professor Apellániz, because it is so similar to the paintings in the caves of Covalanas and La Haza, located in the town of Ramales de la Victoria, in Cantabria. This group of caves is also formed by La Pasiega A, and other sites discovered more recently, like Arco A, Arco B-C and Pondra, about five kilometers from Ramales, and El Pendo, which is near the Bay of Santander. Red animal figures in the caves of Salitre, or the Lower Passage of La Garma also show certain similarities, while other figures in El Castillo, Trescalabres or Llonín have a more distant relationship. But all these sites can be attributed quite clearly to Leroi-Gourhan's Style III, and were probably painted in the Solutrean period.

The features which best define the art in Arenaza are common or similar to the ones in the caves mentioned above. Hinds are the most frequent theme in many of the caves, like Covalanas, Pasiega or Pendo. The figures are usually only represented by their outline. The only interior details that tend to appear are an eye, represented by a dot, and a partition line crossing the body from the withers to the start of the forelimb. Some figures have a wider line in their jaw, and in the angle between the jaw and the top of the neck.

As regards the painting of the outlines, again there are some special characteristics. The most obvious is that the outlines are open, in other words, they are formed by lines which do not meet up. Thus we often find hinds with open mouths, because of a gap between the lines of their face and their jaw. Similarly, the forehead line may not join up with the line of their back, and the ears are usually painted at the ends of these lines, often forming a "V"-shape. The cervical-dorsal line is normally prolonged to represent the tail, and a slight separation is left between the tail and the top of the rump.

The limbs do not seem to be represented with a similar common tendency, either in their number or in the degree of completeness. Thus, we can find figures with their four limbs, compared with others which are reduced to the head, ears and cervical-dorsal line. The degree of realism varies too, and the same panel may have figures where the hoofs and hocks are represented, and others, which are the most common, whose limbs are reduced to a simple line from the elbow or hock to the hoof, and occasionally one line for the whole of the limb.

Perspective is not expressed correctly, so that, for example, the ears are represented in the same plane. In contrast, it can be seen that attempts were sometimes made at showing perspective in the limbs, especially the rear limbs when both were painted.

There is also a typical technical procedure: the dotted lines. This technique consisted of the construction of lines as a series of dots, which may be separated or overlapping. The artist always used red paint, which was not mixed with other colors. Furthermore, different tones of red were not applied, although different shades were sometimes used in the outline and the interior of certain figures of hinds, for example in the caves of Covalanas, Arco B, Pendo and La Pasiega. The combination of the techniques of dotted painted lines and engraving is extremely rare. In contrast, engraved lines do occasionally complement outlines painted as a line, and above all, the masses of color wash.

At present, Cueva de Arenaza, like several other caves in Cantabria and Asturias, is seriously threatened by the proximity of a stone quarry, scarcely 100m away. The explosions that happen every day in this quarry are causing pieces of the cave wall to break off, and will completely destroy this important example of cultural heritage if the Administration of the Basque Country does not impose a little common sense.

References

Apellániz, J. M. 1982: El arte prehistórico del Pais Vasco y sus vecinos. Desclée de Brouwer. Bilbao.

4-3 Cueva de Santimamiñe

Cueva de Santimamiñe is located in the hill of Ereñusarre, very near the village of Kortezubi, four kilometers from the town of Guernica, in Vizcaya. The cave's name comes from a nearby chapel of Santimamiñe, which in the Basque language means San Mamés, or St Amandus, to whom the chapel is dedicated. Equally, the name of the hill comes from the Basque word ereñotz, which means bay-tree, and which refers to the abundance of this plant.

The cave is situated in an area of great natural beauty, in the heart of Urdaibai, an area of 220 square kilometers which was declared a "Reserve of the Biosphere" by UNESCO in 1984. It is crossed by the estuary of Guernica, and also encloses the coastline around the mouth of the River Oka. Numerous species of birds use this space as a resting-place during their migrations from north Europe to Africa. Although the environmental conditions, and the position of the coastline, must have been very different in the Upper Paleolithic, the hunter-gatherers who camped at Santimamiñe would have had easy access to areas of estuary and shore that were rich in animal species, and where they would have had all the facilities they needed for their hunting, fishing or gathering activities. The excavations carried out in the archaeological deposit have thus revealed abundant remains of their presence.

The cave was already well-known by the local inhabitants when in January 1916 a group of young men, among whom was José F. Bengoechea, saw the first of the paintings. Their discovery reached the attention of the great musician and composer Jesús Guridi, who visited the cave a few months later. As he saw the importance of the find, he informed the authorities of the Province of Vizcaya. In the following months more important visitors came to see the site, including the French prehistorian Henri Breuil. He was followed by F. de la Quadra Salcedo and A. Alcalá-Galiano, members of the Comisión de Monumentos de Vizcaya, who produced the first copies of the prehistoric paintings.

The excavations of the deposit, and the full documentation of the cave art, began in 1918, by a team led by Telesforo de Aranzadi, José Miguel de Barandiaran and Enrique Eguren, true pioneers of scientific prehistoric research in the Basque Country. The site was dug in a number of seasons between 1918 and 1926, and in a second phase, between 1960 and 1962. These digs uncovered stratigraphy with levels going from the Aurignacian to the Roman period, one of the most important deposits in the whole of the Cantabrian region. The same archaeologists also carried out the basic study of the cave art in Santimamiñe,

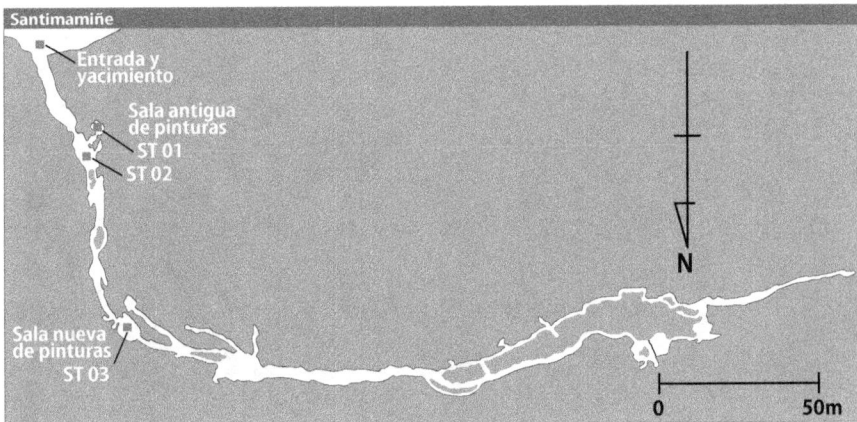
Santimamine Ground Plan

although a few new figures have since been found in several parts of the cave. The art in the cave is currently being revised by X. Gorrochategui Nieto, who has prepared a full study about Paleolithic art in Vizcaya, now in press.

Therefore, Cueva de Santimamiñe is important, not only because of its large archaeological deposit, but also for the interesting group of Paleolithic paintings and engravings inside the cave. Although it is a very long cave, with many side-passages, and shafts which apparently descend to lower series of passages, the known cave art is located in just four areas. The first is about fifty meters from the entrance, on the right-hand wall of the main passage, where we find black paintings of an ibex and a possible bison.

The main group of paintings is in a side-passage to the left of the main gallery, very close to the figures mentioned already. This side-passage is formed by a first small passage, leading to the so-called "ante-chamber", and a final room or chamber. Both spaces have important Magdalenian paintings. The way into the side-passage, which must have been quite difficult in the Paleolithic, has been made easier by a metal ladder. Climbing up this we reach the "ante-chamber", a small passage about 5m long, whose walls have several animal figures; a number of bison and horses and the head of an auroch. As well, other motifs can be seen which may have originally been animal depictions.

At the back of the Ante-chamber, more ladders lead to the best known part of Santimamiñe: the Chamber, whose wall displays some of the most interesting Paleolithic figures in the east of the Cantabrian region. On entering the chamber, the visitor comes straight to a stalagmitic column, with three figures of bison in a vertical position. The two best-drawn bison are in the upper part, looking downwards, while below them the third bison faces upwards. Despite the dif-

233

4-3: Cueva de Santimamiñe

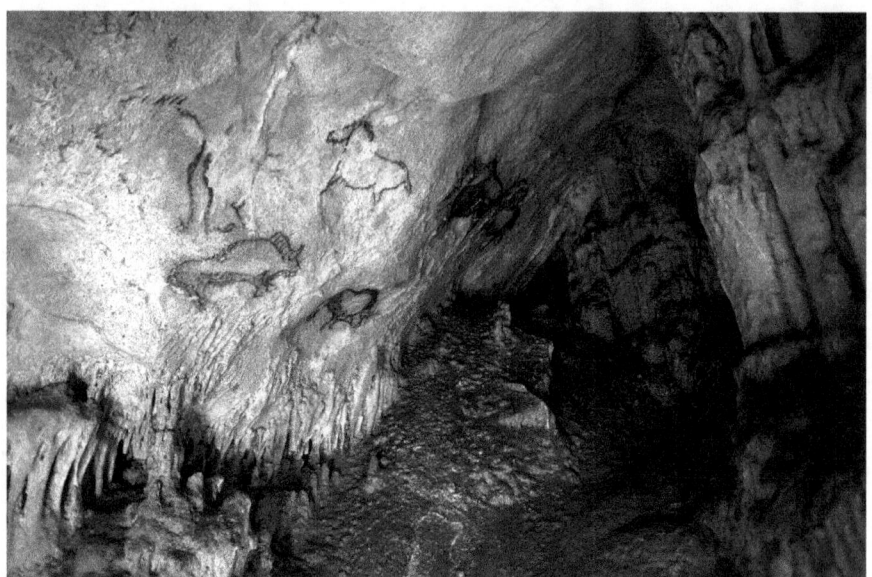
Large panel of black paintings

ferences they show, especially regarding the quality of their execution, the three figures have many features in common, for example their tails are raised. This is an unusual detail in the depiction of other animals, and it may represent a state of excitation in the bison.

The walls on the right of the entrance into the chamber have the paintings with the least firm lines in Santimamiñe: an ibex, several bison and other figures which are difficult to classify as they are incomplete, or badly drawn. or poorly conserved.

Situated to the left of the vertical bison is the panel which, in 1916, was first noticed by the discoverers of Santimamiñe. It is formed by a group of black paintings, including an acephalous horse, a bear (the first figure they saw), and two incomplete figures of a stag and an ibex. These four paintings form a curious composition. The most complete figures, the bear and horse, seem to be facing each other, although it is now difficult to appreciate this as the horse is in a lamentable state of conservation, and has practically disappeared. The stag and ibex, only represented by their heads, back, neck and a horn, are also facing each other, but this time in a vertical position, with the ibex head upwards and the stag head downwards.

The zone to the left of the entrance has the best composition in Santimamiñe. The largest and smoothest wall in the chamber was chosen for this pan-

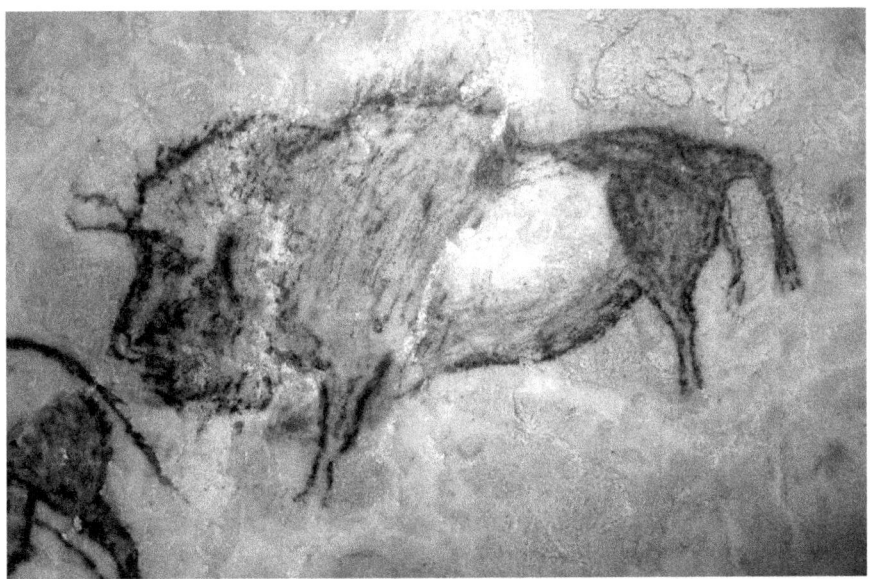
Black bison with two tails

el of a horse and seven bison. The figures are arranged in a very striking way. The horse seems to occupy the central position on the wall, and it is surrounded by the bison. The ones on the left, nearest the entrance, are the least complete. Only one of them represents the whole animal, despite being affected by calcite which partially covers it and makes it hard to see. This bison, and the one further to the left are in a vertical position. To their right we find the central horse.

The four bison situated below and on the right of the horse show very similar features. They were all depicted whole, usually with two horns and four limbs, except the bison on the far right which only has one fore and rear limb. It also has two tails, as if the artist wanted to correct the figure. The technique used is again black paint in the outline, with the interior filled with a wash in the same color. It is noticeable how the figures are out of proportion, as the front quarters are much larger than the rear-quarters, which exaggerates the natural asymmetry of the animals' bodies.

Returning to the main passage, and continuing a further 100m along this, we reach the chamber known as the "New Hall of Paintings" . It is a small rectangular chamber, about 5m wide and 8m long. The first figure we see is an ibex, of which the fore-quarters are very poorly conserved. Below it, a strange construction of lines is interpreted as depicting a bison, although its form is unique in Paleolithic art. About 3m away, the figure of a horse can be recognized, with a bison on the opposite wall, and both face the back of the chamber.

4-3: Cueva de Santimamiñe

The art of Santimamiñe shows certain homogeneity in themes and techniques. One of its most noticeable features is the total absence of conventionalized signs. Among the figurative art, bisons are the most frequent species, with eighteen depictions, followed by horse and ibex, of which there are five figures. The other themes represented are aurochs (four figures), a stag and a bear, as well as two bovines which are difficult to classify as either bison or aurochs, and another four unidentified animal figures. Horse and bison are the only animals present in each of the three main decorated areas: the Ante-chamber, Chamber, and New Hall.

Regarding the techniques used, black paint is almost exclusive, as it appears in thirty-two animal figures, and is combined with engraving in another two depictions. Engraving alone was used in only four figures.

Another very striking feature is the large number of animals in a vertical position in the Chamber, where 30% of the animal figures are represented in this way. According to our statistics, this position is only adopted in 6% of the total number of figures in Cantabrian art, where it is usually due to a number of factors. Most of the vertical animals are on sections of wall whose longest axis is itself vertical, so that the Paleolithic artist adapted the animal figure to the available space. However, this is not the case in the Chamber of Santimamiñe, where it seems that the artists wanted to make the maximum use of the space in the Chamber, painting some of the figures in places which are not the most suitable, such as the column opposite the entry into the Chamber, with the three vertical bison, or the bison on the left of the main panel, where the small available space was used as fully as possible. The wish to make use of the whole surface area can be understood in small caves, or in those where the character of the cave walls means that only small areas are suitable for decoration. But this is not true of Santimamiñe, a large cave which offered its prehistoric visitors numerous walls appropriate for painting. The only explanation for this large number of vertical figures in the Chamber must therefore be linked to the interest this area held for the Paleolithic artists. The virtual absence of superimpositions among the figures may indicate that the group of figures is relatively synchronic. A more difficult question to answer is why the artists who painted in Santimamiñe were so interested in painting in this chamber and not in others. If we accept the first interpretations of cave art, which saw Paleolithic art from a magic-religious point of view, we may consider the Chamber in Santimamiñe as a ritual site, or a shrine.

The chronology normally accepted for the paintings in Santimamiñe is within Leroi-Gourhan's Style IV, basically in the Magdalenian period. This is shown by certain characteristics of the figures, such as the frequent depiction of interior details and partition lines, the correct perspective seen in the bison in the main panel in the Chamber, the naturalism of many of the figures, as well as the association between the techniques of black paint and engraving, which is so common in this period in the Cantabrian region.

References

Aranzadi, T.; Barandiaran, J. M.; Eguren, E. 1925: Exploraciones en la Caverna de Santimamiñe. Memoria 1ª. En Barandiaran, J. M. 1976: Obras completas. Vol. IX, pp 13-89.

Apellániz, J. M. 1971: La caverna de Santimamiñe. Publicaciones de la Exma. Diputación de Vizcaya.

4-4 Cueva de Ekain

Cueva de Ekain contains one of the most interesting groups of cave art on the Cantabrian coast, not so much for the number of figures it has, but above all for the exceptional artistic quality of many of its paintings, and the good state of conservation of the art and its surroundings inside the cave. It is located on the eastern slopes of Ekain hill, very close to the village of Cestona, belonging to the municipality of Deba, in Guipúzcoa. The Goltzibar and Belioso brooks surround the hill, and they unite a few meters away from the cave, and form the Sastarrain rivulet, which flows into the River Urola at Cestona.

The cave is not very far from the present coast line, just seven kilometers away in a straight line. However, at the time when the cave was decorated, the accumulation of ice in the immense glaciers that existed then, resulted in a lowering of sea level. In the Cantabrian region, this meant that the coastline receded over seven kilometers to the north during the coldest periods. In any case, the cave's archaeological deposit has relatively little evidence of shell fishing. Cueva de Ekain is not an isolated site; in its surrounding area other significant Upper Paleolithic deposits are known, with particularly important occupations of the Magdalenian period (16,500 to 11,500 BP approximately). They are in the caves of Ermittia, Erralla, Urtiaga and Altxerri, and the last of these also has an important group of parietal engravings and paintings. They were used occasionally by the human populations who lived in this eastern part of the region, and whose subsistence was based on hunting red deer and ibex, and sometimes other species of ungulates, the fishing of salmon and trout in the rivers, and gathering vegetables, or shell-fish and other animals on the shore.

Cueva de Ekain was known to the people in the village of Sastarrain, when A. Albizuru and R. Rezabal discovered the cave art in June 1969. It was a small cave only thirteen meters long and barely two meters wide. To the right of the entrance, some boulders blocked a small opening, and when they pulled these boulders out, they were able to enter a new, larger passage, and find the splendid panel full of paintings of horses. They immediately informed José Miguel de Barandiaran of their discovery, and this well-known Basque archaeologist and ethnologist visited the cave the following day.

The Paleolithic cave paintings were soon studied and published by J. M. de Barandiaran, together with J. Altuna. Later, in 1978, a second, larger and more complete study was carried out by J. Altuna and J. M. Apellániz. Besides, a magnificent study was made of the archaeological deposit in the vestibule by a

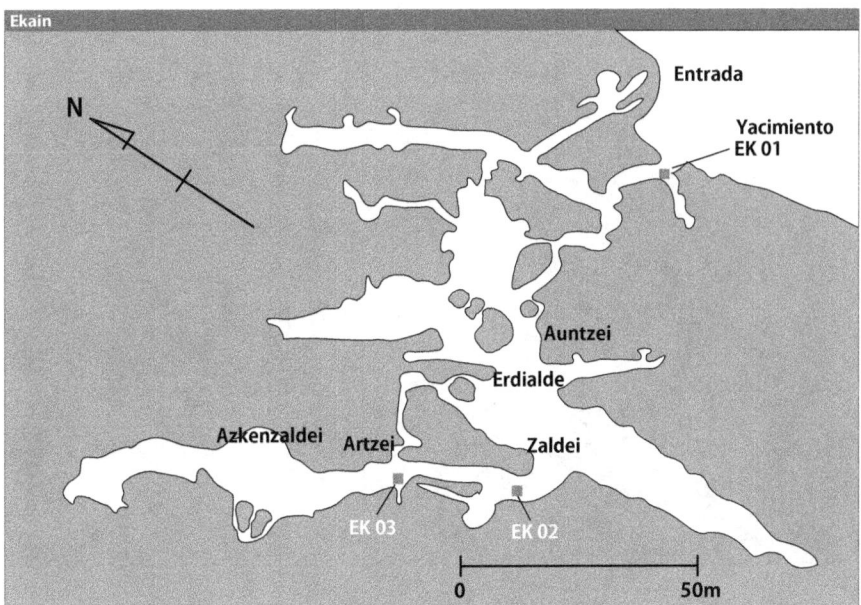

Ekain Ground Plan

team from the Aranzadi Science Society at San Sebastián. They had excavated the deposit, and were able to document frequent occupations of the site, especially during the Magdalenian, when the paintings were produced, and in the later Epipaleolithic and Mesolithic periods.

Like most of the caves in the center and east of the Cantabrian region, Cueva de Ekain was formed in Cretaceous limestone of the Urgonian facies. It is a fairly small cave, consisting basically of a main passage a little over 100m long, with a few short side-passages. The entrance, which faces east, divides into two passages. The one on the left, which was known before 1969, is where the archaeological dig was carried out. The passage on the right leads to the inner decorated parts of the cave.

The first signs of cave art are found in a small side-passage, which has a simple black line. A little higher up, on the left-hand wall, we can see a large horse's head, also painted in black. A few meters further on, another side-passage on the left is known by the Basque name of Auntzei, or "Place of the Goats". The left-hand wall of this passage has a pair of engravings representing a stag and a hind; and then a salmon, and an ibex viewed from the front, as well as other lines which are hard to interpret. These are all painted in black. The opposite wall has at least one more depiction of an ibex, with its body in profile, and its head turned to face the spectator. These figures of ibex are represented there-

4-4: Cueva de Ekain

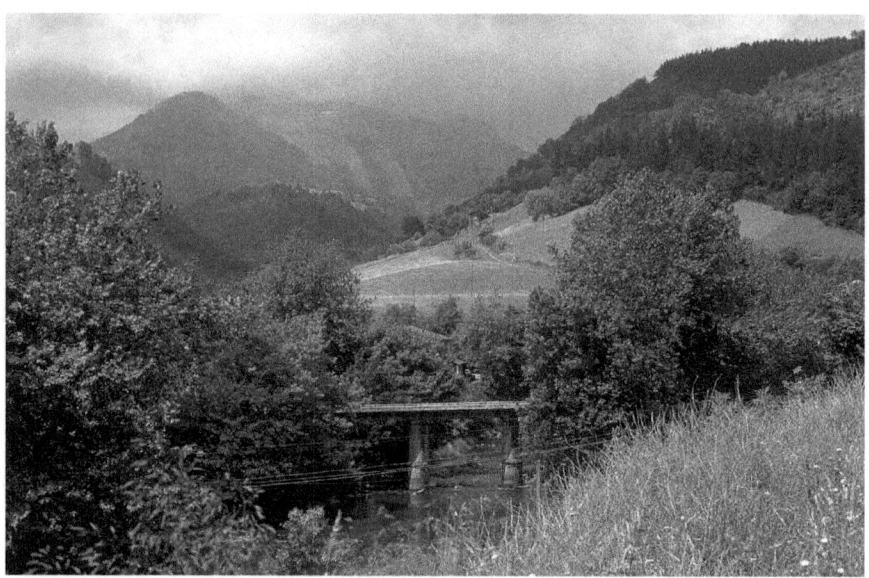

fore in a very common posture in real life, and one that was very familiar to the Paleolithic artists, who systematically hunted herds of ibex from Ekain during the Magdalenian. The posture is repeatedly depicted in Upper Paleolithic mobiliary and cave art, in such sites as Otero in Cantabria and Ker de Massat in Ariège.

Returning to the main passage, we reach the central chamber, and a horse painted in black as a very simple outline figure, with proportions that are not too naturalistic. The greatest densities of figures are located at the back of this chamber, and several successive panels have depictions of bison, horses and other non-figurative motifs around a large block of stone. They announce the main compositions in Cueva de Ekain, situated on both sides of the next section of the main passage, called Zaldei or "Place of the Horses" .

Each part of the chamber must be considered in turn. First, the block at the back of the central chamber has a magnificent whole bison, where the natural shape of the rock was used to represent its cervical-dorsal line and tail. Other figures of bison and horses are found nearby.

The best-known panel in Ekain is found on the right-hand side of Zaldei chamber, on a large oblique section of wall. It has an accumulation of a dozen horses, with four bison, a hind, an ibex and a fish, apparently a sole. A further bison has been seen recently, whose outline was scraped very superficially over some of the painted horses, so this should be added to the total number of fig-

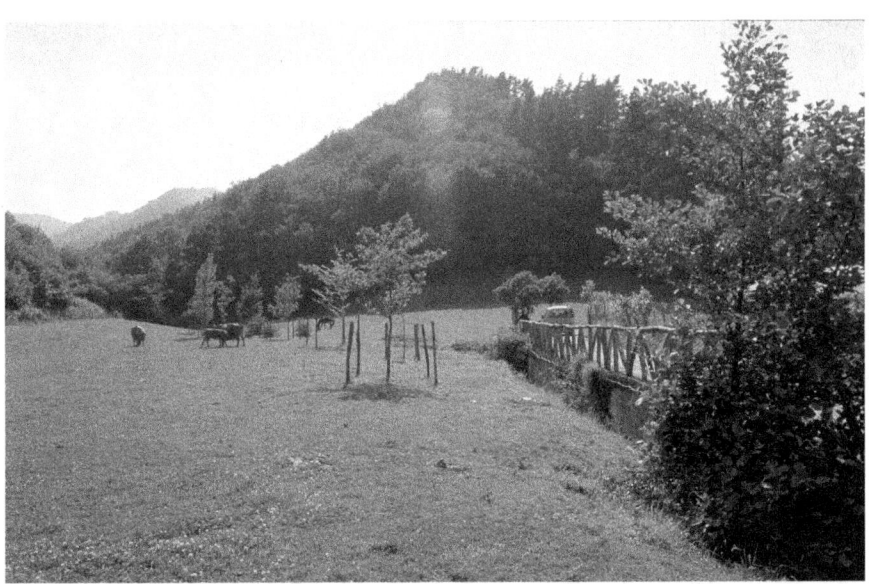

ures mentioned above. The first impression the panel makes on visitors, after their initial amazement, is that it is a scenic composition, representing a herd of horses, with a few other animals on the edges of the scene. Several factors help to create this feeling in the spectator. Nearly all the horses are facing in the same direction, towards the back of the cave, and with a few exceptions, they are all similar in their size, compository scheme, and stylistic conventions. The other animals appearing around the edge of the panel, outside the central composition, are drawn in a much simpler way.

The opposite wall has further panels, which again contain a few bison, and above all horses. They are all very similar to some of the figures in the main panel, although two of these horses seem to be wounded with spears.

Ten meters from the panel of the horses, we find that the low roof of the passage has, on its left-hand side, two figures of brown bear together, one of which is acephalous. Both animals were painted in black, and the larger one is also engraved in its cervical-dorsal area. Like the example of the pairing of an engraved stag and hind, seen in the first part of Ekain, this is a composition of two animals in clear association, and in this case, of one of the least common species in cave art.

Practically at the end of the main passage, another group of animal figures includes horses again, as there are six examples, and engraved lines,

4-4: Cueva de Ekain

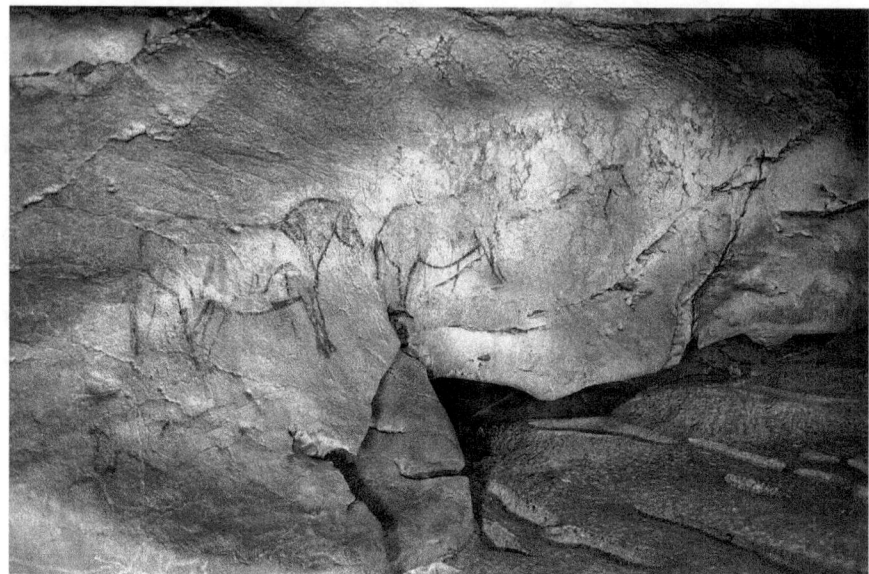
Horses in line

arranged in non-figurative vertical and parallel series. Some of the horses in this area also have spears in their bodies. The art finishes at the very end of the passage, with engravings that, with many, very reasonable doubts, have been interpreted as possibly incomplete depictions of rhinoceros.

The central and final areas of Cueva de Ekain therefore contain a group of Paleolithic art, with several aspects which need to stressed. The figures are mostly paintings, and engraving was used only for two animal figures, a few series of non-figurative lines, or to indicate the profiles and other details of certain of the paintings in black or, less often, in red. In this way, Ekain is different from other sites, where the techniques are more balanced, such as Cueva de Altxerri, one of the nearest examples temporally and geographically. And it is similar to sites like Santimamiñe, or Las Monedas, Covaciella and El Covarón, which have even fewer engravings and are presumably closer in their Magdalenian chronology.

Black paint is clearly predominant over red, as happens in many Magdalenian sites. It was applied with procedures ranging from simple lines, to color wash extended totally or partially over the figure, in order to shape the different parts of their bodies. Above all, different procedures were used in the same figures; sometimes in two colors, the bichrome figures, or in any color or in both together with engraving.

The animal figures, and particularly certain of the horses, were painted

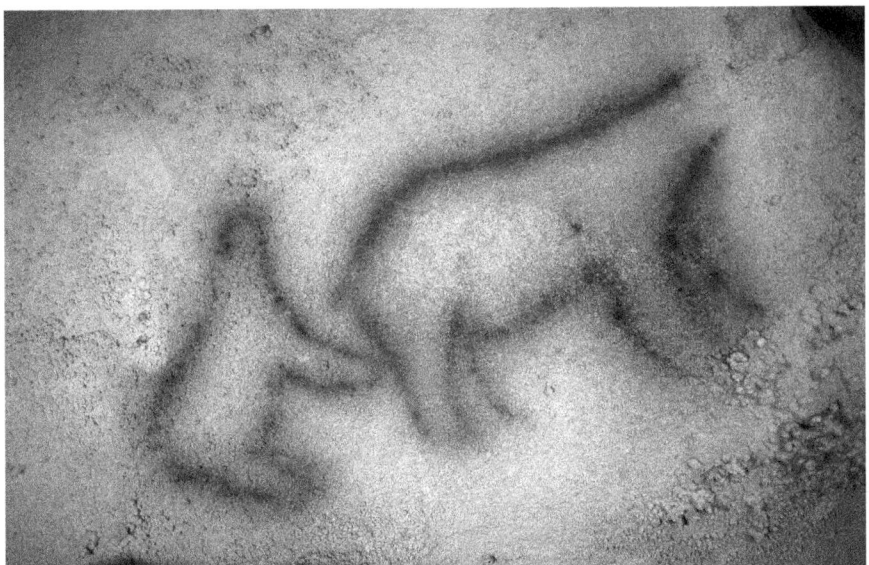
Couple of bears painted in black

with great naturalism. It is therefore frequent to find manes, eyes and nostrils, lines of the withers, ventral "M" -shaped lines separating areas of the horse' s coat with different coloring, stripes on the upper parts of the limbs, and hairs on the under-belly. But some interesting features do not seem to fit in with this supposed desire for realism of the artists. For example, the forequarters of many of the horses were worked much more, and show more details and more precise techniques, than the rear-quarters, which are often simple sketches. The exaggerated size and prominence of the croup and rump of the horses is equally characteristic. This hypertrophy is conventional, and similarly found in sites in the western Pyrenees (Cueva de Sinhikole) and in central and eastern areas of the Cantabrian region (Santimamiñe, and the Lower Passage of La Garma).

The art left by Magdalenian artists in Ekain is of great interest from the iconographic point of view. It contains 71 depictions, mostly animals: 33 horses, 11 bison, 4 ibex, 2 hinds, 1 stag, 2 fish (salmon and possible sole), 2 possible backs of very doubtful rhinoceros, and a few series of lines. The figures are clearly polarized between horses and bison, with few complementary animals, such as hinds, which are so common in other Cantabrian sites. Conventionalized abstract signs are absent, just as in other caves that were decorated in middle or late Magdalenian phases, such as Covaciella, Las Monedas, Santimamiñe and Altxerri, but in contrast with Cullalvera and Pindal. It is also interesting that the composition in the main central panel is the same, but inverted, as on the roof of Altamira, in the central panel in Santimamiñe, or in Covaciella. That is to say that

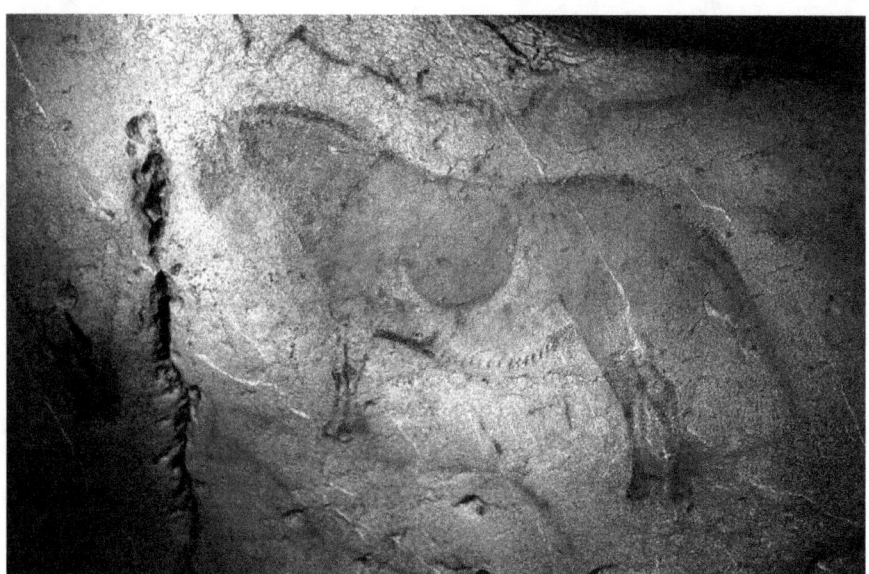
Bichrome horse

here horses appear to play the role that was taken by bison in the other sites; and not only in the number of figures, but also in their degree of completeness and realism. In all the caves mentioned, the degree of completeness is greater in the most numerous animal, whether that is bison, or horses as in Ekain.

The characters that we have described allow the art of Cueva de Ekain to be attributed to A. Leroi-Gourhan's Style IV (from 16,000 to 11,500 BP), and it is likely that it was produced during the middle or late Magdalenian, at some time between 13,500 and 12,000 years before the present.

References.

Altuna, J., Apellániz, J. M. 1978: Las figuras rupestres paleolíticas de la cueva de Ekain (Deva, Guipúzcoa). Munibe 30, 1-3.

González Sainz, C.; Cacho Toca, R.; Altuna, J. 1999: Una nueva representación de bisonte en la cueva de Ekain (Pais Vasco). Munibe 51, pp 153-159.

4-4: Cueva de Ekain

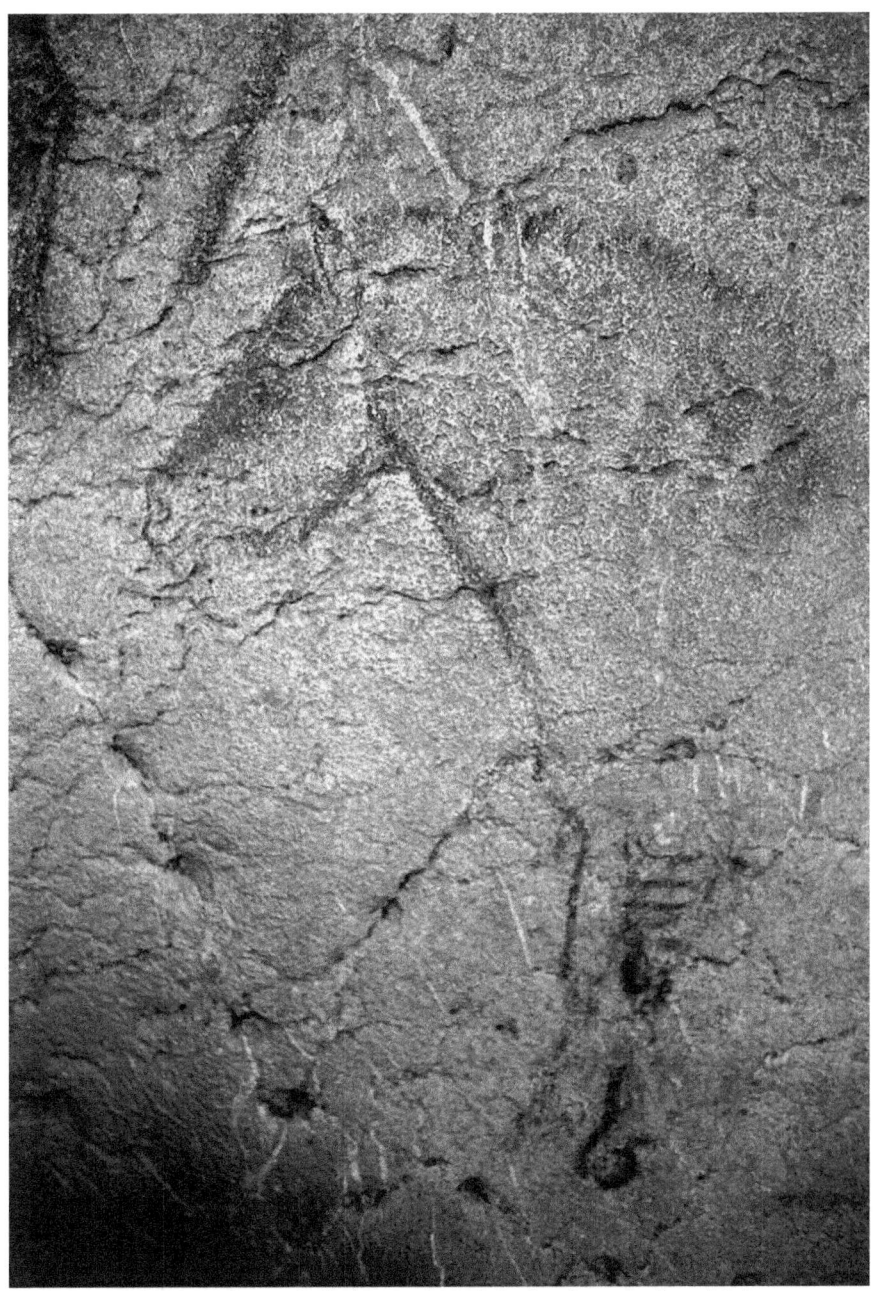
A bichrome horse. It displays great technical and compository detail.

Biblioglaphy

ALCALDE DEL RÍO, H. 1906. *Las pinturas y grabados de las cavernas prehistóricas de la provincia de Santander: Altamira, Covalanas, Hornos de la Peña, Castillo.* Impr. de Blanchard y Arce, Santander.

ALCALDE DEL RÍO, H. 1906. *"La Préhistoire aux environs de Santander. La station humaine d'Altamira".* En Cartailhac, E.; Breuil, H. 1906. pp. 257-275.

ALCALDE DEL RÍO, H.; BREUIL, H.; SIERRA, L. 1911, *Les cavernes de la Région Cantabrique (Espagne).* Imp. Vve. A. Chene, Monaco.

ALMAGRO BASCH, M., 1973: Las pinturas y grabados rupestres de la cueva de Chufín. Riclones (Santander). *Trabajos de Prehistoria,* 30, pp.9-67

ALMAGRO BASCH, M.; CABRERA, V.; BERNALDO DE QUIRÓS, F. 1977: Nuevos hallazgos de arte rupestre en Cueva Chufín. Riclones (Santander). Trabajos de Prehistoria, 34, pp.9-29

ALTUNA, J., BALDEÓN, A., MARIEZKURRENA, K 1985: Cazadores magdalenienses en Erralla (Cestona, País Vasco). Munibe, 37.

ALTUNA, J., MERINO, J. M. 1984: *El yacimiento prehistórico de la cueva de Ekain (Deba, Guipúzcoa).* Sociedad de Estudios Vascos, Sociedad de Ciencias Aranzadi.

APELLÁNIZ, J. M. 1971: *La caverna de Santimamiñe.* Publicaciones de la Excma. Diputación de Vizcaya.

APELLÁNIZ, J. M. 1982: *El arte prehistórico del País Vasco y sus vecinos.* Desclée de Brouwer. Bilbao.

ARANZADI, T., BARANDIARAN, J. M. 1935: *Exploraciones de la caverna de Santimamiñe (Basondo: Cortézubi). 3ª memoria. Yacimientos azilienses y paleolíticos.* (reed. 1978: Barandiaran, J. M., Obras Completas, IX:

249-344, Bilbao).

ARANZADI, T., BARANDIARAN, J. M., EGUREN, E., 1925: *Exploraciones en la Caverna de Santimamiñe*. Memoria 1ª. En Barandiaran, J. M. 1976: Obras completas. Vol. IX, pp.13-89.

ARIAS, P.; CALDERÓN, T.; GONZÁLEZ SAINZ, C.; MILLÁN, A.; MOURE, A.; ONTAÑÓN, R.; RUIZ IDARRAGA, R. 1998-1999. Dataciones absolutas para el arte rupestre paleolítico de Venta de la Perra (Carranza, Bizkaia). *Kobie* XXV, pp.85-92.

ARIAS CABAL, P.; GONZÁLEZ SAINZ, C.; MOURE ROMANILLO, A.; ONTAÑÓN PEREDO, R. 1999. *La Garma. Un descenso al pasado*. Catálogo de la exposición. Gobierno de Cantabria y Universidad de Cantabria.

BALBÍN BEHRMANN, R. de, 1989. L'art de la grotte de Tito Bustillo (Ribadesella, Espagne). Une vision de synthese. *L'Anthropologie* 93/2, pp.435-462.

BALBÍN BEHRMANN, R. DE; ALCOLEA GONZÁLEZ, J.J. 1994. Arte paleolítico de la Meseta española. *Complutum* 5, pp.97-138.

BALBÍN BEHRMANN, R. DE; ALCOLEA GONZÁLEZ, J.J.; GONZÁLEZ PEREDA, M.A. 1999. Une visión nouvelle de la grotte de El Pindal, Pimiango, Ribadedeva, Asturias. *L´Anthropologie* 103, pp.51-92.

BALBÍN BEHRMANN, R. DE; ALCOLEA GONZÁLEZ, J.J.; SANTONJA GÓMEZ, M. 1996. *Arte Rupestre Paleolítico al aire libre de la cuenca del Duero: Siega Verde y Foz-Côa*. Fundación Rei Afonso Henriques, Zamora.

BALBÍN BEHRMANN, R. DE; GONZÁLEZ SAINZ, C. 1993. Nuevas investigaciones en la cueva de La Pasiega (Puente Viesgo, Cantabria). *Boletín del Seminario de Estudios de Arte y Arqueología*, LIX, pp.9-38.

BALBÍN, R. DE; MOURE, J.A., 1982. El panel principal de la cueva de Tito Bustillo (Ribadesella, Asturias). *Ars Praehistorica I*, pp.47-97.

BARANDIARÁN, I. 1967. *Paleomesolítico del Pirineo occidental. Bases para una sistematización tipológica del instrumental óseo Paleolítico*. Monografías Arqueológicas III. Universidad de Zaragoza.

BARANDIARAN, I. 1972. *Arte Mueble del Paleolítico Cantábrico*. Monografías Arqueológicas XIV. Universidad de Zaragoza.

BARANDIARAN, I. 1994. Arte mueble del paleolítico cantábrico: una visión de síntesis en 1994. *Complutum* 5, pp.45-79.

BARANDIARAN, I., UTRILLA, P. 1975: Sobre el Magdaleniense de Ermittia (Guipúzcoa). *Sautuola* I, pp.21-47.

BARANDIARAN, J. M. 1947: Exploración de la Cueva de Urtiaga (en Itziar, Guipúzcoa). *Gernika-Eusko Jakintza* I: 113-128, 265-271, 437-456, 674-696

BARANDIARAN, J.M. DE, 1950. Bolinkoba y otros yacimientos paleolíticos de la Sierra de Amboto (Vizcaya). *Cuadernos de Historia Primitiva* V, n°2, pp.73-112. Reedición en J.M. de Barandiaran, Obras Completas XII, pp.393-433. Bilbao 1978.

BARANDIARAN, J. M. 1960: *Excavaciones en Atxeta. Forua (1959).* Imp. Prov. de Vizcaya, Bilbao. (reedición en J.M. de Barandiaran, Obras Completas, XII: 297-312, Bilbao).

BARANDIARAN, J. M. 1965: Excavaciones en Aitzbitarte IV (Campaña de 1964). *Munibe* 1-4: 21-37

BARANDIARAN, J. M. 1966: Breve reseña de las excavacinoes de Lumentxa (Lequeitio), de Aizbitarte (Rentería), de Marizulo (Urnieta), de Lezetxiki (Mondragón) y del dolmen de San Martín (Laguardia, Álava). *Noticiario Arqueológico Hispánico,* VIII y XI, cuadernos 1-3: 33-63

BARANDIARAN, J. M. 1966: Excavaciones en Aitzbitarte IV (campaña de 1964). *Noticiario Arqueológico Hispánico,* VIII Y IX, cuadernos 1-3: 24-32

BELTRÁN, A. 1971: Los grabados de la cueva de Venta de la Perra y sus problemas. *Munibe,* 23, 2/3: 387-398.

BOSINSKI, G. 1990. *Homo sapiens. L'histoire des chasseurs du Paléolithique supérieur en Europe (40.000-10.000 avant J.-C.).* Editions Errance, Paris.

BREUIL, H. 1952. *Quatre cents siècles d'art pariétal. Les cavernes ornées de l'age du renne.* Centre d'etudes et de documentation préhistoriques, Montignac. (Reimp. Max Fourny, Paris 1974).

BREUIL, H.; OBERMAIER, H. Y ALCALDE DEL RÍO, H. 1913. *La Pasiega à Puente Viesgo (Santander) (Espagne).* Institut de Paléontologie Humaine. Imp. Vve. A.

Chêne, Monaco.

BREUIL, H.; OBERMAIER, H. 1935. *La Cueva de Altamira en Santillana del Mar.*
Tipografía de Archivos, Madrid. (Reimpresión Ed. El Viso, Madrid, 1984).

CABRERA VALDÉS, V. 1984. El yacimiento de la cueva de "El Castillo" (Puente Viesgo, Santander). Bibliotheca *Praehistorica Hispana*, XXII. Madrid.

CARTAILHAC, E. 1902. Les cavernes ornées des dessins. La grotte d'Altamira, Espagne. "Mea culpa" d'un sceptique. *L'Anthropologie* XIII, pp.348-354.

CARTAILHAC, E.; BREUIL, H. 1906. *La Caverne d'Altamira à Santillane près Santander (Espagne).* Imprimerie de Monaco. Monaco.

CORCHÓN RODRÍGUEZ, S. 1986: *El arte paleolítico cantábrico: contexto y análisis interno.* Monografías Centro de Investigación y Museo Altamira. Madrid.

FERNÁNDEZ-TRESGUERRES VELASCO, J. A. 1980: *El Aziliense en las provincias de Asturias y Santander.* CIMA, Monografías N° 2.

FERNÁNDEZ-TRESGUERRES, J.A. 1981. Cantos pintados del Aziliense cantábrico. *Altamira Symposium*, pp.245-250.

FERNÁNDEZ-TRESGUERRES, J.A.; RODRÍGUEZ FERNÁNDEZ, J.J. 1990. La cueva de Los Azules (Cangas de Onis). *Excavaciones Arqueológicas en Asturias 1983-1986*, pp.129-133. Servicio de Publicaciones del Principado de Asturias. Oviedo.

FORTEA PÉREZ, J. 1989. Cuevas de La Lluera. Avance al estudio de sus artes parietales. *Cien años después de Sautuola,* pp.187-202. Santander.

FORTEA, J. 1992: Pindal (El). En: *El Nacimiento del Arte en Europa.* Unión Latina. pp.246-248.

FORTEA PÉREZ, J. 1994. Los "santuarios" exteriores en el Paleolítico cantábrico. *Complutum* 5 pp.203-220

FORTEA PÉREZ, J. 1997. Pintura paleolítica. *El Arte en Asturias a través de sus obras,* n°43, pp.693-708. Suplemento de "La Nueva España". Oviedo.

FREEMAN, L.G. 1978. Mamut, jabalí y bisonte en Altamira: reinterpretaciones sugeridas por la historia natural. *Curso de Arte Rupestre Paleolítico,* pp.157-179. UIMP. Zaragoza.

FREEMAN, L. G. GONZÁLEZ ECHEGARAY, J. 1982: Magdalenian mobile art from El Juyo (Cantabria). *Ars Praehistorica* I, pp. 161-168.

FREEMAN, L.G.; GONZÁLEZ ECHEGARAY, J.; BERNALDO DE QUIRÓS, F.; OGDEN, J. 1987. *Altamira revisited. And other essays on early art.* Institute for Prehistoric Investigations y CIMA. Chicago-Santander.

GARCÍA GUINEA, M. A. 1985: Las cuevas azilienses de El Piélago (Mirones, Cantabria) y sus excavaciones de 1967-1969. *Sautuola*, IV:13-153

GARCÍA GUINEA, M. A. 1986: *Los bastones magdalenienses en Cantabria. El hallazgo de Cualventi (Oreña).* UNED de Cantabria. Lección inaugural del Curso 1986-1987

GARCÍA GUINEA, M.A.; FUENTES, C.; MEIJIDE, M.; MADARIAGA DE LA CAMPA, B. 1975. *Primeros sondeos estratigráficos en la cueva de Tito Bustillo (Ribadesella, Asturias).* Patronato de las Cuevas Prehistóricas de la provincia de Santander, XII. Santander.

GARCÍA GUINEA, M. A., RINCÓN VILA, R. 1978: Primeros sondeos estratigráficos en la cueva de Cualventi. Oreña-Santander. *Revista de la Universidad de Santander.* 361-389

GÓMEZ FUENTES, A.; BÉCARES PÉREZ, J. 1979. Un hueso grabado en la cueva de "EL Cierro" (Ribadesella, Asturias). *XV Congreso Nacional de Arqueología* (Lugo 1977), pp.84-90. Zaragoza.

GÓMEZ TABANERA, J. M. 1978: Para una revisión del arte rupestre de la cueva de La Loja. *Boletín del Instituto de Estudios Asturianos*, 93-94, pp.385-449.

GONZÁLEZ ECHEGARAY, J. 1974: *Pinturas y grabados de la cueva de Las Chimeneas (Puente Viesgo, Santander).* Diputación Provincial de Barcelona. Instituto de Prehistoria y Arqueología. Wenner Gren Foundation for Anthropological Research. Monografías de arte rupestre. Arte paleolítico, nº 2. Barcelona.

GONZÁLEZ ECHEGARAY, J. 1985. *Altamira y sus pinturas rupestres.* Ministerio de Cultura. Madrid.

GONZÁLEZ ECHEGARAY, J. et alii. 1980. *El yacimiento de la cueva de "El Pendo" (Excavaciones 1953-57).* Bibliotheca Praehistorica Hispana XVII, Madrid.

GONZÁLEZ ECHEGARAY, J., BARANDIARAN MAESTU, I. 1981: *El paleolítico superior de la cueva del Rascaño (Santander)*. CIMA, monografías n° 3

GONZÁLEZ ECHEGARAY, J.; GONZÁLEZ SAINZ, C. 1994. Conjuntos rupestres paleolíticos de la cornisa cantábrica. *Complutum* 5, pp.21-43.

GONZÁLEZ MORALES, M. 1974: El colgante decorado paleolítico de la Cueva de Collubil (Amieva, Asturias). *BIDEA*, 83: 837-842.

GONZÁLEZ MORALES, M. 1983. Fragmento de placa ósea decorada del Magdaleniense final de la cueva de La Riera (Asturias). *Homenaje al Prof. Martín Almagro Basch* I, pp.355-361.

GONZÁLEZ SAINZ, C., 1982: Un colgante decorado de Cueva Morín (Santander). Reflexiones sobre un tema decorativo de finales del Paleolítico superior. *Ars Praehistorica,* I, pp: 151-160

GONZÁLEZ SAINZ, C. 1984: "Sobre la plaqueta grabada magdaleniense de la cueva de Urtiaga", *Munibe* 36: 11-17

GONZÁLEZ SAINZ, C. 1989: *El Magdaleniense Superior-Final de la Región Cantábrica*. Ed. Tantín, Servicio de Publicaciones de la Universidad de Cantabria. Santander

GONZÁLEZ SAINZ, C. 1993. En torno a los paralelos entre el arte mobiliar y el rupestre. *Veleia* 10, pp.39-56.

GONZÁLEZ SAINZ, C.; CACHO TOCA, R.; ALTUNA, J. 1999. Una nueva representación de bisonte en la cueva de Ekain (País Vasco). *Munibe* 51, pp.153-159.

GONZÁLEZ SAINZ, C.; GONZÁLEZ MORALES, M.R. 1986. *La Prehistoria en Cantabria*. Tantín, Santander.

GONZÁLEZ SAINZ, C.; SAN MIGUEL LLAMOSAS, C. 1997. Avance al estudio de los conjuntos rupestres paleolíticos del desfiladero del río Carranza (Ramales de la Victoria, Cantabria): las cuevas del Arco, Pondra y Morro del Horidillo. *Actas del II° Congreso de Arqueología Peninsular* (Zamora, 1996), pp.163-172.

GRAPP. 1993. *L'art pariétal paléolithique. Techniques et méthodes d'étude*. Ministère de L'Enseignement Supérierur et de la Recherche. Paris.

GUTIÉRREZ SAEZ, C., BERNALDO DE QUIRÓS, F., 1989: Dos arpones decorados de la cueva de La Pila (Cuchía, Cantabria). *XIX Congreso Nacional de Arqueología*, vol. II, pp. 27-35.

GUTIÉRREZ SAEZ, C., HERAS, BERNALDO DE QUIRÓS, 1986-1987: Arte mueble figurativo en la cueva de La Pila (Cuchía, Cantabria). *Ars Praehistorica* V/VI, pp. 221-234

HARLÉ, E. 1881. La Grotte d'Altamira près de Santander (Espagne). *Materiaux pour l'histoire primitive et naturelle de l'homme*, 2e série, XII, pp.275-283.

HERNÁNDEZ PACHECO, E. 1919. *La caverna de la Peña de Candamo (Asturias)*. CIPP, n°24. Madrid.

HOYOS GÓMEZ, M. et alii, 1980: *La cueva de La Paloma. Soto de las Regueras (Asturias)*. Excavaciones Arqueológicas en España. Ministerio de Cultura.

JORDÁ CERDÁ, F. 1954. La Cueva de Bricia (Asturias). *Boletín del Instituto de Estudios Asturianos,* XXII, pp.169-196.

JORDÁ CERDÁ, F. 1981. El Gran techo de Altamira y sus santuarios superpuestos. *Altamira Symposium*, pp.277-286. Madrid.

JORDÁ CERDÁ, F.; BERENGUER ALONSO, M. 1954: La cueva de El Pindal (Asturias). Nuevas aportaciones. *Boletín del Instituto de Estudios Asturianos,* 23, pp.3-30

JORDÁ CERDÁ, F., GÓMEZ FUENTES, A. 1982: *Cova Rosa A*. Departamento de Prehistoria y Arqueología de la Universidad de Salamanca.

LEROI-GOURHAN, A. 1965 *Préhistoire de l'art occidental.* Lucien Mazenod, Paris (2ª ed: 1971).

LEROI-GOURHAN, A. 1983. *Los primeros artistas de Europa. Introducción al arte parietal paleolítico*. Encuentro, Madrid.

LORBLANCHET, M. 1995. *Les grottes ornées de la Préhistoire*. Nouveaux regards. Errance, Paris.

MENÉNDEZ FERNÁNDEZ, M. 1984: La cueva del Buxu. El arte parietal. *Boletín del Instituto de Estudios Asturianos,* 112: 755-801

MENÉNDEZ FERNÁNDEZ, M. 1992: Excavaciones Arqueológicas en la cueva del Buxu (Cardes, Cangas de Onís). *Excavaciones Arqueológicas en Asturias* 1987-1990: 69-74.

MENÉNDEZ FRENÁNDEZ, M.; OLÁVARRI, E. 1983. Una pieza singular de arte mueble de la cueva del Buxu. Asturias. Homenaje al Prof. *Martín Almagro Basch*, I, pp.319-329. Madrid.

MENÉNDEZ FERNÁNDEZ, M., MARTÍNEZ VILLA, A. 1992: Excavaciones arqueológicas en la cueva de la Güelga. Campañas de 1989-1990. *Excavaciones Arqueológicas en Asturias* 1987-1990, pp.75-80

MONTES BARQUÍN, R. *et alii,* 1998. Cueva de El Pendo. Nuevas manifestaciones rupestres paleolíticas. *Revista de Arqueología* 201, pp.10-15.

MOURE ROMANILLO, A. 1974: "Bastón de mando" descubierto en el Magdaleniense Superior de la cueva de Tito Bustillo (Ribadesella, Asturias). *Boletín del Instituto de Estudios Asturianos* 83, pp.843-853.

MOURE ROMANILLO, J.A.1975. *Excavaciones en la cueva de Tito Bustillo (Ribadesella, Asturias). Campañas de 1972 y 1974.* Instituto de Estudios Asturianos, Oviedo.

MOURE ROMANILLO, J.A. 1981. Algunas consideraciones sobre el "Muro de los grabados" de San Román de Candamo (Asturias). *Altamira Symposium (Madrid 1979),* pp.339-352. Madrid.

MOURE ROMANILLO, J. A., 1982: Espátula decorada procedente del magdaleniense de la cueva de Tito Bustillo. *Boletín del Instituto de Estudios Asturianos*, 107: 667-681

MOURE ROMANILLO, J.A. 1982. *Placas grabadas de la cueva de Tito Bustillo*. Studia Archaeologica n° 69. Valladolid.

MOURE ROMANILLO, A. 1984. Representaciones femeninas en el arte mueble de la cueva de Tito Bustillo. *Boletín del Museo Arqueológico Nacional*, pp.69-76.

MOURE ROMANILLO, A., 1985: Escultura magdaleniense descubierta en la cueva de Tito Bustillo". *Ars Praehistórica II:* 169-176

MOURE ROMANILLO, A. 1991-1992: Documentación del arte rupestre cantábrico: la cueva de Santián (Piélagos, Cantabria). *Zephyrus,* 44-45: 7-15

MOURE ROMANILLO, J. A., CANO HERRERA, M. 1976: *Excavaciones en la cueva de Tito Bustillo (Asturias). Trabajos de 1975.* Diputación Provincial de Oviedo. Instituto de Estudios Asturianos (corte: fig. 2).

MOURE ROMANILLO, A., GONZÁLEZ SAINZ, C., BERNALDO DE QUIRÓS, F., CABRERA VALDÉS, V., 1996: Dataciones absolutas de pigmentos en cuevas cantábricas: Altamira, El Castillo, Chimeneas, Las Monedas. En Moure, A. (ed.): *"El hombre fósil" 80 años después.* Servicio de Publicaciones. Universidad de Cantabria. Santander, pp. 295-324.

MOURE ROMANILLO, A.; GONZÁLEZ SAINZ, C.; GONZÁLEZ MORALES, M.R. 1991, Las cuevas de Ramales de la Victoria (Cantabria). *Arte rupestre paleolítico en las cuevas de Covalanas y La Haza.* Universidad de Cantabria, Santander.

OBERMAIER, H., VEGA DEL SELLA, C. de la, 1918: *La cueva del Buxu.* CIPP, Memoria nº 20. Madrid.

PÉREZ PÉREZ, M. 1975: Algunas piezas inéditas de la cueva de La Paloma. *BIDEA,* 86: 731-754.

RIPOLL PERELLÓ, E. 1972: *La cueva de Las Monedas en Puente Viesgo (Santander).* Diputación Provincial de Barcelona. Monografías de Arte Rupestre, 1.

RODRÍGUEZ ASENSIO, A. 1990. Excavaciones arqueológicas realizadas en la cueva de "La Lluera" (San Juan de Priorio, Oviedo). *Excavaciones Arqueológicas en Asturias 1983-86,* pp.15-17. Oviedo.

RUIZ IDARRAGA, R.; APELLÁNIZ, J.M. 1998-1999. Análisis de la forma y de la ejecución de las figuras grabadas de la cueva de Venta Laperra (Carranza, Bizkaia). *Kobie XXV,* pp.93-140.

SANCHIDRIÁN, J.L. 1987. Arte rupestre en Andalucía. En: Arte rupestre en España. *Revista de Arqueología,* nº especial, pp.96-105. Madrid.

SANZ DE SAUTUOLA, M. 1880. *Breves apuntes sobre algunos objetos prehistóricos de la provincia de Santander.* Imp. y lit. de Telesforo Martínez. Santander. (Facsimil en Madariaga, B., 1976, pp.67-96).

STRAUS, L.G. 1992. *Iberia before the Iberians. The Stone Age Prehistory of*

Cantabrian Spain. University of New Mexico Press, Albuquerque.

SAURA, P.A. et al. 1998. *Altamira*. Caja Cantabria y Lundwerg. Barcelona.

UCKO, P.J. 1987. Débuts illusoires dans l'étude de la tradition artistique. *Bulletin de la Société Préhistorique Ariège-Pyrénées* 42, pp.15-81.

UCKO, P. 1989: La subjetividad y el estudio del arte parietal paleolítico. *Cien años después de Sautuola. Estudios en homenaje a Marcelino Sanz de Sautuola en el Centenario de su muerte,* pp.283-358. Diputación Regional de Cantabria. Santander.

UTRILLA, P.1976. El Magdaleniense inicial en el Pais Vasco peninsular. *Munibe* 28/4, pp.245-275.

VALLADAS, H.; CACHIER, H.; MAURICE, P.; BERNALDO DE QUIRÓS, F.; CABRERA VALDÉS, V.; UZQUIANO, P.; ARNOLD, M. 1992. Direct radiocarbon dates for prehistoric paintings at the Altamira, El Castillo and Niaux caves. *Nature* 357, pp.68-70.

VEGA DEL SELLA, C. DE LA, 1916: *Paleolítico de Cueto de la Mina (Asturias).* CIPP, memora 13.

VEGA DEL SELLA, C. DE LA, 1930: *Las cuevas de La Riera y Balmori (Asturias).* CIPP, memoria 38. Madrid.

VILLAVERDE BONILLA, V. 1994. *Arte paleolítico de la Cova del Parpalló. Estudio de la colección de plaquetas y cantos grabados y pintados.* S.I.P. Diputació de Valencia.

VILLAVERDE BONILLA, V. 1994. Arte mueble de la España mediterránea: breve síntesis y algunas consideraciones teóricas. *Complutum* 5, pp.139-162

VVAA. 1992. *El nacimiento del arte en Europa.* Catálogo de la exposición organizada por la Unión Latina. Paris.

VVAA. 1996. *L'art préhistorique des Pyrénées.* Musée des Antiquités nationales, Saint-Germain-en-Laye. Ed. Reunion des musées nationaux. Paris.

Continued to

"Palaeolithic Cave Paintings in Northern Spain
 Catalog I: Cantabria"

"Palaeolithic Cave Paintings in Northern Spain
 Catalog II: Asturias & Basque Country"

"Introduction to Palaeolithic Mobile Arts in Northern Spain"

www.ingramcontent.com/pod-product-compliance
Lightning Source LLC
Chambersburg PA
CBHW050202230526
45470CB00001B/201